The Politics of Gender, Community, and Modernity

The Politics of Gender, Community, and Modernity

Essays on Education in India

Nita Kumar

OXFORD
UNIVERSITY PRESS

OXFORD
UNIVERSITY PRESS

YMCA Library Building, Jai Singh Road, New Delhi 110 001

Oxford University Press is a department of the University of Oxford. It furthers
the University's objective of excellence in research, scholarship, and education
by publishing worldwide in

Oxford New York

Auckland Cape Town Dar es Salaam Hong Kong Karachi
Kuala Lumpur Madrid Melbourne Mexico City Nairobi
New Delhi Shanghai Taipei Toronto

With offices in

Argentina Austria Brazil Chile Czech Republic France Greece
Guatemala Hungary Italy Japan Poland Portugal Singapore
South Korea Switzerland Thailand Turkey Ukraine Vietnam

Oxford is a registered trade mark of Oxford University Press
in the UK and in certain other countries

Published in India
By Oxford University Press, New Delhi

ISBN 13: 978-0-19-568273-1
ISBN 10: 0-19-568273-4

Typeset in ClassGaramond BT 10/12
By Laser Print Craft, Delhi 110051
Printed in India at Ram Printograph, Delhi 110 051
Published by Oxford University Press
YMCA Library Building, Jai Singh Road, New Delhi 110 001

For SOM
For the NIRMAN that he worked for
For all the people of Banaras that he died for

Contents

Preface

I am pleased to be able to bring these essays to the attention of a new set of readers, and perhaps some of my older readers. These essays have been presented and published over the last four or five years, but have been researched and written with a commitment to a larger vision of South Asian history and sociology that emerged during the course of my work on education from 1985 onwards. The larger vision implied such a magnum opus, however, that although I have been pursuing this book of my dreams for a few years now, I would like to take a break from that huge task and present smaller statements of that vision now.

That will not prevent me from making a statement about the larger vision, however. The study of education has presented several fundamental insights. One, that indeed there is agency in history, and that the structures seemingly in place are thus because they are reproduced; that reproduction occurs primarily in sites of education; and that education therefore is the site from where any action to produce continuity or change has been and can be launched. This insight gives one the ability to pursue a number of intriguing questions: How could we talk about the different paces of change in different contexts of activity, for instance, the rapidity of change in the teaching of history versus a very different change in the teaching of music? How could we formulate the relationships that obviously exist between the politics of status and the politics of aesthetics? What are the conditions that produce a situation of threat to a community and what produces a sense of comfort? How are responses possibly divided in the spectrum ranging from resignation to violent defence? It seemed to me that much that was worth pursuing in the understanding of history, ranging from discursive control and hegemony to the possibilities of agency and change, was accessible through the data on education.

Another insight is that an epistemological shift, such as was produced by colonialism, is actually the model for how history works. It is not that the structure–event movement exemplified by Captain Cook's presence in the Hawaiian islands is the exception; it is the rule. The smoothness of the transition of the modern Indian intelligentsia to a situation of allegiance with a different authority, languages, discourses, and professions suggests that the open-endedness of allegiance was the norm.

Then there is the whole question of development. That term is nowhere used in the essays here, nor elsewhere in my writings. I was aghast at Amartya Sen's uncritical deployment of it when I agreed with so much else in his theses, but that is only because of the negative connotations of the term for me because of developmentalists' relative ignorance of the details of people's lives. But all the details, the subtleties, and the ironies aside, I must admit that the history of education reveals to me the starkness of the inequities of history, and one in which *scholars* participate. As the main agents for teaching, they effectively block any filtering down of the growing refinements in their sciences to ordinary people—we could posit—since all their labour does not apparently lead to any improvements in the lives of ordinary people, but does lead to improvement in scholars' professional statuses and lives. Whether we accept Amartya Sen's liberal articulation of the matter or a starker Marxist reading of the exploitation of the working class by the intellectual leisured class, we have to confront the fact of scholarship abetting in inequality through education, and not aiding equality.

To keep this brief, the topic of education has acted as an exciting lens for me through which I can look at historiographical, anthropological, and development questions. It is also exciting because of its proximity to lives, especially of young people, and to the wonders of learning. I hope my essays impart some of my excitement to their readers.

I would like to apologize for a slight repetition in some chapters—slight because it concerns some three pages in the whole book—that I chose not to re-write for fear of disturbing the 'architecture' of the essays concerned. I would like to thank all my colleagues, editors, and publishers over the years of these essays. The essays have seen previous incarnations as:

Chapter 1, published in *Modern Asian Studies*, May 2006.

Chapter 2, published in Diana Mines and Sarah Lamb, eds, *Everyday Life in South Asia* (Bloomington: Indiana University Press, 2002); and Suvir Kaul, ed., *The Partitions of Memory* (Delhi: Permanent Black, 2000).

Chapter 3, presented at a conference at the University of Michigan, Ann Arbor, September 2003, on 'Alternative Histories of the Family'.

Chapter 4, published in *Seminar*, June 2003.

Chapter 5, published in *Indian Economic and Social History Review*, vol. 38, no 1, 2001.

Chapter 6, published in *Gender and History*, vol. 17, no. 1, June 2005.

Chapter 7, published in *Economic and Political Weekly*, 27 April, 1991.

Chapter 8, presented at the Institute for Research on Women and Gender, University of Michigan, March 2003.

Chapter 9, published in Geetanjali Shree, *Mai* (Delhi: Kali for Women, 2000).

Chapter 10, published in *Les Jeunes: hantise de l'espace public dans les societes du Sud? Autrepart*, no 18, 2001.

Chapter 11, published in Martin Gaenszle, *Visualized Space* (Heidelberg, 2005).

Chapter 12, published in Derek C. Mulenga, ed., *Post-colonialism and Education: Challenging Traditions and Disrupting Boundaries* (NY: Palgrave Macmillan, 2004).

Chapter 13, published in *Economic and Political Weekly*, 19 July, pp. 3049–55, 2003.

Introduction

'Education' is a subject area that is very broadly defined by me in my work. Each of the essays in this book presents an empirical case study of education. The essays include studies of sites such as homes, neighbourhoods, cities, buildings, and families; and of sources and semantic fields such as reform efforts, texts, languages, and the media. The essays are grouped into three parts. The first part is about the nature of history in South Asia. It argues that possible writings of history must engage with the divisive processes of history *in* South Asia (as well as globally), and with the enabling and disabling practices of history *within* communities in South Asia. The second part is about the nature of modernities in South Asia, in which the essays work towards producing a politicized, gendered, and community-oriented history of modernity in South Asia. The third part is called Post-colonialism, which proposes that postcolonialism is an appropriate term for discussions of history and modernity that include reflections on the scholar's particular position within the history and modernity.

While the grouping of the essays is done with a view to isolating their arguments more coherently into three sets, there are certain other arguments, hypotheses, and key concepts that span the whole book. The grouping is done in retrospect; the concepts themselves have been struggled with at every stage of writing. They are large questions, even dilemmas, as I see them, such as of the implication of narratives, and the power of pain. These are perhaps the most interesting contribution of the book, and if I take time over them in the Introduction, it is because I find them stimulating, generalizable, and useful. Let me then discuss some of them with reference to the three groups of essays in this book.

THE HISTORIES OF SOUTH ASIA

It is a tribute to the discipline of history and the contributions made to it by scholars of South Asia recently that there can be such a range of challenges to the norms of history-writing, all of which go towards enriching and empowering the discipline. Among these I would mention Burton (2003), Goswami (2004), Katten (2002), Mayaram (1997), Skaria (2001), Sundar (1998), S. Kumar (2003), as well as outside the discipline questionings such as Bhabha (1990), Chatterjee (1993), Gold (2002), Nandy (1999), and Spivak (1999). After pondering on how to best make my points on the further possible histories for South Asia, I decided to begin by engaging in polemic with one stimulating author, Dipesh Chakrabarty in his *Provincializing Europe* (2000). My aim is to further strengthen the scope and imagination of historians regarding the practice of history, and to contribute from my own work and arguments in doing so. This section is based specifically on the first four essays of the book here and alludes in passing to some of the others.

What could be a justifiable subject matter for a proposition about history writing to be grounded in, that could enable conversation? Anything at all. Chakrabarty's subject is seemingly twofold—the educated Bengali middle class of which he is representative, whose 'mental world [was] transformed through its interactions with the West' (Chakrabarty 2000: 4); and the 'peasant', which refers not to a class, but is 'a shorthand for all the seemingly nonmodern, rural, nonsecular relationships and life practices that constantly leave their imprint on the lives of even the elites in India and on their institutions of government' (Chakrabarty 2000: 11). Further, the ground on which he locates himself is that of a modern university, or at least that of the site of a high universal intellectual discourse where European intellectuals are alive and are taken seriously as of contemporary relevance. As we locate this we can glimpse that the peasant is already the one who has been rendered irrelevant from this vantage point. This is the very issue for Chakrabarty. He is located within a discourse that is his subject of critique. This discourse is the subject of his critique *because* it belittles the peasant. The peasant is *not* the subject of his critique.

My own subject is also twofold: the Indian intelligentsia, as lodged in South Asian metropolises, produced by colonial and national education, of which I am representative; and the provincial and rural in South Asia that produces other histories and modernities to those of the colonial and nationalist intelligentsia (close to Chakrabarty's peasant). The ground on which I locate myself is that of a colonial–national academic discourse which is derived from the European, but does not coincide with it. Like Chakrabarty's ground, this is one that has to be interrogated discursively but also accepted pragmatically. Unlike his political modernity, however, this ground does not have a prior theoretical being. This ground may be located only practically, in its very production, at infinite sites of production. I have looked at the sites of schools, and equally, at the sites outside schools, such as homes, communities, and neigbourhoods. The discourse from within which I speak is that of the production of this modernity. I critique it, both for what it is and what it lacks. But I also speak from within a different discourse, a feminist and gendered historical discourse, and a reflexive anthropological discourse, and from this vantage point I critique the provincial and rural.

It is crucial to note how the *duality* of the subject of each of the authors above is differently deployed. Chakrabarty's first subject, Europe, is jeopardized precisely by the second one, the peasant, and for his argument the two have to be juxtaposed in his text and its reading by him. My first subject, the Indian intelligentsia, is sought by me to be assigned its proper place by narrating it along with other valid narratives, such as of the provinces and of the family. But I would make an argument for their coevality, making for two self-conscious moves. One is for an intellectual challenge to the intelligentsia by the uneducated. The second is for a political challenge to the uneducated by the educated. The intelligentsia may not be understood except via its conception of the other and its self-definition via the other. The uneducated should be understood as an existence not so much conceptually but politically crafted by the other. So, whereas both Chakrabarty and I position ourselves vis-à-vis two subjects, we do so with different readings of their relative power. The difference between us is minor with reference to the actual dual subjects of each, but significant regarding the politics of each subject to the other.

My first essay lays out the broad map of education in South Asia. The colonial state in the mid-nineteenth century plays a crucial role in realigning power, defining meanings, formulating rules of legitimacy, and coding value. That the centres of colonial power which are the capital cities of the three Presidencies, are placed at the centre of the new power structure is a necessary corollary, and that other parts of South Asia are variously defined as 'backward' is equally necessary. This is the working of the hyper-real 'Europe' in South Asia. It is important, however, to not regard this process of provincialization as inevitable, which is what would happen if this was the only narrative told. It is not inevitable and *could have been different.* The provinces could have been successfully colonized too, as the centres were. We have to read the absence of this successful colonization as not a lack, but as the production of other histories. The family and the community acted as active sites for the teaching and training of their youth, and they considered that they were being normative, correct, and even perspicacious. In this sense, another history *did* happen. It is not that only the state-centred history transpired and we should regret the marginalization of any other agency. It is that we typically *tell* only the state-centred history. We should regret, not the mono-causality of history, but our mono-narrativization. We should find ways to narrate the other histories, such as of communities, which *of course* happened.

I have resolved this impasse through the technique of multiple narratives to tell their different stories—in the essays of the first part explicitly; in the essays of part two and three, implicitly. The lure of multiple narratives for me, discussed further in chapter 1, is threefold. It seems to prevent an artificial closure in allowing several voices to represent themselves (a lá Jane Austen, see Handler 1990). Secondly, if one's aim is also the pursuit of justice, but with a desire to avoid the appropriation inherent in the justice-vision of modernization (as in Gupta 2000) and assume a more complicated politics, then a narrative on the side of the weak that is equal and parallel to the narrative of the strong seems to be a beginning in this direction. And finally, it allows for a solution to an already familiar problem: How to insert the self into the narrative. Why, through adding *another* narrative of the self, or the scholar. This works excellently for the pursuit of justice too, because it makes explicit what is so awkward to express otherwise, that in any particular case, the scholar is on a certain side, not because other sides were insufficiently legitimate or articulate, but because such is her politics. In my story of education it was clear that even at the simplest level, there are non-congruent positions occupied by the state or school owner, the teacher, the parent or family, and the student. The scholar could choose one position or she could represent them all. Or she could present the several positions while underscoring which could be considered her own, and why.

Chapter 1 presents the narratives of state history, of elite history, and, as I call it, of provincial history. I split the last into two, the narrative of provincial power and that of provincial powerlessness, which I call pain. The history of the province is not inferior or static in its own vision, only in that of the metropolis. Yet it has a tremendous lack, for my purposes the lack of mobility, change, or choice in the future. That particular narrative of pain is one in which the scholar is directly embroiled, because comprehending the pain implies a particular political position.

In chapter 2, I look at one of the provincial communities, that of the Ansari weavers of Banaras. They possess powerful histories that seem normative and correct from their own perspectives and have been discussed by me elsewhere (Kumar 1988, 1987). I suggest that the two alternatives are not a universalist, nationalist history such as learnt by metropolitan children, and the absence of it for provincial children. This is certainly how the picture presents itself when we ask the first question about schooling, or about progress and modernity in general. This picture is inspired from the case of locations like France where the position of the citizen subsumed completely that of the artisan, and everyone else (Kumar 1998). In India the relationship has been, and continues to be, a symmetrical one between the provincial and the metropolitan child. There are *always* community and family histories, *and* there are national histories. The child who is pushed by the family and the school into mastering the national history, is also aided by the family and the school in erasing the community history. The child who is taught the community history, is not taught seriously the national history and never masters it.

But I am deliberately wrong in suggesting that it is a symmetrical relationship. I am doing so to first demarcate the difference with Chakrabarty who does not find any symmetry whatsoever, and then to follow up by delineating my own lines of asymmetry. The national and the local are *not* symmetrical in that national histories bestow power, and celebrating the community does not. Power is, of course, not unitary. Of its many sources I take the case of freedom here, and freedom is, importantly, not singular. Both our subjects experience freedom and therefore power. The Ansaris enjoy the freedom of time and lifestyle and independent work, or as I have described it, the freedom to wander around spitting pan anywhere. The educated elite, or present-day middle class, in Calcutta have the freedom of choosing jobs, careers, residences, and future lifestyles, within limits. The Ansaris sacrifice the second kind of freedom, of mobility, but enjoy the first, of wandering around, by not disciplining themselves. Middle-class Calcuttans enjoy mobility, but sacrifice the Ansari kind of freedom, that is, they discipline themselves continuously.

In this chapter I have presented it as a stark and balanced choice, but I clearly observe that the balance is in favour of the middle class. Their participation in the national discourse makes them privileged, and they know it and defend it. They do not envy the Ansaris, and believe themselves, rightly or wrongly, to be envied by them in turn.

An important question then is also: How far are these different histories matters of choice at all? In the case of the Calcutta middle class, a further zeroing in discloses that choices are extremely circumscribed by the direct or indirect actions of the state. In chapter 3 I describe how different kinds of families collaborate to different degrees with the state. The citizen family of Rajendra is doing 'exactly' what must be done. It is circumscribed by the processes of Partition and loss of estate in 1947; the circumstances of a middle-class life produced by the economy of Calcutta; and by the demands of the best kinds of school that the family can choose from within a range of narrow choices in a certain educational formation at that moment in history. The family is cooperating willingly, even with pleasure, but it is cribbed and controlled nevertheless. Back among the Ansaris, and a parallel group, the Vishwakarmas, the upwardly mobile family is trying to do a very similar thing, within similar circumstances, to the upwardly mobile Calcutta family. When the family thus cooperates, its choices are minimal within the discourse of the state, of middle-class mobility, of the private school, and the larger world of education. We could not possibly begrudge in its satisfaction in doing its job well.

When the family does not cooperate with the state, and celebrates its freedoms, it is important to see that the controlling factors are as unrelenting. Ansaris often perceive a choice only of madrasa education for their children, or none. Madrasas are designed in a way to reproduce the weaver ethos of the Ansaris. What weavers experience as freedom therefore, can be seen by us as a choice of non-cooperation with the state, but it is a choice made *not by themselves*. Indeed, if they had a *choice*, they would choose to have the benefits that the middle-classes seem to enjoy—proper modern education for their children, future career prospects, health, material domestic comforts, economic security, and mobility. They would choose schools that teach a strong narrative of nationalist history.

With this I come to the second dilemma that the essays here grapple with to different extents: How to place within a history of South Asia the important sites of justice, equality, and redressal? I argue that the politics of the community are abrasive and violent, restrictive and destructive, much as the politics of the nation state are in their different ways. The two politics are parallel in their oppression, as also argued by Das (1996). The politics of the community are *worse* because of an additional reason—they produce a subject who occupies an unrewarded position in the state. We can use history—both the discipline of history in the classroom and the story of the past in the community—as a shorthand for education, and assess how far education equals progress. There is no question that it is the discipline of history that produces progress. *You can lead a more materially and socially successful life when you know 'Indian history' than if you know only the history of your community.* Another education, in the history of the community, produces stagnation, thus, arguably, pain.

The narrative of Indian nationalist history as taught in schools, I show in chapter 4, is a good one. It is coherent and interesting, and it gives power to those who master it. The problem with this narrative of course is that it is false and perpetuates stereotypes. It is equal in this regard to that of every other nation state in the world. This problem of the Indian madrasa is shared, moreover, by all the schools in the state of India. Neither the Islamic madrasas nor the Hindu schools, the two often-cited cases of prejudice in history-teaching, are at all exceptional in their prejudices. They teach the same national history as the others, and the national history itself is prejudiced. The line of difference must be drawn between those who learn this national history and those who do not, and learn, rather, other community-based histories.

Many scholars emphasize another line of division entirely, that between varying visions of history depending on political affiliations. Indeed there are at present in India aggressively Hindu versions of history, fading into softer, less aggressive ones which still insist on a vision of Hindus as the only proper natives, and at the other end there are varieties of liberal positions ending up in a totally materialist-determinist position. Similarly, as I show in this chapter there are Islamic versions of history that range from the intolerant to the benign and fade into liberal positions. But these are not the divisions I am speaking about. Such divisions exist at the lay level among the citizenry of any state, and they occur in professional fields in all disciplines and academies. The division I am making is between 'Western' knowledge by which I mean the product of the European–North American liberal arts curriculum, which is the one used in all institutions of formal learning in South Asia based on the colonial educational model, and other ways of conceptualizing, expressing, debating, and teaching history.

Because the history of South Asia has been produced through colonialism and nationalism, and because the processes of colonialism, nationalism, and modernity in South Asia have in turn relied immensely on colonial and modern education, the structure of inequality in the region is largely a product of its differential educational history. This difference in education lies most of all not in principle, but in the execution. School curriculum is not significantly different in different schools. The implementation of it is. As I show in chapters 4 and 5, history consists of the same 'facts' in all the schools, by and large. In the best schools, history teaching is 'good'. It includes maintenance of proper notebooks, commendable memorization of facts, the ability to write and narrate clear English or Indian language prose predetermined as correct by the teacher, and so on. In the worst schools, history teaching is 'bad'. The students cannot do any of the above and the teachers and administrators do not have a clue as to how to change the situation, or do have a clue or two but express their inability to execute the changes.

Nor does the actual problem with the history of India lie in the division it presents between a history constructed on a certain ground (Europe) and an actual archive elsewhere that should be its ground (India), as argued by Chakrabarty. The problem is that of another division between a visible, represented history of India (Europe-based) that is imbibed in 'good' education, and a poor version of it, that is, its failure, and the complementary success of myriads of community histories all around. The (Europe-based) national history of India is defective, but powerful, and the poorer version of it is the more defective still, and while accompanied by the power of other histories, transmits no lasting power to its learners. The difference in histories of India is to be found within India itself and not between Europe and India. It is illusory to subsume under one umbrella "the everyday subalternity of non-Western histories" (Chakrabarty 2000: 42). Almost everything that Chakrabarty argues makes a valid point as I see it, and yet his argument does not describe the histories of South Asia. The world he surveys seems to be empty of histories in a way that is exactly opposite to the one I observe, that is full.

MODERNITIES OF SOUTH ASIA

The next question is one of the location of history itself. I agree with Chakrabarty that to historicize history would not do. That would be to play its own game of evolutionism and progressivism, that is, historicism. But I do not see historicization as being this accomplished thing as he seems to be able to do. Thus, the use of the past perfect: '...the imaginary waiting room in which Indians *had been placed* by European historicist thought...' (Chakrabarty 2000: 10,9) could of course be a slip, but seems not to be, supported as it is by the other semantics of the book. As I see it, the use of the past continuous would have been more appropriate—Indians *were being placed* in a waiting room, all along during the time of their education in the nineteenth and twentieth centuries, and throughout that time they were negotiating in several ways the fact and the fancy, the burden, but also the imaginariness, of the waiting room. This use of particular form of a verb would not be an issue if it did not have resonance with the largest possible question, *Is history in fact finished?* That is, the history of historicization? Have the habits of thought bred by Europe, its categories and concepts, indeed become, in Chakrabarty's words, *inevitable, invariable, unavoidable, and impossible to think without?*

Maybe the real legacy of Europe's creation of a self-centred intellectual ontology is the Indian educated class (whether Bengali or not could be disputed separately) that then finds this intellectual legacy problematic because of its nationalistic ambitions to see a more India centred historiography. I argue that such a class, this continuum from Rammohan Roy (of the impressively early time of 1772/4–1834) to Dipesh Chakrabarty and (with gender and regional modifications) Nita Kumar, rejects or, as I would prefer, *transcends,* European historicism in a more central and effective way than Chakrabarty describes. For him, the rejection is a familiar, nationalist one—'the national elite's own rejection of the "waiting-room" version of history when faced with the Europeans' use of it as a justification for denial of "self-government" to the colonized'. My proposition is quite different. I suggest that the nationalist elite transcended historicism because they were not produced exclusively by it, but by other discourses as well and that these enabled them to theoretically *and* practically work with the possibilities of other histories, past and future. In chapter 6, I argue that we need to shift our gaze from an enlarged, hyper-reading of nationalism as the genitor of identity to a more dispersed look at the socializing processes in class and community locations that produce identity.

Although Chakrabarty's quixotic denunciation of historicism is breathtaking in its elegance and hypnotic in its allure to an extent that one cannot initially imagine opposing it, oppose it one must. Because the only residue left after a denunciation so total is that of essentialism. The essentialism affects every single party in the story. We do not have to worry about a real geographical region of the world called 'Europe' to worry about this essentialism. Because Chakrabarty's Europe is an imagined one, he would suggest that this imagined thing is what is essentialized. But he makes a connection next which is what deserves scrutiny. Europe, he says, 'fabrication or not', comprises 'the genealogy of thought in which social scientists find themselves inserted'(5). When he talks about the insertion of the Indian intelligentsia into this conceptualized Europe, we long for a sense of process and dialectic. We are talking about some eight generations of educated people after all, between Rammohan Roy and ourselves (not that any single one among us has that lineage). In the practices of those generations, practices ranging from the infantile-formative to the mature-political, there has been both contingent and deliberate variation of influence, response, approach, and position. Grounding the generations sociologically, one can see that at no point is it evident that any Europe, fabricated or not, comprised a determined genealogy for us to point at.

I feel uncertain of my criticism when I allow myself to savour what Chakrabarty is arguing. His *pain* is very evident to me, and touches a chord within me. I have found myself to be similarly touched scores of times over with all the generations of the intelligentsia that I have studied in the nineteenth and twentieth centuries. Chakrabarty is relatively matter-of-fact when he mentions the treatment that would be given to a Gangesa, Bartrihari [sic], or Abhinavagupta, because Indian social scientists would simply not 'have the training that would enable them to make... [their] concepts into resources for critical thought for the present'(6). But other members of the intelligentsia have been outrightly, and often emotionally, critical of this trick played by history. The weight of their response together with my own makes me read Chakrabarty's factual proposition as laden with pain. I am, in my nationalist mode, in agreement with the overall thesis: colonialism was destructive, and *our* epistemologies, historiographies, and sciences have been at the receiving end of this destructiveness.

In my historian mode, however, I want to complicate the argument further. The idea of history as progress was a fundamental aspect of the colonial practice. But it was, significantly, an aspect of the colonial *dilemma*, in that it could be proclaimed with confidence, but practised only unsatisfactorily with some coercion applied to the practice (Guha 1997) and a great deal of inefficiency and other failures (chapter 1). The idea of history as progress was not imposed, and not imbibed by the elite, in the totalizing way that Chakrabarty suggests— not even by the Bengali middle class. Otherwise why would they not be able to display this totalized product?

This is perhaps the most important difference in the visions of Chakrabarty and Kumar. We would both agree that all South Asians were not equally colonized in the epistemological sense of having to think inside Europe. The elite were more so. This much has been documented by all studies that describe how the Indian mind was made or shaped through exposure to the ideas of the Enlightenment, particularly the ideas of Rationality and Progress, especially in schools and through reading (Kopf 1979, McCully 1940). Even a larger perspective such as Cohn's (1992) would argue that history originated as a technical exercise of control of information, and was made acceptable through the agency of the school. Education caused the displacement of Indian by Western modes of thinking, but not in a way that liberated Indians, rather in a way that enslaved them, or more mildly speaking, disoriented them. My research reveals that instead of being merely a trap, which of course it largely is, this Europeanization of the imagination provided a valuable resource for the elite. My argument of the empowerment of the elite through their Europeanization goes beyond these familiar and valuable studies to show that the elite were perspicacious enough to merge their English learning with the learning of Indian languages and worldviews. Perspicacity also varied: often this was done involuntarily by the men; progressively, into and across the twentieth century, it was done deliberately. It was also done both voluntarily and involuntarily by women. The salience of gender in these histories and the complex roles of women in these gendered histories is investigated in chapters 6–9, and discussed in the next section.

My argument about elite empowerment through elite intimacy with plural intellectual worlds is different to the long, partially fruitful but largely debilitating, debate on tradition and modernity. I suggest that there is no *inherent* conflict between these two experiential worlds because to live in plural worlds was a norm. The conflict in their discourses has been put up by modernity as essential to its own self-definition. In different terms, the singularity of the conceptual world of Europe (or modernity or capitalism) is exactly what Europe needs in order to survive. Chakrabarty is correct to use all the hyperbole available to describe its power. But that describes only *it to itself*. It does not describe the power or powerlessness of South Asian modernities, and certainly does not describe the experiential world of South Asians. To do that we have to go outside the constructs of Europe, beginning with the use of different categories. An analogous case would be that of gay or lesbian history of a period, say, the seventeenth century (Traub 2002) when the categories of gay or lesbian were inadequate to describe the fluidity of identities. A familiar historiographical problem, then: How to harness the past to the uses of the present, including to empower the present, without abusing the past by representing it through our present categories? I argue that the nineteenth- and twentieth-century South Asian intelligentsia were not monolingual, mono-cultural, mono-scientific, or mono-discursive; that they were not under the conceptual rule of Europe, and that we cannot see this from within the categories of Europe itself. This problem of the domination of Europe did not exist for the Indian elite because they did not think in those categories; they did not *live* in those categories. It is indeed an important problem for us. Our history writing, however, must include a search for their categories.

My argument is one for modelling plurality as the norm. Plural mothers, mother tongues, identities, learning, epistemologies, histories, truths, and modernities, can all be taken as the norm rather than their singular opposite. The pluralities existed throughout the modern period and are extant today not only because the centralizing and homogenizing mission has failed, but because plurality was actively courted and welcomed, and continues to be not merely tolerated today but considered normal. My further argument is that every normalization, as well as every failure, is an aspect of a politics.

The dichotomous discourse of tradition and modernity in its suggestion that there was a choice, a negotiation, a conflict, a compromise, a dilemma, a split, etc., between these two poles of experience, my essays propose, is limited and faulty. It is derived from the European experience, where given the history of Europe there was indeed such a negotiation and conflict, and where one triumphed over the other. The key to escaping any essentialist statement of the nature of South Asian difference, while respecting the fact of a difference, is to see the differences as a politics and to ground these differences sociologically. Because my essays focus on the actual sites of learning where discourses are produced and transmitted, we are made aware that it is 'natural' for people to inhabit plural worlds, to speak several languages, to have access to varying notions of truth, to share cultural meanings between the so-called 'East' and 'West'. It is *normal* for them to be comfortable and at home in the epistemologies of their grandmothers as well as that of their formal syllabus in colonial schools. 'Tradition' and 'modernity' are not actual experiences that are at war with each other. They are rather the names of a politics nominated by modernity for disempowering and derecognizing that there are other sites and contents of knowledge than that claimed by itself as normative, that may or may not share much with modernity, but certainly they share power, reflexivity, and history, all of which have been sought to be monopolized by modernity.

The connection of this larger argument to education in South Asia is the following. The history of modernity in the West has been accompanied by industrialization and the growth of the nation state, and has been fuelled by colonialism, but the *secret* of its success is that a centralized educational system has normalized a concept of history, the self, science, and ontology. Even when nationalism, capitalism or androcentrism are questioned, the schema of normalcy of this modernity remains the same. The history of such a modernity was produced by several factors, described by various scholars, but it was *disseminated* by schooling, with the support of popular culture and official discourse. Over the same time in South Asia, approximately mid-nineteenth to mid-twentieth centuries, there was an effort to put a similar centralized set of norms of historical, scientific, social, and humanistic truths in place. The project was not successful. The students who learnt one historiography in school, learnt yet another one, or other ones, outside school, and even in school from their peers and teachers, outside the government- controlled syllabus. They learnt one science in school and another, or others, outside. They learnt one sociology in the classroom and others outside. If we take the historical processes of South Asia seriously we are bound to recognize its plural sites of identity and community formation, its plural consciousnesses accessed through the knowledge of languages, and its tied politics of colonialism and the indigenous.

Modernity in South Asia is, thus, plural and can show the world how to take plurality for granted. A study of the intelligentsia in India, from the nineteenth century to the present, shows us that their ways of being modern were multilingual, multicultural, multi-vocal, multi-valent, and multi-discursive. These have not been given recognition for the sociological and political power they have exercised for over seven generations of the modern period in South Asia. And the lesson to be learnt from this history has not been theorized and made applicable elsewhere.

But what about the population that is not the intelligentsia? What is their relationship to modernity and is there any theoretical lesson to be learnt there? The smooth, non-conflictual, creative and empowering relationship of the elite to modernity appear to be certainly missing for the masses, for whom there seems to be rather tension and resistance. The intelligentsia is the section which marches with the state and is happy to cooperate. It has the pride that it can exist in multiple worlds and that English education is not a threat. The masses are the sections which resist the state and are happy to reassert their community identities. English education is a threat to them and their worlds remain comparatively narrow. In both cases there are exceptions. Low-class and low-caste people take advantage of colonial schooling to widen their worlds and achieve the same mobility as upper caste and upper class people, a good example being that of Jyotiba Phule (O'Hanlon 2002). Upper caste and upper class people resist colonial schooling, such as merchants everywhere (Dobbin 1972).

The history of education in South Asia shows that neither the narrative of colonization nor the powerful counter-narrative of resistance tells anywhere near the full story. Nowhere in these do we find the story of those who were left out of this whole saga, and did not even form a part of the colonial educational system. My ethnographic work made this for me more than a trivial lapse. In my ethnography I was seemingly *only* dealing with those left out of these major narratives of education. Nor were these subjects to be pitied or defended: they seemed to live in a world of games, performance, subversion, and irony richer than those more characteristically depicted in history. They were, moreover, self-centred and confident of their being. One answer to the riddle of why they should not be represented in history is definitely the answer given by Chakrabarty, that our colonized social scientific imaginations cannot see them. But anthropologists have always seen them, and it should be easy then, because of that encounter, to see them in history.

The data that permits me to make propositions about modernity consists of a variety of different contexts taken as sites of learning, and the different histories of these, all read as educational histories. In learning and teaching, schools are only one institution that is pivotal (chapter 11). Very influential are several other institutions such as the family and the community. Equally formative are several sites of action such as the neighbourhood, the village, and the city, and sites of consumption such as the media. All these may be explored to tell us how they produce the subjects of modernity in terms of the subjects' participation in nation-building, citizenship, consumption of goods and images, and identities of the self. I have barely begun an investigation here on two sites outside the school—the institution of the family, and the site of the home, neighbourhood, and city (chapter 11)—and barely touched on a third—poetry and song lyrics. This preliminary exploration already suggests important qualifications to our understanding of modernity and its history in South Asia. If we look at the second subject for both Chakrabarty and myself, the provincial/ peasant, we see that the problem of the domination of Europe was also not a problem for them because they were simply not colonized in that epistemological way.

A different plurality needs to be considered here: that based on an internal division in South Asia between the elite and the non-elite. Both are characterized by modernity, but while that of the elite is plural in its creative manipulation of different epistemological worlds and subjection also to the politics of these worlds, the modernity of the non-elite is more picturesque in the ways Doniger describes in her study of copies and originals (2005). Provincials imitate the elite while striving to be true to themselves, thus producing a self that is forever a mirror of a mirror, which is always claimed as authentic and produces no agony about authenticity.

An attendant puzzle does, however, raise its head. This is a suspicion of the actual weakness of one's informants. Because my artisans, traders, labourers, and professionals in small-town India were *my* informants, and their stories were hitherto unknown, and also wildly exciting, the anthropologist in me was triply prejudiced in articulating their stories as elegant and strong. But the historian in me was undergoing a tension she was not trained to resolve. This is what I have introduced as 'pain' in chapter 1, and as I discuss under 'Postcolonialism', it has to do with *justice*, the realization that even when the subjects of one's study were strong in their beings, they were structurally weak, and were themselves aware of it.

TOWARDS A GENDERED HISTORIOGRAPHY

I do not claim a unique South Asian agenda here. I would rather like to emphasize the *universal* nature of the attempt to produce more gendered histories, although these could always be pushed further. Even the authors of *Western Civilizations: Their History and Their Culture* (NY: Norton, 1980) begin their book with the complaint of Jane Austen's heroine from *Northanger Abbey*, that history 'tells me nothing that does not either vex or weary me. The quarrels of popes and kings, with wars or pestilences in every page; the men all so good for nothing, and hardly any women at all, it is very tiresome'. How much more consensus can there be on the importance of gender-sensitivity, together with class sensitivity, in history?

In order to do justice to my own arguments about a gendered history of modern South Asia, I would like to recapitulate the main narrative of the history. Although there had been contact with Europe for a long time, the significant contact for South Asia came with the political activities of the East India Company. The most important events occurred under the tenures of Governor-Generals Warren Hastings (1772–84) and Lord Cornwallis (1785–93). Both were interested in South Asian languages and cultures, and well aware of the recklessness of trying to rule foreign territories with complex histories with the help of untrained and profit-seeking servants of a trading company. Being ambitious administrators, both took bold steps to control the greed of the Company's employees while successfully maximizing benefits for the Company through organized tax collection and maintaining law and order. The story of their efforts could be told at length but I will encapsulate it here as the combined results of their new system of law and administration for India, efforts in the realm of law, of scholarship such as the Asiatic Society of Bengal, and of revenue collection such as the Permanent Settlement of Bengal.

New law courts were established in every district of British India with procedure based on the lines of British courts. More importantly, the law to be administered was, in civil cases, so-called 'Hindu personal law' for Hindus and 'Muslim personal law' for Muslims. The judge, a British covenanted servant, was assisted by *maulvis* for Muslim law and pandits for Hindu law. Bernard Cohn has written drily about how the new system of law worked less than perfectly (1992: 463–82): not only was it a struggle for the administrators, the judges, the lawyers, and the public to keep it functioning, it did not satisfy any of them regarding fulfilment of the aims of justice and produced long-lasting suspicion between these different actors. As he says regarding one set of relationships:

I would suggest that at the end of the eighteenth century, structurally, there was no place for an independent profession such as Cornwallis and his aides conceived it. Almost all social, political and economic relationships in India at the time were hierarchically ordered, and even relationships between buyer and seller in the market had some non-economic and non-contractual qualities. The rich and politically powerful had their agents to deal for them with other rich and powerful persons. Those without economic and political power needed to be clients of those with power to get 'redress and justice'. The idea of an agent to whom one has only a non-recurring, one-dimensional relationship—that of lawyer-client—must have appeared alien (p. 477).

Where other historians have stepped in to add to this story of blundering and strain, is to add the story of a new discrimination that is gendered. South Asian men did find themselves obliged to perform some crucial social and economic activities differently to what they were accustomed to. But the new system of law not only set up new professions, codes, and definitions for its practice, it refined what were a diverse and fluid set of practices into a small and regulated number that were discoverable through the treatises that were considered ancient. This act of refinement and solidification was particularly inimical to the interests of women who had in practice more rights than were articulated in the treatises.

What we have to yet research and write about is the gendered nature of the new classes and professions. In mainstream history-writing in South Asia, just as elsewhere in the world, modernization was spoken of approvingly, and the self-evident role of the woman in this history was that of the silent partner and helpmeet.

The first notion that the history of modern South Asia could be read as gendered began to appear in the 1990s, and was limited to the colonial capitals and the big events of colonial history (Sinha 1995). Events such as the Age of Consent Act of 1891, raising the age of consent for sexual intercourse for Indian girls from ten to twelve, and the 1884–8 litigation in Bombay against Rukhmabai, who presented the challenge of refusing to cohabit with her husband, were carefully interpreted to be about masculinity and femininity as constructed by both colonialists and nationalists (Chandra 1998). The patriarchy of South Asia was recognized as not being either one identifiable thing over time, nor autonomous and pure in itself. but rather profoundly formed by historical, most recently colonial, influences. More radically, colonial masculinity was interpreted as composed by metropolitan interests and activities in the colony, and in no case as a reflection but rather as a constituting element. Gender came to be seen as crucial to historical analysis, as economic, political, and social processes were.

If some of the larger events of South Asian history were amenable to gendered analyses, so were some of the larger processes. Events included the Mutiny of 1857, in which the British used the defence of their women as a central trope in the articulation of their need to defend their empire (Sharpe 1993). Processes included the nationalist movement from the later nineteenth century onwards, which saw women as a metaphor for the traditional and the authentically national (Sarkar 2001). Various scholars pointed out that the way gender operated in the colony was inimical to the interests of women. The separation of the private from the public sphere, one of the processes accompanying modernity, was characterized in the colony with the private as the special domain of the woman. This has also been seen to be the gendered history of modernity in the metropolis. The difference in the colony is that this particular process then sits on the top of, or with, already complex indigenous gender divisions with their linkages to caste and class. Some of the other conditions of modernity, the expectations of a self-determining subject, with choice and agency, also seemed to lessen the legitimacy of women's worlds and to minimize their spaces for actions rather than to widen or heighten them.

Curiously the history of women in the pre-colonial periods was neglected. Some literary scholars kept mining the Hindu epics or Buddhist literature for their discourses of women, but we know relatively little about the playing out of patriarchy throughout South Asian history. Literary data by itself can tell us about both the structures and the particular individuals depicted, but the quality of literature of being relatively open-ended will remain. In *Udayan*, for instance, the two wives of Udayan are both rational, balanced, utterly dignified, happy people, whereas the king is often torn, disturbed, and confused—or so the author makes it seem. It is a patriarchal society with polygamy, with a kind of androcentric fantasy similar to the Ramayana's, but also with characters who have powerful voices and personalities, as if the author could not bear to not recognize real life in his art.

Gender analysis in the post-colony was aided by two related developments in the humanities and social sciences. One was the deconstruction of the culture concept, so that feminist scholars could now proceed to unravel how indeed 'culture' was only the 'culture' of a section of the people, and whereas there had always been class differences to suspect its putative holism, the largest split in the middle of culture was surely that of gender. The second development was the powerful paradigm of orientalism. Colonization was so apparently a violence and a hierarchy on lines parallel to that of gender; what could have been read as a metaphoric parallel was seen clearly now a constitutive deep-grammar parallel.

What I propose through my essays here is to build further on this wonderful scholarship of certain colonial events and processes that displays their gendered core. I would like to expand the notion of 'critical events' to encompass many everyday events, structures, and processes. The data on education easily permits this. In the essay 6 'Mothers and Non-Mothers' (Chapter 6), I argue that because South Asian education is so transparently a history of those who did not go to formal schools together with that of those who did, women are easy to include in its telling. Because, further, South Asian education is so clearly a history of the process of learning that takes place outside formal schools along with those that take place within (Chapter 5), women are easy to include in its telling once more. Then, precisely because women are so totally implicated in the reproduction of patriarchy (Chapter 8), it is easy to include them in the history of education where through numerous ways, from socialization at home, to choosing mainstream schooling for their sons, to setting up institutions for girls (Chapter 7) women are key actors.

However, apart from merely broadening the scope of a gendered history of South Asia to go beyond specific events and processes to everyday life, I propose that discussions of education make some other important points as well. The most important one is about the methodology of studying gender. To ask certain questions about women's voices in history is to confront the methodological challenge of 'How shall we find out?' We could keep experimenting and going around in circles if we keep to familiar data and interpretation. But if we were to use literature, folklore, art, or geography, or indeed any unconventional source, I suggest, we would find new openings. In my discussion of the novel *Mai* (Chapter 9), I found myself arguing that 'the method should follow the subject'. A mother in general, and in this novel, presents certain challenges to interpretation, which themselves, at least in the novel, offer obvious solutions as well. If a mother, or a woman, often retreats from subjecthood, we have to see it not as a 'retreat' in our terms with its negative connotations, but as an expression of choice, agency, and power (all laden with connotations too).

By expanding our methods and sources, we can glimpse wider interpretive possibilities for other related topics in Indian history as well, such as that of reform. In Chapter 6, I make an explicit comparison between the (failed) reform efforts of Rammohan Roy, at least vis-à-vis his mother, and the failed efforts of the young protagonists in saving their mother in the novel *Mai*. I had struggled with the question of women's role in reform for a long time. I could see (chapter 7) that it consisted of women being the targets of reform; women being the domesticated helpmeet of men; women being an ungendered category who could also act; and women being an obstacle to reform. What the perusal of the novel *Mai* taught me was that a woman is also an educator, and that she, of course, produces the adults whom she teaches and socializes as children. The novel itself, and I in many instances, speak of a specific mother in each case. But the argument holds even more appropriately for surrogate mothers and mother-figures. Thus, I propose that rather than emphasize how the intelligentsia, nationalists, and reformers in nineteenth-century India produced women as a particular category, we could start learning a lot about nineteenth-century history if we looked carefully at how the intelligentsia, nationalists, and reformers *were produced* by their women.

POSTCOLONIALISM

The nature of modernity in South Asia rests very closely on its historical felicitator, schooling. There are two wide-open wounds in South Asian modernity, peculiar to its history. One is that because education was colonial and seen as an arm of the state, and because the colonial state was anti-Indian community, a huge section of the Indian population has voluntarily or involuntarily been shut off from the advantages of schooling. I discuss this problem with regard to maidservants in the essay, 'The Scholar and Her Servants' (Chapter 12). The second is that because education was colonial it was also weak in its infrastructural resources, just as science and industry in South Asia were. The modernity that such education facilitates, therefore, is slow to change, quick to imitate, solemn regarding rote-learning and regurgitation of facts, suspicious of innovation and risk-taking. I discuss this problem in the essay 13 'A Postcolonial School in a modern world' (Chapter 13).

The questions raised by historicism, as Chakrabarty uses the term, arise again. As I argue in Chapter 12, how do you dispense with historicism when you do not want to create an is-ness for the other but a sense of process, with a past and a present that does not foreclose the future because of the *desire* of the subject? History is emergence and self-realization for Hegel et al. in a totally different context to ours in the post-colony, where history is the perception of some of privilege and of others of the denial of privilege and the *desire* for it. And, history is the awareness of the scholar of the differential weakness produced in each, the haves and the have-nots *because* of history.

I recognize that there is a tension in my argument, and although I can glimpse its resolution, it needs further research to be able to document that. I am arguing that the nineteenth- and early twentieth-century elite educated classes were well adapted in the synthesis they experienced between their colonial schooling and their early learning of Indian languages, their grounding in local and family histories, and their socialization into Indian epistemologies. But that in the later twentieth century and today, those classes in pursuit of a modern education are losers with regard to family and local histories, Indian languages, and epistemologies. For the masses, the nineteenth-century slowness to become intellectually colonized continues today but its results are even more markedly dubious. English education opens the door not only to employment and income, but to comfort and confidence in the modern world. The absence of English, and often any formal, education, keeps all the doors closed and produces only comfort and confidence in a limited range of activities in a limited space.

But I experience a tension in the very confrontation with moder-nity itself. Taking it as a historical phase, one with modern medicine, academies, services, and media, I would be ashamed to condemn it for some when it is already a fait accompli for others. I would like everyone to have equal share in the spoils of modernity insofar as they are delivered by the state in South Asia. However, there is no gainsaying that this modernity is extremely problematic. As I argue in chapter 13 this modernity denies dignity to difference, avoids confronting the dilemmas raised by science, blinds itself to environmental needs, and worsens stereotypes of gender and class. It would seem desirable to leapfrog, if one could, this modernity for even those who have not achieved it yet, and move on to a postmodern phase. I have called this postcolonial because the modernity I discuss is largely colonial.

My particular dilemma of postcolonialism is one internal to the nation state. The decision of the kind of history to write is one that should take into account the inequitable distribution of the advantages of education. I could add that attention from taking this necessary step has been diverted by our looking outside into Europe's monopolization of history, but I would prefer to more charitably say that such a gaze outwards was perhaps the necessary first step. Indeed there were many necessary first steps. Decolonization had to be followed by this exposé of orientalism (Said 1979, 1993) and 'ontological imperialism' (Fabian 1983; Wolf 1997), but there were also other intellectual transformations such as the growing influence of feminist scholarship, poststructuralism, and deconstruction. If these developments could be summed up in a sentence, that would be to say that the ground has been cleared for a proposition about postcolonialism.

The arguments in the two chapters of the section called Postcolonialism are that there is no escaping the problematic weight of an approach that recognizes the scholar's own historicity. The scholar can only write a history that does justice to the subject by recognizing the dual legacy of colonialism—a poor infrastructure and a problematic domination of self by other—as a history that continues, and that the scholar is complicit in from the very fact of producing a written history. The approach that has to be forged is one that recognizes the presence of the scholar in history, her pain in recognition of her subjects' pain, and her desire in response to her subjects' desire. Because the approach has to be forged I like to call it postcolonial.

A New Historiography
for South Asia

1

Provincialism in Modern India
The Multiple Narratives
of Education and Their Pain

'Provincialism', or the separation of inferior spaces from normative ones, is seen in this essay as a key trope for interpreting modern Indian history. Provincialism, or provinciality, is a space recognizable instantly. It is marked by slowness, by absence of the new and recent, by what is seen at the national level as a brake-effect in an otherwise promising march forwards. Cities, which is what I concentrate on in this essay, are characterized as provincial by a certain appearance: a topography of narrow streets, by the sloppy merger of the inside and outside, by an absence of discrimination between the jungle and the civilized as animal life proliferates on the roads. Their space is marked by a lack of discipline, and this lack is further exacerbated by an attitude almost aggressive, at any rate stubborn, that seems to embrace every other dimension of life. The provincial citizen is one whose body identifies with the provincial space. It revels in an indifference to the rules of obedience to arbitrary external exercises of power. The provincial space and its citizen are marked in the use of languages by the dominance of regional language over English. Overall, the provincial space is signified in the state as an obstacle, political, economic, and most of all cultural, to what could otherwise be the smooth march forward of unfettered forces of rationality and order. But it signifies itself by an alternative code. That which is indiscipline to the centre is freedom to the margins; that which is coarse, is cultured; that which is backward, is rich; that which is alien is intimate; and that which is unable to keep step with a march forward is precisely the intelligent and crafty that refuses to play a non-reflexive, mechanical game.[1]

Although I limit myself here to a discussion of the production of provinciality by schools, I would make the largest possible case for this conflictual metropolitan–provincial relationship, equating it with modernity itself in our present understanding of 'alternative' modernities (Gaonkar 2001).[2] I want to look at the intertwined problem of schooling and of provinciality from c. 1850s to today through one of many possible lenses, those of technology. The minimal technology of schooling consists of: buildings and spaces, furniture and textbooks, teachers and curricula, routines and rituals. Rather than touch on so many diverse areas, each of which deserves an essay in itself, I will focus mostly on buildings and physical spaces here. The purpose can indeed be accomplished with any single chosen aspect of technology, because technology is never neutral and always suffused with politics. Every school building is itself a citadel of the empire, or of the nation, and together with other processes of education does or does not create a particular kind of subject, and a particular positioning, in this case, of provinciality.

I discuss the relationship between provincial schools and the production of provinciality in three parts: as incompleteness, or the role of the state; as local power, or the role of the family; and as pain, or the role of the child and the role of the scholar. In doing this I adopt the technique of alternative narratives, each of which, in the way of narratives, forefronts and empowers a certain subject position, both expressing and controlling desire. A narrative is not only empowered through its very narrativizing techniques, it can have a base or epistemology in explicitly normalized, powerful, other narratives, typically sacred. By using multiple narratives that run parallel to each other, that contribute reciprocally to each other, and are in conflict with each other, when again, they constitute each other through their negation, we are also able to confront multiple paradigms and epistemologies.[3]

PROVINCIALISM AS INCOMPLETENESS: THE NARRATIVE OF THE COLONIAL STATE

Lancelot Wilkinson, Political Resident at Bhopal, made the following observation perhaps in 1839:

Much progress has been made as well at Bombay as at Calcutta, through means of English. Hundreds of youths have received, through that language, an education, which would be held to be liberal and sufficient, even in Europe; still no man of any experience of *the interior of India*, can for a moment uphold that the system which is found to answer at the Presidencies, should be applied also to *the Mofussil*. The acquirements of a youth, educated through the means of English, would be found almost utterly useless for contributing towards the advancement of his success, in any branch of business in *the Mofussil*. A few students might here and there be collected to prosecute the study; but, *even if their education in English was completed*, they would have extreme difficulty in gaining a livelihood by its means. The parties so educated would be, and are, regarded with suspicion by *the mass of the people*, who receive their announcement of new and strange truths, with almost as much distrust as they do those taught by ourselves. The truths, which have cost so much labour, time and expense in inculcating, do not spread, or take root among *the people*. (Indian Statutory Commission 1930, p. 388; italics mine)

This early observer of education characterizes provinciality as 'mofussil'-dom, that which may be contrasted to the Presidency capitals of Bombay and Calcutta. He explains provinciality as a sort of local politics of 'the people', where they are stubborn in their distrust and suspicion of the new. But most of all he suggests that there was an incompleteness—'even if their education was completed....' Provinciality, therefore, is spatial, temporal, and a product of a failure in completion, and it is these characteristics that I will tease out before moving on to the cultural politics of the people.

It is, of course, difficult to generalize for a period of over hundred years, but it is possible. The first generalization concerns the production of provincial space at the overall level of the colony. The whole topographic–discursive definition of centre and periphery in the colony was changed over the nineteenth century. The prior presence of the British in the three Presidency capitals and then in chosen locations inland, meant that the institutions which were to be the shorthand symbols of the empire would also be built in this order. Thus the islands of Bombay and the swampy villages of the Hooghly delta became the grand capitals of the Company's Bombay Presidency, Calcutta Presidency, and then the Indian empire. The advanced, sophisticated heartland of the Mughal empire became the provincial interior. The re-inscription of centre and periphery was done with the tools of a new architecture. New institutions marked a new power. Buildings were the most corporeal, material, and impressive forms of the new institutions. What was visible in the capital city, say, in Bombay, was exactly what the provincial town lacked in the second half of the nineteenth century:

It must have been a great pleasure in the nineteenth century to walk along the Mayo Road, starting with the Wellingdon Fort to the Queen's Statue with a row of splendid buildings to its right, the New Secretariat (1874), then the Convocation Hall (1874), the University Library and Rajabai Tower (1878), the High Court (1878), and the Public Works Building (1878). Across the Churchgate Road stood first the General Post Office of those days (1872) and then the Central Telegraph Office (1874). (Tikakar 1984)

Instead, what the provinces had was a gap that in the observer's embarrassed gaze stood for an essential backwardness:

In 1898 the Lahore Mall was not attractive, being a dusty road with berms [sic] two or three inches deep in dust or mud according to the weather. There were no footpaths.... The resulting depression of a new arrival was not relieved by the grounds of the College, which were dreary in the extreme. There were no gates and no fence, and the grounds were the rendezvous and resting place of cattle from the city. (Garrett and Hamid 1964:108)

Clearly, the resident of such a place would be associated with the dust, mud, and cattle, and the absence of footpaths, gates, and fence. Such a small town resident visiting Calcutta or Madras at the turn of the century, like a Russian traveller to St Petersburg at the same period (Berman 1988), found himself entering new worlds different to his familiar ones. 'Provinciality', which must have always been a state of mind of some compared to others, came to have a new, clear configuration in the space of colonial India.

This new spatial configuration of imperial legitimacy was created partly through a new temporality. History on a grand scale was divided up into the Ancient, Middle, and Modern Ages, and this History was communicated specifically through schools, and differentially through types of schools according to their location in the centre or the margins. The learning and internalization of such a History itself became the march of change and progress, enshrined in the colonial mode of schooling, recognizable first by its building. This History remains meaningless to many Indians even today, depending on the provincialism of their education. The inconsistency in two coexisting models of History was echoed in education and its spaces: what was best was in the past; but also, whatever was the older was the backward, and what was the brand new and imported was the progressive. Thus, old buildings could be monuments to be preserved; but the most desirable were the new monuments of the empire. 'Oldness' and the 'past' was an object of desire strictly when it was produced by newness—by new technology, speeding forwards—and the present/future.

The models for the new education were the Hindu College, Calcutta (f. 1816), and the Elphinstone College, Bombay (f. 1827), both set up in temporary locations by committees of local gentlemen, then moved to their proper sites and aided and co-administered by the government. By the 1850s there were 11 English colleges and 40 high schools in British India being run by the government. Additionally there were 92 English-language missionary schools. These, with their 9,000 and 13,000 students respectively, comprise the 'system' we are talking about. For system there was: it was a new education, characterized by a *technology* (to repeat my list) of buildings, spaces, furniture, textbooks, languages, teaching methods, routines and rituals; by a *philosophy*, of the relationships between student, teacher, text, and the world; and by a *politics*, of control by a central power over definitions of truth and meaning. In 1857 were chartered the three universities of Calcutta, Bombay, and Madras which affiliated all these schools and colleges. This was the new educational system.

Every new school, college, or university that was set up after the 1850s had to approximate the definitions of proper institutions in Europe, 'scientifically' adapted to India, with reference to temperature and winds, and, such being the political nature of science, to the grandeur of the ruling class. In each case, a foundation ceremony was conducted with great pomp, where it was emphasized that the building was an expression of the spirit within. Lord Mayo said of Bombay University, 'The building now commenced will give a fresh impetus to these objects for which the University has been founded'. The objects, it was elaborated, were 'a moral and social training…a change in the character' (Tikakar 1984). The architect of Bombay University was Sir Gilbert Scott, the dreadful English Gothick, who planned and directed it from his London offices, in the tradition of most buildings in India in which well-known architects had a say without visiting the place. 'He could not, to be sure, actually build a chapel (such as he had already built for Exeter College, Oxford, and St John's College, Cambridge), this being a university mostly for Hindus and Muslims, but he managed to imply nevertheless that a Christian purpose lay behind the institution, and that the Christian God was hallowing it' (Morris 1983:105).

The details of the styles patronized comprise an interesting story in themselves. The universities were marked by the earlier passion for the classical, 'white classical silhouette... majestically untroubled, reincarnations of the antique'... 'similar to what we may conceive of a Grecian city in the age of Alexander'. This was the triumph of reason over barbarism, and 'the elegant order of the classical styles was used in pointed antithesis to the riotous tangle of Hindu architecture' (Morris 1983: 25). Their grammar was less than impeccable, 'but the symbolism was the thing, and anyway few of those who saw these buildings, whether indigenes or imperialists, really knew a pilaster from an architrave' (Morris 1983: 26). School buildings, specially, could be amazing combinations of the scholarly-utilitarian, the aesthetic-antiquarian, and the political-symbolic, in their deployment of domes, towers, clocks, courtyards, quadrangles, staircases, pillars, and verandahs.

The new architectural ideal for schools was in stark contrast to the dominant Indian view of learning as unwalled and spatially unspecific, or, as in its Hindu version, 'Saraswati can dwell anywhere'. I want to clarify that I am not making a statement about 'Indian' architecture. I do not imagine that there is one 'Indian' model for me to talk about. Not only have different aesthetics and politics produced the buildings of different regions at different times, there is no reason to not include the colonial in this assortment of Buddhist, Gupta, Sultanate, Mughal, and so on as 'Indian' (even if these categories were distinct, which they are not, see Tillotson 1998: 4). It is also difficult to imagine what would distinguish, in this complex, a building as 'Indian' or, indeed, as distinguishable by any canonistic feature, in a static and non-historicized way. How was the Taj Mahal regarded by those who viewed it in the eighteenth century, before it acquired its aura of romance, history, and the status of an 'Indian' 'wonder'?

However, I *am* claiming that a radical shift in the category of 'space' took place in the discourse of education in the nineteenth century, from what had existed in pre-colonial 'India'. At the heart of the change was not only the nature of a new school building, but that the school building was there at all, and grandiose enough at times to be included in surveys of 'Indian architecture' of the colonial period, whereas there had been no such building that may be labelled a 'school' in pre-colonial periods (see Kumar 2000; Metcalf 1982). This new school building not only became the norm of the new age, symbolic and actually denotative of power, but also an unequivocally negative comment on hitherto existing practices. Both learning and popular culture had been oriented to the outside, and the continuities of the indoors and outdoors. School sites as visible in compilations of 'Places in which the school is held' included in most government surveys (Education Commission 1884b:10; see Kumar 2000), well documented in fiction (Bandopadhyay 1968), and even visible today, consisted of temples, pilgrim houses, mosques, roofs, and verandahs of private and public buildings, and public and private gardens. In these same surveys, the description of sites was accompanied by a coded critique 'There are no proper school buildings', and replaced within the second half of the nineteenth century by a single unquestioned norm: the closed, four-walled room with wooden desks and benches.

This model worked incomparably better in the capital cities than in the provinces. The very first modern schools in both Calcutta and Banaras were set up in 1816–17. In the provincial capital of Calcutta, the Hindu College was set up by a local committee which was weighty enough to work for modern education without including a seeming westernizer like Rammohan Roy with his radical and disturbing politics. In the old central, now rapidly provincializing, city of Banaras, the first school was set up not by any local committee but by an expatriate Bengali. The landlord benefactor, Jai Narain Ghoshal, was cured of a disease by an English doctor and wished to show his gratitude. One may imagine the doctor's response when asked what form a gift to him should take, indigenous forms being wells, pilgrim houses, charity kitchens, and gardens. What is even more significant here is that the first close dates are followed by a very different metropolitan and provincial chronology. In Calcutta, there was a succession of similar schools to the Hindu College followed by the University itself in 1857. In Banaras, the next important school was the Anglo-Bengali High School in the 1850s and then the Central Hindu School in the 1890s, set up respectively, by the expatriate Bengali community and the Madras-based Annie Besant and her followers. The University in this case was founded only in 1916 as an explicit Hindu nationalist response to colonial educational endeavours. The difference in the two histories is reflected in a difference in the study of the two. There is a fair amount of work on Rammohan Roy, and the educational endeavours of other liberal residents of Bengal apart from him. There is not a single work on the founders of the educational institutions in a city like Banaras, such as on Jai Narain Ghoshal, Chintamani Mukherjee, or Bipan Bihari Chakravarty.

It was not that the norm of the modern school building as a neo-Gothic structure with a material statement of a new order, a civilizational legacy, and the power of both Europe and Christianity was not accepted even in the provinces. It was accepted, but as one of at least two ideologies. The strength of metropolitan modernity decreed that the modern building may be planned and built. The strength of provincialism dictated that then there would typically be an unembarrassed disinterest and distaste towards maintaining the building as befits its original purposes, and certainly towards treating it as an active agent for developing a new consciousness. The school building was accepted as a sign of legitimacy and power, but was not accepted, perhaps, as a necessary location of learning and knowledge, or, in the Hindu case, as the most compatible home of Saraswati, the goddess of learning and the arts.

But I choose to write the narrative of the colonial state in order to speak of it as agent, and will resume that track. If we keep at the centre the Director of Education and those instrumental in the new policy-making, we see that the aim of the new education could be thwarted in two ways, one substantial and the other subsidiary. The subsidiary was represented by the state as the helplessness of sheer distance from England, and the location in tropical conditions:

[The styles] were all, like the empire builders themselves, slightly mutated *en voyage*....The architectural styles got cruder, looser, wider and very often larger. They were making the sea change from a highly advanced Western country, whose art stood in the direct line of descent from Greece, Rome, the Gothic master-masons and the Renaissance, to a country whose educated architecture sprang from different roots altogether, and whose vernacular styles were evolved to meet the demands of extreme poverty and simplicity of material....Throughout the long building period of British India, the constructions were, so to speak, roughened by their setting. It was inevitable (Morris 1983: 14).

The substantial and major undermining of the new policy occurred with funding. The resources available for education were meagre, and it was consensually agreed that almost no school could be properly housed or staffed. The problem lay partly in a structure of distribution, with less going to the provincial than to the Presidency towns. But it lay largely in the size of the total outlay. The distance between the amount needed, say Rs 33.7 million, and the amount available, Rs 4.2 million, was incommensurable (Nurullah and Naik 1964: 155). The 'filtration theory' favoured in different parts of the subcontinent at different times, but influential everywhere for a large part of the time, advocated concentration on higher education. A major cause of its advocacy was the realization that the funds government was willing to part with were quite inadequate for mass education (Education Commission 1884b: 12; Chaube 1965: 307–11).

Apart from directly setting up schools, funds were needed for giving grants-in-aid to the schools set up by concerned individuals and bodies, in line with the top-heavy philosophy of downward filtration. Local taxes were used for this purpose, and they could not be raised above a point. There were differences between the three Presidencies and then the North-Western Provinces and the Punjab (see differences in Education Commission 1884b: 168–71 and Education Commission 1884a: 18–21) but two things were in common. Very few of the vernacular schools came to be aided, and these were not the provincial ones. 'Almost all the schools were situated at Bombay or Poona and were maintained by the Missionary Societies' (Education Commission 1884b: 34). Second, the criterion for receiving grants-in-aid was made progressively more stringent, which was then followed by observations about the inadequacies of the schools. People simply failed to run them according to the new norms, and their failure was then characterized by the state as 'the want of enlightenment in Native communities' (Education Commission 1884b: p. 34).

There are records of local dissatisfaction with various government requirements (Kumar 2000), but I do not have much information on how these requirements were circumvented or dealt with. My ethnographic research suggests, however, that the criteria laid down for grants and recognition must have been inappropriate to the small towns to begin with and over the decades came to be treated as meaningless requirements simply to be manipulated as best as possible. In a typical small town today, an interesting state of affairs is visible. Less than half of the hundreds of schools will have government recognition, a reflection of an ideological conflict that was first set up in the mid-nineteenth century between the government's statement of needs and the needs of a neighbourhood. What the government demanded then, and demands now, are papers certifying that the school owns a given extent of land, that it has classrooms of a certain size, that it possesses laboratories, a library, and a games room, and the books and materials to go into them, and that it provides toilets and drinking water. What the neighbourhood perceives as its needs are typically satisfied by buildings that are residential homes, without the expected open land, classrooms, or additional facilities. These model features are never discussed by educator or guardian as crucial to an assessment of the educational quality of an institution. A school is judged to be sufficiently good if it has 'discipline'. 'Discipline' does not include the administration's discipline in complying with government rules, but refers only to the unilateral disciplining of children by educators.

The irony lies in the nineteenth century origins of this impasse. The state either did not have the funds for the number of schools that should be aided, or its aid was not sufficient (Bruce 1933: 116; Garrett and Hamid 1964: 119). Its criteria for giving aid were inappropriate for the people to begin with. Instead of being made more liberal with experience, the criteria were further narrowed in principle, and emphasized in practice, over the years, and when not fulfilled, no aid was given (Education Commission 1884b: 35–8, 74–5). Many of the few schools that did receive aid, did so through progressively popular techniques of manipulation of papers, false records, and influence-mongering. This seemed to suit the impoverished Directorate of Education.

And the last problem was insufficient staffing, for which our record is most expressive for top institutions, although the shortage of trained teachers was bemoaned at every level (Nurullah and Naik 1964:119). The charters of the first universities, as laid out in 1857, could not even then be carried out for lack of funds. Qualified teachers could not be hired and there was a shortage of staff. This underscored what was already an ideological propensity; to promote languages and the humanities at the expense of the sciences. The professor of chemistry at Elphinstone College, lecturing without benefit of laboratory or demonstration apparatus, dismissed his efforts in 1875 as 'a waste of time on the part both of the professor and of the students' (Tikakar 1984). In 1880, when the Bombay University course was reorganized, only three out of the nine science fields provided for could actually be offered for shortage of funds. This being the case with the capital cities, we can be certain that smaller cities and towns suffered a shortage of teachers even more severe (Garrett 1914: 132–5).

Now, in a narrative that deliberately forefronts the role of the *state* in education, we could find a cause for empathy with even the actors here. The dilemma—we may even call it the *pain*—of the professor at least is quite evident to us if he does not have the facilities he needs and considers his teaching wasted. The *political* dilemma, which I have not had a chance to mention, but which is well documented in the literature, lay in balancing a pragmatic approach of creating a class of trained servants with a hesitation caused partly by the glimpse of a new politicized identity that would demand independence in the future (McDonald 1966). The *administrative* dilemma arose in balancing the bridge on the gap between policy—the world's largest experiment in centralization, and that in a foreign language—and achievement, never over 25 per cent literacy. The *discursive* dilemma lay in the very nature of colonialism, in the exercise, over a fairly extended period, of control without hegemony. There is something touchingly solemn and tragic (in the sense of futile, doomed) about the to and fro of discussion and decision-making on all educational issues in the British colony of India, as it emerges from the voluminous archival record. Such an ambitious effort, such an idealistic experiment, such a faith in sense and reason, in definition and law! And all understood to be futile even from the first step. As if it were a structure to be created with words, where the strength of the words would go on sustaining the effort, when all the words echoed was the hidden statement, 'It is not happening':

Even if the zealous educationist concentrates his efforts on the development of simple literacy, he encounters obstacles which he cannot quickly remove or evade....Nine-tenths of the Indian population...live in the villages of India....There are formidable obstacles arising from caste and communal feeling. It is not too much to say that the establishment of a really satisfactory system of mass education in India...constitute one of the most tremendous problems which educationists have ever had to face. (Indian Statutory Commission 1930: 381)

One could come to a sort of poetic view that makes the tragedy internal to colonialism. But interesting as the dilemma of the colonial state is from its own point of view, we should move on.

PROVINCIALISM AS LOCAL POWER: THE NARRATIVE
OF THE INDIGENOUS SCHOOL

If there were certain reasons why the project of a modern educational system remained incomplete from the point of view of the state, what was the story for the indigenous school? Powerful as the new model was, it was not a case of one system of education replacing another. All the varieties of schools that existed before colonial education varied in language, standard, design, and purpose. They were not thought of as one 'system' and not named or categorized under one rubric by patrons, participants, or observers, until the British labelled them 'indigenous'.

Among many differences were that Sanskrit schools shared some key premises with colonialism, such as the welding together of power and knowledge (Pollock 1993), and vernacular schools did not. The new policy chose to make a deliberate and total discursive break with all of them, and from the 1860s until approximately 1900, indigenous schools gradually became extinct. Some were reformed out of existence. Many were systematically marginalized and starved of funds and recognition. The local social leaders who had been their natural patrons found their role transferred to the colonial state and themselves reduced to figureheads on committees. A few old schools continued as the choice only of those under duress, the poor, politically helpless, and lacking any vision of progress.

But why did this project remain incomplete? That is, even when the schools were weakening or finished, why in the provinces did the relationship of people to the environment, to space, time, mud, water, the indoors, the outdoors, and their body and their selves in the anthropological sense of substantial, key concepts, not disappear over the nineteenth century? One explanation lies in the different functions addressed by the two kinds of education. The new schooling was initially useless in the provinces because the training it sought to provide was for professions in which the provincials could see no future, whereas the older schooling did have relevance. If, and when, it was understood that these new schools were not merely workshops for teaching another language, script, general knowledge, and at the best, etiquette, but in fact would strive to wield 'moral influence' over the pupils, they were treated as irrelevant for a more positive reason, that they taught the wrong and *failed* to teach the right, ethics to students.

To make a positive case, however, and one of agency such as the narrative mode should enable, one must go beyond the argument of non-utilitarianism. There was a positive wielding of power over the processes of social and cultural reproduction. This can be understood by looking at certain sites not typically regarded as sites of education: the family, the caste, and the community. These were institutional sites that have vanished from our vision because of the norms set down for 'institutions' in the nineteenth century. They deserve a great deal of attention because apart from any resistance they offered to the state, they were sites that reproduced themselves in a tight discursive way, and were determined, not always consciously, to be equally, if not more, hegemonic than the state.

The 'family', 'caste', and 'community' are, of course, foreign words with no exact Indian language matches. Indians took happily to the English words 'caste' and 'community' and they entered local lexicons. 'Family' was not adopted as comfortably, perhaps because the other two subsumed the realities that it could refer to. I will here speak of the three as largely overlapping spaces.

The *family* was tied up with education in a very direct way, in that the location of 'indigenous' formal teaching could be the home as often as not. But, for the Education Commission in its data-collection, 'We employ the term "school" or "institution" to mean an assembly of pupils belonging to more than one family or house, and receiving instruction together from a teacher, who has set up on his own account, or is not solely employed as a family-tutor. The inclusion in our returns of single children or of groups of children of one family privately instructed at home, *might possibly have added large numbers of pupils to the total, but the returns themselves would have been confused and misleading*' (Education Commission 1884b: 67, italics mine). That is, unlike what all the government documents tell us, the 'indigenous' school, when located in the home, did not vanish; it was simply not recorded. Every single person interested in the subject of modern Indian education believes, fallaciously, that indigenous education was altogether replaced.

The relationship between caste and education is even more hidden, and deceptive for the scholar. Historical discussions of caste have tackled different problems, but have failed to pin down its power or meaningfulness as a system of social-cultural reproduction. As anthropologists, we could choose to consider a caste best defined by its interactions or its attributes (Sharma 1999; also Quigley 1999,

Searle-Chatterjee and Sharma 1994). But in either case, it would be the reproduction in the family that ensures the continuity of the caste. Its techniques should be classifiable with those of education (Reagan 2000).

Yet, 'education' is never conceptualized as such and never spoken of as a training in profession, the arts of life, or ethics, but exclusively as formal, liberal education. Thus, in one of the recent-most studies of caste in modern India, the author, Susan Bayly (1999), speaks of education in only two senses: one as the liberal education that enabled Indians to plan a future for India that would be caste-free; and two, as a kind of failure, in the contrary case of those Indians who had a similar liberal education but chose to speak in defence of the caste system, attributing to caste a scientificity and rationality.

But apart from being an object of representation that could be condemned or defended, caste had a more experiential meaning for Indians. At the most elementary, there has always been a backbone of professional specialization running through the caste structure, which implied, and implies, that not only do people have different life trajectories, they are trained differently as children to follow these. A corollary to a professional or technical training is an ethical one. This includes definition of the self, relationship with 'society' and 'others', understanding of hierarchy and duty, of citizenship and age, of the good life and pleasure. This varies from caste to caste, group to group. It has been noted in the education literature that those castes, such as certain Brahmans and Kayasthas, which had the business of working with the pen or with paper, and were often masters of Sanskrit, Arabic, or Persian, and often of the vernaculars, could switch comfortably to colonial education, other conditions being right. What has not been equally noted is how other castes, in occupations that demanded specialized education, including of certain scripts and systems, kept to their own training, and found no value in English education at all (Dobbin 1972). To merely see in this a 'problem' to be explained means that we have assumed a hard core narrative of modernization, where the choice of the new, colonial offerings marks rationality, and whatever is opposed must be orthodoxy or conservatism.[4]

And of course there was a technology to the social reproduction of castes, which could be more or less formal. An example is the Gaud Saraswat Brahmans for whom we have a detailed description in the work of Frank Conlon (1977). They chose a *smarta swami* from whom they sought guidance and teaching periodically. Splits in families, while often ostensibly on matters of devotion, were professional splits, such as that of the Shenai or 'learned' who supplemented their landed income with teaching, writing, and accountancy. When a split was imminent or had occurred, a primary method of ensuring the distinctive qualities of each subsection was through the training of younger generations in certain codes of conduct. Apart from teaching in the sites of temples and *maths*, and by swamis, the guidance of the larger body was undertaken usually by the elders in groups of ten or five. More precise instruction, as in accountancy for a son or sons when the family was otherwise in farming, would be given by a teacher chosen from the locality.

Yet, as with Bayly, Conlon makes his first mention of 'education' only as equivalent to colonial education, and at the very end of his chapter 3, after he has discussed the genealogy of the Saraswats, their techniques for maintaining purity and unity, their migrations and work. At the start of his discussion of education, he mentions their 'cultural heritage of literacy, education, and scribal employment', which is for me the lost world in our story, and which becomes so difficult to retrieve because of its cloak of 'culture' and 'heritage'.

If the world of social-cultural reproduction in castes and communities is un-reconstructed yet, the world of infantile socialization and early childhood learning within the family is equally un-investigated. The sociological role of the mother in not only 'mothering' but in active teaching—of languages, narratives of the region, the community, and the self—is unknown compared to what we know of the new disciplining activities of the nineteenth-century mother (Bose 1996). This emerging power of the mother, in conjunction with other changes in the public sphere, could lead the son to emphasize his masculine qualities and the necessarily masculine nature of his activities in the public as well as private sphere. It led to a particular woman's and mother's role being emphasized for the woman. Public work and action in general became more gendered over our period and was accompanied by the separation of the man's and the woman's sites. If we look at the new middle classes of the metropolises, we see the recast woman, with her new duty, goal, and virtue, certainly circumscribed in herself, but a figure of discipline for her sons, working to make her sons the best possible colonial citizens. This modern Foucauldian disciplining of the child in which she participated was more extensive and thorough than the pre-modern version.

However, this happened cleaner and faster in the Presidency towns than in the provinces. Such a disciplining did not quite arrive in the provinces. But what did exist was another disciplining, equally powerful, that of the caste and the community. Even as the so-called indigenous school vanished, the indigenous held firm in its site of the family. In the metropolis, the differential participation in the public sphere came to mark a modern-traditional division. While the new family and new mother themselves enabled a smooth adaptation to new employment and economic opportunities, they permitted a new loyalty to 'tradition', which was feminine, while the pledge to it was rhetorically and epistemologically masculine, and indeed politically rewarding for men under colonialism.

This argument is important to broach even if we do not have the space to develop it, to emphasize how complex a narrative of education we could have if we were to place indigenous and family education at its centre. My point then is equally about history-writing. The older family was authoritarian, disciplinarian, and pain-inflicting enough for us not to romanticize or valorize it. Indeed, it was so subtle and natural-seeming in its procedure that those of us interested in the production of modernity, or simply in the social and cultural history of South Asia, have not considered giving it its dues as a politics. The ink spelt on the study of the production and representation of colonial discourses is not matched even with a token gesture of attention to the space and politics of the family, the community, and local cultures. These are, apparently for contemporary historians, merely the givens of 'community' or 'culture'. Or they are responses to colonial hegemony; not themselves domination or hegemony, but the marks of their absence. The victory of colonialism lies in that it has not only monopolized all representations, it has made us afraid of seeking out other representations in case we err on the side of under-presenting the power of colonialism and mistakenly valorize 'tradition'. Thus does colonialism disempower other discourses from being interpreted, and 'unplace' spaces (Ranciere 1994; also Ahmad 1992).

PROVINCIALISM AS PAIN: THE NARRATIVE OF THE CHILD

No narrative of the child exists in modern India, perhaps because the child as a category has not been discovered or invented yet, along the lines of Philippe Aries' argument (1973). In doing a history or ethnography that may seek to focus on the child, one would be pursuing the unrecognized, trying to locate the undefined. The 'child' or 'childhood' has no resonance yet, particularly in small town India. But surely what we mean to say by this is that the 'modernist' invention or discovery of the child and of childhood has not occurred in India yet outside metropolitan centres. It is clear from all evidence, linguistic and otherwise, that the overall discourse in society is emphatically not of discrete, self-sufficient individuals and of the child as one such individual in the making. But certainly the child exists as a structural, semiotic reality (Jenks 1996), as other evidence—most impressively from fiction—shows us. My small claim here is that a narrative of the child may be fitfully reconstructed from the technologies of the provincial school, that the discourse of the child in turn allows us to glimpse better the nature of provincialism, and that both may be partly comprehended as pain.

For a class of children such as those destined to be the new educated elite, the colonial re-inscription of the centre and periphery, and the growth of new metropolitan centres, meant that as they grew up, childhood typically came to be in another place and became distanced in space as well as time:

Opu's eyes, as he journeyed on, were taking in all the colors of the landscape and the beauty of the over-spreading sky; but on the canvas of his mind appeared and faded many a dream picture of the childhood which this day had brought to an end. He had left his village. It was now a thing of the past. He was on his way to places distant and unknown, perhaps to those many lands and that wonderful life he had seen in his dreams. (Bandopadhyay 1968: 352–3)

Because the child departed, he began to treasure his childhood experiences, and envisioned the land of his childhood as located in the new status of the 'past' and 'tradition'. The child became more 'rooted' in childhood space for moving away. This geography of an 'unearthly beauty, with its fields and rivers, its untrodden forests and the changing glory of its moonlit face' (Bandopadhyay 1968: 354) became available as an asset for the regeneration of the nation, its history, its future.

Opu's case also tells us about the pain of the moorings and mobility that characterized many Indian childhoods in colonial India. Opu's acceptance of poverty and struggle was uncritical when it concerned himself: he was preoccupied with discovery of the world and suffered relatively little. It was when he remembered his hungry, neglected, unloved sister who died as a child, unfulfilled in her desires to own things, ride on a train, and marry, that he felt pain. His childhood home was inextricably part of him because of the people who populated it. The past became not merely a crystallized consciousness, it became a resource for the future, a 'religion', as Shree (2000) calls it.

The discourse of the Presidency child, so to speak, is relevant here because the elite idea of Indian history and a usable past was produced in the Presidencies in a way that did not happen in the provinces. In the provinces, the home and the school were not spatially separated in the same way, there was no departure and no parting, and the past was not identifiable as a specific geographical location. Not only was there less mobility (for education) in non-Presidency India, there was less of a performance of the 'surrogate functions' of a modernizing project by the colonial school (Naregal 2001). The colleges and libraries, hostels and eating houses, discussion centres and meeting places described for Calcutta and Bombay did not exist in the scores of small towns and cities, many of which had been centres of education in an earlier period (and had boasted such colleges, libraries, and hostels, known by other names). There were hardly any new colonial schools in non-metropolitan India; 'new' schools were typically housed in buildings that were continuous with life around. The past, childhood, and tradition were not elsewhere, but immediately present, not objectified but lived. 'Saraswati dwells everywhere' continued to be both believed and acted out.

An observer of the provincial urban scene today can see this in relation to the technology of education. The rules of the government regarding space and buildings from mid-nineteenth century onwards are based on assumptions concerning the nature of childhood, the nature of learning, and the duties of educators.[5] Provincial schools and their public *have not* shared these assumptions. The criteria for government recognition of schools have been, and are, so distant from people's worlds that whether affiliated or not, *all* provincial schools are in fact similar. If the requirements for affiliation are classrooms of a certain size and facilities such as a library, laboratories, and play-ground, and unaffiliated schools do not have them, affiliated schools in the provinces *do not have them either*. They may have them 'in name', that is, there are spaces that may be pointed out to the visitor, and may be noted for the record, as library, laboratory, or games room, but these spaces are never used by students for the named purpose. Real facilities actually used by children, as required for the running of a modern, liberal school by affiliating boards, have not existed, and do not exist, in *any* schools in a provincial town.

Most schools in small towns have come to be housed in residences donated to the school committees by philanthropists. One example would be Bipan Behari Chakravarty Higher Secondary School in Varanasi, housed in an old, ornate, late nineteenth-century aristocratic home, with deep verandahs and high ceilinged shady rooms—all wonderful as a home, but unsuited for use as classrooms of a modern school. Such buildings are donated, and accepted, with grace and gratitude and named after their donors. As expansion became inevitable, new classrooms are created with tin or asbestos siding, on the roofs, all around in the compound and spawning all over corridors and verandahs. I wish to emphasize the range this includes. There is W.H. Smith Memorial School, founded by an Englishman's widow, and immensely popular because of its suggested resemblance to a 'convent'. There is Sir Syed Public School started by the Aligarh Old Boys' Association as a 'reply' to Christian and Hindu schools. There is Sunbeam in Annapurna Nagar, a closed box of a building that grows upwards, ever more closed and crowded, seen as a model of an avant-garde modern school. In all these cases, all semblance of an original model was long lost as classes met in the verandahs, in the courtyard, in front of offices, and literally in nooks and crannies—in the case of residential buildings, in bathrooms and garages. Clearly, any acquired space may be used for any stated purpose, and failure or success in achieving the purpose is not attributable to the space. In all these cases, the crowding has never been of interest to the educators, including all those who have enthusiastically discussed the 'problems of Indian education' in article and speech.

We come then to the question of 'pain'. I propose that there is pain for the provincial child at two levels. First, there is an awareness exemplified by the adult that one lives within a structure of necessity from which certain ideals are necessarily banned. In response, for instance, to the question of why school buildings may not be more clean, adequate, purpose-specific, there are two reactions from educators. The first is of agreement with the questioner, a confirmation of knowing the same approaches, perhaps of having attended several workshops, of having taken training courses and got degrees. But there is an underlying separation into 'theory' and 'practice', marked by a separation between book knowledge which is imported or elite, and practical knowledge which is shared by all intelligent people on local ground. The separation is caused, as I see it, by an omnipresent colonial discourse about learning which blocks out at the very outset the possibility that book knowledge could be practical knowledge, or its corollary, that local knowledge could be legitimate knowledge. In a historical perspective, I see it as caused by the experience of colonial education which established this equation time and again: 'What you learn on the ground is unofficial and unrecognized, but very useful. What you learn officially is compulsory but not useful'.

The second reaction is also premised on a shared understanding that of course we are all trained, sophisticated educators who know the tricks. They do not need discussion. What we are also is practical, experienced adults who know exactly how the world functions. *In places like Banaras. In the real India.* So we can agree that many of the ideas, in fact *all* the ideas of liberal education are totally inoperative in local situations. The first argument teaches the child to think of himself as cleverer because he (the provincial) can be practical as well as theoretical; the second argument broadens the case beyond all dispute, as the child is taught to essentialize himself as absolutely, always different to the metropolitan other.

The pain lies not in any lack of agency, but in this very self-enactment. People in the provinces, even while paying lip service to the ideology of the colonial state, did not 'modify' modern school buildings beyond recognition because they were *ignorant.* There was certainly a clash of two contrary discourses: a modern one of properly conducted specialized space, and an anti-modern or pre-modern one indifferent to the specific qualities of organized space. But in modifying modern buildings or finding alternatives, provincials were distancing themselves from the play-acting of Calcutta, and theatres like the Hindu/Presidency College.[6] They were sceptical of the colonial state, are now of the postcolonial state, openly dismissive of its civilizational claims, and finally, not overly threatened by its coerciveness. There was also a double loop: the mimic-man of Macaulay was the one produced in Elphinstone in Bombay or La Martiniere in Calcutta, and an other of that was the one produced in the provincial school. We can interpret this as mimesis if we also question the implicit claim that there exists a purer model of which this was an unstable copy. The model even of the stablest buildings was most likely a hybrid hyphenated one: Indo-Saracenic, Hindu-Gothic, Renaissance-Mogul, Saracenic-Gothic, Swiss-Saracenic. I propose that mimesis itself is the ultimate in creativity: when a representation satisfying certain criteria, functional and aesthetic, is made by the actor, not particularly because he is a certain *kind* of actor (colonized, South Asian) but because mimesis is the condition of life. How 'real' does a copy have to be? Provincial schools fail our realist tests of modernity; they show no *fidelity*, in the sense of both *accuracy* and *loyalty*. But the magic of mimesis lies in that while the copying may be quite imperfect, it nevertheless accomplishes some purpose of the actors and bestows power.

Or, *it should* accomplish the purposes of the actor and bestow power. If we interrogate the modernity of the provinces, we find ourselves on sites where subjects are produced and reproduced who have no access to the science, language learning, discursive skills, and the secular, liberal, values of the elite. They access a range of other options, none of which, certainly, are primordial or ignorant. Theirs is not the narrative of a colonial takeover of various discourses, of caste, religion, and history, as regularly recounted for the metropolitan centres. But we would do well to go beyond the deconstructive historian who would critique modernizers in the past for their promotion of science, or question the allegiance to 'progress' displayed by the educated elite, and question instead: why, in the provinces, was modern science not loved and promoted *more*?

This has brought us to a mini-narrative of the historian-observer. In this narrative what is fore-fronted is the historian's point of view, and not the state's, the elite's, the family's, or the self-satisfied locality's. Such a historian should describe the child's experience at the micro level, stuck in overcrowded classrooms with inadequate light and air, body trapped in synthetic uniforms and badges, threatened by the ogres of homework and examinations, altogether victim to over-disciplining. Such pain might seem to be partly the fate of every student everywhere, something we accept as pedagogic violence. All students might always thus suffer at the hands of adults, certainly in metropolitan India. As a champion of working class history would do for workers, and a subalternist history for subalterns, I, the historian forefronted here, would still like to render this on behalf of the children as pain. The particular provincial gloss on it is that *this disciplining is for nothing*. The students of provincial schools are denied the rewards of the national-global. As opposed to the earlier school that taught specific skills, the new school was designed to make over the child in a new image with the minimal virtues of punctuality, uprightness, and masculinity, and the promise of modernity and success. But the colonial school in the provinces could not and did not do it.

In the history of education and modernity, there have clearly been winners and losers, both economic and symbolic. Provincial schools have *not* succeeded as little theatres of the nation to play out, or little workshops to create, the spokesmen, the elite, and the intelligentsia (Srivastava 1998). Their discipline has been sufficient to cause pain at the micro level of everyday life for the children. But the discipline has been insufficient to produce the inwardly directed citizen subject of the modern nation state. Provincial schools certainly reproduce the ever-wandering, pan-chewing, pan-spitting, free and satisfied human being of the small town, and not the progressive, successful citizen of the nation—perhaps the secret as to why they continue. But for children and for the historian of children, a source of a doubled pain resides in their subjecting children to an inadequate disciplining and not even giving them a share in the spoils of modernity and citizenship. It is no coincidence that the provincial schools evoke the goddess Saraswati, since she is and always will be, invisible, while for metropolitan schools she is a figure who is passé compared to their more tangible icons.

NOTES

1. This is not a topic, fascinating as it is, that has been rewarded with much attention. The vision of Gideon Sjoberg (1965) remains relatively empty of empirical content for India. For an evocative description of Lucknow as seen in its (problematic) provincialism by the British after 1857, see Oldenburg (1984), and for a celebration of the same kind of unreformed space, see Kumar (1988). The most interesting recent description I have read of the discourse of provinciality is by Srivastava (1998) specifically produced as a negative, or an absence, by metropolitan subject-hood. One could make much of the contrary positions of fiction and film. Hindi fiction, as that of Bismillah (1996), Nagar (1973), Renu (1963), and Shree (2000) talks engagingly about the province in all its multidimensionality, but this fiction has not been tapped as a source by history and anthropology. Film, in its pursuit of the hegemonic nation-building discourse, lingers lovingly on the metropolis, and exclusively so, with only a backward glance at the province that has been left behind by the reformer (see Srivastava 1998: 165–7).

2. As opposed to Srivastava (1998), I do not perceive that there is *one* discourse of Indian modernity, which is the secular, national one, positioning itself in opposition to the communal and backward. The defeat of Gandhian to Nehruvian discourse in history did not mean a permanent defeat of non-metropolitan India, as the appearance of the popular provincial political leaders, Lalu Prasad Yadav, Mulayam Singh Yadav, Mayavati, and others should announce. The nation's metropolitan identity might valorize itself with a distancing from the provincial, and thus pose as modernity and Indian-ness, but this pose is flattering and convincing *only* to the metropole itself. It either rings hollow in the provinces or is actively resisted and counterposed by another discourse, for which the *real* India, the spirit of the nation, its power, and beauty, reside in the provinces.

3. A word must be added about the doubly constructed self of the narrative. I am a reader of the nineteenth-century narrative(s), whose narrators in telling their story *of*, and telling it *to*, include in their audience and subject-matter me and my quest for a certain knowledge, often leading me to frustration and alienation, even as they sometimes convince me. I am, in turn, a writer of the nineteenth-century narrative(s) and would be quick to proclaim its constructiveness, specially when it poses as a full and authentic report. The two kinds of construction are different, the one I read and the one I write, because the first one includes a naturalized one and a humanist one, whereas what I write is a counter-humanist one and a narrative of performance (Sheehan 2002, especially pp 2–19). The shortcomings and pain I record are equally the 'tyranny of narrative' on me as a reader, its breaking of an epistemological and representative contract. In retrospect, the narratives can be told in the ways I choose because such is the configuration I perceive from my end. There was no closure in the events as they unfolded; there was contingency and much else. But from my positioning, in my retrospective examining, feeling eye, I perceive this structure that I lay out.

I am dominating therefore with my own 'tyranny of narrative closure' in that I could be said to inject an inevitability in the narratives. By presenting more than one narrative, and by imbuing them and my own placement as 'pain', I seek to rework this inevitability. But a contradiction persists that perhaps should not be relegated to a footnote. To propose a telling of multiple narratives, to confess to being a 'narrator' with particular interests, and subject to the formal constraints of narrativity, proposes a real-world multiplicity that I have uncovered (and, implicitly, prior writing has repressed)—and readers are asked to accept this post-Grand Narrative strategy as an ethical feat (see Punday 2003: 3; also Ranciere 1994). Beyond this, I am excluding certain narratives in this telling: among others, that of the elite (Weiner 1991), that of nationalist patriarchs (see Alter 1992 and Chatterjee 1993 for two different kinds), and that of educators (PROBE 1999).

4. All the older studies of education problematized this upper caste-colonial education nexus as a kind of shortcoming in the correct liberalization of Indian society (McCully 1940; McDonald 1966). Older studies of nationalism explicitly suggested that Indian politics was faulty because its leaders were both the old upper castes and the new educated (Seal 1968; Gallagher, Johnson and Seal 1973). For an un-reflective statement, see Basu 1925.

5. For the administrative structure of the school system in the nineteenth century, see Restructuring (1996: 1); for the grant-in-aid system introduced by the Wood Despatch, see Chaube (1965: 345–6); for present-day locations, see Primary Education (1997); and for specific affiliation rules, see the guidelines of the Indian Council of Secondary Education and of the Central Board of Secondary Education.

6. The fate of the two schools founded together in 1816–17 is significant. Jain Narain Ghoshal Inter College in Banaras has been reduced to a heap of rubble for sometime now, its original building overshadowed by a 'coaching centre'. Hindu College in Calcutta became Presidency College, the premier institution in the state, some would say the country, and continues to look impressive with its columns and arches.

2

History and the Nation
The Learning of History in Calcutta and Banaras

Why do Hindus and Muslims fight? The partition of India in 1947 into 'Muslim' and (putatively) 'Hindu' nations forces one to pose this grave question—or so one would presume. But for those citizens of India born after 1980—that is, for those who were teenagers when the research for this essay was done—the partition of 1947 is only a distant event with which they have at best tenuous relationships. To investigate these relationships is to raise questions about the way history and histories are created and how the arts of memory are exercised.

At the very least there is an official history to which all historians have a certain relationship. Set beside these official histories are other ways of grouping the events of the past, and we experience or observe their presence as alternative or competing histories. The children of modern India may be: (1) aware of their official history, which they integrate into other aspects or their being; or (2) aware of their national history but separate from and uninvolved in it. Alternatively, they may be (3) unaware of their official national history but aware of other histories; or (4) unaware of their official history and of any other history.

This essay is chiefly about children in the first three categories, and indeed these may be the only three that are socially possible. In the first and longer section, I look at children of category (3), children who clearly have other histories. How are the arts of memory exercised in their case? This section, prefaced by a set of two interviews, concerns the children of Muslim weavers in Banaras. I have chosen weavers because this community has been historically regarded as communal, bigoted, and backward, and today its members are regarded as much of the same, but more eloquently as resistant to the secularizing and modernizing efforts of the nation.

In the second section, I look at children of categories (1) and (2). They are from the class that forms the backbone of the nation, that wants liberal education and secure service jobs for its sons, marriages into service families for its daughters, and maybe now careers as well, if in proper establishments. This class reads and comments on national politics and takes issues of inflation, corruption, production, distribution, etc., very much to heart. The children confidently regard the lessons of history and society which they learn in school as gospel truth, and, what is important to my argument, there is no contradiction to these lessons at home.

I want to show how weavers' children fall between the arts of memory of a *pre-modern* and the history of a *modern* epoch. They certainly know their history. But a secular and disciplined national identity is created only through suppression of minority, or local, or deviant cultures. Given their stubbornness in sticking to their own histories, it is the weavers who are losing out on their legitimate place in the nation. But what is not often recognized is that the middle-class children are losing out on the memories and cultural funds that should be theirs also.

SECTION I. MADRASA EDUCATION: WEAVERS IN BANARAS

1. Interview with the son of a weaver in Banaras, about thirteen years old

Q: Who are you?
Shahzad: My name is Shahzad Akhtar. I am in class IV, in Jamia Hamidia Rizvia.
Q: What do you like to do?
A: I like to play marbles in my free time. I play bat and ball in the field occasionally. I don't like to stay at home.

Q. What do you know about 1947?

A: 1947? I can't remember. I don't know.

Q: You must have studied it in your history?

A: History? We don't do much .... Nothing much is taught in our school. We will have our exams soon. Yes, I know, the Slave Dynasty...the Slave Dynasty....

Q: Yes?

A: I don't remember. The Slave Dynasty... blast! Many of our periods go free. Let me tell you what happens. The teachers get together in groups, talk, eat, and drink. They eat in the classroom and don't let the children eat anything. No, we don't have tiffin time. If we try anything, they beat us.

Q: You do have a history book don't you? Maybe *Hamari Duniya Hamara Samaj*? ['Our World and Our Society'—the government Board textbook in social studies].

A: Yes, but we—er—we haven't begun it yet.

Shahzad is then asked many random questions in history but cannot answer a single one of them. He keeps explaining that he has forgotten or they haven't done it yet. Then he volunteers certain answers he remembers, in a subject called *Malumat-e-Amma* (General Knowledge). He repeats the answers in a monotone, accompanied by a swaying of his body, as habitually done by those reciting what is learnt purely by rote: 'What is *haj*?.... What is *namaz*?... What is *roza*?... Who invented the needle?... Who invented soap?'... The speed of his answers precludes getting them down exactly, and he is unable to repeat them slower. His mother enters at this point and interrupts occasionally.

Q: How will you do your exams?

Shahzad (doubtfully): Yes, they are in May, no, in June....

Mother: We want him to change schools. He is not learning anything.

Q: Is he fond of learning? (*shauk hai?*)

Mother: No, his father is very fond of having him learn.

Q: Are there any activities or functions in the school? Do they celebrate 15 August? 26 January?

[I refer to the Indian Independence Day and Republic Day.]

Shahzad: Nothing. Nothing at all.

Mother: There were when I was small. I studied in the same madrasa, you know. On 15 August we were all taken to Jai Narain [the oldest 'modern' school in Banaras] to participate in a parade. The management of this madrasa eats up all the money. They do not bother about studies at all.

Q: Can you not complain about this as a guardian? And about their not getting time for a snack?

Mother: No, because we are "low" (niche hai). (I am not sure of her nuance here but cannot ask her because she leaves the room.) Shahzad has a younger sister of six or seven whose doll has recently had a wedding with a doll in her paternal aunt's house. Shahzad recounts it with enthusiasm. The two children, with two other siblings, show all the store of things now owned by the doll: fridge and kitchen items, clothes, jewellery, and furniture. Shahzad is very interested in every part of the proceedings and exhibits a necklace that he had made, one of many such little pieces he has made for the doll's dowry.

Q: Do you have any teachers at all that teach?

A: Mansoor master is a good teacher. He even jokes a little.

2. Interview with the teacher 'Mansoor Master' at Jamia Hamidia Rizvia

Q: Who are you?

A: Mohammed Mansoor Alam Khan, from Bihar, here for ten years. I teach maths in classes VI and VII, Urdu in IX and X, history in VI and VII, geography in V, VI, and VII.

Q: What is special or different about the teaching in this school?

A: For a long time, this school was till classes V–VI only. Those who are in the sari business do not want their children to get ahead. Then it was till VIII for a long time. For the last four years we have IX and X. There are obstacles from guardians.

Q: What kind of obstacles?

A: Greed for money (paise ka lobh). Also, the economic condition is not good.

Q: Regarding that—if the children need to sit at the loom—why not adjust the school timings?

A: We have. The timings are 7.30 a.m. to 12 noon. About 40 per cent work at the loom besides studying.

Q: How are the studies here?

A: Good. Which subjects are good? Hindi and Urdu are good. Sociology [sic] is okay. Science is not. Why? It is tough for them. They cannot work hard enough.

Q: What is the advantage of learning these things if they will only weave in the future?

A: Oh, there has been some improvement in the condition of the people.

Q: Is there any direct teaching on the subject of citizenship, social interaction, behaviour, etc.?

A: There is *Dinyat* (Religion), a subject from class II onwards. There is civics, part of the U.P. Board syllabus from VI onwards.

Q: Is there any indirect teaching ? Do you gave any functions or programmes?

A: On Republic and Independence Days, we have flag hoisting, sweets. On 23 December, ten days before Ramadan, we had our annual function. We gave awards and a farewell to class X. There were seven this year. Their guardians came. No, we have no plays, music, recitation, satire, etc.

Q: What are the main problems you encounter as a teacher?

A: There are many. Guardians don't take enough responsibility. There is poor attendance at parents' meetings, or the guardians simply never come. We tried monthly meetings, classwise. There is great illiteracy among them. In my own class, V, out of some twenty-eight, twenty do come. They listen, but they cannot do what they are told. They drop out after class V because they've finished the Qur'an Sharif. This place has no society, no culture. Since this madrasa is free, only the poor send their children to it. They are also indifferent to other schools because there is no Urdu there.

Q: What do the children learn at home?

A: How to weave. The traditional work (*gharelu karobar*). Things related to weaving.

Q: Anything else? What about TV?

A: The influence of TV is restricted to clothes.

Q: What about cricket?

A: Yes, now cricket is such a thing that you can get carried away during a game. But it only lasts as long as the game. They cheer for the Pakistani team. Then they forget. It is a temporary phenomenon. One of my friends currently supports the South African team.

Q: So it is not an indication of communalism?
A: No, it is only cricket.

Let us explore the art of memory as it is exercised by the weavers. Weavers' children, like Shahzad, have the following experience. A son, for a weaver, is an extension of himself. As an infant he is only semi-human; the other half of him is divine, toy-like, prince-like: 'A child is an emperor' (bachche to badshah hote hain), people say. Fathers give sufficient indication of this by enthusiastically playing with their small children in their free time, cuddling them, commenting on their abilities, indulging their whims. From as early as four or five years onward, a weaver's son becomes streetwise. He is sent to the shops for tea and pan (betel nut), for small purchases, to send and bring messages. He is not disciplined regarding his use of space or time, and he is expected to be mobile. In this respect he is a miniature version of his father and other males in the family, whom he begins to resemble more and more. He shares in the male popular culture of Banaras.

Of the many leisure activities of the weavers, such as fairs, festivals, processions, annual celebrations at shrines, gathering for music and poetry, and wrestling and bodybuilding, the most important for them is ghumna phirna (wandering around), including both wandering around the city and gong 'outside' for sair-sapata (pleasure trips). In all these activities, especially the last, 'freedom' is a concept idealized by weavers and all artisans. It reflects partly the actual freedom inherent in the piecework that characterizes artisan production, and is partly an ideological reflex to the insecurity and inflexibility of such labour. That the idealization of freedom reaches the heights it does is a testimony to the self-conscious ethic of the city, based on its corporate character, its patronage of the arts and letters, its pride in more mundane pleasures associated with open air, mud, and water; and a refinement of 'tradition' as expressing the excellent in many areas of cultural life.

While Muslim weavers hold this view of the city, of freedom, and of themselves as inheritors of this tradition in conjunction with other artisans, their view of history and geography is parallel to but separate from that of their Hindu counterparts. Certainly, if we reflect upon it, they could not be expected to share in the familiar, dominant Hindu view of the city as the centre of civilization and the bestower of release after death, or in its fecundity with regard to temples and icons and holy bathing places.

For the Muslim weavers history dawns with the coming of Islam to the region, approximately around AD 1000 when Salar Masaud Ghazi, a semi-legendary general of Mohammad Ghori, was supposedly martyred nearby and the remnant of his force settled down in the region. They became the kernel of the present population of Muslims. Bearing evidence to this history are scores of graves, shrines, and mosques to the *shahid*(s) (martyrs) who sacrificed their lives for the spread of Islam. This history is kept alive in everyday existence by the weekly worship and annual celebrations that mark the most popular of these shrines, as well as in their quieter role as places of rest and meditation at any given time.

While women, children, and whole families go together to shrines on special days, the places are cultural centres for males typically, as are mosques and *chabutaras* (open cemented platforms) in every neighbourhood. A small boy may accompany his male relatives and experience in ever-increasing degrees the openness and benignity of the city. Like them, he wanders around anywhere in his free time, may be traced to one or two favourite haunts, like an outdoor space, playing or watching cricket at a friend's home, or simply 'in the lane' (*gali men hai*). He does not get embroiled in domestic activities, unless, like shopping, they involve the outdoors. Teenage boys, when interviewed, provide reports of the outdoors, of free time, and open space that are identical with those provided by adult males.

Shahzad Akhtar stands at a bridge between childhood and the teen years. He was 'spotted' by me on the street, engaged in nothing in particular, accompanied by a few friends who hastened to blend into the background. Rather than surround me with curiosity, they preferred to remain 'free.' To shake me off, Shahzad first reported that he was on his way to weave. But when my insistence made him surrender and we were sitting and chatting in his home, two of his friends looked in to find out where he had disappeared. At the same time, he showed evidence of enjoying quieter, more 'feminine' pastimes at home, including sewing and threading necklaces for his little sister's doll, although he did not mention any such interest when reporting on his pleasures.

He began weaving at least two years ago. The vocation of the weavers lies with the pit loom, and the training of all of them starts with their sitting at the loom from about the age of eight onwards. This may be with the father or with a master weaver in exchange for a small apprenticeship. He starts with the simplest processes and is made to 'embroider' the narrow borders at each end of the sari under the adult's guidance. He is simply inadequate physically to use the loom fully until he matures.

Shahzad Akhtar lives in Madanpura, the centre of the silk-weaving industry. To be from a weaver's family is to 'be' an Ansari, a nomenclature adopted by weavers in preference to 'julaha,' the derogatory term commonly used for weavers up to the 1930s. Upward mobility through a change in name and the composition of valedictory histories is a process that characterizes every caste and caste like group in twentieth-century India, and began too far back for any weavers to retain oral memory of it. Ansaris consider themselves a lineage and an endogamous group. They cite as their specific personality traits pacifism, kind-heartedness, and love for freedom. The last is expressed and reconfirmed in lifestyle and leisure activities. Pacifism and the less easily translatable *narmdil* or *dilraham* (kind-hearted) are perhaps demonstrated in their relations with middlemen and agents. Weavers are consensually accepted as being easy to deal with in matters of buying and selling. Their love of freedom does pose a danger in that they miss deadlines and shut up work at any small pretext, but in the process of transaction, they display no acerbity or aggressiveness.

It is difficult to state precisely where a weaver's son like Shahzad would pick up these preferred qualities of Ansaris except to say that he does spend hours with male relatives, first while sitting at the loom in the dusky workshop amid the clatter of anywhere between two to eight looms, then in occasional trips with his father to Chauk, the central wholesale and retail market of Banaras, carrying finished saris. Otherwise he hangs around in his neighbourhood and rarely if ever goes outside it.

The founding of Shahzad's school, Jamia Hamidia Rizvia, and other such madrasas or Muslim religious schools in Banaras are both cause and result of the educational history of colonialism. The Despatch of Sir Charles Wood in 1854 provided grants-in-aid to establish new schools in India, for both vocational and ethical reasons. The new schools were favoured by some because they trained boys for an official or professional career, but local Muslims failed to 'take advantage' of them. As the government was told by assorted members of the public, 'The Ansaris already have a profession'. Nor could the weavers resign themselves to sending their children to schools where no character formation would take place. Together with other castes and communities, Ansaris came to found their own institutions, in which they believed a synthesis between the spiritual (*dini*) and the worldly (*duniyayi*) could be effected. In the process of doing this, they worked along denominational lines. The Muslim sects Deobandis and Ahl-e-hadis set up separate madrasas, as did the Barelwis (Shahzad Akhtar's sect). Their teachers were hired accordingly and their textbooks chosen or even written according to sectarian loyalties.

Shahzad Akhtar's school, Jamia Hamidia Rizvia, like other madrasas, had to develop its own curriculum once a government Board syllabus was substituted for the accepted classical Islamic syllabus. Histories and geographies had to be written, since such subjects did not traditionally form part of the Islamic syllabus. Let us look at only one issue as it is treated by the school's fourth-grade social studies text. The book discusses the name and location of the Jama Masjid or Friday mosque in the heart of Banaras, the Gyanvapi mosque, one of significant interest to historians because of the threat it poses today as a target for the wrath of fundamentalist Hindus, who consider it symbolic of Islamic iconoclasm. Then: 'This Jama Masjid was built approximately 315 years ago in 1070 *hijri* (c.AD 1664) by the renowned emperor of Hindustan, Alamgir. Hindus claim that it was built by destroying a temple on this site. This is wrong. The foundations of this mosque were laid by the great-grandfather of Emperor Alamgir, Akbar, and Alamgir's father, Shah Jahan, had started a madrasa in the mosque in 1048 hijri that was named "Imam-e-Sharifat"' (Salam n.d., p.15).

Of course, the status of the iconoclastic activities of Alamgir, better known as Aurangzeb, and the origins of the Gyanvapi mosque are far from resolved. While Indian textbooks have unreflectively presented, and continued to present, Aurangzeb as among the most fanatic of Muslim rulers (and for them there are many to choose from), and the destruction of any temple by him as a most credible, unquestionable fact, contemporary research has also shown that complex political motives lie behind seemingly simple religious ones. The Hamidia Rizvia textbook is therefore 'right' in its denial of guilt to Aurangzeb but 'wrong' in the reasons it gives for this.

What is of immediate relevance here is that textbooks of this kind create a history and consciousness on questionable premises. In this case, a community is being set up which includes Alamgir, an emperor whose sway extended over the whole of Hindustan, and weavers in

Banaras, mostly poor and illiterate. The dividing line is between this community, whose members worship at and therefore build mosques, and those who worship at temples and therefore mourn their destruction. Such divisions and constructions do not have to be anything more than suggestive and associative to make an impression on minds of every age. The most powerful kinds of evidence used in these constructions seem to be those from the most fantastic and dramatic epochs of the past, those in stark contrast to the humdrum existence of poverty-ridden everyday life.

Does all this, however, match what we hear from Shahzad Akhtar about his own experiences? We can discount his mother's testimony that things were much better in her student days as the romantic nostalgia of a parent frustrated by a child's failure. But while in conversation, Shahzad and I were surrounded by four other children from the same madrasa who assented to everything he was saying, qualifying it for their own teachers and classes. Shahzad is an attractive, cheerful, intelligent, sociable boy, who is articulate on all subjects, but specifically effective on certain chosen ones (his teachers' injustices, his sister's doll).

Shahzad does not know what happened in 1947. Shahzad cannot remember any episode or personality from Indian history. More than that, he cannot make up, improvise, or just invent anything, as one might imagine a child to be able to do who has some elementary training in answering questions of a 'textbook' character, or demonstrate experience plus an active imagination in dealing with questioning adults.

His responses constitute a damning indictment of his school. First, no history has apparently been taught him even within this rote-learning system. Second, no overall pattern has been revealed to him regarding how to field questions or spin tales, that is, to construct narratives. Third—a fault the madrasa shares with most other schools in India—no connections have been suggested between his own life and larger historical developments.

If we turn to the second interview, with the teacher that Shahzad admires, we find part of the key to the puzzle. If master Mansoor may be taken as spokesman for the madrasa, as he and I both consider him to be, his answer to the poor learning of students like Shahzad is that Ansaris in general are apathetic to learning. They should support the schools and the students. In 'other schools' (that is, where guardians are more active) schools do 25 per cent of the teaching, guardians do the rest, but here the school has to do 95 per cent of the teaching. The Ansari guardians are not only lacking in 'society' and 'culture' (that is, they do not share in middle-class ideals of progress); they are particularly *udasin* towards schooling (indifferent, because interested only in the child's learning the Qur'an).

The guardians, on the other hand, imagine that the child's learning will naturally take place in the school (what percentage was not specified to me, but I repeatedly got the impression that it was almost 100 per cent). Since madrasas are known to be government-aided institutions, which also receive charitable endowments, it is a common speculation that their managers are misusing their funds. Why else would the kind of descriptions that Shahzad gives of classroom conditions be given? Why else would the child learn so little?

My approach to the problem is to try to see it as a condition within a certain fault line between discourses, that of the modern and that of the pre-modern. The madrasa would like to expect the guardians to behave like modern, participating citizens and prepare their children socially and psychologically for an educated future. Such a future would be bounded by practical considerations such as health, nutrition, and family planning; and by ideological ones such as awareness of constitutional rights and participation as a full citizen of a democracy. The guardians, on the other hand, are still part of a pre-modern world, one that has been trying for at least the whole of the twentieth century to come to terms with the demands of modernization and that has claimed to leave the task to schools. If indeed it was still an older world where an Ansari world view was fully legitimate and the outside world condemnable, socialization could be left to the family. If, similarly, it was a newer world where a modern nationalist world view was hegemonic, socialization could be left to the schools.

As things stand, Shahzad learns little in the school. The school blames the parents for their ignorance of the modern educational agenda. The parents blame the school for not fulfilling the agenda, conscious that they are being treated as inferior in this old-new dichotomy.

Of course, while Shahzad does not know what happened in 1947, what is important is that he does know and is learning many other things. Together with other Ansari boys, he is learning the craft of weaving, both its technique and its ethic, or how a weaver is expected to conduct himself. He is learning the pleasures of the outdoors and the established pastimes in Banaras' popular culture. He is gradually being socialized into gender role-playing (even the sewing and necklace making that impressed me so much has much to do with his learning to weave and embroider). Every part of his work and leisure underlies his maleness first. And since he does go to school and passes exams, he is learning to think of himself as 'educated'. An educated person is necessarily superior to an uneducated person, but inferior to others educated in more normative ways. Madrasa education is on the brink between non-education and education in the eyes of the system and its supporters, and almost everyone else as well.

There is a structural congruity here. Either Shahzad will become a well-educated person, or he will become a good weaver. Good weavers, the majority of weavers, are those who are tied to their occupation as an inevitable one, justified to themselves as the best occupation in the world. They are free and not reformed, sceptical of the values of control, discipline, citizenship, and progress. The practices of Jamia Hamidia Rizvia effortlessly guarantee Shahzad's fitness for this role. And all madrasas are like that, erring, according to educators, on the side of religion and in the balance they try to maintain between spiritual and worldly instruction.

One conclusion that emerges effortlessly is that community-based schools such as the madrasas of Banaras must be sacrificed for national(ist) schools. The needs of a community, whether religious, occupational, or linguistic, have to be erased in deference to the needs of the nation. This is a violent, arbitrary, colonial solution. Madrasas and such schools may be pedagogically weak, but they are not 'symbolically violent' (Bourdieu 1977a); they do not impose the 'cultural arbitrary' of the dominant group of society on other groups. At the same time, they are repressive in that they restrict the choices of children. If we acknowledge the value of freedom, not in the weavers' sense of strolling around and spitting everywhere, but in the sense of the equality with other citizens to choose occupation and lifestyle, then it is the madrasa that precludes such freedom totally.

Part of being a good weaver is to be rooted in local culture, protective of a particular history, ignorant of and indifferent to the nation and its history, unaware of 1947, aware of being a Muslim, a Barelwi, a Banarasi, and an Anasari, unreflectively supportive of the Pakistan cricket team, and resistant to the condemnations of ignorance and backwardness because the community is self-sufficient in itself. There is a close tie between history teaching and citizenship. The madrasa children do not reproduce their lower-class identities through resistance to their schools, as do the working-class children in a modern British school (Willis 1977), but directly *through* their schools.

SECTION II. NON-MADRASA EDUCATION

1. Class V in Qudrutullah Gulzar-e-Talim

I teach history in class V in Qudrutullah Gulzar-e-Talim, a Muslim school (not a madrasa, or religious school) for girls in Banaras. Class V has fifty students, of which some five are absent. It is a spacious, well-lit, airy classroom, with bare walls, serviceable desks and benches, and a large blackboard (for which a child produces the chalk from inside her desk). They are all wary of me in the beginning, and warm up slowly.

I ask them about 1947. There is a prompt response from the same child regarding both aspects of the event, independence and partition, as well as to my other question, regarding five important freedom fighters. The hesitation in answering among the other students is so extreme, with the same child attempting the next few questions also, that I wonder aloud if she stands first or second in the class? She does not. Now the two who do shake themselves up slightly.

I ask them to attempt a map of India on the blackboard. They will not. I show them the trick of making it with a triangle. With vast prodding and help from me, some two or three come up and make a hash of it. None of them have a picture in their minds of India, its states, or its neighbours. They cannot place any of them on the map, or any cities, or anything else. When questioned orally, they know the main mountains, rivers, and cities. They have obviously never used the blackboard, drawn anything, or attempted anything visually or tactically.

Does anyone know a story or song regarding 1947? No. With some help from me, a couple of girls mention a song or two, such as *Sare jahan se achha Hindustan hamara* ('Our land is the best in the world')—a popular children's nationalist song, and scenes familiar to me from television. It seems to me that their general knowledge, even regarding television and film content, is very poor. Even more, their level of interest is very poor in what is shown or could be shown on television.

I try to probe into their identities. What is their father's occupation? After a long bout of tongue-tiredness, one ventures the euphemism *loom ka kam* (working on the loom). Almost all are from weaver's families. Do their mothers work? Upon their saying 'no', it is to their credit that they all look embarrassed when I wonder aloud if housework is not work. They vow to never consider their mothers non-workers again.

Their identities are securely gender-based. They laugh heartily when I suggest that their fathers may provide them with clean uniforms for school. They associate intimately with their mothers and are eager to claim a share in her work: washing and ironing clothes, washing dishes, cooking, and cleaning up. They love it when I ask a question regarding their dolls and how many were married. Hands shoot up with alacrity. Smiles flash on most faces.

Their subjects are all the same as in a madrasa, including Urdu, religion, and Arabic in addition to the Board-required subjects. Many of them have tutors. When I discover they have no music, dance, or drama, and that the school merely gave a holiday on Republic Day instead of celebrating it, I heave an involuntary sigh of disappointment. 'One should have some music, dance, or drama' escapes me. Such is the rapport built up in the class by now that they wistfully agree with me.

2. Class XI in Qudrutullah Gulzar-e-Talim

I interact with class XI in the same school, Qudrutullah. There are eighteen girls, most between fifteen and seventeen years old, sensible, confident, and pleasant looking. They are sitting temporarily in a classroom not theirs, so when I look around for their *naqabs* (full-length veils), I don't see them; they are hanging up in their own room. A couple of voices murmur, 'We don't all wear *naqabs*'. (The principal had earlier told me that naqabs were compulsory.)

Throughout the class, the teacher of economics, Indrani Tripathi, sits with me. They have no choice of subjects: all do Hindi, economics, and home science. They are just the second or third batch to be in class XI, and the second one from whom the school can hold some hope of future collegians.

They answer promptly all my questions regarding 1947 and freedom fighters. They remember at least the film *Gandhi* and have heard nationalistic songs on television. They even have some idea of what to do for the country—work to solve the problems of poverty, illiteracy, and so on—especially one who is a doctor's daughter.

They are unselfconscious about Pakistan. Many have relatives there who visit often. One narrates the tale of an aunt who does not like it there because she does not feel at home (*apnapan*) there and this is greeted with empathy by others.

All help at home. One even makes candles and pickles, presumably helping in her mother's work. They meet each other, go out for shopping, and watch TV, read Urdu magazines and film magazines. Two respond 'yes' to having Hindu friends, one the daughter of her father's friend, the other a neighbour in the mixed Hindu-Muslim neighbourhood of Shivala.

The girls seem relaxed about themselves and their future. Some five will seek a Bachelor's degree from Vasanta College. One can picture them as promising undergraduates, in veils or not.

In my view the greater secularization and national identification of these girls are due partly to their belonging to a different class of Ansaris, those who would prefer non-madrasa to madrasa schools. Within these schools, it is due further to their having some Hindu teachers like Indrani. Teachers, like Indrani, are modern, secular, nationalist women who are subtly Hindu; friendly observers of the girls, but their critics and reformers as well. My most powerful impression of the teacher was that she was a trifle bemused by Muslim customs and commented negatively on them to the children's faces, neither of which would happen with Hindu children getting a Muslim teacher. The students learn in a myriad of subtle ways how to conform to 'majority religion' and 'national' culture, and because they and their families have the will to do so, they conform and 'progress'.

3. Middle-class children in Calcutta

The second part of this second section moves to a different stage of action, Calcutta. The children studied here are all sons and daughters of refugees who left East Pakistan in 1947–8. The families are Hindu, but secular and liberal. They are upwardly mobile and universalist, and believe in progress. All the children go to schools that are overtly religious: Loreto House (Christian), Future Foundations (Hindu, based on Aurobindo Ghosh and The Mother's teachings), and Ramakrishna Mission School (based on Vivekanand's philosophy). I had taken these schools as typical of those that project a national secular version of India's history. The families concur in this version, regardless (or some may say because) of the past that individuals from these families have experienced.

a. *Interview with the daughter of a refugee from East Bengal, ten years old, student of Loreto House, a christian missionary school*

Q: Who are you?
A: I am a girl. I like badminton and cycling and my favourite food is cheese. My hobby is reading. My favourite subject is science.... I'm short, I have black hair and brown eyes. [There is no response to stimulus from my side for more community-oriented definitions of the self.]
Q: What do you know about 1947?
A: It was an important year but I can't remember what happened. Yes, India got independence from British rule.
Q: Do you know about Partition?
A: There were lots of riots going around. India got divided into two. All the Hindus came to India and all the Muslims went to Pakistan.
Q: What are Hindus?
A: It's a...religion? [I encourage her.] Hindus are a kind of people.
Q: What kind?
A: Their language is Hindi and most of them live in India.
Q: Who are they different from?
A: Sikhs.
Q: Anyone else?
A: Muslims?
Q: What are Muslims?
A: Muslims are just another kind of people. They go to mosques and do a few other things differently.
Q: Do you know Muslims?
A: No.
Q: How would you know a Muslim if you saw one?
A: They dress differently. The girls wear veils. The boys wear salwar-kameez—no, kurta-pyjamas—and caps.
Q: Do they speak Hindi?
A: Yes. [She realizes sheepishly that earlier she had said that only Hindus did.]
Q: What about Masroor [a friend of hers who is Muslim]? How is he different to you? What is the difference?
A: He is not. There is no difference.

Q: What is your father?

A: He is the director... [gives occupation].

Q: His religion?

A: He is a Hindu.

Q: How do you know?

A: I know he is.

Q: Does he do puja or go to temples?

A: He does not go to mosques. No, he doesn't go to temples. He *visits* temples.

Q: Puja?

A: [Doubtfully, then humorously] I've seen him light a wick.

Q: Tell me about your father's father.

A: He was a zamindar and used to own a lot of property and then he sold it all. I don't know when.

Q: Was he a Hindu?

A: I don't know. I think he was. No, I haven't seen any pictures of him in his house. [I know that such pictures hang in their family house.]

Q: How do you know all this?

A: My father told me.

Q: Do you know where he lived? Anything else?

A: In Bengal, but I don't know where. I don't know anything else.

Q: Would you like to know?

A: Yes.

Q: Do you know any stories about Muslims?

A: Id is their festival. They go to mosques and they pray. Once in my old school on Id we had a poetry competition. In one book I saw they were hugging in a special way, on both sides of the neck.

Q: Do you know that Hindus and Muslims fight?

A: Yeah, I don't know about what. I know that one of our neighbouring countries wanted to take Kashmir...it was China or Pakistan....

Q: Why Kashmir?

A: It makes a lot of things. It's clean and pretty.

Q: Would you like to fight? For Kashmir?

A: Yeah [grins]. No! I don't like fighting. I would not do it because I would like to do something else.

Q: For yourself? Or for India?

A: I don't know. Yes, for both.

b.   *Interview with the son of a refugee from East Bengal, thirteen*
     years old, student of class VIII in Ramakrishna Mission
     Association

Q: Who are you?
A: My name is Dibyarka Basu. There is not much to say about
me. I am a boy. I read in RKMA Vidyalaya. My hobbies are
reading storybooks and watching cricket.
Q: What do you know about 1947?
A: It was a year that brought much hope to the Indian common
people. But the independence of India also brought the partition
of Bengal. A catastrophic [pauses, gropes for the word] riot began.
It gave the Indian people an opportunity to develop their country,
but it gave the political leaders a way of exploiting the country.
Q: Who is to blame?
A: Mahatma Gandhi is partially involved but I think the real...was
Zinnah [sic]....
Q: How do you know all this?
A: General information...what I hear from people, what I read in
books.
Q: Do you study about it in history?
A: No, our textbooks have nothing on this. Our syllabus is not so
much attached with politics.
Q: Do your teachers talk about it?
A: Our history teacher is not so good, although he has
knowledge, but my English teacher in my previous school was
very good.
Q: Did you see anything on TV in this connection?
A: Yes, two or three films....I can't remember which. *Gandhi?*
Yes, I know some songs.
Q: Which ones?
A: *Bande Matram, Bharat amar janani* ['Long live our
Motherland', 'India is my mother']. On 15 August we have a
march or parade, and flag hoisting.
Q: Do your parents tell you about this?
A: My father does. No, he is not like the textbook.
Q: Do you know anything about your grandfather?
A: Yes, he [sic] was a professor of English. I heard that he was
wise. He lived nearby. The second grandfather I have forgotten. At
one time, he lived in Bangladesh. I don't know where. His occupa-
tion? I don't know.

Q: Would you like to know?
A: Yes. I am interested.
Q: Are you a Hindu?
A: Yes.
Q: How is that different to others?
A: There is no difference. Customs are different. That is not very important. All the gods are all the same. My father and mother are Hindu by name. They celebrate Durga Puja. They worship Goddess Kali. But all the gods are the same.
Q: Do you know any Muslims?
A: Yes. [He names cricketers, at least four of them.] No, I have no friends. I have one uncle. Not a direct relation. A friend of my father's. No, there is no difference between his house and mine.... Yes, the construction is different. The kitchen is very big. There is a big roof. The house is large. They are rich.
Q: Why do Hindus and Muslims fight?
A: It is a perfect example of stupidity. There is no reason to fight. It is due to orthodoxies. They are stubborn. No, I don't know this from my teachers, but in general...but I don't know the way of removal of this.
Q: Would you like to do something about it when you grow up?
A: It depends on the political situation of the time. There may be no need.
Q: What religious books do you know or have read?
A: The Veda. We have *slokas* in our school. *Amader Gan* ['Our Songs'] has Veda *path* [excerpts from the Vedas]. We have a subject, 'Indian culture'. We memorize slokas and learn the meanings. No. I have not read the Qur'an.
Q: Would you like to read it?
A: No. I mean I have not decided.

The Muslim school Qudrutullah Gulzar-e-Talim described above sets itself apart from madrasas; in the tradition of the nineteenth-century Muslim reformer Sir Syed Ahmad Khan, it states its intention to produce a well-rounded, modern, progressive person, but one who is also a good Muslim. To achieve this goal, the principal and teachers of Qudrutullah depend far more on the guardians of their students to accomplish their purposes than madrasas can. Qudrutullah guardians are required to actively cooperate in the school's mission, to complete daily homework, and pass periodic exams, and the guardians in fact do so—or remove their wards to a madrasa. The guardian's failure to meet these standards is exactly what madrasa teachers deplore but have to tolerate.

The corollary of this greater cooperation is the undermining of the arts of memory as practised in daily life. The school, in performing its job better, co-opts the home, weakens home culture, and weakens a world of intangible traditions, rituals, practices, and role playing that helped—and continues to help in the case of madrasa children—in the perpetuation of histories. The modern school's student will not have the time or inclination to learn, and her guardians will not have the will, the coherence, and sometimes the very courage, to teach seriously in any way an identity and relationship to the past that is different from the officially preferred one. The project of modernity, secularism, and nationalism becomes a family project, with the child at the vanguard.

Subsection 3 above highlights the second process at work. The school's history teaching is imbibed by the child but with no connection to the child's own identity. Nor does the child have an alternative culture or history. The schools these two students belong to are respectively, an old, well-established Christian missionary school, a model for a kind of modern English-medium institution; and a Hindu reformist school, which, denominational differences aside, has an Annie Besant philosophy for producing modern, scientific Hindu citizens. In both cases the overwhelming experience of the child is one of homogenization, where no part of the home culture is acknowledged or tolerated, unless it be targeted for reform. Guardians of these public or missionary schools cooperate with the project of homogenization even more fully than in the case of the modern Muslim school. Indeed, they do not follow, but lead the school in its mission, being either products of such institutions themselves or consumed by the ambition of seeing their children 'succeed' in a frankly competitive world. Whatever they retain of an alternative history—as in the case of the above interviewees, the parents having been refugees from East Bengal in 1947—is consigned slowly to oblivion. All linguistic, regional, sectarian, and caste identities of the child and her family are purposefully erased.

It is perhaps natural for us to regard the socialization effected by Qudrutullah, Loreto, and Ramakrishna Mission Vidyalaya as more successful than that of Jamia Hamidia Rizvia. The Muslim, Christian, and Hindu reformist schools—all claiming to be secular in practice within their sectarian ideological pronouncements—teach students with more professional acumen. They are closer to the model of a modern institution, with less soul-searching and conflict regarding the validity of the model. Their students are better able to answer factual questions regarding their history, and they are altogether better trained in the art of answering questions. As one student responded:

I think Partition was the fault of some leaders who wanted to satisfy their own interests, like Jinnah; they knew they were in a minority in India, they would never become big leaders—now I'm talking like my textbook—they aroused communal feeling among Muslims. The Congress had to agree. Were some of the Congress leaders not at fault? [Pause] Some of the Congress leaders might have also wanted Partition but the aim of the Congress was to keep India united so they couldn't openly support that demand.

Both the level of knowledge of the student and her self-consciousness that she sounds like her textbook are noteworthy. Also noteworthy is the reflexive sense of humour of the child in interview 3 as she admits that she would 'rather do something else' than fight for her country even to save the clean and pretty Kashmir, or as another child of the same age responded, 'I do not want to fight because I might die, and I prefer to be alive than to be dead'. Similarly, the self-conscious dignity of interviewee number 4 is notable when he refuses to commit himself to what he would do to resolve the communal question when he grew up: 'It would depend on the political situation of the time'.

How far the 'history' learnt as a subject gets assimilated by the child as part of his or her identity is not possible for me to say conclusively, given our relatively simple ethnography here. The evident indifference in response to questions related to history in general and Indian history in particular points to a weak relationship between the subject as studied and the child's sense of herself. The child's world does not incorporate a sense of the nation and its birth. But then, there are the occasional insights, which indicate at least the possibility of a strong relationship between the sense of self and the sense of the nation. For instance, a child of an immigrant father from Pakistan and a non-immigrant mother explained:

Am I sorry about Partition? My grandfather was a zamindar; he had a lot of property. They had to leave all their property. Later on, the government gave some of the money to the refugees, not all the money, that would have been too much. My grandfather had a really nice library, which they had to leave behind. [Pause] If it hadn't happened, if they'd stayed there, our lives would have been different. He wouldn't have met my mother, I wouldn't have been born. It must have been very sad for them though. My father said my grandfather didn't want to leave.

This interesting philosophical point came quite unselfconsciously to the child, that what happens in history, when seen from our personal vantage point, is very likely the best, since if things happened differently we personally would not be here at all to discuss these questions.

But these glimpses aside, the child in South Asia—not only the disadvantaged working-class child whose school does not teach national history, but also the privileged middle-class child who learns history lessons well—grows up without a sense of personal certainty about her national history, where she belongs in it, and what her 'duties' within it are. This is all due to various reasons that I have not discussed here, such as the unimpressive pedagogic approaches used even in the mainstream nationalist schools, and the absence of all debate about what are the best processes by which the child may be wooed to participate in the construction of a national identity.

However, these inadequacies provide a vacuum that could possibly be exploited by those who choose to confront the dilemma described here. How should we formulate the relatiohship between our official history and the senses of history created in routine, everyday ways? That is, how could one write or talk about the national, or implicitly assume the nation, while doing the least possible violence to—indeed, while respecting and celebrating—other higher- and lower-level histories? How could we educate a child about her nation and yet protect that brilliant innocence that makes her admit that she would not like to fight for its boundaries because she 'would rather do something else'?

3

The Family–School Relationship and an Alternative History of the Nineteenth-century Family

My interest in the family is part of an interest in the multiplicity of the educational narratives of modern India. But as I try to broaden the discussion of 'education' and become embroiled in issues concerning family, community, and neighbourhood, I find that I can perhaps broaden the discussion of 'the family' as well.

The historian and the sociologist of the family in India speak at two different levels. The historian speaks to the question of how the family is produced, and its power struggles with the state and its institutions, and in turn to a smaller extent about how *it* produces its subjects (Chatterjee 1993; T. Sarkar 2001; Sinha 1995). The sociologist marks the cycles and patterns of change in the constitution of the family, but does not seem interested in its power struggles with its outside, stressing rather the power struggles 'within' the family (Raheja and Gold 1992; Shah 1973, 1998). I am interested here in the internal as well as the external politics of the family; in it as a site of reproduction for a certain kind of adult as a result of the complex interaction of both these politics. In this preliminary essay, I have explored the inequality at the heart of the history of the family, and the reproduction of this inequality, both inter- and intra-family.

THE GHOSH FAMILY OF DINAJPUR-CALCUTTA

Narendra Ghosh was born in 1916, the son of a zamindar in Dinajpur in East Bengal, with relatives in Calcutta who were in trade and commerce. Together with his brother, Narendra was brought up in luxury, with its own mix of discipline. The brothers learnt from private tutors, mastering English, Bengali, and Sanskrit, and some maths, science, and History. They learnt accounts and estate-management. They became skilled in playing the tabla, the sitar, and the *tar-shehnai*. The footnote here would be that this system of education has disappeared after that generation, with some lingering remains in aristocratic families till the 1930s.

In 1936, on one of his visits to Calcutta, Narendra's father fixed up matches for his sons with two eligible Calcutta girls. Narendra's wife; Madhumita, was sixteen and had completed her F.A., or two years after high school. She had throughout been an excellent student and had always 'stood first' in her Calcutta schools. Of the two or three she had attended, the most impression made on her was by Sister Nivedita's school, because everyone there seemed so smart and serious about their work. It would be fair to say that she came from a family that was attracted by the promise of the new education, reading it as enlightenment and progress, but wished to play it safe in the paths its women would follow in life.[1]

Once married Madhumita was supposed to take care of the household. But the household was a bustling one with its own motors: a mother-in-law to supervise, servants to work, routines for everyone to follow, diverse family members and hangers-on with resolved avenues for their eccentricities. Madhumita liked to read and was able to find time for this. Only on the birth of her three sons, Rajendra, Rabindra, and Birendra, in 1940, 1942, and 1944, respectively did she have a progressive burden of cares and duties. She had five daughters between 1947 and 1956, and lost two or three children along the way. She was a full-time mother for over fifty years. It was only in 1995 that she finally gave up her full-time occupation of mothering when her youngest daughter was married and she began to live with Rabindra and his wife who would permit her to do no chores.

In 1947 the Ghosh family migrated from Dinajpur to Calcutta. Their estate had seemed safe, their Muslim tenants friendly. Everyone was knit together, shared each other's joys and sorrows, celebrations and sufferings. At the end of the year, the winds changed. It seemed safer to flee. With trunks full of silver heirlooms and zamindari papers, they abandoned their property and came to live as guests of Madhumita's parents. From this unsatisfactory arrangement in North Calcutta, they moved to their own house in Netaji Nagar, an immigrants' colony in south Calcutta. Narendra Ghosh became an active member of the Communist Party of India; Madhumita tried to make ends meet, especially as many children were born and grew up.

Rajendra, the eldest son, studied well but chose technical courses in college and started working as an engineer in a private company. His earnings over the thirty-nine years of his working life were always just adequate. For the first twenty years he was responsible for two unmarried sisters and his parents. When his father died in 1981 and his sisters got married the next year, he was left with an almost natal household of four and his mother. It would be fair to say that whatever he became and did was the result of many factors related to the changing fortunes of his nation state. This decided his course of education, and that in turn decided his career and his life. From being a zamindar's son to becoming a junior engineer was a transition that moulded him—through the avenue of his education. The only choices he had was to become very highly qualified through further and more intense study, which he declined because the imminent impoverishment of the family inclined him to start working early. Nor could he have chosen a different, humanities-oriented course of study because there were no quick job prospects after that.

His was a typical middle-class Calcutta existence; a rented house in Netaji Nagar, marriage to a hard-working housewife, a son and a daughter in nearby schools, an aging mother, a fixed routine of work, relaxation at home with tea and bolsters on his bed on his return from office, TV, dinner and a walk-cum-shopping trip to the market. Most of his time in the evenings was taken up with helping his children with their homework—every subject but Bangla, which was supervised by his wife. At various points they kept tutors also. Their lives revolved around the education of their two children. Rajendra's was what may be described as the citizen-family, in that he read the papers and took them seriously, he talked to his family about the news, and was totally part of the discourse of development, progress, and mobility (although he personally had not experienced much of these). He believed in system and structure and regarded the law, railways, the telephone, post and telegraph systems as bits of invincible machinery. He spoke of the metro with awe. He loved the bomb.

Rajendra's was also what may be called the tutoring-family. He loved books and home-work. Contentment was to him being surrounded by piles of his children's books. It is possible that from them and from tutoring with their help, he relived his student days, recreating any excitement he had experienced, and compensating for what he would have liked to learn and discover but did not. This would certainly explain his forays into book exhibitions and College Street, his liberal spending on books, and his loving care of them by covering them and arranging them in cupboards. He even designed desks with special drawers and double cupboards which could contain more books.

His wife cooperated as an equal partner. She had hot rice ready before school time for the two children, their clothes ironed, their shoes polished, their tiffins packed. She gave them fruits when possible, milk twice a day, and looked critically at hoardings that announced snacks that were good for the mind. When they returned she was on her toes with a late lunch prepared. Then she made them rest, get up—sometimes that took half an hour of calling and persuasion—wash, and sit down to study, with her husband or with tutors. Whether it was making tea and tending through the evening, or even as she cooked her fish, rice, and vegetables for dinner, the noise was kept low so as not to disturb them. At any moment, any of them could call out, *Ma!* or *Ai, shunchho? Jol dao.* (Are you there? Give me some water).

Let us jump over to the third brother and look at the case of Birendra. He had gone to study in Europe after getting a postgraduate scholarship but had mysteriously not completed anything there. However, he managed to do odd jobs and save a lot of money. He married late and took early retirement. After twenty years of student-bachelor life, and ten years of married life abroad and a daughter five years old, he decided to return to Calcutta. With his immediate purchases of an apartment, a car, huge amounts of furniture and drapes, hiring of a driver and a servant, and admission of his daughter into an expensive private school, he became as clearly a member of the upper middle classes as Rajendra was of the middle classes. He occupied himself with freelance writing. His was a citizen-family too, of the kind that remains sceptical of the nation because it takes one reflexive turn further (he described his daughter's plaid school dress as 'a Scottish Highlander's' but would only put her in that modern private school) and such citizens too are needed by the nation state. He had no discernible politics, certainly not the Communist Party of India (Marxist), but he took politics itself seriously, and most of all 'the problems of India', its apathy, corruption, inefficiency, and so on. As opposed to his elder brother he sneered at the postal and telephone systems, was aloof about politicians and newspapers, and believed that chaos was around and impending further.

Birendra's was even more a tutoring family, but with a stronger gender division. Birendra was almost always closeted in his computer room or glued to the television. His wife was equally closeted in the bedroom with their daughter. She cooked and ironed and had everything always ready like her elder sister-in-law. She also 'sat down' with the little girl for all her free time in the evening to revise her homework, prepare her lessons, make her do extra work to stay ahead in her class. In addition she took her to dance class on Sundays, drawing class on Saturdays, and swimming every weekday. She gave her *chhana* (the 'cottage cheese' almost worshipped by Bengalis as 'good' for you), sprouted lentils (another protein-rich 'good' thing), and rare fruits (a precious thing) to eat. When the girl was nine she was still being fed her rice and fish by her mother, because the mother wanted to make sure that enough fish got into every round mouthful.

Between them these middle/upper middle class brothers exemplify the middle-class family in a metropolis like Calcutta. Such a family is what I would call 'the citizen-family' and the location of the domestic educational economy. Such a family is frightened, because education is its only investment and recourse, although it appears to be comfortable because it has come to terms with it. It is not a risk-taker, so it is exceptionally eager to play the game according to its rules. It is browbeaten into a submission to an external will, although it might claim to have made its choices voluntarily. It is defined and performs totally according to the orchestration of the state and its discourses, but with so much charm and enthusiasm (as in the loving covering of books after searching them out in sales) that it has a pathetic dignity of its own.

When we say that Rajendra and his wife created a citizen-tutoring-family, we do not imply that they were not critical. They had chosen the Future Foundations School for their children because it was nearby, and though new, seemed promising. They interacted closely with it and closeness brought on tolerance. But they were critical, in the time of the second child specially, of what was taught, how it was taught, when it was taught, and why it was taught. They would question the 'project work' given to the student, but would rush around to acquire and photocopy materials to complete it. They would not like the standards of explanation of almost all subject teachers and begin explaining at home from the basics up—to the dismay of the child. They disapproved totally of the policy of keeping all the students one step ahead in the system by teaching them the next year's course in the present year. They watched their son carefully when he was six and seven and discussed having him kept back one year so that he could cope better. The discussion came to nothing, as does every family's discussion of its issues with its school. Regarding other changes in the curriculum, such as making maths compulsory or optional, they were also aggrieved, largely because there was not enough information and debate.

But the fact remains that this family was and remained the tool and the victim in the triangulation of the state, the school, and the family. Each, logically, should have its 'rights' and make its 'sacrifices', if adversaries they must be, in the power game that is development. The adversary positioning is already an overdetermined one. In the nineteenth century, the edifice of colonial educational policy was built on the ignoring of the fact that education up to that time had been decentralized and was generic to the community. That is, it depended on the family rather than the state. The shift that occurred was a profound and dramatic one. The location of legitimate education shifted from both formal and informal sites supported by the family to formal schools that were extensions of the state. They could be directly run by the state, or financed by it though under private management, or financed privately but affiliated to the state—but in all cases, teaching only state-legitimized curricula. The family had no say in their running. The family was, on the contrary, the target of reform, not directly as a meaningful category of the population, but as an already-entrenched rival that was undertaking socialization, apprenticeship, and cultural reproduction.

These developments affected classes and school-going populations differently. The case we have looked at is in the 'middle', and allows us to approach the extremes at either end of the continuum. The mobile nineteenth-century family responded to the changed political situation with alacrity. Its children would be students of the new learning, whatever it took. What it could take was: a break-up of the family as some members lived near the student's educational site and others lived wherever they needed to. Or, a certain job was decreed for one member to enable others to study. There was the killing of desires and hushing of dreams of some, to such an extent that even in the most committed history-writing, the tools simply do not exist to present a narrative of someone like Rajendra's wife—even her name seems irrelevant—who was herself a student until eighteen, got married, and had her first child, and from the point at which she assumed the mantle of motherhood was never anything other than a mother. What the new education demanded was the full-time dedication of the mother and often other females to the needs of those who were studying. Then there was the learning by the parents of new codes and languages that belonged to the new education. Besides all this, there was the other intangible thing: a silencing of other possible narratives, stories, pleasures that earlier came 'naturally' to the family but now, not required by the school, seemed a waste of time.

How did the family seek to subvert the rule of the school, because it must of course have resisted an out-and-out utter domination? If we look back at the first decades of the new educational system we have an answer. The learning of English and of all the subjects in the medium of English, the orientation towards annual examinations, periodical tests, and the textbook, and the disciplining of the self through punctuality, dressing, body language, and so on translated into an immense burden that was impossible to bear in some cases and was weighty, difficult, and at least somewhat meaningless in all cases. A publishing industry burgeoned that provided 'keys' and 'guides' to the new learning. A class of professionals emerged who could act as the middlemen between the new learning and its tests and those for whom their lives depended on it. These middlemen could simplify, explain, and guide towards success. Tutors and coaches became the norm. The family sought to subvert the school by finding its own aids and maps in the new unfriendly terrain. It further sought to subvert the school by the technique of hollowing out the school's rituals and pouring its own meanings into them. (For instance, children must be picked up by a parent at a certain time. Mothers gather at the gate a good half an hour ahead and have organized the equivalent of a club to exchange news and to buy and sell saris lower than in the retail market.)

But subversion can also be subsumed by the normative. Schools did not back down before the relative failure of the families which were supposed to benefit from them. Schools became only all the more fortresses of precious secrets that had to be acquired through whatever tools one could organize. The response to the keys, guides, coaching, tutoring, and wiles of the ambitious family was a kind of enlargement of the system to encompass all these practices. Not only did the family become the accepted, normative collaboration in this vast enterprise, but the family became the essential partner without whom the system would not run. It was a discriminated-against partner, we should add, one with no rights, and only a burden of guilt and anxiety. Even at their most broken, parents would insist that what they wanted was not a change in the education but the know-how and the techniques to make their son (sic) reach the pinnacles of high marks. What started as sub-version, then, became the corollary to the domination.

The child was caught in this family–school power struggle. A student in the nineteenth century had relatively more freedom because the result of poor performance was an exercise of will by the teacher and not a strike by the whole system to award him failure that could mean failure in life. A student could have been late, stayed away, acted up, and shown other idiosyncrasies—and been merely caned for it. Now he was defined as poor, dull, worthless, unpromising, and simply, failed. Nor could he have recourse in his home or his neighbourhood. A good parent would remove him from such dangers as bad company, euphemistically called 'playing in the streets.' Families that choose to leave their inner city ancestral houses and live in modern neighbourhoods state simply that they had to remove their children from 'those' influences: *us mahaul se dur karna tha* (We had to remove him from *that* environment).

THE FAMILIES OF GULISTAN, NAZIR, VIKAS, AND VINOD

When visiting her family, I asked eight-year-old Gulistan to read a few lines copied verbatim from her book, the familiar poem '*jisne suraj chand banaya, jisne phulon ko muskaya...*' she began to read at such a speed that there was no question but that it had been learnt by rote by her and that she could not have been asked at random just words and phrases in the middle. She could not stop and then continue, nor could she start anywhere but in the beginning. Nor could she be questioned about anything else on the page. She had memorized it, she had not learnt to read, and she could not read *a thing*. Her family beamed in delight.

Somehow that was one of the saddest discoveries ever made by me in my fieldwork. I sat there disconcerted, not knowing what to make of the laughing child, her happy siblings, the proud family showing off her home-work. The thought that possessed me was, 'Her school is playing a bad joke on this child. The whole system, the *nation*, is playing a bad joke. They are supposed to make this child literate, and then educated, but they don't seem to know what literacy and education are. No matter how hard she works and how much motivation she has, she will always remain 'backward'. So overwhelming was this impression of the pathos of the encounter between the student who knew so little and should be learning, and me, a potential teacher who was not teaching as she ought to but only *studying* her, that I could almost not continue. Then the feeling passed and I continued to study her.

Gulistan's is a family of *zardozes*, or embroiderers. Children start learning some embroidery from as young as possible, and all of them know it, whether they decide to pursue it professionally or not. Those who continue to go to school are the ones who are able to balance their home-work with their embroidering. The children who cannot are described by family members as '*baithta nahin hai*' ('not able to sit down'). There are the few who will not learn the family work but seem to fare all right in school. Of them, the complaint is that they will learn up whatever the madam tells them but will ignore what is taught at home. For most of these children, the attraction of the school lies in its structure, its clear commands, and promises of reward, and perhaps its relative simplicity. I looked at little Nazir's English homework copy. There were hard words and translated words and simple sentences. The questions and answers he had done for homework seemed amazingly accurate. I asked him where the work was from. 'From the CW [class-work] copy,' Nazir told me. 'And where did you get it from for the CW copy?' I asked. 'From the blackboard', I was told.

It is possible that the implication we hold regarding 'child labour' versus formal schooling needs to be reversed for some children. Children are attracted by the challenging and perhaps by the meaningful. They do not like school not because it is so difficult but because it is non-stimulating, over-easy, mechanical, and meaningless. Much craft training is not only located in a comfortable setting, it is provocative and stimulating.

The families of Gulistan and Nazir are on the verge of becoming citizen-families and any day they will discover the merits of tutoring their small children, turning their household into an educational unit.

The family of Vikas has already become so. Vikas is the grandson of Tara Prasad, who was a very talented maker of wooden images and figures. He carved them by hand, sitting on his haunches in the space by his front door leading to his courtyard. His wife cooked on another side of the courtyard, and they lived in one room which was bare during the day. After his death his wife and twelve-year-old daughter managed for four years by working as domestic servants in a house and she arranged the girl's marriage to a maker of the jacquard machine. The son-in-law came to live in the Khojwa house. His own family—father and three brothers—lived and had their shop of jacquard machines in the far north of the city. He commuted by cycle everyday. They had a son, Vikas.

The business did well and they planned carefully. First, the one room that was *kachcha* was made *pukka*. The courtyard was improved and a good handpump installed. The upstairs was gradually built up for two sets of tenants. A third tenant was given the original room in which Tara Prasad had managed. With the rent from all this, and alongside the steady, prospering business, all the paraphernalia for a rising middle-class family was acquired: double bed, rug, chair and table, stereo, toys, accessories. Part of this same paraphernalia was Vikas's admission to a neighbouring private school called Diamond English School. He was also given a private tutor who came daily to supervise his homework and give him then further homework in all his subjects. Vikas was then in kindergarten. We will never know his inner state. But he developed an ulcer within a year, had to be carefully treated till he recovered, and lost one year of school. When he went back, he was a 'poor student', but continued in his routine of school, homework, private tutor, more homework, discipline at home, revolt.

His mother, Tara Prasad's daughter, Mangra, has spoken of him since at least the age of four as *badmash* and *harami*. She says boastfully that like his grandfather, Vikas is an artist. He draws beautifully, but then gets in a rage and destroys his work. She says he does not listen to her and will not 'sit down' when asked. He is restless and always trying to run around. Vinod's mother says the same things about her two sons, the third being too old now to comment on. She calls the eldest one *fasadi*, which I had thought referred to someone who caused riots.

Mangra is herself educated till class V. She has never considered helping Vikas herself with any of his home-work, including the alphabets and elementary arithmetic. One may wonder why. She, like a very disciplined housewife and also landlady, believed her primary duty lay in cooking, cleaning, and running the house, and this she did with unrelenting efficiency. So the primary reason she gives when asked is that she has no time.

But most of the time when mothers give such an excuse or reason, the underlying conviction in their minds is that they *cannot* help with the work. That they are too uneducated, behind-the-times, they know no English, they know none of the rules that are the backbone of English schools.

I went to Diamond English School. The front room of a house had been converted to an office. There were four other rooms, housing the kindergartens, 'LKG' [Lower Kindergarten] and 'UKG' [Upper Kindergarten], and classes I and II. Other classes were pointed out to me on top but we did not go there. Children were all in uniform, the girls in shapeless skirts, the boys in better fitting trousers, all in ties and socks and shoes. They were from the neighbourhood, that meant the sons and daughters of lathe workers, shopkeepers, weavers, and oil pressers. The classes I visited at the kindergarten level, consisted of endless rote learning of the English and Hindi alphabets and numbers (in English) up to 100. Given the four tiered structure of schools in Banaras, Diamond belongs to rung two, above the municipal and district school, and below the madrasa or Hindi medium private school.

A SCHEMA OF SCHOOLS AND FAMILIES

One could make a ranking of schools that revolves around the family–school relationship. The municipal school is ranked lowest in my schema because it is totally an arm of the state and antagonistic to the community and family to the point that they can never do anything right. In its alienating and intolerant atmosphere, parents and children find themselves stigmatized in advance and predictably fail. The school *makes* them fail. It starts with the proposition, 'These families cannot produce educated children'. Then it dedicates itself to proving it. Its formula is a simple one: to counterpose the qualities of 'culture', time-discipline, social mobility, and literacy, with those of 'backward-ness', unstructured lifestyles, poverty, and illiteracy; to demand the former set of qualities; and then to fail the family for not possessing them.

Even *The Journal of Indian Education*, a publication of the prestigious National Council for Educational Research and Training, says:

There is no doubt that the majority of students studying in govt primary schools belong to poorer sections of the society. Many a time, the parents are unable to provide them with uniform and necessary stationery items. Moreover, due to the illiteracy of the family they do not get any academic support, proper guidance or encouragement. On the other hand, they are supposed to help the family in household tasks, such as kitchen work, looking after younger siblings or taking care of animals, etc. During harvest seasons, children miss their classes to supplement the family's income. Parents are too busy with economic and domestic problems to take any interest in the performance of their children at school. The atmosphere at home is one of frustration compounded by use of abusive language, alcoholism, and above all, lack of love which are harmful for students' psyche (Kaul, Singh and Gill 1996: 14).

Vinod, eight-years-old, who was mentioned in the title of the section above, was left out here to avoid repetition since he is *fully* described in the quote here. He has no history or story—he is only a problem. His family is too poor to afford what the school considers necessary. They are illiterate so helping him with home-work is out of the question. He is constantly running around on domestic errands and in a few years would become an apprentice to a carpenter or plumber, like his elder brothers. His single mother is absolutely too busy making her meagre wages to 'take any interest in the performance' of her child. Only the last sentence of the quote above is incorrect.

The second rung of the educational ladder from below is occupied by the 'convent' and 'English-medium' schools like Diamond English School that exist in the scores in small towns and even villages. They imitate missionary and public schools in their outward trapping and paraphernalia, such as uniform and disciplining. But with their untrained teachers and absence of philosophy on the questions of children and pedagogy, they are afraid of being deluged by the very surroundings that their 'kind' of school (missionary, reformist) has historically been set up to counteract. Their understanding of the family of the student is not much different to the municipal school's, including in the liberal use of *pichhra varg, neech kaum,chhote tapke ke log* (backward class, lower class, small people) for it. It is different only in that they are marketing a commodity, English education, and have to therefore please their customers at least a little. For the same reason they have to assume an air of mystery about the special formula they own that will produce the alchemy of changing backward people into modern ones. The mystery baffles the families enough to make them need middlemen.

Someone who wants to do well, be seen as doing well, enjoy and sport the accessories of prosperity and progress—*taraqqi*—like Mangra and her husband are as obliged to send their children to an 'English' school as to now own some furniture at home. If a sensitive child, like Vikas, he gets ulcers. If intelligent, like Vikas, he revolts, and tears up his work.

The third rung of the ladder from below is composed of the madrasa or Urdu-teaching school and the Hindi-medium school, both of which are typically affiliated to the state Education Board. Such a school has a better building and staff than the others. It is community-based,[2] founded, administered, and staffed by people from the constituencies it represents, which are typically based on region, language, and religious sect. The school ranks higher for me because its reforming ambitions are very modest. It is critical of the family and community but totally rooted in it. All its policies, such as those regarding school dress, school hours, holidays, and activities, tend to be in line with community wishes. Its teaching, being in the mother tongues of the students, tends to be more palatable. This is the kind of school that Rajendra and his brothers studied in, in Calcutta. While studying there, neither Rajendra nor his family got into a frenzy regarding his studies. But he felt deprived of choice, which is the mark of a 'vernacular' school. The feeling of being trapped stayed with him, and turned into a permanent one. As a father, he continued to act towards his children as if they were trapped too, thus effectively ensuring their entrapment.

Finally, the topmost rung of the ladder is the authentic, original missionary, English-medium, or Public School. These may be found only in the metropolises, large cities, and specially chosen locales such as hill stations, and do not exist in small towns or villages. They produce the kind of modernity described so eloquently by Sanjay Srivastava, largely by distancing themselves from the rest of the population which is responsible for the backwardness of the nation, a population which is ignorant, illiterate, superstitious, communal, hierarchical, and so on. Rajendra and Birendra's children study in such elite schools. In another context it would be important to see how the distancing inherent in their school's teaching may be partly offset and diluted by a more socially responsible teaching by their parents.

CONCLUSION

The four types of schools all have in common an antagonistic relationship with the family, but to different degrees and of different kinds. The municipal or district board school is worst in this regard and children like Vinod are guaranteed to reproduce the poor conditions their parents inherit. Slightly above this school is the local 'English' school, which enjoys the subservience of the family. If Vinod will suffer in the long run and all his life, he is at least happy as a child in his running around in the lanes. Vikas and soon, Gulistan and Nazir, suffer twice over. They are in pain now and will probably not experience much mobility in the future. For the Hindi/Urdu/Bengali medium school children, there is much less trouble, but a compensation effect as all the unsatisfied ambition of childhood is worked out in adulthood with their own children, as by Rajendra and Birendra and their wives. Lastly, the elite school child is as great a victim as the municipal school one, but for totally different reasons: deprived of local narratives, little freedoms, unplanned pleasures, secret escapes; placed at the vortex and pulling the whole family into the vortex, of the great project of progress in India.

NOTES

1. Bengalis in other parts of north India are reputed to be consistently the most educated and progressive, such as in permitting their women to work. Of any single regional group, Bengalis have been in a majority in the teaching profession in the cities of U.P. When asked about the impulses for this educational forwardness, however, Bengali fathers and heads of household consensually maintained that they want(ed) their daughters educated so that they would be ready with qualifications *in case* they were to be widowed or abandoned by their husbands, or—with some hesitation—*in case* they could not get married at all.

2. It is time to qualify my usage of the term 'family' appropriately. It is not a term ever used by my informants and I have no useful equivalents of it in their languages. What they would use in the contexts in which I use family are the terms *qaum, jat*, and *samaj* (otherwise commonly translated as caste, sub-caste, and society). *Ghar* is household, and *ghar ka vatavaran* (literally, the atmosphere at home) is family.

4

History at the Madrasas

HISTORY IN MADRASA JAMIA IRFANIYA[1]

It is class VIII, a class of some forty young men. They are sitting on benches and not on *daris*, only about four in the stereotypical caps, all looking smart and modern. And they are open. On my arrival, they get over their smiling and staring quickly and then ignore me and get on with their work.

The teacher gives them a brilliant lecture on the topic of the day, 'The Expansion of British Rule in India', sub-topic, 'Control by the English over Bengal'. A familiar narrative falls on my ears. *Alivardi Khan...Companies...Calcutta...Chandernagore...fortifications...Mir Jafar...Treaty of Murshidabad...Battle of Plassey.* The children are listening enraptured. Naturally. He is telling it like a story, like 'literature', even as he is peppering the blackboard at odd angles with scribbled names and dates. We come to the Treaty of Allahabad, and the signing over of the *lagan* of Bengal, Bihar, and Orissa. At this point he alludes to the movie *Lagaan*. It is an appropriate reference, in that it is one all the children would get, maybe the whole nation would get. It is good technique. As an old-timer at developing techniques for teaching history, I only wish the young teacher had not been so unsure about his reference to a popular film, had not lowered his voice and implied, 'This is a mere aside, you understand; not part of my otherwise very serious history lesson'. This excepted, I have no differences with him. He is spinning the same grand narrative of Modern India that is familiar to me and thousands of others from school, college, university, and our own work. He is a knowledgeable historian and consults no notes. He is a fluent speaker and is narrating it at the level of the children. If I was a student in the class, I would respect him involuntarily for being a strong authority figure, and for opening up so effortlessly a window into this exciting world of adventures for me.

But there is one grave flaw in his narrative, which he shares with all other teachers of history. He does not manage to communicate in any way, 'This place was called Bengal, but was an incipient India. It is *you, your* story. Alivardi Khan dressed like us, spoke like us. He was different because he was a nawab and had his own calculations. Should we discuss the priorities of a nawab?' What is not taught effectively in Jamia Irfaniya is not taught in any school in India: that a nation can have immense convolutions, and still emerge, injured, and imperfect (as a kind of miracle) *a nation*, which means (still more miraculously) that you and I and everyone else who lived here past and present *are one*. That we want to believe it and make it true. Let us jointly exercise our imaginations to see what this idea could mean (and what it leaves out).

But the students, as I said, are enraptured. Given the narrative as it stands, the teacher is a talented performer. The class is successful. If there is a shortcoming in the teaching of history in madrasas like Irfaniya, it is a shortcoming shared by all the schools of the country.

This particular teacher, Mr Saiyad for convenience, also gives the explanation for this 'shortcoming'. The course to be covered in classes VI, VII, and VIII is huge: the whole of Ancient India (including Pre-History and Early Man), Medieval India, and Modern India, respectively, with a large dose of civics in each textbook as well. Nothing is left out. The narrative is more condensed than one would find at higher levels but is the same compilation of facts. As Mr Saiyad puts it, 'If you teach properly, you cannot just mention an event, as the textbook does. You have to explain it. You have to use five sentences instead of one. Then they need to write everything. For them, nothing will be learnt if they do not write. So, how to use the half-hour period three times a week (the other three go to geography)? Lecture? Have them read? Have them write? Correct? Discuss?'

It sounds impractical to me to suggest map work, classroom activity, or innovative methods after this. In any case, no such methods have achieved legitimacy yet in Indian schools. There are many problematizations of the writing of history by sophisticated historians. They have no time for, and there is no discussion by others of, alternative classroom techniques to the present Grand Narrative-delivered-as-boxed-knowledge-to-empty-receptacles. Comparing this technique at its best, as at Irfaniya, and post-modern history at its best, the moral I see is: A straight narrative is more interesting for children than an ironic, reflexive, open-ended one not at their level.

THE NATURE OF JAMIA IRFANIYA

All this comprises 'History at the Madrasas', but, as the four white caps remind us, we must ask: What makes this specifically a madrasa? Irfaniya is a modern building of three storeys, the rooms built three sides around a courtyard, a wall on the fourth. They own a whole *katra* with some twenty shops. Their classrooms are large and all open to the central courtyard through verandahs and balconies, as well as have windows on the opposite side, so are well-lighted and airy. Let us go to an Arabic lesson in class I.

There are about twenty boys and ten girls, all small and sweet. They wear an assortment of clothes although some students' appearance tells us that the uniform is supposed to be white.

The little children could look like an illustration in the entry 'Education' of the *Dictionary of Islam* by Thomas Patrick Hughes published in 1885 (repub. Rupa 1988). Children sit on a jute mat on the floor and recite loudly to themselves. When bored by reciting, they talk among themselves. The teacher says, '*Aiye! Sabak sikho!*' (Hey you! Learn your lessons!) And the boys I am looking at suddenly seem to fall over, sideways. No, they are beginning the recitation of their lessons. They sway and learn some five lines each every day. During the recitation they look away into the distance with glazed eyes.

The *maulvi* can call them names, can hit them or threaten them with a cane, and make them stand up in awkward positions. He summons them one by one and hears the lines they have learnt and 'gives' them the next three or four lines to learn up. They use the terms 'read', 'learn', and 'recite', but all that the children are doing is deciphering the Arabic alphabet to read the Qur'an line by line, with no understanding of any word of its content. Separately, they learn at an elementary level what the duties of a Muslim are, in subjects called by the equivalent of *Dini Talim*, or, Religious Education.

The children could look like a benign illustration, but our modern pedagogic sensitivities, or mine at least, would question the validity of such rote learning and abuse. I would consider it 'pain' at two levels: at the daily level of how children are treated, and at the long-term level of their being denied choices in their future.

But this is a different problem to that of history teaching. The primary schooling in madrasas like Irfaniya, up to class V, is in Urdu-medium. They are moved into Hindi-medium in classes VI, VII and VIII, then go to High School elsewhere. They have a platter-full of languages: Arabic, Urdu, Hindi, and English. They are learning in the Basic Shiksha pattern and use the Basic Shiksha textbooks for all the subjects. Two extra languages and their initial Religious Education aside, children who study in Jamia Irfaniya are like all children in other institutions. The history they learn is shared by all children. Insofar as this history is inadequately conceptualized and taught, all children, including those in the madrasa, are ill-fitted to be part of India. The failure is one of historians who write textbooks, administrators who design them, and teachers who work out pedagogic strategies.

MADRASAS

In the archival records of the British colonial state, as well as in the private records of members of the Indian intelligentsia, the indigenous school of north India is referred to by the generic term 'madrasa'. There is no exclusive implication of this institution as Islamic. This is close to the literal meaning of 'madrasa' which is 'the place of dars': dars being teaching, instruction, a lesson, or lecture.

Today, the term 'madrasa' stands for Islam. It does so, moreover, not in a neutral sense in which 'masjid' still means place of congregation, but rather in a heavily loaded sense of a place of biased and distorted learning. It is regarded, loosely, as a hotbed of terrorism in Pakistan and Afghanistan, and in India, of opposition to modernity and progress, by which is consensually implied both Western modernity and progress as well as indigenous versions of the same. 'Close down the madrasas', demands the popular press as part of its analysis of Islamic resurgence. 'These institutions, funded by external sources' is their description by a certain kind of layperson, meaning, 'anti-national external sources'. Madrasas are treated as the index of backwardness even by secular Muslim intellectuals. The curriculum is not supposed to have changed from about the thirteenth century to the present.

In order to understand the nature of history teaching in contemporary madrasas in India more fully, we have to agree on the following:
(1) Muslims are also heterogeneous, with sects, schools, ideologies, classes, gender divisions, subcultures, and territorial and linguistic identities. One has to balance between generalization that reveals patterns, and contextualizing that is necessary for precision.
(2) There always exist several approaches to history, as written, taught, and passed on. To judge any of them as right, wrong, correct, or false, we must specify *for whom*, and *according to which criteria*.
(3) Muslims are not otherwise nice people who have somehow gone wrong on certain points. They must be ceased to be understood as 'in opposition' to something normative and better. They are just themselves. Yes, to be 'oneself' is to have an oppositional identity, insofar as most identities, at all times are articulated in opposition to an 'other'.

THE HETEROGENEITY OF MADRASAS

When students finish with class VIII in the madrasa described above, they go to other High Schools in the city and continue in the same stream as in their Middle School. I would call this a secular, nationalist stream, in intention, with failures in both the secularism and nationalism. Perhaps the biggest aspect of failure is that this education is relatively meaningless in their lives and some 90 per cent of them drop out after class VIII. Almost none of the students goes on to Irfaniya's own higher classes. The equivalent of High School, Intermediate, and B.A. are the *Munshi, Maulvi, Alim,* and Fazil diploma/degrees awarded at 2 year intervals. These classes are housed in a separate building, also called Madrasa Irfaniya, under the administration of the same committee, with a different principal and headmaster. *This* Madrasa Irfaniya is under the Arabic and Persian Madrasa Board of U.P. (and in the respective state, in each case). Such Boards run the four exams mentioned above, as well as others such as Qamil and Mumtaz-ul-Muhadassin.

Madrasas belong to a certain sect each, such as Barelwi, Deobandi, or Ahl-e-hadis. For some, including among the madrasa administrators, the difference between the sects is of utmost importance; for others it is trivial merging on inconsequential. Anyone who walks around to observe classes in, say, Madrasa Hamidia, Madrasa Dar-ul-Islam, or Madrasa Umahut-ul-uloom, each of a different sect, cannot distinguish how the sectarian differences play themselves out. When asking about the textbooks, one learns from some teachers that there is a difference between Barelwi and Deobandi books, and from others that there is not; and typically that the differences are minor ritualistic ones regarding how to pray and whom to address. Reading the textbooks does not explicate the differences either. There are good, better, and worse textbooks, independent of affiliation. They are written by diverse people, and published differently, with Deobandi ones written and published from Deoband (but also from Nadwa). Much as one would like a clear pattern to emerge that would match sectarian loyalties, it does not.

In history teaching, particularly, there is little chance of pinning down a Barelwi version of history as distinct from a Deobandi one. While there certainly exist claimants to a significant difference, the educators I personally have met are mostly of the opinion that the differences are greatly exaggerated and that the colonial state particularly distorted the relationship between them by exaggerating differences.

The most startling difference is not between the sects, which certainly do have separate institutions and constituencies. It is between the madrasa which is affiliated with the State Board or the Basic Shiksha Parishad, and is secular and nationalist (plus teaching the Qur'an on its own and using Urdu as a medium at lower levels), and the madrasa which is affiliated with the Madrasa Board, and is explicitly religious. When marking this difference, we must also remember that for every hundred students educated in the latter, religious system, some one thousand are educated in the secular, nationalist system. This may seem to mark the victory of the nationalist over the religious sectarian, but if there are certain rewards that come for students from such a victory, they are small and elusive.

Before discussing this further, there is another important difference to be noted within the catch-all term 'madrasa'. Many children being educated are taught only at home. Either in their own home or in another's, children ranging from three to twenty gather to learn the Qur'an from a maulana or *maulani*, simply someone who has in turn read the Qur'an. Again, these children are never explained, and never understand, a single word of what they are reading. The *tarjuma*, or translation, of what they are reading, can be pursued, according to their educators, when they grow up—if they wish.

What history do these young students in domestic madrasas know? I tried to answer this with a group of one dozen girls ranging from six to sixteen years, from beginners to those who had read half the holy book already. What we would consider historical facts were unknown to them. They did not know who was Babar or what he had done. They did not know when India became independent (and if it had). Certainly, there is a gender difference too. Females are a notch more ignorant than males of modern narratives and facts, and no doubt more knowledgeable of histories of the family and community. But, as my previous research revealed, boys are ignorant also, even those who are in the primary sections of madrasas, and in such startling ways that the notch they are higher becomes invisible.

There are other children who do not study at all, neither at home nor outside, neither the Qur'an nor secular subjects. They begin working early, and are among some of the most 'cultured' people otherwise. They go towards forming, however, the vast pool of India's illiterates. I mention them here in the understanding that a question about madrasas is really a question about Muslims, and the absence of madrasa education among Muslims is also a statement about madrasas.

To end, the heterogeneous nature of madrasa teaching is a product of class, sect, and history. The upper classes and socially mobile Muslims will ensure that their children receive the best cosmopolitan kind of teaching beyond madrasas. Provincial Muslims of almost all classes will choose from among a range of madrasas, or of Muslim schools with no 'madrasa' in their name but with the same combination of national curriculum, Urdu, and religious education. Poorer Muslims may be satisfied with no other teaching but the Qur'an at home. A very small number of the two classes above may send their boys for the religious education necessary for a professional religious career. The very poorest may dispense even with Qur'an learning at home, but would certainly ensure that their children learn their vocation.

THE HETEROGENEITY OF HISTORY

There are two kinds of nationalist history. There could perhaps be a 'good' Indian nationalist history, but it does not exist yet. It does not exist anywhere, and it does not exist in the madrasas. The best that exists, as I see it, is articulated in a textbook like *Hamara Itihas aur Nagarik Jiwan* (Basic Shiksha Parishad, U.P., 2002). It could be taught excellently too, if used as a guide, and followed in principle and not in letter. A good teacher like Mr Saiyad dislikes this textbook because he does not find in it enough of a clear and strong narrative, and finds it too much like 'literature'. He does a wonderful job of teaching it anyway because he in turn makes history 'literature'.

Apart from the general problem that a nationalist history is a distorted and artificial one if not cross-questioned and related to actual people's lives, this history has specific problems. Aurangzeb is always vilified, Akbar celebrated, heroes like Rana Pratap or Shivaji treated like saviours or martyrs, rather than all as complex personalities. The long-term damages of such distortions are immeasurable. Children grow up into adults thirsting for some kind of revenge because they actually believe that 'In 3000 years of our history people from all over the world have come and invaded us, captured our lands, conquered our minds...all of them came and looted us, took over what was ours...'[2].

The second kind of nationalist history is a very weak version, where the teachers are unenergetic and unsuccessful in communicating any sense of a nation, including the elementary facts. All the teachers, including the good ones like Mr Saiyad, consider this failure to be a function of the 'backwardness' of their students' families. Families should not be so ignorant, so uninterested in education, should somehow magically not be illiterate and pre-modern themselves. The subtext here is that parents should be able to help their children with homework and do their share of the teaching as it is supposed to be divided between home and school.

There are two kinds of non-nationalist histories. The first is that taught in Munshi, Maulvi, Alim and Fazil sections. This is *Tarikh-e-Islam*, or *The History of Islam*, such as written by Sheikh Moinuddin Nadavi, published by Darul Musannafin, Azamgarh. Importantly, it is abridged by Asir Adravi from its original four parts to four thin booklets of some seventy pages each. These are the 'notes' that students actually memorize for their exams. It is consensually agreed that teachers do not need to explicitly teach or explain this history. It is there in the notes, and students can 'manage' on their own.

There are several versions of this history as written and published. In a Shia version, the position of Hazrat Ali will be different to that in a Sunni version. In Sunni sectarian versions, there may be barely distinguishable differences, although an institution might prefer to teach its own publication. One version which is never taught in madrasas is the Western version of the 'Venture of Islam', or even the histories of Islam written (in English) by Western-educated Indian or Asian scholars. These are taught in the Arabic history courses of Indian universities, but not in madrasas. One may question whether the 'History of Islam' as taught in Board Madrasas follows the norms of disciplinary history. Like other textbooks, it sounds biased in little ways. Its biggest bias is to speak, not 'objectively', but as a concerned insider, thus: 'Before the coming of Islam, there was no worship of the Supreme God anywhere'. Another bias could be that it is one-sided. This history concentrates on Arabia and does not mention India at all. In justification of this and their total course, Board Madrasas maintain a career orientation logic. Their students are trained to preach and to teach Islam, and all others can and do study in other types of schools and madrasas.

The second type of non-nationalist history is the local history not explicitly taught anywhere but known and cherished by children as they grow into adults in lieu of the teaching of other kinds of history. We should take this history seriously, for two separate reasons. If we were worried about a threat to nationalist history, we should know that it came from both a sectarian history such as the History of Islam, *and* from a local history that flourishes in the absence of deliberate nationalist teaching. If we were worried about a threat *from* nationalist history, we should also know that one of the ways to fashion a more humane, imaginative, and correct history in the future would be to take seriously these local histories at present confined to the 'illiterate'.

THE OPPOSITIONAL STANCE OF MADRASAS

There is an immense variety of positions from within those who grapple with the question of the appropriate education for Muslims. We can barely touch on a few.

The question, according to Dr Muqtada Hasan Mohammad Yasin Azhari, the Rector of Jamia Salfia, is not one of East versus West or Islam versus the West, but of what is practical and desirable. Those structures which are practical and useful are taken over by Muslims regardless of whether they originate in the West or not, such as written exams. Muslims open the institutions needed by them. Thus, for

Salfia, it was necessary to have an educational institution where together with a high-level study of Qur'an and hadis, there would be higher study of Arabic language and literature, and there would be also the work of writing and publishing books, where books of hadis would be written and distributed...' (*Tarjuman*, Delhi, 1 January, 1964, p. 10, quoted in *Jamia Salfia* 1998: 30).

This is a fair description of the identity of a Madrasa Board madrasa. It is criticized by many educated people such as Masooda Khan, the Principal of Umahut-ul-uloom, who is against religious education. She considers other cities more forward than the provincial one she lives in, with its preponderance of 'traditional' cottage industry. Although not expressed by her openly, I understand that she is a Pathan, or an *ashraf* of some kind and she considers weavers who do not value modern education backward. She is vehement in denouncing those who behave like frogs in a well, who provide services only to train maulvis, and who make religion the staple and be-all of their lives.

On my part I would like to separate the Arabic madrasas as specialized vocational institutions comparable to other narrow training institutions. Then I would propose we understand the bulk of madrasas in the larger context of schooling in India and modernity in India. In this perspective, I see schools in India as covering some five parts of a range of schools, each fading into the other. At one extreme, the institution with the weakest link to modernity is the municipal or *mahapalika* school. It has all the paraphernalia of a modern school except the teaching. It also has a colonial attitude in its core distinction between us, the enlightened, and them, the ignorant. Next to it comes the local 'English-medium' school, which has all the same structural features such as age-graded classes, as well as furniture for children and the requirement of uniforms. Neither the students nor their guardians nor the teachers nor the administrators fathom the meaning behind the modernist features they live out, but compared to the first kind of school, they live more of them out and more strictly so.

Next in the range comes the madrasa. Yes, it is indeed more modern than the mahapalika and the neighbourhood convent school. On the face of it, it is nothing but traditional. In the lower classes boys all wear caps, girls all cover their heads. All learn the Qur'an. But their buildings are cleaner and more solid, the classrooms better laid out, the books less in tatters, students and teachers more in harmony. The rote learning of the Qur'an with swaying of the upper body and recitation at a speed which cannot he coded finishes off in the first years. Then there is the execution of the modern requirements of the writing of questions and answers, the preparation for exams and revision, and the grappling with several subjects in an age-graded way.

And, just to complete the argument, the next two phases are the imitation convent schools, and then the actual missionary and public schools. The history taught here is the same as in the others. Only its facts are better memorized by students and they are taught how to be more adept at spinning out narratives. The best cases aside, one could argue that these schools, for all their liberalism, are more violent towards the child than the madrasa and more successful in transforming his being according to external ideological formulations.

CONCLUSION

A madrasa can be of many kinds; its history teaching of many kinds. When it is Islamic, it is geared to a profession. When it is secular, it is nationalist in the way prescribed by various Boards and common to all schools. This history is inadequately taught almost everywhere and is also faulty in its layout. If our aim is to have a successful teaching of secular and nationalist history, the madrasas are not the main defaulters at all. Insofar as they offer free or subsidized teaching to children, try to preserve a continuity between home and school, and invest in most of the paraphernalia of modern schooling, they are indeed institutions to be emulated. Their teaching of history is not as bad as in our municipal schools and little private schools, and sometimes as good or better than in our grand private schools. It can certainly be improved in numerous ways, but none of these ways would be specific to the madrasa and would apply equally to the large variety of institutions and children in India.

NOTES

1. The name of this madrasa and most others, unless in a citation, has been changed.
2. Speech by the new President of India, APJ Abdul Kalam, in Hyderabad, July 2002, for which I presume his speechwriters should be held responsible.

Modernities, Communities, and Genders

5

Languages, Families, and the Plural Learning of the Nineteenth-century Intelligentsia

One often hears it said, within India and outside, by foreigners, and by Indian intellectuals themselves about other Indian intellectuals, that the Indian intellectual is uprooted, that he has lost contact with his country and its culture, that he belongs neither to India nor to the West—and all this because he is an Indian taken by Western ways and ideas. In consequence of this, he is alleged to be neurotic, schizophrenic, ambivalent, suspended between two worlds and rooted in neither (Shils 1961: 60-1).

Let us imagine—or remember—three educational practices:

The first is *teaching*: A (previous) knowledge is transmitted by oral or written discourse, swathed in the flux of statements (books, manuals, lectures).

The second is *apprenticeship*: The 'master' (no connotation of authority: instead, the reference is Oriental) works *for himself* in the apprentice's presence; he does not speak, or at least he sustains no discourse; his remarks are purely deictic: 'Here', he says, 'I do *this* in order to avoid *that*'. A proficiency is transmitted in silence, a spectacle is put on (that of *praxis*, to which the apprentice, taking the stage, is gradually introduced.

The third is *mothering*: When the child learns to walk, the mother neither speaks nor demonstrates, she does not teach walking, she does not represent it (she does not walk before the child): she supports, encourages, calls (steps back and calls): she incites and surrounds: the child demands the mother and the mother desires the child's walking...(Barthes 1989: 336-7).

My essay discusses this problem of the 'suspension between two worlds' through the solution of 'three educational practices'. I suggest here the importance of an empirical sociological enquiry regarding the locus of ideas, the patterns of learning, and the source and effect of intellectual development. In the larger work, I would like to further ground in historical and biographical data what Shils calls the 'composite' culture of Indian intellectuals, a combination of their 'local culture' and the 'world' that 'transcends' it that they would like to participate in. While doing so, I hope that my work can also evoke some to the complexity and excitement of the multiple processes of learning, and the drama inherent in any learning whatsoever.

The relevance of Barthes' quotation on educational practices lies in that he reminds us of the breadth of the phenomenon we otherwise without reflecting call 'education'. We might question and modify him on each of his three points. We might suggest that formal teaching is not always previous knowledge, but that in the best of rare cases, it can be knowledge formed partly in the process of transmission itself. As for the second and third processes, they need not be separated if we take the business of living itself to be a 'craft': how adults fit into their worlds. Then we glimpse the apprenticeship for life to be given also by the same mother who teaches the more 'natural' processes—that is, the implication of the last process should be more heavily laden with 'culture' than suggested by Barthes. One could well use walking as a metaphor. There are many ways to walk, as we know well from the experience of colonial India where a certain body language was interpreted positively by local people, and negatively by their rulers. The mother teaches the language, body and otherwise, that she knows and considers appropriate. Barthes' threefold division may more accurately be converted into a two-fold one.

As for Shils' dual vision of 'India' versus the 'West', of a local tradition versus a universal one, I would suggest that there are not so much two phenomenal objects to be contrasted, but two levels of historical enquiry that should not be held discrete but merged in the interest of greater perspicacity. One is a meta enquiry which inevitably uses terms such as 'tradition', 'modernity', and 'conflict'. As part of this enquiry we inevitably confront the omnipresent question of History itself: How does the will and the desire to have a history arise

among a class? How is modernity created? How does, or does not, a
class accomplish a necessary work, marked by the pain—as in India—
accompanying this vast labour of bearing forth the historically
imminent while confronted by a non-cooperative political economy
and a powerful religious tradition?

But, as this last question can tell us, the weight of this meta-
enquiry is on the side of 'modernity': how the discourse of science, of
nationalism, and the unilinear temporality of History, succeeded. Not
treated as discourses or construction are the other epistemological
formations subsumed under 'tradition' which, either as material
practices or spiritual beliefs, come to be seen as the dead weight of
conservatism.

Indeed, although Shils himself is speaking about the middle of the
twentieth century, it is the 'new' intelligentsia that was produced by the
new system of colonial education in the nineteenth century that are
excellent exemplars of his kind of 'dilemma'. This level of enquiry
produces a model of the Indian intelligentsia that is even, ironically, an
'emic' one, reflected by the intelligentsia in its self-presentation: as the
leader of reform movements, the builder of a nation, and the unifier of
a civilization. From Rammohan Roy onwards, all members of the
intelligentsia have been concerned about this seeming conflict between
their tradition and their modernizing role, between their continuity
with the past and their integrity as reformers. Rammohan's 'crisis of
identity', as well as Jawaharlal Nehru's 'despondency' one century
later, is an expression of this level of self-conceptualization.

At another level, we could look at the intelligentsia ethnographically. It exists and reproduces socially like other groups, rich in occupational and lifestyle characteristics, captured in its very nomen-
clatures: babu, pandit, lala, munshi, vellalar, sardar, maulana, mian,
and so on. These local and variant characteristics preclude flattening,
being as ethnographically and discursively rich they are, and pose a
problem only when categorized as 'tradition' from the perspective of
those, like Shils, who take Western-style modernity for granted. They
are perfectly well comprehended otherwise by anthropology, which we
know can handle non-modern epistemologies and cultures with more
acumen that it can modern ones, if it can do the latter at all. My
interest lies thus in rendering both the self-presentation of the
intelligentsia as modernizer (and our theorization of them as such), and
the so-called 'local culture', more transparent through a gendered,
ethnographic exploration of their learning. And to move towards

suggesting that this is not a case of conflict between the 'old' and the 'new' so much as a case of plural learning.

The distinction of the two levels, as I have made it, may seem to echo Gramsci's distinction between two kinds of intellectuals, the 'organic' and the 'essential' or 'independent'. In line with what I have suggested above, the former, for Gramsci, are those rooted in their strata, class or profession, and the latter are those who have the specific function of intellectuals. However, my own distinction, and then the bringing together of the two levels are meant to emphasize that other notion of Gramsci's which is expressed as: '*Homo faber* cannot be separated from *Homo sapiens*' (Gramsci 1971: 9). I hope to show that those who performed the function of intellectuals were also at the same time organically rooted in their communities and families. They were formed intellectually by formal learning as well as by processes of acculturation and apprenticeship. Unfortunately, the latter processes are rendered invisible to us when we classify them as 'tradition', and also when we separate, like Gramsci, intellectuals' function from their class and community base. I should add that I am emphatically not claiming that my difference with Gransci lies in that I am presenting a colonial case, where, it has been imputed, the home represents the private, the pure, and the preserved domain, of which women were the high priestesses.

The home, as I see it, was progressively marginalized by the state and its schools for the nineteenth-century Indian intelligentsia. Yet, it continued to perform an important sociological function, which we may be interested in, not to reiterate the discourse of its sacredness nor to otherwise define it as in opposition to larger structures but to complicate our understanding of the learning and knowledge of the Indian intelligentsia.

Because my interest is in the processes and sites of learning, and in how intellectuals or social leaders are formed in these and in turn form them, I also scrutinize our assumptions about who or what 'creates', 'declares', 'refuses', 'divides', and 'launches' domains and projects, and suggest that it is not 'nationalism', but institutions, languages, and everyday workers who do so (Chatterjee 1993: 10–13). In other words, we will pose again Ranajit Guha's promising question, 'Where does historical criticism come from?' answered by him with a 'From outside the universe of dominance... from another and historically antagonistic universe....' (Guha 1997: 11) He expands this very tentatively with Marxist explanations of an ideology antagonistic to the bourgeoisie before the bourgeoisie have even become dominant. And we are left asking, but where *does* historical criticism come from? I suggest that we may never find the answer to that question unless we look specifically at the sites and contexts for the construction and transmission of ideas.

In the two succeeding sections we will look at the formation of the intellectual, and touch on the familiar areas of education and social criticism in the less familiar light of languages and the family. Throughout there is a commentary on how, while being formed themselves, the intelligentsia in turn created their master narratives, a commentary that ends in the second section with some hypotheses about social reform.

LANGUAGE AND SCHOOLS

Our discussion of languages should begin with a brief mention that the importance of language learning in this context lies in the closeness of the comparison between language and culture learning. As research on 'maintenance-loss' models of the capacity for cross-language speech perception has shown, infants exhibit capacities that adults no longer possess, specifically to distinguish between categories in 'foreign' languages (Werker 1989: 54–9).

If this early capacity to detect a sound contrast in foreign tongues is kept alive through even a small amount of initial second language learning during the first two years of life, it is maintained into adulthood. Typically however, it disappears by the end of the first year of life, with the onset of exclusive single language learning... (Shweder 1991: 6).

In bolder, more philosophic terms, 'language is the abode of Being' and gives form to the world (Arendt 1978: 174). When new words are learnt, new cultural worlds are discovered and created. New grammars put new structures of power in place. But old words, as long as not forgotten, keep old worlds alive. Old grammars keep older structures of power alive. Indeed, poetry, philosophy, and science (if we may use the term) come together on the subject of language. Words are 'prismatic, vehicles of hidden, deeper shades of thought. You can hold them up at different angles until the light bursts through in an unexpected color. The word carries the living thing concealed across millennia' (Morrow 1997: 4).

In the nineteenth century, *most*, if not *all*, members of the Indian intelligentsia were educated initially in their own language at an indigenous school or at home. The languages learnt by them were their mother tongues: Bengali, Urdu, Hindi, Marathi, Gujarati, Tamil, Telugu, and Malayalam, to mention only some. Apart from language(s), some proceeded to a more advanced level of literature, grammar or philosophy in Sanskrit, Arabic, or Persian. In the beginning, the reasons for keeping up with vernacular and classical learning were career-oriented, as before. The East India Company needed judge-pundits, teachers, and translators. Among the public there was a demand for Sanskrit and vernacular teachers. Indian languages were learnt among literate communities also because English teaching was not available everywhere. English was not immediately seen as more useful, and the East India Company did not make teaching into a policy. Ishwar Chandra, born in 1820 in the village of Birsingha, fifty-two miles west of Calcutta, did not study English because there was no English school in his village and his prospects lay with the learning and teaching of Sanskrit like his peers. His career took a different turn only because his father, Thakurdas, decided to take him to Calcutta to join the Sanskrit College there. Its system of teaching was an improved one, the father had heard, and there were good prospects for its graduates, such as the post of judge-pundit.

The progress of English merits a narrative in itself, one that respects the markets and constituencies in the different parts of India. Rammohan Roy was perhaps the first Indian, followed in 1831 by the 'citizens of Bombay', who petitioned to the government that no Indian be employed in government offices without English. From then on, there was no looking back, as the model of colonial schooling came to be seen as 'natural' and inevitable at different paces in different parts of India. Within a generation, the importance of English for new and old occupations had grown to such an extent that the sons of *mahamukhopadhyayas* were all being given an English education. Later nationalist demands could be made for several kinds of amelioration—such as for more scientific and technical education, or for a more 'Indian' content—but the model itself came to be accepted and no alternatives seriously imagined. English was the language and also the discourse of a new kind of schooling.

However, as a study of the progress of English shows, there were three clearly demarcated parties to the endeavour: the government, Christian missionaries, and Indians. Each used English for its own purpose. For the East India Company, English teaching began with employment of Indians in a subordinate administrative or translating capacity, moving on to a climactic normalization when 'English' was the only knowledge desirable and necessary. Individual members of the government saw the history and future of English education in India as leading towards either a permanent bulwark of British rule in India or, conversely, a political challenge that testified to the acute learning by Indians of British political philosophy.

Missionaries had an agenda of spreading Christianity, which made them more troubled about the failure of the foreign tongue and distant ideas to reach the mind of the student, leaving him to simply regurgitate words and passages. They were, therefore, inclined to be far more pedagogically alert, and both bemoaned the failure of English learning by Indians on the whole, and celebrated its success among the elite when it did occur.

Indians of literate and upwardly mobile classes were interested in the new employment opportunities. They considered the match of these new opportunities and the mastery of a new language natural. Those in direct contact with missionaries could get worried that the latter's vitriol against their culture could be disruptive of students' morale, but they could not and did not take the threat of religious or even cultural conversion seriously. As Alexander Duff put it, missionaries believed that

In the very act of acquiring English, the mind, in grasping the import of new terms, is perpetually bought in contact with the *new ideas, the new truths...* so that, by the time the language has been mastered, the student must be *tenfold* less the child of Pantheism, idolatry and superstition than before (Laird 1972: 207–8).

For most Hindus, on the other hand, Christianity was not a real danger, and its discourses impinged little on their daily lives. Lal Behari Dey's father expressed the extreme in caution. He planned to let his son study English in Duff's school up to a useful point, and then withdraw him when scripture teaching began to have discernible influence (Viswanathan 1989:13).

English education was voluntarily chosen by the Indian intelligentsia and empowered them in a multitude of ways. Knowledge of Sanskrit and especially Persian continued to remain important because of their use in law. But over the nineteenth century they came to be seen as no longer directly related to jobs with the monopoly gradually established by English. Sanskrit, Persian, and the mother tongue became non-utilitarian choices: not good for careers, and progressively as 'of little or no use in the development of [the] mind' (Mitra 1880: 7). At the same time, the colonial state succeeded in marginalizing and making extinct all types of indigenous institutions of learning. The history of indigenous schools shows them to be ignored by the government in the first half of the century. In the second half, they were systematically discouraged and replaced by new primary schools. We know from the Surveys of Education that their figures dropped markedly after the 1870s and that they had almost become extinct by 1900 (Basu 1974; Dharampal 1983; Howell 1872; Kempson 1867-77; Monteath 1887; Reid 1852; Thornton 1850).

But over the whole century, while formal indigenous education declined, it continued informally for the intelligentsia at home. All those who grew up to be active in state bureaucracies; who were at different levels of the professions of law, medicine and teaching; who wrote, spoke and led from different platforms, had a vernacular education in early childhood. To mention only a few cases at random: Bankim Chandra (b. 1838) learnt Sanskrit as a child; Kali Prosunno Singh (b. 1841) had Bengali and Sanskrit lessons in his childhood; U. Ve. Caminataiyar (b. 1855) began learning Tamil at seven or eight; Pandit Ajudhianath (b. 1840) studied Arabic and Persian; Surendranath Banerjea (b. 1848) learnt Bengali in his childhood; Kashinath Trimbak Telang (b. 1850) learnt Marathi very well; Shankaran Nair (b. 1857) learnt Sanskrit as a child; and Motilal Nehru (b. 1861) read only Arabic and Persian till twelve.

It can be shown, I think, that the continuity of vernacular and classical education was an amateur, non-ideological, non-discursive attempt by the older intelligentsia and elite to reproduce themselves culturally in the face of the ambiguous threat of the colonial school. Here, while we are speaking literally of the language, we must remember that a language can never be divorced from its discourse, its mode of teaching, its power. English schools were at first taken by the older intelligentsia to be shops where the child merely mastered the craft of a new language and an associated science. They were only gradually understood to be educational in a wider sense, as including an ideology and an ethics in their training, therefore acculturating children into worlds that were alien to surrounding ones. We may speculate, and in part document, that the cause for the continuity of indigenous education was this new understanding. The documentation would come from the scores of caste journals and caste association papers that emerged all over India from the end of the nineteenth century onwards, all with the common theme of losing something valuable—that is, both precious, and also something possessed and regarded as inalienable—and speculating on how to protect it (Kumar, 2000: ch 4). However, I cannot help but add the additional speculation that intellectuals everywhere, at all times, tend to be more wide-roaming in the spaces they make available for social and cultural reproduction for their younger generation—not out of any philanthropic unity with universal humanity, but as part of their professional practice and cultural identity.

The results of this continuity may likewise be speculated on and in part documented, and divided, for heuristic convenience, into the conscious and unconscious. Its most evident conscious result was to generate a continuing interest in the languages, literatures, and philosophies of India among the intelligentsia. Old languages were revamped, new technologies of print and journalism used, older literary models were refined, new ambitions for the self and the public developed. What did not exist in formal articulation in the language, such as 'history', was freshly expressed or composed. The act was a deliberately constructive one. The construction of 'new' as opposed to 'traditional' was not intellectually problematic, particularly as the activities of the intelligentsia of the 'upcountry' provinces show us. It was logical to use a new epistemology to reinterpret familiar facts, or to fit in new facts into a familiar epistemology. Sayyid Ahmad Khan (b. 1817) remained a product of Delhi's pre-colonial cultural and intellectual milieu, in spite of serving the British government for some twenty years. As late as 1846–54, when posted in Delhi as *munsif*, he took again to his studies of the intellectual traditions of Shah Waliullah and Shah Abdul Aziz. Other examples were Zakaullah (b. 1832), Nazir Ahmad (b.1830), and Altaf Hussain 'Hali' (b. 1837) (Minault 1986: 290–1). In the Northwestern Provinces, the vernaculars remained the most important medium right through for all those who were in traditional occupations, such as Kayasthas, Brahmans or various trading and commercial castes, even while all the boys learnt English. Bharatendu Harishchandra (b. 1850) epitomizes some of these complex trends in his use of the new print technology, his literati creativity, and ambitions for a new nation, all in vernacular language and idioms (Dalmia 1997).

In the Presidency capitals, and especially in Calcutta, this re-discovery typically took place in later years, after an adolescent and youthful reception and digestion of Western learning had had its time. Then the memories of childhood training leavened with an urge of creativity, led to a relearning, rediscovery and recognition, of the 'traditions' of India. Interests might include an extreme of near worship of language or motherland, or language as motherland, such as of Tamil by U.Ve. Caminataiyar, for whom the love of Tamil was a 'marker of moral character' (Monius 1997). At the other extreme was a merely practical belief about the necessity and commercial efficacy of English, and the cultural value of the mother tongue or indigenous classical language.

The other, less conscious, more resounding result was that the possible absolute rule of 'reason' in India was postponed. That is, although children were learning 'only' languages, what they were actually learning, as already mentioned, were 'discourses'. The learning and the intellectual work of the first generation definitely (born before 1800, such as Ramram Basu and Mritunjay Vidyalankar), and that of the second and third generations to a large extent (born in the 1820s – 30s and 1850s–60s, such as Degumber Mitter, Ranganada Sastri, and Salar Jung), was coloured by the understanding of history, society, and the truth that they imbibed both in their colonial and in their indigenous educational settings. The less than perfect reproduction of the Western models of history, society and truth were not due to any failure of capacity on the part of educated Indians, or in the very nature of imitation, or due to an inherent conflict between modern and pre-modern or West and East. It was due to the other education that they had also received.

Although intellectual traditions all over India have not been studied as 'education', there are certainly sufficient allusions to them, and sometimes very detailed discussions of them, by literary historians. 'Non-idolaters' and 'rationalists' may be particularly noted, including the Kartha Bhajas, the Balramis, and the followers of Ram Prasad Sen in Bengal—the region most influenced by English education, where society was seen as 'crumbling', having 'lost her links with her own supreme realizations, her universal and eternal thought', where 'dead, meaningless habit and decadent traditions stifled all creative efforts in the fields of art and culture, religion and politics' (Laird 1972: vii; Ray 1995). Outside Bengal, there were more vigorous traditions of cultural assimilation and continuity. The eighteenth-century scholar, Shah Waliullah of Delhi, continued to exert, through his disciples and scholarship, tremendous influence on scholars of Urdu and Arabic.

While adapted to British rule and keenly aware of the need for social reform, the springs of inspiration for the intelligentsia would necessarily include the intellectual-Sufi approaches already laid down over the last two centuries; and also be motivated by the obvious benefits to *sharif* culture and status that such learning provided. Delhi renaissance men could even be ambivalent towards the advantages of a new education, and consider English a necessary but subsidiary subject (Gupta 1973; Minault 1986).

What I am calling 'plural education' then, has been clearly noted by many scholars in diverse terminology. Brian Hatcher calls it the 'convergence of bourgeois ideology with norms of indigenous discourse' and gives convincing examples from the lives of Ishwar Chandra Vidyasagar and Girischandra Vidyaratna. He cites Barbara Metcalf whose study demonstrates how Abul Kalam Azad 'was profoundly shaped by the complex convergence of the colonial period', in whose life we see 'the overlapping and interpretation of indigenous genres and the hegemonic bourgeois model of self-narration introduced by the West' (Hatcher 1994). Indeed, it would be difficult for a scholar to *not* recognize such a convergence, overlapping or interpenetration, in whatever terms she chose to discuss it (Robb 1993: 1–21, especially 13–21).

A study of the sociological present such as Edward Shils' makes many of the same points but cannot support them with ethnographic data or a complex historical narrative. He mentions, for instance, the upbringing of the Indian intellectual within an Indian household in the middle of the twentieth century, with its caste and other vibrant traditions; the closeness of the intellectual to his mother tongue; and the hold on him of religion and astrology. A typical comment is:

The third and fourth stages [of the asramas or stages in life]....continue to have a tremendous power over those we interviewed....The transcendence of the concrete self, detachment or unattachedness, renunciation, escape from the routine and the compromise of market, hearth and committee room—these are some of the ideals of the third and fourth stages and they are common ideals of Indian intellectuals (Shils, 1961).

What is fascinating about Shils' discussion is its perfect prototypical representation not only of the intellectual's 'conflict' but of the unspoken critique of 'tradition' by 'modernity', as in Shils' statement that Indian intellectuals are more 'religious' than their Western counterparts, implicitly, against their wishes.

We are familiar with another version of this plural learning in the notion of the 'renaissance'. Directly the product of two streams of learning, the renaissance worked at two levels. At one level was the new creativity in languages, genres, and media that has come down to us as the achievement of the nineteenth century. The creativity arose from the workings of new Western knowledge not on some abstract 'past', but on other bodies of knowledge encountered in quasi-formal and informal settings outside the school. The same creativity, I suggest, may be seen in everyday life, in average careers, and their pragmatic adjustment to domestic milieus, in answers to private/public questions, without any of this reaching the stage of publishing, lecturing, or demonstrating. In this sense, all the first and even later generations of the Western-educated participated in the 'renaissance' because they were all brought up in two worlds; socialized by other teachers, elders and womenfolk as well as by their new teachers and new work experience. These two streams of learning did not stay discrete in their lives but were actively amalgamated in ways that may not necessarily seem compatible to us in our search for some elusive holism—and are certainly not sufficiently known by us.

We are further familiar with this in discussion of nationalism. The 'progress' of the nationalist movement from a 'moderate' to an 'extremist' phase was due, of course, to large changes in politics, economics, and ideology. But it matched a similar process within the lifespan of single individuals who seemed to discover the missing dimension in their lives. Surendranath Banerjea (b. 1848) thundered when he was about thirty years old:

We are an astute people. We are not as wholly devoid of sagacity and common sense as some people take us to be. Well, then, our fathers, with the astuteness characteristic of our race, at once saw that England's greatness was, to certain extent at least, due to her noble literature, to the immortal truths taught by her science, and to the sublime morality which breathes through the burning words of her great writers and thinkers.... Might not Bengal freely grope about, in the same direction, and under the same guidance? (Banerjea 1878: 6–7).

On the occasion of the inauguration of the Banaras Hindu University, when he was about seventy years old, he spoke—together with all the other speakers on the day—about the importance of incorporating 'Indian culture' into the modern curriculum:

We who have profited by experience are not going to make such mistakes. In our curriculum, Hindu ethics and metaphysics will occupy a foremost place, the Western system being used only for purposes of contrast or illustration. Special attention will also be paid to a knowledge of the country, its literature, its history, and its philosophy (Sundaram 1956: 147).

The relationship of nationalism to the plural learning that characterized the intelligentsia is, of course, a very complex one. We are familiar with one side of the relationship, that between colonial education and nationalism, and especially how all nationalists were educated in the colonial mode, were aware of the greatness of Western nations as based in their intellectual pursuits, and were then engaged in the discovery of their own nation's past glories as being related to excellence in education in the past. The contribution of languages to this discussion lies in that a language is precisely what is not fixed, or traditional, or essentialist. It is duplicitous and offers ceaseless possibilities for play and difference. Even more, a language opens the gate to a literature, which is in itself a repository of ethics, common sense and philosophies of the self. But most of all, a language is a discourse in itself, with a critical definition of everything in its purview, and beyond so that the continuities in language learning equalled discursive learning. The intellectual structures inherent in these discourses could be objectified, expanded, and marshalled for various purposes, with breathtaking possibilities for a nationalist 'science' in particular, and nationalist pride in general.

THE FAMILY, EDUCATION, AND SOCIAL REFORM

The locus for the new, synthetic, syncretistic consciousness of modernity of the intelligentsia, then, was largely the language(s) they worked with, that they comprehended the world through, that they had learnt both in school and outside school or in less formal schools. But what they learnt went beyond language, as we have already suggested, and as we shall explore in greater detail now. Let us imagine the life of an intellectual in the nineteenth century. Let us look at the extreme case of Aurobindo Ghosh. Born in 1872, Aurobindo had a father who, lost in admiration for the British way of life, wished to preserve his son from any contact with Indians. Aurobindo was, therefore, sent to a convent in India at the age of five and to the care of an English family in England at the age of seven. Ten years of English education later, he was master of Western knowledge. He was as anglicized as his father would have liked and knew almost nothing about India. But it seems that his father had slipped up somewhere. Otherwise how would Aurobindo have known the little Hindustani and Bengali that he apparently did know? And how was his father to take care of his colour and his name, so that when at Cambridge, Aurobindo could not be kept immune from Indian politics? By 1890, when he failed the Indian Civil Service examination, he was already on his way, at the age of eighteen, to being a full-blown nationalist.

If we look at the course of his life and his education, we may find at least one missing clue. His mother, the daughter of the Vedanta scholar, Rajnarain Bose, was 'an orthodox Hindu lady'. The two sources of his 'alternative' knowledge were his own independent study upon his return to India, and what he must have learnt in his first five years in India from her.

This is one pattern in the history of India that could be given more attention. The fathers of these early generation new intelligentsia were themselves members of the 'old' intelligentsia (their famous sons' names are in parentheses): *darogas* (Akshay Kumar, b. 1828), diwans (Rammohan Roy, b. 1772; Raghunath Rao, b. 1831), other kinds of court officials (Syed Ahmad Khan, b. 1817; Mahadev Ranade, b. 1842), clerks (Haracharan Ghosh, b. 1817; Vembankum Ramiengar, b. 1826), and pandits (Ishwar Chandra, b. 1820). As pillars of society, the fathers typically honoured caste and sectarian rules, practised gender and age hierarchies, and believed in child marriage. Akshay Kumar and Mahadev Govind Ranade were married at thirteen, Rammohan Roy at nine and ten, Sivnath Sastri at twelve, Bhabhanicharan Bandopadhyaya at nine, Gopal Hari Deshmukh at seven, Lajpat Rai at twelve. Gopal Krishna Gokhale and Bal Gangadhar Tilak at thirteen, and Dhondu Karve at fourteen.

The mothers of the first and second generation intelligentsia were often widowed, such as those of Akshay Kumar Dutt, Baladev Palit, Gopal Hari Deshmukh, Kandukuri Veerasalingam, Krishnachandra Majumdar, Pratap Chandra Majumdar, Shyamacharan Sarma Sarkar, and Surendranath Majumdar. One may suppose—even without recourse to psychoanalytical discussions of the strong mother–son bond in India (Carstairs 1961; Kakar 1989)—that after the father's death, the mother's bond with the son became further strengthened. The reappraisal of the status of the 'female' in India that is already being done must also be done with reference to the identity of the intelligentsia. Anthropological and feminist work tells us that the maternal and the feminine may be more central and multi-vocal in Indian society and culture than allowed for. We know particularly of the high evaluation of androgyny and sexual inversion. Historically, we also know that the tie between mothers and sons was especially close in some regions, such as Bengal, but that the tales of 'bleeding female lingams' and 'male yonis' come from diverse regions (Ferro-Luzzi 1987; Borthwick 1984). It is relevant to evoke here all these various ideas, each with its own scholarship, in order to emphasize that we should particularly worry about a current contradictoriness: our present understanding is, on the one hand, hazy about the meaning of the domestic, maternal, parental, and 'traditional'; on the other hand, it has preconceived, fixed, non-discursive ideas about this realm of the woman.

For a variety of reasons, therefore, the notions of 'masculinity' and 'femininity' in the Indian context are particularly relevant to childhood socialization and need to be further investigated. My particular proposition here is that because of the nature of gender in India, the demographic facts of the nineteenth and early twentieth centuries, and the nature of childhood, the mother has a profound influence on the making of the adult identity of the intelligentsia. She does this not only through her work of biological reproduction, child-rearing and utterance, but through imparting visions of alternative sensibilities, values, narratives, and mental worlds to the ones being imbibed in public institutions such as the school and the workplace.

The biographies of men reflect, it is true, an idealized cultural expectation of nurture, and emphasize the 'nature' of their mothers rather than their 'culture'. The case of Gooroodas Banerjee (b. 1844) sums up this image eloquently. Widowed,

the mother on whom the task of bringing up the child now devolved was a woman of great sweetness and force of character, and the gentle but firm touch of her hand had been in no mean degree responsible for the character of her distinguished son (Rao 1983: 70).

Even with a little reading between the lines, we find that what the mother is being attributed with is, in specific cases, the precise qualities of thrift, forethought, strength, and often her own physical labour. Vembankum Ramiengar (b. 1826), 'the first Indian in Madras to keep his house in European style, to teach English and European music to the females of this family and to invite European gentlemen to parties at his residence' attributes his good education to his mother through exactly these qualities: thrift, foresight, and strength (*Some*

Noteworthy Indians 1992: 198). In other instances, the mother could oppose the iconoclasm of her reformer-son, but support him, and in cases like Rammohan's, where she opposed him, still exert great influence on him. Sometimes, it was her position as member of a particular caste and class that made her the socializing influence that she was, such as Hatcher argues for the grandmother and, less so, the mother of Vidyasagar, The former spun yarn to support her children as many in the Bengal countryside had to at that juncture in history. Both of them in their own ways were Brahman matriarchs, who, we suspect, maintained the ethics of their clan through the generations (Hatcher 1996).

In numerous cases, it is the language-culture that is attributed to the mother, sometimes implicitly as a contrast to the paternal schools that the child was later subjected to. Subhas Chandra Bose, at sixteen, 'was more an ascetic than a political activist perhaps owing to religious instructions [sic] he received from his mother. As a result, his attachment to Shaktism and Vaishnavism was clear' (Chakrabarty 1990: 22). When educated, such as in the cases of Syed Ahmad Khan or Rama Verma (b. 1837), the mother was actively and directly involved in the son's training.

The mother's role, however, was far from restricted to a 'maternal' as opposed to a 'paternal' school. Even while her husband survived, and especially when she was widowed, the mother could be actively on the side of English education through not only the typical means available to her, such as thrift, labour, and self-denial, but by making the active choice of English education. In Akshay Kumar's case, the widowed mother was responsible for the commitment to his schooling. Veerasalingam's mother, Purnamma, widowed when he was four, 'wanted to give her son the best possible education. So she sent him to the Government District School' (Chatterjee and Mukhopadhyaya 1931: 115,127). Again, we must read between the lines at times. Dadabhai Naoroji's mother, widowed, 'worked for' her child. Illiterate, she was still his wisest counsellor. 'She made me what I am', he reminisced (*Indian Worthies* 1906: 167–94). The case of Dhondu Karve's (b. 1858) mother, widowed when he was in school, illustrates the complex interplay in the mother's subjectivity and agency. Her almost total illiteracy went with 'religiosity', which, while otherwise opposed by her son in public life, was transmitted to him as 'charity' and 'love'. Her devotion to her son was part of the task of motherhood and, upon her being widowed, became intensified. She became very 'careful' with his upbringing, particularly with his education, because that was where the future lay. The decision to continue with English schooling, sometimes in the face of great financial odds, was necessarily taken by her. Her 'old ideas' notwithstanding, she 'fully appreciated the great work being done by her Dhondu...' (Paranjpye 1915).

The position of the mother in Indian history has been unjustifiably obscured by the discourse of the 'mother', available at first hand in the recollections of their sons and the sons' biographers, and then interpreted ironically by historians. She is seen simply as the idealized nurturer of all material and spiritual resources in the otherwise colonized male, and then as the idealized land and nation itself. And the difficulties of historiography are undeniable. No great person's biography gives a description of the earliest years spent with his mother, as Walsh points out (though Walsh in her turn gives attention exclusively to the father when discussing 'growing up' (Walsh 1983: 137). Great men feel obliged to remember their mothers only in the most generalized ways: 'About my mother I can only say that she was the typical ideal mother described by everybody...' (Kolhatkar 1963: 137). There is no evocative scene from a dim, past store of images, such as we find in the fictitious description of Nabin Singh, modelled on some nineteenth-century Calcutta grandee, perhaps Kali Prosonno Singh, who spent his days, as a toddler, with his mother, feeding her pet birds and so on, one corner of her sari tightly clasped in his fist. She 'didn't know one letter from another' (Gangopadhyaya 1981: 24).

The point here is not to attribute to a 'mother' a particular set of characteristics, and certainly not those of wisdom or sacrifice. The point is to restore, even while problematizing it, the sociological status of the mother—and of the surrogate mothers of the family—as the primary caregiver(s) and socializer(s) in the child's infancy, and, when widowed, in diverse ways even afterwards. In doing this, we also unravel one more strand of the extra-scholastic influences on the intelligentsia. The women themselves certainly experienced their lives as larger than that contained in the overdetermined category of 'mother', as the occasional writing by women, spectacularly that by Rashsundari Devi, can reveal to us (Chatterjee 1993; Lalitha and Tharu 1991; S. Sarkar 1998; T. Sarkar 1999). We do not intend to drain her being by restricting her to one static identity. We do not see her as '*the mother*'. We see her as engaged in the work of mothering, and in the process, as engaged in a productive labour that goes beyond physical reproduction and nurturing to social and cultural reproduction (Glenn, Chang and Forcey 1994; Jetter, Orleck and Taylor 1997; Nair 1990; Okin 1981, 1991; Phoenix, Woollett and Lloyd 1991).

Mothers, like all females except prostitutes and *Vaishnavis/sadhvis*, belonged to an 'inside' that was being further bifurcated from the 'outside', to popular culture and in formal learning, to indigenous education. What they transmitted to the child were therefore, naturally, ideas from the general pool of the 'indigenous', the 'vernacular', and the 'traditional'. These could be mythological tales and histories, read or recited. They could be the verses of the poet-saints, the lore of reformist devotional poetry. They could be the epics, in Sanskrit or the vernacular. They could be nursery rhymes or stories about the family. They could be *abhangas*, nonsense verses, and literary games. They could be any stories about the region or about the Hindu pantheon (Ranade 1963). The few writings that speak directly about childhood mention, typically in a very casual manner, how mothers performed various skilled jobs beyond housework. Ramabai Ranade's mother, formally uneducated, knew about medications and regularly told her children stories from the Puranas. Parvati Athavale's mother, similarly uneducated, helped, in her husband's trade (Ranade 1938). It was only by the turn of the century that a *bhadramahila* mother could be educated enough to teach her son English, but even then Shudha Mazumdar had herself been trained in fasts, rituals, and their narratives. When she mentions her English teaching exclusively, we may assume that it is largely the expectation of the 'modern' in her narrative that makes her not mention any other teaching (Mazumdar 1977). But whatever the formally retrievable content, in all cases, the early years spent with the mother would comprise an early education.

The education we are speaking of is close to what a Hindu calls *samskara*, or the ethical dimensions of living as learnt from one's ancestors. Here I am speaking of the term not in its dictionary meaning of the Sanskrit term *samskara* as 'essential rites', but in its colloquial (specifically, Hindi and Bengali) usage. In all fairness, transmission of values, or *samskara*, is not the monopoly of the mother, and for a more complex reason than the workings of patriarchy. It is because 'mothering' is not exclusively the domain of one parent. The same processes that made the woman more private, in need or protection, a bearer of tradition, the synonym for home and religion, made her play a progressively larger role in the upbringing of the child over the nineteenth century. But this did not always occur at the same pace between regions, town and countryside, classes and occupations. The English-educated class was minuscule. Even while its ideology of family life was progressively based on the European model, 'a husband's relation to his wife was subordinate to that with his mother' (Borthwick 1984:12). But by the same token, mothering was not a full-time occupation or a science and the husband and children were not seen as exhausting a woman's whole world. The father, and various other members of the family, also continued to be domesticated, bearers of traditions, and synonymous with religion and lineage. Our argument is not for a mother as a somehow unique personage, but rather for recognition of the spaces within which the child learnt apart from his government-recognized school.

If the cases of Aurobindo Ghosh and others named earlier tell us of the hidden link of the mother, that of Ishwar Chandra Vidyasagar tells us of the role of *samskara*. Hatcher calls it the vernacular or Bengali traditions, and Ishwar Chandra's own presentation of the self, a case of Brahman identity. We know that in the retrospective gaze of history, we often impose categories on our subjects that had little meaning at the time they lived. Families, kin groups and networks, clans and lineages, sub-castes and *biradaris* comprised the social experience of people. Hatcher describes rather perspicaciously the experience of a Brahman family, and more, of a gifted individual of a Brahman family. There were identical experiences in all other castes: Baniya (Agrawal, Khatri, Gujarati, Marwari); Kayastha; Kasera, Lohar, Barhai; and in Muslim lineages (Ansari, Pathan, and so on). A Brahman is more easily locatable and retrievable historically, but Hatcher's study exemplifies the way in which the 'natural' cultural characteristics of any group should be problematized. The ethical dimensions of identity were as central to the selfhood of the subject as other material or social dimensions and do not deserve obfuscation as 'tradition'.

Because English education did not and could not take over the whole of life, and language teaching continued, and because ethical teaching—the passing down of *samskaras*—was so central to the existence of the 'family', the process of education that actually occurred is what may be described as that of plural acculturation. There is little empirical description of this, since we have as yet no interest in the Indian child or childhood, and no strong analysis of it beyond the metaphor of the child as a battleground of cultures, where the old and the new thrash out a compromise (Nandy 1987). But we may want to question this metaphor as well. Learning is continuous and, rather than confrontational, is creative, enriching, and empowering. To make this plural, creative learning a subject of serious inquiry and positive evaluation, we have to attribute an importance to family and community history such as has not been done so far, and pay new attention to the quotidian sources of ideas outside the classroom.

If we take stock of the processes briefly described above, we come up with the following generalization. The mother and father prepared the child for a career by cooperating in the disciplines of the new education, whether it took their physical labour or their mental compromise. The father's profession and the parents' caste and lineage positioning necessarily meant a consciousness in the growing child of his 'identity'. Even as the father and mother ensured that their son got the English education the father himself may not have had, they taught values that were important to them, and that were as 'real' as anything in their world (Nanda 1977). Yes, they were not professionally relevant, and they were not always objectified or available in articulated form. The growing son's *samskara* was not confined to certain rituals and practices that he might well abandon. It consisted of an unspoken acceptance of an epistemology and ontology that may be glimpsed in all his later writings and actions. Some of the best insights may be gleaned from attitudes towards the body. Even those totally anglicized through their formal schooling might continue to believe in the *akhara* as the preferred site for working out and exercising (Banerjea 1925: 4–5). A 'modern' intellectual such as Sigvaswami Aiyer (b.1864) spoke in the Madras legislature against government support of the Ayurvedic and Unani systems but used them in his own home in treating his wife, praising them as superior to the 'allopathic' system (Sastri 1965). At the other end of the spectrum would simply be glimpses, in different degrees of clarity of abstract world views and cosmologies. To take from Surendranath Banerjea's story again, he talks of the natural-ness of the 'reverence for the head and the elders' of the family shown both by him and his English-educated father (Banerjea 1925: 2). What seems to us as a 'natural' movement towards novelty, individualism, and modernity in the reproduction of generations is difficult to pin down anthropologically.

Again, both the father, but more typically the mother, since she was often widowed and always in the position of nurturer, taught the child a fund of stories, views, and images, to which we have little access yet. But an excellent instance is the continuing popularity of the *Ramayana* and *Mahabharata* corpus of stories, which have never been part of the formal school curriculum, and which are not taught in Hindu homes through any formal religious teaching, and are not to be confused with 'religion' in any institutionalized sense. Can we dispute that these corpuses of stories have gone into the making of the Indian intelligentsia? Given the nature of 'Hinduism', with its absence of church and priesthood, where would the so-called Western-educated elite of India have learnt of these stories if not through their parents, both biological and surrogate? To ignore the family as a site of learning means, in the colonial case most of all, not so much to neglect 'family history' as to short-circuit the history of education.

Then we come to the troubled case of 'reform'. Here, we will barely touch on one aspect of it: the context of the learning of the reformers, which was more wrapped up with the family and the mother than is understood. We can glimpse how the experiential location of the child within a home conceptually structured on a certain philosophy, his own early marriage, his constant interaction with servants, if any, and with the world of the streets and popular culture in every case, meant that the stimulus to his reform-mindedness as an adult came equally from his experience and his intuitive interpretation of the home, as from his late intellectual appreciation of it as injustice and oppression in the light of certain teachings. What are regarded as obstacles and inconsistencies in reformist thought must also be understood largely as the complexity of the encounter between experience and its plural theorization.

Indeed, there was a dilemma for the reformer. It lay in the nature of active intervention in society, in the nature of violence, and the question of degree. The indigenous reformer is always different from the colonial reformer in a crucial way—in the consciousness of violence. Some of this comes from familiarity. Reform, change, and rejection are all easier when the people, relationships or values being changed or rejected are unfamiliar, strange, and other. But when, through infancy and childhood at least, and in ways that continued to surround and bind in later years, the relationships or values were familiar and at least unilaterally 'yours', then the action that changes or rejects them was one of violence. This awareness of violence creates the dilemma. Colonialism defines problems and then sets out to correct them. The indigenous cannot philosophically define itself as the problem, but must rather separate a part of itself as immune to the definition and label the rest of it. But every such separation is violent because there are no discernible lines. So some are drawn, some etched darker, some shifted, and realigned. That between the masculine and feminine is one such. Another is between the low and the high. A third is between the popular and the classical. Reform and progressiveness resulted almost consistently not only in unequally distributed new rights and favours, but also in extensions of older repressive structures.

Once we have further studies of the links between reform and plural learning, we would find the data to substantiate this 'dilemma' further. For the moment we can take a small detour to explicate the point. In the novel *Mai* we have three main protagonists: two who want to save and reform the third, and the third who is the victim (Shree 2000). What makes this illustrative for our purpose is the author's tracing of the process whereby the 'victim' comes to be understood by one of the projected reformers as someone with a mind of her own and with the choice to fight or not, or, with yet more sensitivity, fight in one of several possible ways. At the same time, the business of being a 'victim' becomes complicated as scenarios unfold themselves where she is bullied by the evident oppressors into acting a certain role, but, equally, she is bullied by the saviours into fighting back. There is little to choose between the bullying, the domination, and finally the accusation of weakness hurled against the victim, by either side. Yes, the aims of the two sides are different: the oppressors wish to have her conform and to deny her any subjectivity and being; the reformers want her to be herself and stand up for her subjectivity and being. The trouble arises in that neither considers what *she* is or wishes to be. The former assume she is nothing, and the latter assume she is nothing—for two different reasons. The former seem to be indifferent to her, but perhaps love her in their own way. The latter certainly love, even worship her, but seem quite indifferent to her preferences.

The dilemma is the outsider-insider's. Indeed, those very terms are used in the book:

We had risen above caste. Above tradition, community, nation, everything. We were not superstitious, not religious, not middle class, or caught in any other binds...our freedom lay in our being 'outsiders'. At home we were no longer of the inside, so we were free. Abroad we were outsiders anyway so we could do what we liked. Everywhere we were 'outsiders' and therefore alone. Drunk with our freedom... (Shree 2000: 111).

There are two insights to be gleaned from this. As the book goes on to demonstrate, one at least of the 'outsiders', totally knowledgeable about and in love with the West as she is, realizes that she will never escape completely to the outside, because the 'inside'—the house, its traditions, her mother, her foremothers and forefathers—are all right there inside her and she has been travelling with them all along. Perhaps one cannot ever become an outsider to every place, as the passage just cited claims: outsider to one's inside, and outsider to the outside as well—outsider both at home and out of it, both to one's nation and abroad.

Second, maybe it is not even desirable to be an outsider. Because that implies rejection, condemnation, and a grossness and falsity of understanding. Some truths, at least, are only known from the inside, if they are known at all. Some battles can only be fought from the inside, if they can be fought at all. Once one has rejected or condemned, one may suffer in an unpredicted way, and in some cases, revert to a previous imagined state with impassioned repentance.

If, in terms of the use of sources and data, it seems a travesty to bring in a novel about a contemporary mother into this discussion of reformers in the nineteenth century who have no precise words to say about their own mothers, let us erase all gender considerations and consider the problem of the novel solely as one of reform. Reform implies that we recognize something—it may be 'us'—as in need of change. But 'us'-ness implies inter-generational continuity and the feeling of 'inside' that recurs at some point even if it disappears in adolescence, and the glimpse or recognition of why some things are the way they are. To quote Shweder, the insider recognizes that: 'Reason and objectivity may lift us out of error, ignorance, and confusion. Yet error, ignorance, and confusion are not proper synonyms for tradition, custom, and folk belief' (Shweder 1991:8). What Shweder is calling 'tradition. custom, and folk belief', are, as this article argues, more precisely understood as the content of other processes of learning.

CONCLUSION

We are not speaking of perfect reproduction or of functional adaptation over the nineteenth century. The assumption is of a society in profound self-questioning and change, and the lens is that of children located in their families and societies and their experience of learning.

The argument is that the combination of certain features in the lives of the early intelligentsia—the recurrence of certain patterns, as I have called them—needs a higher evaluation than it is given. Our data may be empirically less than adequate at present, but while they may be improved with labour, certain hypotheses enable us to stretch them further already. Notwithstanding the limitations in the present state of the study of 'education' in India, it would still seem defensible to argue that the early grounding in one system of thought, however partial, ensures that there will be a complexity in the subsequent mode of thinking. The explanation sought today for 'alternative modernities' and the 'local in the global' lies largely in that children grow up into adults knowing more than what their schools (and, in contemporary analyses, the media) teach them (Duranti 1997: 351). In the nineteenth century, the first generations of the Indian intelligentsia discovered a cosmogony, an epistemology, and a science in their formal schooling that enchanted them. But they were also familiar with another that was taken for granted by those around them. This constituted a mental 'home' from which they could wander afar, but to which they could always return; a home that did not necessarily forbid—if correctly manipulated, negotiated with, and won over—all possible intellectual adventures, such as those related to rationalism, universalism, freedom, equality, and change. Many searched for these correct negotiations till the end; others were confident of them from the beginning.

Second, an emphasis on family, on childhood experience, and on the extra scholastic dimensions of education will enable us to give a place in intellectual history to those who seem otherwise mysteriously silent and absent. This article is a study of the production of intellectual cultures and educated people, but it is certainly a statement about the gendered nature of history as well. Given the power and emotive relationships within the family, women had a further role to play, not only in intellectual history as discussed here, but also in the history of reform, as can only be suggested at this point. A man's wife, mother, sisters, and daughters may be expected to play an active role in arousing in him an awareness of his grounded-ness, the first three at least deliberately. Further, rather than simply being objects, women surely sometimes used, as it were, the man as an instrument to achieve for them their needs: of female education, widow remarriage, raising the age of marriage, and other social reforms. At other times, they used their position as mother, wife, and so on, to preserve for themselves some enclaves of autonomy and power, and when doing so, seemed to resist reform. All these goals were not uniform, and could and did conflict with each other. But the interlinked activity of women in both creating, learning, and producing reform is utterly lost so far in the histories of reform, nationalism, and modernity.

The dangers in this line of interpretation have to be recognized and avoided. The first is a political one. Even as we show the work of childhood socialization and early teaching to be 'essential'—an indispensable and irrefutable part of the history of education—it is 'non-essential,' that is, not 'natural' to its practitioners but rather the institutional product of forms of patriarchy. Moreover, we may not be personally interested in mothers, mothering, families, or the implications of fertility as lying at the centre of women's lives, and therefore may hesitate to make such a large case for the value of these and related processes.

Another danger is to see each of the bodies of knowledge, the 'formal' and the 'informal', as a 'body', corporeal, solid, or fixed. The 'informal' at least, would better be seen as many evolving systems of thought always discursively open, in their implications, their potential, and their relationships with other systems, if not in their practice. Thus, we could speak of any of the many strands of Islamic or Hindu learning, but more relevantly, of 'world view' and 'popular conceptions', as does Dale Eickelman when he argues for widening the understanding of education (Eickelman 1978, 1986). Another danger lies in our contemporary differentiation of systems of knowledge as 'science', 'religion', and so on. Not only is this a distinction not relevant to the time we are speaking of, but also any system of knowledge may be more incom-plete and internally inconsistent than this suggests, specially regarding ideas of time, of duty and honour, of action and freedom. Further, there is the question of the old and the new, and of the cultural defence of the 'old' which always generates, in the very logic of human activity, 'new' symbols and patterns (Conlon 1994: 46).

Finally, there seems to be one important reason for pursuing the hypothesis of this article further, a reason completely implicated in the arguments cited here for the creativity of learning, and the hidden role of women in history. This is our contemporary interest in discourse, and in many cases in that discourse that relates to women. It is not only the stated and the articulated, the wordy, and the coherent, that go into the making of a prevailing discourse, but even more, and more elusively, the ideas, concepts, images that are only suggested, somewhat familiar, somehow intimate, surprisingly natural and powerful, but always on the verge of vanishing. In any study of intellectuals and reformers, then, it would behoove us to remember that the most formative influences on them may be exactly those relatively invisible to us: those of their early language, their families, and their communities.

6

Mothers and Non-Mothers
Gendering the Discourse
of Education in South Asia

EDUCATION IN SOUTH ASIA

Three issues shape the narrative of the educational history of modern India. One issue is that of the early nineteenth-century anglicist-orientalist controversy, as it is called, which marked the shift from a high evaluation of 'oriental' literatures and languages to a conclusive victory for English both as a medium for higher instruction and as a discourse surrounding the highest body of knowledge. English in both senses then made progress: the number of institutions expanded over the nineteenth century, the curriculum was further developed, and successive generations of students were produced who were at home in the new cultural world of English literature and European philosophy, history, and science.[1] The second issue, taken for granted and poorly documented, is that of the progressive marginalization and final near-extinction of 'indigenous education'. The lack of analytical attention to the possible meanings for those in the nineteenth century of this dramatic change in social relationships and shifts in epistemologies and common sense has produced a unique thinness in the social history of modern India.[2] Finally, the third issue centres on the consciousness of racism and discrimination on the part of Indians, leading to nationalist efforts to create a history and a nation for themselves, including setting up national schools.[3] These three issues produce rich narratives and I will return to them at the end after building up a case for how they may be more holistically recounted by being made into gendered narratives.

However, even with all this wealth of plots, the history of Indian education remains a very constricted one because it leaves out the histories of all those who did not go to colonial schools, government or private. These were groups across the caste and class spectrum: Sanskrit pandits, merchants, and owners of various industries, artisans, petty traders, and workers. By excluding them, the history of education in India leaves out the complex workings of professional apprenticeship, domestic learning, the transmission of samskaras or ethics, and indeed all the processes of social and cultural reproduction that take place outside the school. Those on whom the history of education does focus, the few thousands who did go to colonial schools, from among whom emerged the class we could call the new Indian intelligentsia, are also curiously two-dimensional. They seem to exemplify the despotic machine of capitalist and modernist transformation in the older story of Europe, with the minor modification that they were also the products of colonial transformations as well as that which colonialism failed to transform. In terms of education, they seem to be formed by a fairly coherent and progressively elaborate ideology of English studies and European Enlightenment discourse, and yet to be not so much formed by alternative discourses, as to delve into some kind of raw, pre-discursive material called 'tradition' or the 'indigenous' or 'vernacular' that goes into their making in unspecified ways.

The Indian historical case, I have suggested in chapter 5, illustrates that education is a multi-stranded process occurring at plural sites, not so much contradictory as cumulative, producing results that go beyond the schemes of any one organizer of the process. To ignore some of these sites because they are overtly 'domestic' or 'private' is to entrench those same gendered private–public dichotomies that we should be deconstructing (Nicholson 1986). The share in modern education of those who are themselves not subscribers to it consists of both facilitating modern education and also opposing it by teaching other epistemologies, neither of which processes has been explored yet.

My argument concerns both the field of education and of women and I focus here on the education of the intelligentsia and on women within the discourse of motherhood. The position of the mother in

Indian history has been unjustifiably obscured by pursuing only the equation of the 'mother' with the idealized land and nation itself. True, certain members of the Indian intelligentsia, mostly Hindu, particularly Bengali, collapsed mother with the motherland and found then every reason to keep this mother confined and protected. One may say that this was not necessarily any more imaginary and political than earlier constructions of women, but it was a tighter, more efficacious discourse. More importantly, one may say that recognition of that construction does not remove the onus from us to enquire into how *she* constructed herself or how we might otherwise understand her. Significantly, almost all the description of the new role of the nineteenth-century woman is in the passive voice: 'There was a shift within thinking...'; 'there was a keenly felt need...'; 'there was also a thorough examination...' (T. Sarkar 1995: 98-9). Although the passive voice may be chosen for a variety of reasons, I find that its choice here underscores my point: we do not seem to be sure who the subjects and agents of our story are. Because we are not apportioning responsibility more carefully, we resort to explanations of 'confusion', 'tension', and 'ambivalence' (T. Sarkar 1995: 102-3).

When we do have a description of the new woman in the active voice, the voice is that of the vernacular press, and of reformist pamphlets and tracts, that is, the voice of the male intelligentsia (Forbes 1996; Minault 1994; Orsini 2002). There is not likely to be an equivalent source to give us the voices of women. In the absence of other strategies to present her participation in this social-discursive history, we are left with a story which is, to put it most simply, the story of the 'child' about the 'mother'. It is neither the story of the 'mother' about the 'child' nor, which would be most desirable, a combined story told by both 'mother' and 'child' (Shree 2000).

As a corollary to this, there is a historiographical trend of relegating women as a special case within South Asian education, as self-evidently a kind of community, without problematization, to be approached in studies of 'the education of girls', 'women teachers', specific institutions for girls, and the problems of women (Amin 1996; Forbes 1996; Karlekar 1991; Minault 1998). A history of education in India which is gendered would see multiple positions of women in it. I would also like to add a new problematization regarding the feminist politics embedded here. The gain for 'education', I argue, that is chiefly men's education, was in the mother occupying the particular spaces she did. But this, in turn, was a loss for the cause of womanhood. Our feminism would necessarily side with the reformers. She *should not* have been so much of a mother, and she *should not* have been so confined to inside worlds. Even widowhood, which we might redefine as a chance for her to gain greater agency, was a mixed blessing, if blessing it might be called at all, in that it assigned her to sainthood. She *should* have been saved—but preferably by herself.

Two necessary tasks can be approached simultaneously. The discourse of education in South Asia can be expanded to include other sites and processes than what a Eurocentric, colonial-modernist history writing might allow. And bringing it closer to the actual processes of 'informal' education of the subcontinent means necessarily to pay attention to the family, the community, mothers, servants, and other unrecognized teachers. This wider discourse fills in the more familiar, limited discussion of schooling, and it is gendered.

MOTHERS: IN THE SERVICE OF MODERNITY

The category of mother, as I see it, is an unattractive one. Caught in the web of marriage—which was child or adolescent marriage in South Asia in the nineteenth and most of the twentieth centuries—in the predictable bonds of kinship, household, childcare, petty responsibility, then all too often, widowhood, and social and emotional deprivation, she is difficult not to treat as a victim. The new bourgeois romanticization of the mother starting in the later nineteenth century (Chatterjee 1989) reduced her more pitifully yet to a passive site for male transactions (Bagchi 1990; Chowdhury-Sengupta 1992). Even abstractly, if we take up a neutral definition of mothering as a culturally and historically variable relationship 'in which one individual nurtures and cares for another' (Glenn 1994: 3), mothering continues to seem to be two ironically contradictory things: overblown and idealized, and insignificant and unimpressive.

The first problem here of the unattractiveness of certain spaces inhabited by women is already partly understood in the literature. It lies largely in the categories themselves: 'mother', 'home', 'childcare' versus 'intelligentsia', 'the nation', and 'education'. The former cluster has to do uniquely with women and is private, passive, apolitical, and ahistorical. The latter has to do only with men and is public, important, the stuff of politics and history. The category 'intelligentsia', particularly as defined by class, education, occupation, and ideology, is male, a woman intellectual being not an exception so much as unnatural and an oxymoron. This intelligentsia then bears the mantle of history itself. The intelligentsia of colonial countries like India bears a wider mantle: to develop the will and the desire to *have* a history. Women are accepted well enough commonsensically as having a *place* in history; they do not *imagine* or *make* this new 'history'.

This necessary work of developing the will and then of engaging in the technical manoeuvres of constructing a history, is accompanied by a certain pain and has been described as such, both by the male intelligentsia themselves and by scholars. In earlier versions, it was the pain of bearing forth an immanent idea without support from a non-cooperative political economy (Sen 1977). In later versions, it is the pain of struggling with unspecified obstacles, maybe the dilemma of creative sensibilities confronting conflicting worlds (Kaviraj 1995). In both versions, one of the obstacles is by implication the female dead weight in society, somewhere equivalent to the feudalism, superstition, hierarchy of pre-modernism. Yet, for all the suffering, even in their aborted efforts towards a realization of a destined history, the intelligentsia retains an effect of unity. Surely this is achieved chiefly through exclusions and repressions of important parts of the story. Certain 'men' find themselves confirmed in history, and others, such as 'women' get positioned 'so as to confirm the truth of that operation' (Crosby 1991: 148). The 'essence' of the intelligentsia—troubled, questing, struggling, building—gets predicated on the larger non-intellectual activity of their societies and, specifically for us, on the non-intellectual activity of the women of their class. The history of the intelligentsia is confirmed by the non-essential and non-historical.

How would we reposition the non-historical? Even within this foundational, modernist narrative of the intelligentsia we can introduce elaborations. First, a history of the intelligentsia in the nineteenth century should necessarily be a story of men with wives at home. One focus of our discussion should then legitimately be a reinterpretation of the division of political (public, historical) and 'natural' (domestic, maternal). We could redress the balance by which housekeeping and maternity, while seen as the very bulwark of human survival and reproduction, become an instrument of subordination, and maternal responsibility is 'used as an alibi to exclude a woman from power, authority, decision and a participatory role in public life' (Krishnaraj 1995: 34). In South Asian history, including the history of education, this work has barely begun. In my study of the education of girls in Banaras for instance (Kumar 1994: 211-31), I have a detailed discussion of the historiographical problem of the invisibility of women, but the most cursory mention of the role of women as wives. For the Agrawal Samaj school in Banaras (f. 1896), we have a passing comment that not only are women teachers and staff members absent from the records, so also are those who 'permitted men to have the necessary leisure for all this public activity through management of the homes—the same management that led both males and females to claim when the question arose that women did not have "enough time" for public work' (Kumar 1994: 215). The Agrawals are a trading caste with pride in their work ethic and their social ethic. Like other such groups, they set up modern schools for their children, while keeping their social boundaries intact. This is not merely a case of record keeping, since the whole edifice of this community, the Agrawal Samaj, was kept up through the marriage links in which women were crucial, links maintained sometimes across vast distances and leading to preferred reproductive results. Women were the resources for creating alliances and were at the heart of any notion of the community as 'solid' and 'pure'. Any work, including that of building up educational institutions, was possible for men to undertake because of the roles relegated to women. We need a *structural* understanding of this as basic to the history of education in India. We need to place squarely in Indian educational history the few nuggets of first-person data such as the following:

Sometimes in fun I tell him that although people call him Maharshi, some of the credit is due to me. For if I had not managed the family affairs and set him free to carry out his public activities, he could not have achieved so much. But that is merely in the lighter vein. I consider myself fortunate that I should give him some help in his great work (Karve 1963).

However, members of the intelligentsia are born, not as autonomous actors who then proceed to throw off the yoke of colonization, but as malleable infants who are then socialized into roles sustaining the rationale of their class and time. They cannot possibly be formed *only* by their experience of new occupations, colonialism, racism, nationalist organizing and attendant self-questioning and self-development, as our history-writing seems to imply. Because all history-writing is based on a European model and the European case does not include a story of plural sites of subject-formation, there is an invisibility of this plurality in the Indian case also. The most elementary biographical facts about members of the nineteenth-century Indian intelligentsia are the following.

The fathers of the new intelligentsia were themselves members of the 'old' intelligentsia (their famous sons' names are in parentheses): *darogas* or police inspectors (Akshay Kumar, b. 1828), *diwans* or chief ministers (Rammohan Roy, b. 1772, Raghunath Rao, b. 1831), other kinds of court officials (Syed Ahmad Khan, b. 1817, Mahadev Ranade, b. 1842), clerks (Haracharan Ghosh, b. 1817; Vembankum Ramiengar, b. 1826), and *pandits* (Iswar Chandra, b. 1820). As pillars of society, the fathers typically honoured caste and sectarian rules, practised gender and age hierarchies, and believed in child marriage. Akshay Kumar and Mahadev Govind Ranade were married at thirteen, Rammohan Roy at nine and ten, Sivnath Sastri at twelve, Bhabhanicharan Bandopadhyaya at nine, Gopal Hari Deshmukh at seven, Lajpat Rai at twelve, Gopal Krishna Gokhale and Bal Gangadhar Tilak at thirteen, Dhondu Karve at fourteen.

The mothers of the first- and second-generation intelligentsia were often widowed while their sons were still students (the age of the son on losing his father is given for some), such as those of Akshay Kumar Dutt (19), Baladev Palit, Gopal Hari Deshmukh (13), Kandukuri Veerasalingam, Krishnachandra Majumdar, Pratap Chandra Majumdar (9), Sasipada Banerji (5), Shyamacharan Sarma Sarkar and Surendranath Majumdar. Even without recourse to psychoanalytical discussions of the strong mother-son bond in India (Carstairs 1961; Kakar 1981), one may hypothesize that after the father's death, the mother's bond with the son became further strengthened. At any rate she was obliged to take over much of the double work of parenting.

There were specific ways in which she did this. When her own labour was needed, the means available to her were thrift, forethought, and sheer physical obduracy. She could spin yarn, engage in simple unskilled labour like making paper bags or do domestic service. Typically this was done to see her son through school, where colonial schooling was available. While the biographies of men reflect an idealized notion of nurture and we would be right to discount their hyperbole, there are precise references to mothers' work with reference to schooling. In Akshay Kumar's case, the widowed mother was responsible for his education. Veerasalingam's mother Purnamma, widowed when he was four, 'wanted to give her son the best possible education. So she sent him to the Government District School'. Dhondu Karve's (b. 1858) mother, when solely responsible for his future, became very 'careful' with his upbringing, particularly with his education, because that is where the future lay (Paranjpye 1915). The *bhadralok* in Bengal, an educated middle class, and its equivalent elsewhere, was not a prosperous class *sui generis* and more hardship was sustained for educational purposes than we know only from the well-known cases of Vidyasagar, Akshay Kumar Datta, and Dhondu Karve.

The work aside, the very decision to continue with his English schooling, sometimes in the face of great financial odds, was necessarily taken by the widowed mother. This in itself is an important missing link in the history of modern education in India. The commitment to English schooling was regularly made even when the husband was alive, as in the following rare case of a daughter.

Kamaladevi Chattopadhyay's father died in 1910, when she was seven. Her mother, she records, was a disciplinarian, and where her father would be indulgent, the mother believed in a stricter upbringing. When Kamaladevi showed reluctance to go to school initially because she found the untrammelled outdoors more interesting than the stifling and stultified atmosphere of a conventional classroom, it was her mother who overruled her father's indulgence and insisted that she had to get a proper education, even tricking her into going by pretending to take her on an outing and depositing her straight at the school gates, as Kamaladevi recalled (Narasimhan 1999: 17). Similarly Bipin Chandra Pal recollects in his autobiography (Pal 1932: 34-5) that his father withdrew him from school for political reasons and seemed content to have him stay on at home, unschooled, but when his mother arrived from the village, she was resolute that he return to school.

This missing link has a curious twist to it that goes further unrecognized. Far from accepting, along with our sources, that such support is only 'natural' for mothers, we could consider the conflict in the mother's identity that this kind of decision and its future entailed. We see this in the example of Dhondu Karve's mother. She was widowed when he was studying. Her almost total illiteracy went—in a typical way—with 'religiosity' which, while otherwise opposed by her son in public life, was transmitted to him as 'charity' and 'love'. Her devotion to her son upon her being widowed became intensified. Her 'old ideas' notwithstanding, she 'fully appreciated the great work being done by her Dhondu...'.(Paranjpye 1915: 33).

Indeed her willingness to *travailler pour l'armée* – 'to accept the uses to which others will put one's children' (Ruddick 1980: 354)—is both the problem and the achievement. A problem because she is colluding in her own subordination in numerous ways, indeed, expanding its possibilities through abetting changes without questioning them, and typically neglecting her own daughters for her son. An achievement because she is interested in the growth and success of her son, someone who does not automatically guarantee her continuity as he does her husband's (Sen 1940), and this she works for without reservation. But perhaps an inadequately theorized aspect of 'feminine' or parental thinking is how the parent expands the limits of her own life by working hard to expand the limits of her children's lives. We learn, for former slaves in America, how the 'struggles of these Black mothers and grandmothers, especially to ensure an education for their children, pushed back the boundaries, the limits, set by a white, racist world' (Aptheker 1989: 19). For South Asia we have no documentation or discussion yet about how women imagined their world expanding through the education of their sons, but such an imagining is consistent with the nineteenth-century data.

The more common notation of the mother's labour is therefore in the form of counselling and identity formation. In the case of Gooroodas Banerjee (b. 1844), 'The mother on whom the task of bringing up the child now devolved was a woman of great sweetness and force of character, and the gentle but firm touch of her hand had been in no mean degree responsible for the character of her distinguished son' (Chatterji 1979). Dadabhai Naoroji's widowed mother did more than work for her child. She was illiterate but still his wisest counsellor. 'She made me what I am', he wrote (*Indian Worthies* 1906).

The two characteristics of mothers, their labour, and their decision to support their sons in the pursuit of English education regardless of where it led them, are attested to directly and obliquely. Vembankum Ramiengar (b. 1826), 'the first Indian in Madras to keep his house in European style, to teach English and European music to the females of his family, and to invite European gentlemen to parties at his residence,' attributes his good education to his mother through her two practices of physical service and intellectual counselling (Chatterjee and Mukhopadhyaya 1931). Sometimes it was simply her position as member of a particular caste and class that made her the socializing influence that she was, as Hatcher argues for the grandmother and, less so, mother of Vidyasagar (Hatcher 1996). Pratapchandra Mazumdar's mother was unlettered, like other women of her time, though she had received the high training of her caste and her position. When educated, such as the mothers of Syed Ahmad Khan, Raghunath Rao (b. 1831) or Rama Verma (b. 1837), the mother was actively and directly involved in the son's training.

All these activities of mothers—their labour, their decisiveness, their counselling—should be read more actively as part of the story of modernity. The point here is not to attribute to a 'mother' a particular set of characteristics and emphatically not to discuss these characteristics pre-discursively as wisdom or sacrifice. The point can only be to restore, even while problematizing it, the sociological status of the mother—and of the surrogate mothers of the family—as the primary caregiver(s) and socializer(s) in the child's infancy and, when widowed, in diverse even more intense ways afterwards. I see her not as *the mother*, that is, I see *them* not as *the mother*. I see them as engaged in the *work* of mothering. Mothers are then due to be given their place as subjects of modernity in that they actively chose and laboured for a new education for their sons, and occasionally daughters. But we also glimpse that while engaged in productive labour that went beyond physical reproduction and nurturing to social and cultural reproduction, the work actually went even beyond that, to actively producing a *new* historical subject.

MOTHERS: IN THE SERVICE OF THE 'INDIGENOUS'

What kind of a new historical subject did they produce? Here we encounter several historiographical difficulties. No great person's biography gives a description of the earliest years spent with his mother, as Walsh points out, though Walsh in her turn gives attention exclusively to the father when discussing 'growing up' (Walsh 1983). Great men feel obliged to remember their mothers only in the most generalized ways: 'About my mother I can only say that she was the typical ideal mother described by everybody...' (Karve 1963: 137). There is no evocative scene from a dim past store of images, such as we find in the fictitious description of Nabin Singh, modelled on some nineteenth-century Calcutta grandee, perhaps Kali Prosonno Singh, who spent his days when a toddler with his mother, feeding her pet birds and so on, one corner of her sari tightly bunched in his fist. She 'didn't know one letter from another' (Gangopadhyaya 1981: 24).

Apart from difficulties with data, there are conceptual difficulties as well. If we want to uncover gendered processes that suggest difference to existing models, we have to cast our net wide. Biological nurturance and early infant rearing are unexplored areas for the last 200 years of South Asian history. Nancy Chodorow's psychological location of gender-specific roles and traits in primary parenting (Chodorow 1978) gives an important insight into the subject of *Western* mothers. But even in Europe until the eighteenth century, the family as we know it today, the 'sentimental family' as it may be called, and marriage as we know it, or companionate marriage, did not exist (Cowen 1983; Okin 1981; Shorter 1975; Stone 1977; Trumbach 1978). In South Asia, for many classes and communities, it still does not exist (Harlan and Courtright 1995; Shree 2000; Trawick 1990). Although the diversity of the homogeneous seeming 'mothering' function and experience has been acknowledged, particularly for divisions of race and class (Glenn 1994), and historical period (Hays 1996), cross-civilizable comparisons are rare (Gold 1994), and those that can take into account all the many variables rarer still.

We may hypothesize that, while we progressively recognize that mothers in the past may be different from the contemporary and the Western, and contemporary mothers themselves may be very diverse, we still tend everywhere on the globe towards an over-determination and essentialism of the woman as 'mother'. The corpus of myths and scriptures in Hinduism, on the other hand, shows mothers to be alternatively powerful or helpless, auspicious or malign. Nor is a woman most centrally a mother. The glorification of the powers of motherhood is offset by description of the actual powerlessness of the role. All studies of devi, or the mother goddess(es), in contrast, and all myths with women characters, startle with the unexpected location of power in the mother. All in all, South Asia exhibits fecund complexity of characterization at the ideological, functional, and cultural levels.[4]

Equally troublesome are the very male–female divisions in South Asia. Even if the primary parents are acknowledged to be mothers, with clear work and space segregation, their other traits such as sacrifice, gentleness, non-violence, and nurture, can be comfortably shared by both men and women, whether this is marginalized (Chowdhury-Sengupta 1992; Nandy 1980; Sinha 1995) or celebrated. The binary opposition expressed in Western Judeo-Christian civilization by figures like Eve or Mary is replaced in Indian civilization by a more reciprocal male–female structure, exemplified by Shiva, Durga, and Kali (Gold 1994).

For the new educated class, especially the *bhadralok* in Calcutta and the gentry in other metropolitan centres, there was a striving for the ideology of Europe from the second half of the nineteenth century (Bose 1994; T. Sarkar 1992). But the new educated class was minuscule in India, and its gendered analysis has only yet begun (Amin 1984; Chowdhury-Sengupta 1992; Sinha 1995). On one level, its ideology of family life was progressively based on the European model, including an extended domain for mothering by one specialized parent. There was a new division of the inside and outside, the domestic and public, the private and worldly. The control of women in new cities like Calcutta was stricter than either in the countryside or in older cities. Looser and more dynamic social situations in the cities meant more concern about maintaining social status. Seclusion of women was ensured in the *antahpur*, literally the 'inside'. Other versions of this were the *mol* in Maharashtra and the *purdah* in north India.

On another level, the divisions were far from entrenched, and new relationships worked in connection with the old in complex, unpredictable ways. Even as a succession of young daughters-in-law entered the home, the stress continued to be on fraternal bonds and the mother-son link. 'A husband's relation to his wife was subordinate to that with his mother' (Borthwick 1984: 12; Mandelbaum 1970). The wife's situation improved only upon becoming the mother of a son. She could then look forward to authority over her own sons and daughters-in-law who would continue to stay with her.

There were still other levels of difference with Europe which we should mark to help us with the history of both Europe and South Asia. One concerns how women themselves experienced their lives as bigger than that contained in the overdetermined category of 'mother'.[5] There is no reason to doubt the vitality, creativity, and security of the women's work, leisure, and ritual worlds. Given the limitations of an inherently secluded life, many separate insights into these worlds can be gleaned from assorted interpretations.[6] Even with modernization, mothers in South Asia continued to be, and today can be seen to be, categorized as varied in their characteristics, and not merely as the soft, sentimental, emotional creatures of bourgeois discourse. The family was not (and is not) a nuclear one united by conjugal love and family love. Mothering was not a full-time occupation with its own science and the husband and children were not seen as exhausting a woman's whole world. The female world continued to include the world of popular culture: balladeers and performers, story-tellers and masseurs, ritual specialists, and salespeople of the streets (Banerjee 1989).

The only theoretical statement we have regarding a separate world is the notion of the 'backstage', as in the following:

Confronting man woman is always play-acting; she lies when she makes believe that she accepts her status as the inessential other, she lies when she presents to him an imaginary personage through mimicry, costumery, studied phrases.... With other women, a woman is behind the scenes; she is polishing her equipment, but not in battle; she is getting her costume together, preparing her make-up, laying out her tactics; she is lingering in dressing-gown and slippers in the wings before making her entrance on the stage; she likes this warm, easy, relaxed atmosphere.... For some women, this warm and frivolous intimacy is dearer than the serious pomp of relations with men (de Beauvoir 1961: 512-13).

We need a theoretical statement adequate to the South Asian data where the women's world can be read as not frivolous, but of sociological weight, even as it may be frivolous-seeming. The importance of this for the story of education is that it allows us to unravel one more strand of the extra-scholastic influences on the intelligentsia. According to the discursive-administrative understanding embedded in the colonial archives, there were no proper schools in the nineteenth century, even as varieties of ways of instruction were systematically recorded. Observers like Adam, Thomason, and Munro made a critique of the lack of discipline and totalization in existing Indian practices. Those who followed them moved on from there to further critique. Indigenous schools were reformed out of existence, some systematically ignored, and others deliberately starved of funds and recognition. The number of women who came to be educated in the new scheme was tiny, bordering on non-existent. The rest continued to belong to the world of the 'indigenous', the 'vernacular', and the 'traditional'. What they transmitted to their children were narratives from this world, or rather, these diverse, plural worlds, both narratives in the sense of stories, verses, tales and myths, but also narratives of the self, or how the self could possibly be constructed. It is important to see this imparting of alternative sensibilities, sacraments, and narratives to the ones being imbibed in the school and the workplace as 'work'.

Certainly, nurturing is also work, at which some women labour exceptionally hard, others may be emotionally inept, spiritually impoverished, materially handicapped or voluntarily or involuntarily retired from doing. Yet most do the best they can, and on the whole they are the specialized workers at this. The category of 'maternal thinking' brings the material and the intellectual close in a way crucial to my analysis. Because she is not a machine or an unskilled worker but a reflexive actor engaged in a discipline, making choices, asking questions, and establishing criteria for the truth of proposed answers, a mother engages in a particular kind of intellectual activity (Ruddick 1980). In doing this she exercises a particular influence which is different to more formally organized teaching. It is particularly different when the formal teaching and the domestic narratives belong to two different ideological sets, as in the case of colonial schooling and unschooled mothers in South Asia.

The problem and the continuing paradox of the subject is that even while the work of nurturing is 'essential', that is, indispensable, an irrefutable contribution to human history, it is 'non-essential', that is, not 'natural' to its practitioners but the institutional product of insidious forms of patriarchy. We do not want to elevate its importance as if it was the only thing to say about women's position in education history. If we make a case for nurturing, we are implicitly belittling women's larger work, and if we emphasize the latter, we seem to defensively deny the largest part of the work that they actually did. So, we have to walk carefully here, trying to ensure that in restoring power to women in the history of education we do not in fact restrict them further.

It is important to note that I am not making the claim that what mothers taught was 'authentic' in any sense. It was highly coloured by the snippets picked up by them from the 'media' of that time: gossip, servants, performers, men of the family, and the emerging press. It was generously coloured by their own biases and prejudices and the patriarchal ideology they neither dreamt of, nor aimed at, changing. It was probably very orientalist in its construct of India's past, ranging from less to more orientalist over the course of the nineteenth century. While not educated in formal schools, all women were part of the emerging world of certain public discourses of 'Indian' history and culture (Orsini 2002). But while the teaching of women was thus orientalist in its constructions at the national, class, caste, and even gender level, it was less so in its constructions of the home town or village, as in Satyajit Ray's protagonist Charulata's writings (Ray 1964)—its stories, its gods and goddesses, and the way that a day and a life could be run. We cannot, after all, posit a real, pure, authentic representation out there to which this woman's ideas did not measure up.

I do therefore want to propose a 'woman's world', but also to suggest that it is disempowering merely to interpret it as a discourse that kept the woman 'in place' and served the intelligentsia's purpose of separating a corrupted, colonized world from an unadulterated, privately dominated world (Chatterjee 1989; S. Sarkar 1998; T. Sarkar 1995). Because it does not seem self-evident that the male intelligentsia profited in their nationalism from such a separation as much as they were *formed* by it. Apart from being educated at school, members of the intelligentsia were educated in the home, in languages, ethics, and world views that never left them and were evolved further by them in their maturity. They and their work—political, reformist, insti-tutional—can be understood only in a gendered context in which their work came to be what it was because of the work of women. Women played many roles simultaneously and alternatively. Women were the guides and teachers, they were the exemplars and models, they were the apprentices and helpmeets, they were the objects of reform and, as we shall see below, they were also active opponents of change.

But most of all we must integrate what we know of the intelligen-tsia as the producers of certain discourses with the processes by which the intelligentsia themselves were produced, including by some of the same structures they had helped to put in place. To seek to describe how women *were* or what women did is not a question about authenticity at any point. A gendered history of education reveals that there are *multiple* discourses: women were formed by men through a discourse of reform and the 'private', and *men were formed by women through a discourse of motherhood and family.*

METHODOLOGICAL POSSIBILITIES

I have laid out in this section many of the shortcomings of the current discussions of education, and the possibilities of enlarging it through specific attention to the construction of subjects by the mother. I propose that the woman as the object of the reformer's gaze was equally instrumental in teaching, simply by being more than this putative object, or in our modern parlance, by being *herself* and *a real person.*

First we have in this literature on South Asian women a familiar separation of two academic discourses, roughly speaking, the historical and anthropological. Each is somewhat informed by the other, but the overall disciplinary tendency is to stay aloof from the other's analytical field. Thus, for historians like Geraldine Forbes, Nita Kumar, Samita Sen, or Barbara Southard (Forbes 1996; Kumar 1994; Sen 1993; Southard 1995) it is self-evident that women should be entering the fields of modern medicine, forming associations, and seeking wider freedoms. For anthropologists like Margaret Trawick, Gloria Raheja, and Ann Gold (Raheja and Gold 1994; Trawick 1990) women have different avenues of power altogether. Women's worlds not only exist, they are little known only because of androcentric discourse in both society and the academy. These worlds demonstrate power, structure, meaning, and legitimacy. Such women and such worlds do not find recognition in Forbes or Minault. In Partha Chatterjee (Chatterjee 1989) they are not even given a passing nod as existing. The narrative told is of the man's world, including its encompassment and recon-struction of others.

We can imagine that it was precisely the kind of women described by the anthropologists whose forbears must have been the objects of reformers' angst. In fact, we have direct evidence of this, in the form of the *galis* or abusive songs that women sing on sacramental occasions like weddings. They did so in the nineteenth and early twentieth centuries and they continue to do so today. These were the kinds of songs that reformers directed their ire against, holding them res-ponsible for the backwardness of particular communities.

It seems unlikely that the subjects and sites of the anthropologist (local, usually village-based, little-educated, seen-from-the-inside) and that of the historian (colonial-national, usually metropolitan or at least urban, contextualized-in-a-larger-whole) would come together. This again produces a thinness of interpretation as we speak, seemingly, about two Indias. The anthropologist's women's world is rich and powerful and in no imminent danger of extinction by reform. The historian's is imitation-modernist, reforming, in search of an identity. This analytical separation prevents us from seeing the actual interplay that constituted the reformers and would-be reformed, and from using sources imaginatively to note how each presented a politics and a threat to the other. In the fascinating study of women's work and secrets today by Sirpa Tenhunen, the historical debate on the emergence of a separate sphere for women has a marginal place, when both analytical fields could probably be illuminated by directly being made to shed light on each other.

A similar expansion of interpretive possibilities could occur with taking seriously the insights of literature. If women are written about in history as successfully reformed or else trapped in male discourse, and in anthropology as complex and autonomous, fiction succeeds in representing them at several levels simultaneously and also leaves open the very possibility of multiple discourses (Handler and Segal 1990). I give here a sample of how the subjects of history and literature can be brought together, as in Tarini Devi, the mother of India's first modern man, Rammohan Roy (b. 1772).

In the story of Rammohan Roy's formation a description of the complex factors that go into his making is given by Rajat Ray: Sanskrit and Arabo-Persian classical learning, the mastery of English, and the awareness of problems accompanied by a desire for reform (Ray 1995). In the whole discussion of his formation, we have no mention of his mother, which seems particularly extraordinary since she was a Sanskrit scholar who actually taught him some Sanskrit. But again, even if she had not, her teaching him his mother tongue, Bengali, would be sufficient to merit inclusion in his strata of learning (Garner, Kahane, and Sprengnether 1985). From the little we know, this mother seems to have been a 'conventional' one in her acceptance of social discourses. 'Conventional' too, we should think, in that Tarini Devi was a powerful woman with her own ideas, not quickly swayed by others. Such women arguably bring up their sons to be questioners: 'The determination and single-mindedness that was evident in Rammohan's whole life was in fact the quality bestowed by his mother' (Dwivedi 1917: 14). While for a historian such a hypothesis might remain a weak one, we could, if we were to permit ourselves, take women and their sons in fiction as additional evidence (for instance Gobar and his mother in Premchand's *Gift of a Cow* 1968).

Tarini Devi was conventional again, in that she opposed the iconoclasm of her reformer-son, and opposed him to the end. We have no idea of what influence this had on him but we know that he frustratedly continued to wish for her support until his death. We do know that she showed great determination and agency in choosing what was for a woman in her situation a legitimate cultural choice: to spend her last years dedicated to the service of Jagannath in his temple.[7] Realizing that in a pilgrimage to get *darshan* of the lord there should be acceptance of physical strain, she did not take even one maid with her. Not only that, she made no arrangement for comfort on the way and undertook the pilgrimage like an ordinary sufferer. She spent the last day of her life in the service of the Lord Jagannath. Like a servant, she would sweep the temple of Jagannathji every day (Mishra 1917: 9-10).

The novel *Mai* by Geetanjali Shree bears a startling similarity to the story of Rammohan Roy and his mother. The two stories are different insofar as Rammohan Roy and his mother's story is a lost historical one, about which we can only make educated guesses, and *Mai* is a piece of fiction about Sunaina, the narrator of the story, her brother Subodh, and their mother. Rammohan Roy and his mother's story takes place between 1772 and 1834; Sunaina and her mother's sometime in the 1960s and 1970s, although we should note for the record that both mothers had histories before these dates which belong to their offspring. For me this similarity that spans over 200 years highlights the centrality of certain questions in Indian history. It allows me also to suggest that our historiographical imaginations could well be triggered not only by pondering ethnographic findings, but by reading fiction more carefully.

The narrator and her brother in *Mai* want to save their mother, just as Rammohan wanted to save women. Both sets of reformers saw women as victims, trapped, hopeless people who needed to be given a voice and opportunities to develop themselves, lead autonomous lives, and be fulfilled. Mothering and its attendant housework together with all the limitations it demanded, such as little or no education, total seclusion inside the house, what appeared to be no pleasures or social activity, was seen as a pathology, a problem that had to be taken up and a cause to be fought against. Much like Rammohan, the novel's reformers grew up with a consciousness of being weighed down with the necessity of action and change.

The novel problematizes what I suggest should be problematized in Rammohan's life as well. That is, how did the mother produce the possibility of both the recognition of her problems by the child, and the child's faith in his/her ability to question and change? The first required a bonding, an empathy with problems that were not directly one's own but came to be felt as personal ones. The second required a letting go, to learn from diverse sources, challenge and speak up, and break loose from one's bonds. The children in both cases are impressed forever with the abuse the woman suffers. With schooling (which the mothers actively permit them to pursue) they learn a language for her problems; they think of 'chains'. Their education teaches them that their own solution lies in going out, finally to England, in learning English and becoming the opposite of their parents and grandparents. The education does not offer any solutions or accommodation that are acceptable to the wider society, including their objects of reform.

Most importantly, there is nothing archetypal about the nurturing of these mothers. They nurture their children towards questioning and independence. They themselves make 'sacrifices' with confidence but do not glorify these virtues. Their children love them but condemn their lives and will not be like them. That is, the mothers' nurturing is not cyclical and repetitive; it produces change, but through tactics beyond those we directly grasp, such as encouraging other influences towards change on their children. The mother's contribution to change is certain, but while her labour, nurturing, and guidance are accessible to us, the exact nature of her disclosure of possibilities in the future is difficult for us to grasp.

In both the history and fiction, the mother is mistakenly understood to be a victim. The novel questions again and again whether she is a victim because we can see that she is a strong character with a mind of her own, including in resisting her children's reforms. Tarini Devi was equally not a victim, but a strong character with a mind of her own. We have no words spoken or written by her, but we have a record of her action in opposing Rammohan. Both mothers turn around on their very saviours and oppose the plans for saving them that are being proposed. The offspring in both cases feel betrayed. But they feel that a statement of strength is being made that eludes them: wherein lies this strength? Why is the lifelong dream of emancipation of this beloved mother-figure finally not successful? The novel suggests some answers in the way of fiction. Perhaps it is because there are other ways of 'saving' than those adopted by the reformers. Perhaps the mother 'saved' herself rather than be 'saved' by her son or daughter. In addition, there might be another liberating mechanism at work here. Presuming she was dominated by her father, then her husband, and various other family members, the mother now does not permit her son/daughter to dominate her, thus closing the cycle and demonstrating another alternative to that of domination, as well as averting the next generation's possible guilt in the future. Rammohan Roy did not succeed in saving his mother, but she succeeded in saving him from the doubtful role of saviour.

NON-MOTHERS

The category of mother is further to be grasped through its opposite, the non-mother. The most eminent category of non-mothers is men or women who deny themselves, or allow themselves to be denied, their parenting privileges. In many cases these 'non-mothers' are only seemingly that. I would like to underscore the fact that even in the 'mothers' discussed above, there were plenty who performed the work of mothering but were not biological mothers, and were more literally the fathers, grandparents, uncles, older brothers, and servants of various descriptions—all of whom deserve attention.

Other kinds of non-mothers are women who might well be engaged in mothering, but find that another role determines their identity, such as worker or labourer, skilled or unskilled. Their poverty and insecurity makes their mothering invisible, by implication deficient and unsuccessful. In the history of education, the fate of those who could not for various reasons grasp the opportunity of the new colonial education is often blamed on their mothers. In a continuation of this idea today, the problem of children who do not go to school or drop out is blamed on their mothers.

The non-mother who will concern us in this essay is not the woman who could have mothered, or the skilled or labouring woman mentioned above, but the 'unsexed' woman, the ascetic or nun dedicated to a higher cause. Apart from men and their wives, there were active women in the nineteenth and twentieth centuries, as there continue to be today, who have defined their activity with no reference to the men of their families. They were not married, or if married, were freed of the obligations of that status through widowhood. They were child widows and grew up with no other work but their chosen one, albeit performed through social and intellectual struggle. Or they were adults when widowed, and even if mothers, opted for a role that defined them as something else. They were either privileged in that they were in control of some resources, or were ambitious enough to raise resources. They were active in public life, collecting funds, building institutions, administering them, and recruiting teachers and students.

The case I will look at is that of a north Indian city, Varanasi, neither a metropolitan centre nor a provincial capital, and not in Bengal. This is important because the history of gender and of women followed different paths according to the extent of colonial penetration, economic destabilization, and corresponding self-questioning regarding one's identity. In Varanasi, the penetration, destabilization, and questioning were less severe and different than in Calcutta. The case is therefore important partly to balance the historiographical bias towards Bengal that has emerged in Indian history, equating 'Bengal' with 'India' against all empirical evidence (Conlon 1986), and partly because we want to explore the very avenues of women's activity exemplified by provincial towns. I use for my argument here the case of several schools founded and/or run by 'non-mothers': Central Hindu (1904), Durga Charan (1918), Bipan Behari (1922), Arya Mahila (1933), Rameshwari Goel (1939), Sarojini Vidya Kendra (1930s), Vasanta Kanya (1954), Nandlal Bajoria (1955), and Gopi Radha (1963). Each of these institutions was started by a woman who had no other commitment but to the cause at hand, defined modestly as 'providing education to girls', built up over the years to span primary and secondary schools and often intermediate and then degree colleges, with impressive endowments, buildings and student numbers. Because they were founded by women of various Hindu sects, even while they were open to teachers and students of Muslim sects, their ambience and discourses were all purposefully Hindu. Without conflating Hindu with 'Indian', I am obliged below to discuss educational activity within Hindu terms.

The institutional histories are straightforward and I will not narrate them here. I could problematize their narratives and show how much had been distorted in the records and the subsequent reporting to outweigh the contributions of certain men against other men and women in general. I could construct many interesting parallels between the various efforts to make points about the nature of reform, the changing understanding of education, and the phases in urban social life where women's education was differently emphasized as problem and solution. What I want to stress here, however, is the existence of several discursive spaces that could be occupied by the women educators in question for their own defined purposes against the apparent will of society.

The ambiguity of the category 'mother' that has been alluded to in the first section is a space in itself. The three axes of the contemporary myth of motherhood—'that all women need to be mothers, that all mothers need their children and that all children need their mothers' (Oakley 1974: 186)—are not borne out as central to the ideology of South Asian motherhood. At the simplest, differences arise from the differential workings of capitalism and technology (Rothman 1994), but the workings of epistemological constructs of the body and mind, the senses, human qualities, hierarchies, and so on, if more elusive, demand attention as well (Marriott 1998). Anthropological and literary work tells us that not only the maternal but the feminine may be more central and multi-vocal in Indian society and culture than allowed for. We know particularly of the high evaluation of androgyny and sexual inversion and of tales of 'bleeding female *lingams*' and 'male *yonis*' (Ferro-Luzzi 1987). Most of all, it is in myths that we find the most disregard for any normalization of the mother figure (Bose 1994).

A first glance, certainly, even at education, reveals a seeming obsession with the figure of the mother: in textbooks, in school magazines, in ceremonial lectures and classroom teaching, and in the *vratas* (fasts and their narratives) that among the main teaching for girls outside schools. Yet, even in these very places, there are alternative preoccupations or suggestions that seem to offer the possibility of opening up into wide spaces.

In the 1988-9 annual number of the school magazine of Durga Charan Girls' School in Varanasi, the principal begins her piece on 'Women's Education' with:

Ma. There are so many feelings embedded in the very word. She is both the giver of *shakti* [power] and the giver of *mukti* [freedom]. Mercy, pity, sympathy, and other such feelings are contained in this word. She gives *shanti* [peace] as well. So, from ancient times women were considered a form of *shakti* and were worshipped. A Russian writer has praised the importance of women thus: 'Give me 60 mothers, and I shall give you a great nation...' (Ghosh 1989).

The article continues with criticisms of the doublethink that allows women to be thought of only or primarily as housewives, even when they have careers. As we move towards the twenty-first century, 'it is the call of the times that women should get the same freedom as men to get an education and choose an occupation according to their interest and ability' (Ghosh 1989). This contradiction in the ideas of the opening and closing of the piece is common. If reflective in feminist terms of a dominant ideology—'the oppressor within each of us'—it also acted to provide a space for those who needed it.

The bottom-line argument in favour of girls' education was throughout that they were the future mothers of the country. If we think of the different ways that gender hierarchies were constructed, legitimized, and maintained in Hindu India, it is the *varnashram* (the class and stage of life) and *jati* (genus, literally, caste) discourses that presumed a woman to be constituted by birth as a separate kind of being. Anyone who knew Sanskrit seemed to be able to confirm this. When the first journals appeared that were directed at women, they elevated the *dharma* or duty of women into a religion with highly charged images evocative of Vedic rituals. The wheel of the world rotates on a hub, and if woman, who is this hub, is not disciplined, how will the universe survive? But if we ask who could challenge this discourse, the answer is again: those who knew Sanskrit. It was they who could quote examples of learned and free women in the 'past'. Nationalist discourse often referred to Vedic times as a time when women were educated and competent, so that after centuries of degradation one could recover the ancient glory by returning them to their place. Manu's strictures notwithstanding, there was sufficient variation in the vast corpus of texts and their interpretations to histori-cize the essentialist category 'woman'. That is, the very dis-ourse of the woman as housewife and mother contained within it the possibi-lities of a reversal.

The Sanskrit-based discourse could further be challenged at the vernacular level by those who could cite the case of *viranganas* or women warriors; of *bhakti* or a one-to-one devotional relationship with one's god that did not recognize, and even reversed, gender; and of *Shakti*, or mother-goddess worship.[8] A different case of non-mothers whose position as worker and quasi-professional is ignored are those in artistes' and artisans' families. In the *kathak* (literally, story-teller, performer) community, women are spoken of as private, secluded, devoted to the home, and unsullied by public work or appearance. In fact, *kathak* women are highly proficient in the arts of their families. During the early- and mid-twentieth-century changes, some *kathak* women did go public, and made a relatively smooth transition from being domesticated to being highly acclaimed pro-fessional performers.

In all these cases, the main method of challenging accepted norms seemed to lie through sheer action beyond language and discourse.

Women simply *did*, without lecturing or publishing on it. The internal differentiation into 'mothers' and 'non-mothers' within the overall category of 'women' was never mentioned in the spoken or written word even obliquely, even by the most radical women and the most successful institutions for girls. Education seemingly fit into the reproduction of motherhood and the category of 'mother' seemingly encompassed all women. Yet most of the founders and administrators of schools and a great many of the teachers, were not mothers, but were either widowed and childless, or unmarried or separated and alone. A school like the Arya Mahila School had set up special services for widows to provide for self-sufficient futures, but in public the message reiterated was only about motherhood.

The women who were thus active in the twentieth century, Sarojini Devi, Satyavati Devi, Godawari Bai, Vidya Devi, Gayatri Devi, Krishnabhamini, Ushamayi Sen, and Manorama Chatterjee, among others, all had identical experiences of bereavement, then inspiration to act, and then a lifetime of service. Satyavati Devi was widowed at thirteen, resumed her education at first privately, then in recognized colleges. She became a teacher and upon retirement, started a school of her own with two girls 'under a tree on the road'. She was gradually helped by her family, then the larger Agrawal community, and the school took off to become one of the most popular for girls (co-educational in lower classes) in the city.

The women were similar in that they either had funds or succeeded in raising them and had no children for whom to save directly. They were of different castes: Brahman, Kayastha or Baniya and of different regional origins: Punjab, Maharashtra, Karnataka, Bihar, Bengal, and Uttar Pradesh. Even when supported by a brother or father, they felt alone and claimed that their lack of preparation for supporting themselves inspired them to defend other girls from such a fate. Uninterested in the question of widow remarriage, they worked directly for the education and training of girls.

These non-mother educationists were regarded not as professional workers but in negative terms, as those who practised sacrifice and self-denial—of sexuality and motherhood—a categorization that my own coining of the awkward term 'non-mothers' echoes. Yet I mean my term to be ironic, to celebrate the hidden spaces that are exposed by reversing even the most overdetermined categories. A widow is potentially the most overdetermined category equalling, it would seem, powerlessness and inauspiciousness just as a mother equals fertility and the power of nurture. But the latter ascriptions themselves can be turned around for the widow to equal the 'power' of austerity and asceticism.

All the women I have mentioned adopted and were relegated to the role of ascetics, that is, beyond worldly distinctions including those of gender. Of the several discursive spaces open to women – the *virangana*, *bhakti* and *shakti* already mentioned, the *ardhangini*, or the complementarity of male and female – the most potent turned out to be that of self-fulfilment, or *atman* (self/soul) development. In indigenous terms, it could be said that 'education' comprised a series of disciplines which revealed the truth inside the self. Many of the disciplines related to food, sleep, sexual abstinence, and control of the *chit* or nature, leading to the transformation of gross energy into subtle energy. These were the kinds of exercises that seemed to come painlessly to women, or at least we have no record of any kind—but we could search more thoroughly in fiction—of pain from them.

These women had access to a discourse of *sewa*, or service that permitted them to be respected, even revered, for going beyond themselves as people and, especially women should do. The objects of service were, variously, womankind, the caste or regional-linguistic community, and the nation. The women often came to be not merely revered, but assimilated in turn into the role of 'saints' and 'goddesses', which in turn gave them the freedom and power in public life which is only the ascetic's or god's. What came together for these women, I think, is the reality of a power that was otherwise an abstraction. These women stood forth as powerful by any criteria: raising, controlling, and administering funds; managing people and institutions; starting new institutions and seeing them grow to capacity; given public recognition for their work. This was in return, as it were, for leading disciplined, ascetic lives, for showing themselves to be saintly or goddess-like, in every respect other-worldly. Vidya Devi was eulogized in the following way: 'From the viewpoint of learning, Saraswati; from that of raising funds for her school, Lakshmi; and from that of showing courage and discernment in countering undesirable people, Durga'.[9] Obviously, this was an instrumental technique of the simplest yet most effective kind. Through manipulation of symbols—what she wore, what she ate, how she talked—the public efficacy of the worker was immeasurably enhanced.

This power comes together, I claim, with another which similarly goes beyond gender. Also instrumental, this is the power gained through austerities first to control one's senses and then, through self-control, to achieve single-mindedness of purpose and through that, to control the outside world. In other words, the ascetic non-mothers who turned to education believed in their asceticism as a means of achieving their purpose—and indeed they did achieve it.

In a different way to mothers, non-mothers also made history. The women ascetics of Banaras performed a task that would have been otherwise challenged and found themselves eulogised for so doing. This was the founding of half a dozen important schools for girls that were identical to the schools for boys with no separate curriculum or treatment for girls. In this respect of gross action on the institutional front, Banaras, in spite of having a larger proportion of widows in its population, is not different to any other part of non-metropolitan India.

Nor is it different in the other contribution made by women: that they did not question the new educational system. Their schools, though Gandhian, Aryan, nationalist, and so on in name, were identical in structure, form, and content with all the other colonial schools. This had the advantage of allowing girls to get the same education as boys. It had the disadvantage of not passing on to students any of the beliefs or qualities of the educationists, in an ironical parallel with the case of mothers who also 'permitted' the next generation to choose for themselves. No matter how conservative or, at best, liberal feminist their efforts appear, these educationists were remarkably radical in their own lives and work. The changes they let loose were no less radical.

This radicalism becomes invisible because the women tend to be seen as 'saint'-like beings who should not be spoken of in the same material, aggressive way that men and men's work is narrated, or in the way we might discuss the normative, dominating category of 'mothers'.

CONCLUSION

It is important to be methodologically innovative and perform the elementary service for women of coming up with new insights into the spaces available to women for action. We see that these spaces are prolific and all around and that they are used in creative ways by 'mothers' as well as 'non-mothers'. But the primary aim of this essay has been to expand the discourse of education and simultaneously show that whichever question we ask, whichever part of the process we look at, education in South Asia can only be spoken about in a gendered perspective.

I began by outlining three common plots in Indian educational history: that of a burgeoning English education, that of a faltering indigenous education, and that of nationalism. I conclude by proposing that these should all be shown to be coincidental and interdependent and, equally, interdependent with what they exclude. Thus English education produced the intelligentsia but this was an intelligentsia that was simultaneously produced in the site of the mother's work, a mother that both promoted the English education and also subverted it. Indigenous education died in its formal setting but continued in innumerable locations in the home, family, neighbourhood, and community. Nationalism and reform can be understood only if we ask how the reformers were produced and how their very targets of reform were instrumental in the making of the history. Because of course the reformers belonged to both the modern school and the unreformed family, and marked their difference from colonialism not by a political alliance with 'tradition' but perhaps with their half-voluntary formation by another education. These 'other' processes of education are what I suggest I have no name for as yet, because family, community, tradition, the indigenous, and the domestic all savour of the marginalized and are imprecise, non-evocative categories. My essay suggests that they were sites of central, powerful, discursive processes that we should recognize as crucial to an understanding of education in India.

NOTES

1. All the writing on the history of education and that on colonialism that touches on education, regardless of certain different emphases, follows this unstated plot structure, for instance: Basu (1974); Boman-Behram (1943); Chatterjee (1976); Cohn (1996); Kopf (1969); and (1979); Nurullah and Naik (1951); Viswanathan (1989); Zastoupil and Moir (1999). For a critical essay, see Spear (1971).
2. There is no good single study focusing on this question, which itself is part of the marginalization of the subject; for indigenous education, the best study remains Dharampal (1983). For a study of the change in a socially contextualized milieu, see Kumar (2001).
3. Among many interesting works on the subject, see Guha (1997); McCully (1940); Mukherjee and Mukherjee (1957); and the three I would consider exemplary institutional histories, Lelyveld (1978); Metcalf (1982); and Srivastava (1998).

4. There are too many studies on the subject to be listed here, but the ones I have found particularly useful are: Aklujkar (2000), pp. 56-68; Ghosh (2000), pp. 33-47; Hawley and Wulff (1982); Khanna (2000), pp. 109-23; Pintchman (1994); Kinsley (1997); Doniger (1980).

5. Although she could hardly have been unique in her experiences, someone who was exceptional in that she wrote her experiences down was Rashsundari Devi, discussed in Chatterjee (1993); Tharu and Lalitha (1991); Sarkar (1998); Sarkar (1998), pp. 35-65.

6. Among some of the basic and most interesting descriptions are in Banerjee (1989); Jeffery (1979); Minault (1994), pp. 108-24; Papaneck and Minault (1982); Raheja and Gold, (1994).

7. Rabindranath Tagore's story 'Streer patra (Letter from a Wife)' translated in Bardhan (1990), pp. 96-109, is an eloquent description of a woman's surfacing self-awareness that culminates in her decision to leave her home and spend her days in the Jagannath temple at Puri. For an adverse comment on Tarini Devi's decision to do the same, see Forbes (1996).

8. Hansen (1988); Khanna (2000), pp. 109-23; McGee (2000); Zelliot (2000), pp.192-200.

9. *Shubhabhinandan Patrika*, 1986. In Hindu iconography, Saraswati is the goddess of learning, Lakshmi the goddess of wealth, and Durga the warrior-goddess, even while they are all aspects of the same goddess.

7

Widows, Education, and Social Change

This paper is concerned with a slice of the educational history of Banaras, approximately 1920s to the 1950s part of a larger study. I raise here a methodological question of importance to women's studies. What have been the social and cultural spaces available for Indian women within which to initiate action? Effective action often consists of working, seemingly, within accepted boundaries, but in fact, inverting, subverting, and otherwise manipulating the familiar symbols of dress, behaviours, and lifestyle. How, particularly, do marginalized women such as widows find spaces for action? This is related to the yet wider methodological issues regarding the recovery of the historical subject through the silences of documents and their usually cryptic allusions to one small aspect of a larger action. In asking the question: what are we to conclude when we have no direct speech by the actors? I and many involved in the history of women, share the territory with historians of popular culture and subalternists, am subjected to the same dangers of lapsing into essentialism and humanism, and am engaged in a similar deconstructive enterprise that takes me back by many circuitous routes to my thinking—acting subject.

The paper is divided into three parts:
   (i) the nature of Banaras society and its educational history;
   (ii) The discourses available to women; and
   (iii) The women educationists and how we judge their success.

I

Contrary to the impression created by a Bengal-centred historiography of modern India, indeed a Bengal renaissance-centred historiography, the reformist–nationalist discourse in other parts of India such as the United Provinces did not incorporate women's issues before the 1920s. The nationalist–reformist notion itself became salient only in the twentieth century, and battled in Banaras with another consistently articulated notion best encountered in journalistic writings, of the continued importance of the Indian tradition to which only a pinch of the right purificatory stuff needed to be added. This was not for Banaras, as often labelled, the 'orthodox' reaction. The self-satisfaction of Banaras, compared with, say Calcutta, implied (i) that colonial penetration was far less severe, and hence the need to mould oneself in the image of a master less troublesome; (ii) a smaller destabilization of the economy had taken place, and a positive consciousness of older roles survived; and (iii) there was a continuing viability of local culture with its shared set of meanings, discussed at length by me elsewhere and labelled *Banarsipan* (Kumar 1988).

The metaphors of decay, moral crisis failure, darkness, death, falsity, waste, as presented in Tagore's vision: 'A thousand permanent evils with their ever growing tentacles had amassed under the spell of inertia and are creeping through the myriad cracks of the crumpling edifice of Hindu society.... Bengali society was a graveyard... the shores of Hinduism lay wasted...' were emphatically not shared by the people of Banaras (Tagore 1962: 425).

At the turn of the century, the number of girls being educated in all of India; the percentage of population they represented, the percentage of school-going age girls, and the percentage increase per year, were all low, and lower yet in UP and lowest still in Banaras. In 1885, 92 per cent of the population of the (then) North Western Provinces and Oudh was quite illiterate, and one of 350 females received an education. In Banaras the number of girl students crossed the 1,000 mark in 1924 and 2,000 in 1932 (Annual Administrative Report 1910–11).

The causes for low rates of female education were many, and we will summarize them very briefly here. There was no incentive for women's education, economic or otherwise. Women were not the earners, men were, and the new education did not in any case guarantee jobs. The curricula in the new schools were inappropriate both because they were too difficult without strictly seeming relevant, and because they were simply wrong with religion absent from them. All these were problems that Indians experienced and articulated far more strongly with regard to boys' education (File 48, Edu 1914). For girls it was most of all the infrastructure of the new government or aided private schools that was objectionable. Girls had to leave home, spend many hours away, perhaps be taught by missionaries which especially after the kind of incident in 1870 in which a Bengali widow was converted to Christianity (Allygurh 1870) was highly suspect; and they had to mingle with all kinds of people and be exposed to unknown influences. Both in a vague, general way, and in some very precise ways, these problems continued to be seen as the extension of a discredited Western materialist philosophical system at the expense of a highly refined Aryan way of life (*Bharat* 1914; Lal 1900).

The government's repeated calls for a 'change of heart' among the leaders of society were constantly countered by the realization that there was a doublemindedness even on the part of those who wrote or spoke in favour of female education. 'So long as those who gave education were trusted and refined women', the public would find it acceptable. Sometimes this took the form of a direct call for 'purdah' schools, sometimes more generally as on overall difficulty with government aid. To be acceptable to the public, an institution 'would require to have considerable liberty in the way of teaching and also of a certain amount of freedom in the curriculum' (File 378, Edu A 1916).

Reformist notions in Banaras, as they gathered strength around 1900, were broad based and struck at many roots, predominantly the proclivities towards drinking, drugs, obscenities, patronage of other pleasure activities such as gambling and prostitution, certain superstitious practices and rituals, the over-early marriage of girls, and the prohibition of widow remarriage. The lack of education only gradually came to join the list of vices in the catalogue of problems of the Khattris, the Kurmis, the *halwais*, the *telis*, as well as more 'progressive' castes of the region (*Hamari Jati* 1906; Central Khatri 1938l; Sri Arya Mahila 1962; *Diwakar* 1934; *Kashi men* 1933). If we keep in mind the economy of the city, the fact that these castes were in 'traditional' occupations, most of which did not require a high level; or even any level, of literacy, and then if we note their actual transactions with the new agencies of control of the educational system, we recognize that this is a 'derived' discourse. There is an abstractness to it; education itself becomes a sign of a pace of change rather than a utilitarian action. One of the reasons why there is a three-to four-decade lapse between the local efforts made in this sphere in Bengal and in eastern UP is because the ideas of what should be done are less clear-cut and self-evident in UP and the struggle for education to acquire both form and meaning lasts longer there.

We can delineate three phases in this struggle:

(i) The extinction of indigenous institutions over a period of half a century without proportionate replacement by an alternative system. In its ideology, this alternative system was far more threatening and therefore unacceptable to males than to females. As a Hindi proverb went, '*Angrezi parhi, admiyat jati rahi'* (Learn English, and lose your manhood/humanity) (File 378 Edu A 1916). It was based on a different sociology and psychology to the indigenous system, it offered no less than new definitions of self and new construction of rightness and rationality. In the first phase of the new education system in Banaras, there was a kind of vacuum in public life as citizens took stock of their options: Schooling on the British model? Continuation with a discredited un-patronized, un-funded, un-recognized old model of schooling? No schooling? As for women, their lower status as mediators in society and their particular role as socializer of children and the fulcrum of domestic stability, led logically to their more conservative socialization and greater restrictions on their activity (Ortner 1974; Ramkrishna 1866; *Kya striyon* 1914; Sri Agrasen 1972). This also evolved into the argument of conservatism: if males buy their progress at a price, let females at least remain the repositories of the best in the old culture.

(ii) In the second phase, approximately 1890s to 1920, there was a movement towards the British educational system, with progressive patronage of government Anglo-vernacular schools, Christian schools, and private schools based on this model. Among the large schools funded in Banaras in this period are: Anglo Bengali 1896, Bengali Tola 1898, Central Hindu 1904, DAV 1900, Gujarat Vidya Mandir 1906, Saraswati Vidyalaya 1917. These schools were all private but aided, which meant that under the new dispensation, their curricula were regulated by government agencies. This undoubtedly signals the rise of a middle-class consciousness, but also reminds us of an essential fact about Banaras society. The structure within which public action took place was the 'jati' structure, 'jati' being the term used not merely for caste and sub-caste, but for linguistic identity, and—in rhetorical contexts, not in most practical ones—gender identity. That is, discussion and organization of public activity in Banaras was in groups and subgroups of the following: Khattris, Agrawalas, Marwaris, Bengalis, Marathis, Tamils, Ansaris, and Pathans. This identity meant specifically male identity, and subsumed in this period female as well. Thus all the schools set up included the teaching of girls.

(iii) In the third phase, which followed quickly from approximately 1920 onwards, there were concerted efforts by jati organizations to reach a compromise between modern/progressive and indigenous, a struggle accompanied by many clashes, short-lived victories and defeats, and a remarkable lack of unanimity. The local perspective on change and continuity is of some interest. At the ideological level, there was a perception, more coherent in Banaras than perhaps in other regions, of the continuity of tradition, tradition consisting of texts and discourse, given, challenged, mediated, and struggled over (Suman 1943; *Suyogya pati* 1948; *Doha* 1887) and of a robust give-and-take between popular cultural practice and these hegemonic texts (Kumar 1988) creating a total cultural ambience that allowed for change along indigenous lines. as yet another debate within the tradition rather than a questioning and overthrow of the whole edifice. Modernization (as economic progress, *'taraqqi'*, *'vikas'*) was a real thing in the interest of Indians, but to be achieved through playing a new kind of game with the rulers, by which core values were strategically retained while compromises were made on the fringes (*Bharatiya shiksha* 1935; *Shiksha prachar* 1933; *Dharma shiksha* 1937; *Angrezi shiksha* 1881).

It was in this phase that girls' education came on the agenda. The progressively louder summons of nationalist ideology as it called upon new estates, including women, to participate; the progressively greater weightage given to Gandhian style reform within this ideology; and the expansion in journalism and propaganda techniques in urban centres, including magazines for women, all got together to produce a new consciousness that largely acted itself out through rivalry. The condition of women became for each jati an indicator of its progressiveness and dynamism. Woman is a sign, a language, at this stage, and while the protected woman was a sign of male superiority so far, she becomes within years the sign of male backwardness (*Shikshit* 1934; *Stri Samaj* 1934). While all this is easy to discover in the literature, what is more difficult to perceive is when and how women take action in their own hands, founding schools (Rameshwari Goel, 1939; Arya Mahila, 1933; Sarojini Vidya Kendra, Vasanta Kanya, 1954; Nandlal Bajoria, 1955) administering them, recruiting teachers, inspiring students, and leading the educational movement in new directions. The impression we get from the activities of the 1920s onwards is one of strength, of women shaking off bonds, and playing unpredicted roles. How do they do so? What were the discursive spaces that existed for the new discourse of the public woman to occupy?

II

Had women, to start with, been educated before the British system was introduced, that they were now deprived and going to make up for it?

They had not, of course, been formally educated, but neither, for that matter, had most males. Although 10,000 students were recorded as receiving schooling in Banaras in 1890, Sherring's observation that the term 'schooling' was an exaggeration was biased but factually correct (Sherring 1975). Boys were educated in the nine-teenth century according to their prospective careers. Women did not have careers. But they had duties. The term 'shiksha' as observed by several authors, could not be happily translated into education (as we know that 'dharma' cannot be into religion) so that it would make little sense to Banarasis of a hundred years ago to say that women were 'ashikshit' although they were of course, unschooled (*Hamari dasha* 1907; *Vidya* 1907; *Stri Samaj* 1937). The catalogue of their necessary accomplishments was very long, their job as housewife and server seen as a weighty and specialized one, needing apprenticeship and practice (Lal 1900; Indravati 1940; Sinha 1939). Within this necessarily abstracted, totally dominating discourse which specified the place of women in the private internal domain, and the role of women as mediators, the necessary reproductive link, therefore the preservers of purity, what is significant is the vision of structure, with each duty and its style of execution spelled out as in a shastra. References to it range from the mundane: prescriptions of how the day should begin; to highly charged images evocative of Vedic *yagya* rituals; the wheel of the world rotates on a hub, and if the woman who is this hub is not competent, how will the universe survive? (Chandra 1904; Tripathi 1934).

The sources from which women could imbibe these messages were varied: *vratakathas*, rituals, festivals, performances, and story telling. But primarily it was the *Ramcharitmanas* and the *Mahabharata*, and popular stories and sayings extemporizing within the corpus of their mythologies, that educated women into their wifely roles. A re-exposition of them is not necessary to my purposes. The point I am making here is that the discourse of women in a trained, structured, specialized role as a housewife was a supremely hegemonic and powerful one with almost all (because never possibly all) loopholes plugged in, all kinds of pleasure and fulfilment, this-worldly and other-worldly guaranteed; sufficient mythical models set up, necessary rewards for obedience and punishments for transgression imagined; and centuries of literary eloquence accumulated, to enhance its persua-siveness. At the same time, the notion of structure implied a training, and education, and the case could smoothly be made that the points of weakness lay in the quality of women's performance of their duties, and the solution lay in educating women. The lack of education was already being blamed for all the shortcomings of Indian society, to which list could be and came to be added various short-comings of women, from singing obscene songs at weddings and giving children tasteless, uninspiring names, to sleeping too much or failing to balance the domestic budget (*Vivah* 1906; *Ashlil* 1906, 1907; *Yatha nam* 1943; *Gali gane* 1941; *Apni bahano* 1941).

Equally, their roles as the receptacles for that most precious of substances, sons, ironically gave women a wedge. The story of Narad and Kayadhu, wife of Hiranya-Kashipu, was directly narrated as a clue to how social revolutions can be effected. When Narad wanted to overcome the all-powerful demon, he did not know how to proceed because at the time everyone in all three worlds had 'become like stone' (that is displaying false consciousness, a familiar Marxist prob-lems of where the vanguard will come from). Upon Indra's temporary victory over Hiranya-Kashipu's kingdom in the demon's absence, he (Indra) was about to take the demon's wife, Kayadhu, away as a prisoner of war. Narad intercepted, explained his purpose, and took her to his ashram where he started patiently teaching her. He knew he had no hope of making headway with her because she also had 'become like a stone'. But she was pregnant. And while she was a stone, the foetus inside was a ball of soft, malleable, matter. The teach-ings transformed the child, who grew up to resist his father and avenge the gods.

Women were incapable of public action but by educating them, one was reaching their sons, which was how social revolutions could be brought about, change equalling a re-stabilization of society in this vision. This Banarasi understanding of change fitted in neatly with that aspect of the growing alliance of nationalism and religion where women progressed precisely by keeping to traditional roles. This was one way in which the *grihastini* (housewife) discourse created a space for women's education. There were other spaces being created and widened also.

Women had potentially high status on the basis of an equally old, equally revered discourse, that of the female as '*ardhangini*', or the model of '*ardhnarishwar*', the gods with their consorts occupying one-half each of an androgynous whole. In all kinds of texts—popular rendition for both males and females of sacred classics, magazines, and leaflets, *kathas* and stories—the image is belaboured that the female is essential to all the workings of the world, not as cook, cleaner, and server in this case, but in a more undifferentiated, philosophic, general, and therefore more interpretable sense of helpmeet (Arjun and Subhadra), professional assistant (Kaikeyi and Dashratha), rival in art (Shiva and Parvati), antidote for male excesses as the male is for hers (Shiva and Durga). So the point could be made and it was with total cultural validity that every activity could be co-shared by women.

At the practical level, this was a familiar facet of the economy of Banaras, where, in every craft/occupation, women participated in essential ways towards the final production. Though not defined as workers, and though their training went unrecognized, the level of expertise of their womenfolk was accepted (as one extremist went so far as to say: what was all the fuss about women working if they got educated? They are trained *now* and could work for a living any time they wanted to).

The availability of cultural discourse, of models, and spaces for action, means for one thing that at times of faster change in history stimulated usually by external influences, sufficient individuals take up the opportunity for adopting these alternative, available models to make a trend that gets labelled as 'social change'. Another way to describe it for dominated groups is as occasionally recognizable formations within the ongoing tension between hegemony and resistance, consciousness and action. We see, on adopting this perspective, that those who have seemingly inconsequential histories have been instrumental in making history.

Among the *kathak* (performer) community, for example, the normative discourse is of women as private secluded, pure, unsullied by public work for money. In fact *kathak* women like the women of artisan families, are highly proficient in their field, regularly providing accompaniment privately to their sons and husbands to practise by, and there exists a lore of women taking *tanas* (orginal improvisatory exercises) and *talas* (rhythmic patterns) along as their dowry. The availability of this (silenced) dicourse of women as highly competent means in the middle-twentieth century that some enterprising kathak women did go public, taking to the stage, attaining fame, and acquiring independent name and fortune. They are regarded by kathak as not quite proper, but simultaneously accorded respect as performers, particularly as the rest of the nation showers them with awards and tributes.

In the language of early twentieth century Banaras, if men were regarded as uneducated, so were women, education in a formal sense being really marginal to their trained, skilful, and *'shikshit'* (morally and socially trained), then so had women to be recognized thus. Now if boys were supposed to need an education—without any direct relation to an occupation or new lifestyles—why not girls? A question for which there was no answer.

To take up a third discursive space: a woman's *dharma* could not be rendered. She had no separate *dharma—yagya, dan, tapasya* (sacrificial ritual, gift giving, meditating) were not for her; simply through the merit of *sewa*—service—to her husband she became deserving of all the fruits of these 'karmas' which were so challengingly difficult for men to attain. What, then, about the unmarried female who refused the easy way out, and chose a more difficult path of acquiring merit? Or the widowed female who was no longer in a position to acquire merit through the service to a husband? The category of the widow particularly was an overdetermined one, defined by a discourse that weaved knowledge and power into a coercive structure that forced the individual back on herself and tied her to her own identiy in a constraining way. But the widow was also the Other, not a *grihastini*, not an *ardhangini*; by not being this or that, she had far more ambiguity that could get re-constituted as a space. For the widow was available what I would like to call the larger Hindu discourse of *atman* development.

As numerous popularized writings in Hindi of the period tell us, the 'ancient' system of education in India was based on a model wherein:

(a) Development took place according to the *gunas* of the individual, but in general the education process worked to promote the *satvik* and discourage the *tamasik*.

(b) All the aims of life—*kama, artha, dharma,* and *moksha*—
were taken into account, thus education provided intellectual
resources for earning wealth, living with pleasure, executing
religious duties, and finally attaining release through self-
knowledge.

(c) Most important of all, the *atman* contained all knowledge
within it, and education was the process of disclosing it by
removing sheath after sheath of ignorance. This had to be
done through technical processes that preferably needed a
guru, but could also be accomplished on one's own (e.g., we
do not know of every guru's guru). The *chit* or nature had to
be controlled; the material bases of life recognized and
handled; the body trained through exercise, such as meditation, yoga, disciplines of food, sleep, and sexual abstinence,
so that its *kama shakti*—gross energy—could be transformed
into spiritual *shakti,* knowledge.

This *atman*-revealing process with its necessary disciplines was
what constituted education, and although full coherent accounts can be
found only in the writings of those who were purists about the Indian
way, the discourse could be heard in many different forms: in popular
literature, in the talks of saints and ascetics, in journals, and in newspaper editorials.

The *atman,* the world soul, of which every individual *atman* is an
aspect, has no sex and no gender, and nor does the human *atman,* and
this non-gendered discourse of self-fulfilment was available to the
women, particularly widows, of Banaras.

And then we come to notions of historical time, as another space
existing for women. Here we have two myths or constructions: first
the notion of cycles of time in Hinduism and second the time we are
looking at—early and middle twentieth century—as some kind of a
'period of change' in Indian history. What we see in the first construction is all those concentric circles or spirals of time which Hindus
know in a general sort of way, and when they make a specific allusion,
it can be to a *kalpa* (4,320 million earthly years with fourteen periods
in each) a *yuga* (four in all, of varying lengths of some 100,000 years
each), or to a smaller historical period. Nationalist discourse often
referred to Vedic times as a time when women were educated on a par
with men, so that after centuries of degradation one could recover the
ancient glory by returning them to their place. (I noted that the

present-day viewers of the TV serial *Mahabharata* could spot exactly at which point of time the decline of women set in—thanks to Draupadi's performance in the gambling scene.) Or, as Manu says with his usual flair for the obnoxious: 'In this kalpa' (some 300 odd million year cycle) women do not go through Vedic rites, except of marriage. Their service of their husbands is their *gurukul* (university) and the running of their home their *agnihotra* (domestic sacrificial ritual for twice-borns)' (*Maharaj Manu* 1988). The epics, as we all know, provided a model for women where women followed their husbands to jungles with total commitment, Sita wincing with pain as she crossed boulders and thorns, soles scratched, toes hurt, heels bleeding, her husband Rama in front, strong, smiling, and untouched.

Any of these time-based discourses could be, and were, summoned up according to the preferences and purposes of the speaker. Whatever their desirability as role models for women, they all served to historicize the essentialist category 'woman' (*Parda* 1950; *Prachin Bharat* 1949; *Prachin Bharat* 1941).

Lastly, we have our own construction of a period of change when new discourses based on reform and reassessment of the self are being articulated, so that we feel justified in saying that this was a time when change was in the air. How far 'social change' was a real experience for the people living in it is an open questions as far as I am concerned, because the historical tendency to read coherence, organized movement, and purpose into events of the past is a very powerful and self-legitimizing one. It seems fair to say that the nationalist movement opened up new possibilities for action through its opening up of a third representation of women: beyond (i) Indian, traditional, pure, and sacrificing; and (ii) anglicized, educated, free, vampish, and destructive; now (iii) Indian, educated, pure, motherly, serving all, the nation before family, and society before self. What it definitely did in its self-reflections was to make even more available, through its reliance on history, the range of choices as to which vision of time should be adopted; its practices enhancing the importance of contextuality in correct interpretations (*Striyon* 1940; *Nari* 1940; *Hindi sahitya* 1940; *Gandhivad* 1940; *Wah!* 1939).

So we have a feeling for the spaces possible for women to appropriate as subjects of their own history in twentieth-century Banaras.

III

The fifteen or so women I am interested in were all educationists and may be further characterized as nationalists and/or missionaries. They all were *saints*. Let us enquire into their nationalism and sense of mission a little bit before inspecting their sainthood.

We have the example of Sarojini Devi Bhattacharya, a widow who came to Banaras (as many windows, particularly Bengali, did), and was influenced by Gandhian ideas in the 1930s. She started a school for poor widows, giving them also a means for support by weaving rugs and shawls. Her social work making her more familiar with poverty and illiteracy, she next started a school for children, at first on a very small scale in her spare time. She invested her own capital in it as well as collected donations from others. This school gradually expanded, became recognized and registered, was taken over by a trust, and named Sarojini Vidya Kendra in her memory. It has a student body of some 200 girls and boys at the primary level today, mostly from poor, working class families of the neighbourhood (Dubeyji, Mauryaji 1986).

Another widow with a sense of mission was Satyavati Devi who returned to her natal home in Banaras some years after being widowed at the age of thirteen. From a prosperous Agrawal family of Banaras, her education had been disrupted upon her early marriage. She was supported by her brother in her desire to resume education upon widowhood, studied privately, then at the Banaras Hindu University, finally going to England for a degree. She started teaching in Central Hindu Girls' School and upon retirement fulfilled a long cherished ambition of a school of her own. This school, begun 'with two girls under a tree on the road', was slowly helped by her brothers' families as well as by the larger Agrawal community of Banaras, and is today one of the most popular schools for girls in south Banaras. It is called by the unusual name of Gopi Radha, explained as being 'based on Indian culture', with the nationalist movement invoked to explain its philosophy (Leela Sharma 1988; Karuna Shah 1988; Satyavati Devi 1988).

Leela Sharma was a nationalist who vowed not to marry in unfree India. Upon the death of her father in 1931, she would have returned to the Punjab, but was kept back with her sisters by Godavari Bai, another educationist, who encouraged them to study further and stand on their own feet. ('Get married, and you'll be washing dishes' was Godavari's motto.) Godavari Bai was herself unmarried, a saint, a *'devi swarupa'* or of the nature of a goddess. According to Leela Sharma, the initial opposition to working was changing because of Gandhi, although she continued to face pressure from the neighbours to conform. Most of all, Gandhi made them get out of the house. She and her companions left their veils and took to processions, picketing liquor shops and foreign cloth stores. When Vasanta College suddenly shifted to Rajghat in 1954, she became the principal of the new institution that sprang up overnight on the old campus, and is universally credited with helping it survive and expand into what is today one of Banaras's foremost girls schools (and degree college as well), Vasanta Kanya Mahavidyalaya (Leela Sharma 1986; Vasantshree 1980-81).

Another kind of 'guru' and another kind of mission were those found by the widow Vidya Bai who came around 1920 to Kashi and took *diksha* from Swami Gyananand. Swamiji had founded the Bharat Dharma Mahamandal in 1901 'upon seeing how Western influence, selfishness, atheism, heterogeneity of religion, neglect of *shastras*, and disregard for ancient *sanatan* cultural values were increasing day-by-bay in the *lila* ground of God and the land of Bharat' (*Shubhabhinandan Patrika* 1986). Vidya Devi learnt not only the shastras and philosophy but also to perform all the various public tasks he was engaged in, such as fund raising, managing six different trusts, and publicity. After his death, she took on the endless task of the regeneration of *sanatan dharma*, and her own original contribution to the Mahaparishad's activities was the founding of the Arya Mahila Kanya Vidyalaya (The Aryan Women's Girls' School) in 1933. Today it is one of the four largest and best regarded girls' schools/colleges in Banaras. Vidya Devi's name is usually coupled with that of Sundari Bai, who left her family in Mangalore at the age of twenty-four, and joined the Aryamahila Hitkarini Mahaparished, The Society for the Promotion of Aryan Women. She moved from being teacher to headmistress to principal, and retired as joint general secretary of the Society (Vidya Devi 1986; Sunderi Bai 1986).

Other widows—Gayatri Devi, Krishnabhamini, Ushamayi Sen, Manorama Chatterji—all had similar experiences, first of bereavement, then of inspiration to act from an external source, nationalist, reformist, or missionary, then of adopting a lifestyle of lifetime service. Gayatri Devi is typical in that she was widowed four months after marriage, and lived with relatives (in her case also widowed) after that, rather than remarry. She was a Marwari from a business house, and used her considerable wealth and property to promote charitable causes, such as a school for the blind. Like other widows in a similar position, she invested her own wealth in her efforts and also managed to collect funds from her other caste and community members. High on the list of charitable causes is the education of girls, especially poor ones. Although not educated herself she wished to provide other females with a means to stand on their own feet in the world, particularly if they were to meet a fate similar to her own, namely, early widowhood. Her primary school, Nandlal Bajoria Shiksha Sadan, named after her husband, is also a recognized, large popular school today (Gayatri Devi 1986).

Manorama Chatterji, who came to Banaras in 1933, educated herself and her sister Rameshwari with great difficulty. Upon the latter's death in childbirth, she resolved to continue her studies, even in the face of opposition from family and friends (she often went on hunger strikes to get her way) and declared: 'I will also educate girls for whom there are obstacles in learning' (Rustom Satin 1986). She opened the Rameshwari Goel Balika Vidyalaya in memory of her sister and remained its principal till her death in 1985. Similarly Ushamayi Sen and Krishnabhamini thought of helping poor girls, started classes on a small scale in their own homes, were helped by supportive family members, and gradually saw their dreams of full-fledged schools achieve reality. Bipan Bihari Chakravarty, founded in 1922 by Sen, and Durga Charan School, founded in 1918 by Krishnabhamini, are even today in spite of the generally bemoaned overall 'fall in standards' reputed to be excellent, serious institutions (Rama Bhattacharya 1988).

These women may be classed together in that most of them were women of means with rights over their own property, and no children to save it for. This enabled them to change the terms of gender discourse in their society. They were of upper castes: Brahman, Kayastha, or Bania. The differences in their regional origins—Maharashtra, Karnataka, the Punjab, UP, Bengal—apparently mattered little, a point that holds true for the larger population of Banaras. For all of them, widow remarriage was a non-issue. From a concern with remarriage as the only solution for widows who had otherwise neither the freedom to live or to die, they took up through their actions a vindication of their direct experience of the suffering of bereavement. Alone and unsupported, untrained and unable to support themselves, they turned their situation around to asserting the necessity for action to prevent further members of their sex undergoing the same experience as they.

We can narrate the lives of other such inspired women, and we can bring the account close to the present by looking at present-day teachers and principals. But this is enough presently to derive some significant conclusions. There was no one moment of awakening in the experiences of these women but rather a process of growth. The conjunction of bereavement—most were widowed, one lost her father, and another her sister and took it very hard—and of the gradual acceptability of a nationalist discourse that wanted self-sacrifice and service to the community (how far these women saw their work not as a profession but as service and self-denial, as our sources claim they did, remains to be discussed); and of a sense of mission, that of brightening the future of poor girls—this conjunction provided their motivation. It is important to note that they were directly inspired by a 'guru' figure (often expressed as 'He/she called me to come and join him/her' or 'She came one day and said, "Join tomorrow!"'). Gurus are all-powerful figures in Indian thought, and it is unusual to resist their call. But even when the inspiration was nationalist and came from Gandhi or a local leader such as Malaviya, or it was religious and came from one like Swami Gyananandji, it was not nationalist or publicist religious activity that occupied the women for any length of time but acted rather as a kind of entry way into public life following which other courses were charted.

The most significant fact about all the widows was that their bereavement, their being alone and unsupported, turned out to be a blessing in disguise. They were freed from the duty of 'pati sewa' (service to one's husband) which they would have consensually ranked as first among their duties. Their dharma changed from that of service to husband to service to others. This was, incidentally, a possibility glimpsed earlier by British administrators as they tried to push girls' education forward, but while their idea of training widows for teaching was good it was unacceptable because it came from them (V/26/862/4, V/26/860/11).

The aloneness of widowhood and the sense of vocation in teaching became conflated in the case of these widows where their greatness seemed to arise from the interdependence of the two circumstances, and one seemed a necessary condition for the other. All those who chose to dedicate themselves thus were and are regarded, never as professional, competent teachers or administrators, but as of 'satvik pravriti' or 'saint-like', and 'devi swarupa', or 'goddess-like.' Whereas any man may be glorified by similar epithets, it is not men education-ists who are typically thus glorified. Nor of course are the widowers as a rule. The lifestyles of these women were characterized by eschewing regular family life; by vegetarianism; by early rising and early retirement to bed; by the wearing of plain or coarse cotton, preferably homespun; by sleeping on hard surfaces; and by giving *darshan* with difficulty. Rarely are male educationists associated with such lifestyles, and hardly ever with chastity; it is sadhus, swamis, and other ascetics that are.

The women, of course, came to be genuinely powerful—in controlling, raising, and administering funds; in managing and organizing people and institutions; in being given public recognition and being sought after for favours. This in return (as it were) for being at the last stage of life beyond that of householder, supposed to live simply and think pure thoughts. Vidya Bai was eulogized in the following way, as being: 'From the viewpoint of learning, Saraswati; from that of raising funds for her school, Lakshmi; and from that of showing courage and discernment in defeating undesirable elements, Durga'. She demonstrated perfectly that 'In the "gunas" of service, there is no class and no sex!' (*Shubhabhinandan* 1986)

Two things come together here. One, that all these widows display through their sainthood that training of the senses which has value in Hinduism as a legitimate search for freedom through self knowledge which relies, technically, on a disciplining of the body. For Hinduism it is also an instrumental technique to increase one's powers to achieve whatever goal one sets oneself—the example of Drona and his disciples and the bird on the tree comes easily to mind, as does the practice of celibacy, vegetarianism, etc., in the case of Gandhi, making for a single-mindedness of pursuit that almost guarantees success.

This instrumentality is the second point also. Because by effective deployment of the image of sainthood through manipulation of symbols (a single black bangle on her left hand), the public efficacy of the worker was greatly enhanced. She achieved not only internal power but external power as well. Yet this use of symbols, totally within the accepted discourse as it is, may be called discursive displacement because its ends were subversive. A widow equals powerlessness and inauspiciousness in normative discourse; but a widow also equals austerity and asceticism, which in turn breed tapasya that leads to extraordinary power. Satyavati Devi was so strong, so healthy, and capable of such long hours of hard work, because of her '*daivi shakti*', arising from her renunciation of greed, attachment, and anger (*Smt Satyavati devi* nd).

The cultural practices of these women, to use Mohanty's terms were 'traditional', but politically mature (Mohanty 1988). From their actions we can theorize regarding the identity and concept of woman, and see how it is a relational term where women may be able to actively utilize their position. We see our widows construct the meaning of widowhood rather than merely discover it, or even transcend it.

Thus the woman educator of Banaras found herself eulogized for doing what was not envisioned for her, and to do unto other women that which was highly disputed as desirable and useful. This was no less than the educating of girls in exactly the same curriculum as boys. Perhaps the greatest contribution of the early twentieth-century women educationists was that they never questioned or debated the terms of the education system. The schools they founded, although ostensibly nationalist, Gandhian, Aryan, etc. were modern institutions with the same formal structure, content, and culture as all the other institutions being founded on the British model. There was nothing remotely 'indigenous' about any of them, not even in a general way of emulating one of the four so-called indigenous models of education (the Tagore, Gandhi, Dayanand Saraswati, and Kashi Vidyapith/Gurukul model). One might say, this was inadvertent, that it was their failing that they did not participate in the discussions regarding textbooks (which continue to be sexist), curricula, and educational goals. But what if they had? The education of girls would most likely have been marginalized and treated as a separate sphere where 'appropriate' subjects and approaches for them had to be developed for which there were sufficient calls (V/26/862/4; Sampurnanand 1940; *Adhunik bharatiya* 1938; *Stri shiksha* 1939; Suman 1943; Kaushal 1936). Instead they adopted the liberal feminist approach of equality within existing institutions, on the same terms as males. Their silence on the question of curriculum complemented very nicely the public's overall feeling of unease, throughout the twentieth century, of the irrelevance of the prevalent curriculum. Schools had been seen as failures in that they fulfilled neither the criteria of utility (preparing children for diverse occupations) nor morality (making them responsible members of society). Repeated surveys by the government, such as that conducted in the province in 1911 as well as all the journalistic literature of the period, condemned almost every aspect of the new curriculum— textbooks, choice of subjects, teaching methods, and the philosophy of education itself. But if textbooks were inappropriate, their idioms uncouth and unfamiliar, subjects like clay modelling and drawing irrelevant, the useful Indian systems of accounting and hygiene untaught, all this mattered less for girls than it did for boys. All the constituencies in the city that chose to identify themselves politically, Sunnis, Shias, Arya Samajis, various Hindu jatis and regional and linguistic groups, spoke out regarding their dissatisfaction with the curriculum controlled by the government, but none of them spoke of anything but its shortcomings for *boys*.

This has crucial consequences: the girls educated thus could in turn produce from among their ranks those who could and did shake off normative grihastini discourse because their own thinking was not fashioned by it. They grew up to be, for example, both housewives and doctors, lawyers, and teachers, a possibility never encountered in the texts. I do not want to exaggerate the results, particularly since I do not have any figures regarding the fates of school graduates. The domestication of women who worked, taught, thought, interacted with others, and lived fairly independent lives, is almost too explicit to merit comment. The domestication of girls who left homes, crossed streets and public places, interacted with peers and seniors in schools, and could conceivably use their education for building professional lives, was likewise an easily recognizable part of the hidden curriculum of schools. The virtues of discipline, obedience, motherhood, and sainthood were explicitly promoted: written out in school brochures, stated at annual days, discussed with investigators, gone over in reminiscences, and repeated in class as well as in individual conversations with girls.

But the modern schools such as founded by our women educationists were different to the kind of private schooling most of them had experienced. So the consequence of their moderate liberal action was a radical one. It was also achieved through radical means: the deployment of familiar symbols strategically to their own ends; of preserving their sainthood, because in India, although we may disagree with Dumont about everything else, saints are the ultimate individuals, those who have the sanction to act as they please. Unfortunately, to the extent they are 'outside' society, their visions and their powers are not automatically passed on to their disciples, and neither were the radical qualities of our educationists passed on to their students.

8

Making the Nation
Ansari Women in Banaras

My arguments in this essay are first, that the history of artisan and labouring classes, such as the silk weavers of Banaras, is necessarily gendered, and that the particular processes of gendering are important to inspect for a larger gendered history-writing of India. Second, I argue that after we insert women into history and discover gendered processes, we still confront the problems of nation-building, and any problematizations we bring to the issues of nationalism.

I begin with the chapter, 'Our country' from the textbook used in Islamic Barelwi madrasas in classes one and two *(Hamari Pothi)*:

Our country is called Hindustan. Hindustan is a very large country. It has on its north the Himalayas and to the south the Indian Ocean.

Allah Mian is very kind. He has done many favours to our country. He has made its land very fertile. He gives generous rain. He has made countless rivers and streams flow with which we irrigate our crops, He has made all kinds of animals and birds. From these we have the advantage of milk, meat, and skins. He has made all kinds of flowers, fruits, trees, and plants which we use for all our purposes. Our country has vast fields, long and broad rivers, the highest mountains, rich jungles. For all these reasons our country is very beautiful.

God has put a rich treasure under the earth also. When you dig in places, you find iron, or coal, or petroleum, or gold and silver.

At one time Muslims used to rule in our country. They ruled for a long time. They did many constructive things in the country, but when they became destructive instead of constructive, God snatched our country away from them and gave it to a race called 'English' from across the seven seas. The English also ruled our country for sometime. But when there was more destruction than construction from their hands also then it became impossible for them to stay. They left our country and went away. And thus this country came to its own people's hands again.

After the departure of the English there was a great riot and many innocent people were killed. Eventually this land was divided into two. One part was called India (Bharat) and the other part Pakistan. There are more Hindus in India and more Muslims in Pakistan.

After Partition many Muslims went to Pakistan and many Hindus from Pakistan came to India. The Muslims who went to Pakistan are called *muhajir* and those Hindus who came to India are called *refugees* (*sharnarthi*).

We live in this country. We love every little part of it. While we live we will not let anything hurt it. God has given such a beautiful part of the earth to our countrymen for its safekeeping. We will tell them to run it well, build it, beautify it, and run it according to God's will. Otherwise he will be displeased and will snatch our country away and give it to others. Then we will have nothing. Dear God, give us and our countrymen wisdom. And let them act according to your will. (pp 49-53)

As this excerpt demonstrates in perhaps a touching way, the nationalism of Ansaris cannot be in doubt. It illustrates a larger point about nation-building and history that is important to my argument. In the narratives of Indian history familiar to us, Muslims in India seem to participate in nation-making only at the two extremes, when they are members of the intelligentsia who lead actively in the struggle for a new nation; or, conversely, when they are a deadweight, and will not reform, or progress. By all accounts, Ansaris seem to fall into the second category. They find no mention in any nationalist history except as participants in occasional riots on the cow protection and assorted issues. This 'communal' behaviour is interpreted as rational or irrational depending on the historian, and there are some histories that successfully put the blame squarely on the colonial state, but the bottom line remains: Ansaris play a role in nation-building only on occasions of provocation and reaction (Pandey 1990). As one could demonstrate, however, their efforts, material and discursive, at education, identity-construction and other practices within their industry, community, and city are centrally a part of the story of the nation of India (Kumar 2000). As this excerpt reveals, even when no one is looking, they are silently building up the nation in the most normative ways. The gendered nature of this nationalism, however, and how

Ansari women are at the heart of the 'making the nation' is more obscure. To make an argument for it we need a further contextualization of Ansari history.

The history of the Ansaris goes as follows. The Ansaris are *julahas*, that is, weavers, but Muslim weavers as contrasted with the Hindu weavers in the population of that same region (eastern Uttar Pradesh). They ascribe their origins officially to the remnants of Salar Masaud's army, Salar Masaud being a general who undertook Islamic conquest and conversion in the eleventh century and was martyred in that place and is worshipped as Gazi Mian. Julahas are the descendents of, or converts from the impact of, Gazi Mian's army. According to their own local histories they settled down to the craft of weaving and through innovation and enterprise made it the prosperous industry it is. Unlike many other handicrafts it has moulded itself to changing markets and has not merely survived but expanded over the centuries (Ali 1900; Census 1901-1981, Siddiqi n.d). Hundreds of thousands of Muslims in Banaras are engaged in this industry.

Julaha was the caste name of these Muslim weavers until the 1930s and informally continues to be their name today. The All-India Momin Ansar Conference adopted the name Ansari formally in the 1930s, which alludes to the original helpers of the Prophet in Madina, with which community they have otherwise nothing in common. The choice of Ansari denotes that they would like to be considered *sharif*, or higher class. The first step in such a projected upward mobility is, everywhere in India, a change of name. However, from the 1930s, although almost all weavers use this name of Ansari, and almost all are referred to by this name, at least to their face (not, for instance, in the Police Station records), the signs of social change among them have been mostly in the form of class differentiation (Ansari 1960; Ahmad 1978). Some Ansaris have become international traders in silk, with or without their own firms, and others are dependent labourers who work from piece wage to wage.

Throughout the last century, Ansaris have come together in various groupings for reform. Most explicitly, they have organized as Barelwi, Deobandi, and Ahl-e-hadis sectarian groups to set up schools, publish textbooks, win over supporters, correct their practices, and seek to progress (Metcalf 1982). There is a multitude of local societies and organizations that variously address the questions of how Ansaris can be both ethical and worldly, traditional and progressive, reformed but true to their identities.

This 'History of the Weavers' is marked by a total invisibility of women. It is as if the men fought the battles, practised the crafts, built the neighbourhoods, constructed the codes, peddled their wares, invented new designs, chose their names, elaborated their pleasures and arts, and thus were literally both the makers and tellers of their histories. The only place women have in this narrative is as those who blow at the embers of their domestic fires and cook the food, often to reheat it as the men in the family, all wilful and free, wander around as long as they please, then come home to eat and rest. They blow at the embers and wipe away the water in their eyes from the smoke. They also cough because often chronically ill with TB, and cook and cough and wipe their faces, all in a dirty sari, because they can hardly afford even to touch the beautiful silks being woven by their menfolk for other women in other places. This at least is the picture painted by me as an anthropologist and Abdul Bismillah as a novelist (Bismillah 1986; Kumar 1992). The women of better-off Ansaris are not represented in either genre, and perhaps any genre.

The invisibility of women is an over-familiar and seemingly redundant problem by now. Yet the recognition of it has not resolved the problem of the non-gendered nature of most histories, and even less, the problem of the actual inferiorization of women in every separate case. I would argue that even if at one level, the problem seems identical: women are silent and invisible everywhere, and their positioning in history implicitly or explicitly seen as lower than men's; we still need to recognize the different ways in which this occurs in every case and what is generalizable about it (Nicholson 1986).

Now within Ansari history, women have been crucial. Of course we cannot say we know what 'women' are, so we will look at a specific discourse of women, that is as 'mothers'. As wives of men and mothers of their children, women create, first, the spaces for men to be active in public life. No women, and only men, are members and office bearers of the several committees, beginning from the Momin Ansar Committee, for education, reform, and community identity. The excerpt at the head of this essay is typical of a madrasa's nationalism, a nationalism which is not noticed. Yet, while Ansaris, both men and women, are not remembered for their nation-building efforts, women are doubly ignored. There are several madrasas specifically for girls. But their own all-women staff of teachers explain that although they are in control within their madrasa, the institution itself is managed by a committee wholly of men who prefer them to be neither seen nor heard, that is, in purdah and obedient to the managing committee's wishes. The positioning of these Ansari women as professionals is subsumed under their role as housewife. But then, this housewife's role *is also rendered totally invisible*. The housewife's special contribution, in making the man free and comfortable in every public activity he chooses to engage in (which is glimpsed for a passing moment when he may have lost his wife and quickly takes another wife), is not ever articulated. Obviously it has been naturalized and does not need to be expressed because it is, or should be taken for granted.

The habit of subsuming professional work within the identity of mother-housewife is observable even more dramatically in the weaving profession itself. The person who sits at the loom is typically the man, but almost all the preparatory work for weaving is done by the woman. There would be no possibility of weaving without this work, that is, weaving encompasses other processes that do have separate names but are all subsumed within it. The woman has no identity as worker. Her professional work as artisan is not named or referenced, and of course not paid. She is not worker but mother and housewife, and then as that is not a worker either. Such is Zarina, most skilled a crafts 'man', but with no language in which she may be described. This is particularly ironic within the Banarasi sari industry, because the Banarasi sari, together with Bombay films, is probably the one product of India that is circulated over the whole country and the whole world, in both cases standing as sign of 'India' itself.

Second, women have been crucial in the narrative of the nation's history in actively choosing to have their sons educated. The decision to send their children to schools for a liberal education, as madrasa education actually is (chapter 4), is taken not only equally by both parents, it is taken often singly by the mother upon being widowed or divorced, when she typically supports herself as a single parent in her natal family rather than remarry as men do. One example would be Mehr-ur-Nissa who, upon separation, returned to her natal family with her six-year old son, and supported herself with stitching and embroidery. She educated her son to adulthood, in madrasa and at home, in weaving and in ethics. Today, in his twenties, he is as honourable and competent a young man as any parents could demand of their child, or nation of its citizen body. This particular role of the woman as mother in pushing her children, specially her sons, to fulfil a destiny she herself has never had as an option, is one of the most obvious missing links in the history of the nation.

Then we have the mother who 'teaches' directly, and not merely provides the material and psychological funds for education. She teaches as a master his apprentice and as a teacher her student. She teaches the mother tongue and often, a classical language such as Arabic through the teaching of the Qur'an. The number of women who are learned in the Qur'an and teach it in turn, is very large, though statistically unknown and impressionistically underrated.

The mother teaches, further, the fund of narratives about the family, community, and locality, producing a feeling of closure in the child regarding the location of the self. She teaches the ethics of the community, or what it means to be a healthy, proper, dignified, happy human being. She communicates all the definitions of the self and of a good life before the child is old enough to be streetwise and a wanderer, and these definitions go into the fashioning of the adult self we recognize and interpret without a thought given to this early socialization. Indeed, because of the otherwise well-known fact that the pull of the formal school is weaker on communities like the Ansaris, their grounding in the family is greater, notwithstanding the fact that we are *not* talking about the familiar nuclear family of the modern West, nor of the companionate marriage, with the wife/mother as the predetermined nurturer and carer. We are talking specifically of the role of mothering and of all those who perform the role, who are, besides the mother, aunts, grandparents, sisters, and other relatives.

Thus, the woman, looking at her only in the one positioning of the mother, produces the nation in these several ways. She does this with as much finesse as any other maker of the nation. That is, she also does it uncritically. Mehr-ur-Nissa or Zarina are producing sons who will be ready to die for the nation. It is indeed ironical that the woman who extends herself by thus denying herself an autonomous space of her own in favour of one for her child, and who is always prejudiced against her own sex in favour of the man's, including by favouring the son over the daughter, is not recognized as 'worker' and 'nation-builder'.

We need a double loop of criticism here. The solution is only partly in subjecting our disciplinary discourses to questioning. In every single one of them, there is a prioritization of the public, political, extra-domestic, and masculine which is taken to be an automatic, self-evident forefronting. And, in fact, the woman's domestic and mothering role is neither 'natural' nor 'necessary'. It is highly discursive and political. The possibilities of interpreting it with the subtlety that is expended on the public working man, his associational activities, and his constructions of nationalism, would open up only with the practice of interpretation.

This, I am suggesting, is a practical but limited solution. It would enable us to construct several parallel narratives which jostle each other for importance, and it would enable us to broaden our methodologies and data sources in unpredictable ways. I am personally very interested in seeing the 'family' brought to our gaze as a site of education and social reproduction. The nature of the modern Indian nation, no less than the nature of the modern Indian person, derives from the fact of plural sites of education and learning: in formal schools, and in homes, and neighbourhoods. The reliance on a European model of history-writing makes us adopt a singular narrative of subject-formation, whereas the South Asian narratives must be necessarily plural. I am arguing here that the impulse for change in the nineteenth–twentieth centuries, first as colonial legislation, then as nationalist reform, was sited in opaque ways in 'private' as well as 'public' spaces, each of which supported as well as undermined the other.

Thus, while the man located himself in the reform association, and started a school or wrote a textbook, he was himself formed by his womenfolk. He was taught his languages, his ethics, and his narrative of the self by them. He was informed by them, perhaps without his awareness, of the possible targets of reform. He was given a 'home' to venture from and to return to (Shree 2000). Any story of his public activities must take these aspects of his formation into account. The story that ensues is therefore through and through a gendered one. When looking at the activities that follow, educational, reform, and nationalist, we have to extend ourselves to encompass in their deconstruction the plural learning that went into their making.

I am calling this a limited solution, however, because our other problem of questioning the nature of nationalism is not resolved by it. By performing the sociological roles of mothering and teaching, women are producing and reproducing the nation, but a nation is not thereby made more innocent or benign. On the surface, as in the textbook excerpt at the beginning of this essay, it presents itself as harmonious, a beautiful gift by God of natural resources that must be protected. Under this surface, the nation rests totally on patriarchy and gender hierarchies, and its machinery is one of exclusions and repressions. As the trainers and teachers of young citizen-nationalists, women are responsible for this hidden story and machine. They reproduce the gender divisions. They actively construct women as domesticated, protected, virtuous, and shameful, the constructs which lie at the heart of the nation (Van der Veer 1994). They oppose and resist reforms that challenge these constructs. They confirm the patriarchy of the nation.

Thus the two Ansari women mentioned here, Zarina and Mehr-ur-Nissa, are to be pitied thrice over. First, that they are not recognized as workers. Zarina is a professional embroiderer and Mehr is a mother and informal worker, but neither gets justified economic, political or symbolic-cultural returns for their work. Second, they play no role in any account of the history of the Ansaris and the history of the nation. Third, they cannot possibly be praised for their agency from a perspective of an egalitarian politics. They are agents in strengthening and elaborating their roles of mother and housewife, which they had no hand in choosing, but choose now to affirm and reproduce. They are active in making certain that they themselves live lives of seclusion, and affirm this for the women and girls around them. They seem neither to question nor subvert this discourse but rather to celebrate it. They bring up their sons and nephews to be exemplary citizen-men within this overall gendered discourse of a national space constructed by divided roles. Simultaneously they bring up their daughters and nieces to keep their heads covered and their voices low, to submit to men and to desire the minimum.

The case of Ansari women is deeply problematical—as of any such subjects anywhere. It points us to a possible history of India: one that includes private, inward-looking communities; that describes the gendered formation of the nationalist-active men; and that faces the problem that men, women, community, and nation are all produced by and in turn produce these highly questionable gendered discourses. This essay is the briefest effort to set the stage for these considerations.

9

The Nature of
Reform in Modern India
A Discussion of *Mai*; a Novel
by Geetanjali Shree

I

THE MATTER OF THE MOTHER

Mai, as the title suggests, has at its heart a mother.

The mother is a familiar one. I have one like that at home right now, as I type. She is sitting next to me, bent over. She will not rest against the cushion because of her inbuilt grid of self-sacrifice. We have just had tea. While I was looking at the paper, she carried the tea tray back to the kitchen and sneakily washed the cups and spoons, although that is my job. She will offer anything there is in the house: food, drink, place to sit, newspaper to read, TV channel to watch, window to look out of, bathroom to visit, and so on, endlessly, to all of us while denying that she needs any of this for herself. She does not merely say this in a hundred ways, she enacts it consistently, in subtle, hidden ways, until we are all pawns in her game of supreme self-sacrifice. Like the mother in the novel, while appearing weak, she has the strongest will of us all: we may question and dither, but she knows what she wants. She may seem to change her mind or veer from one position to another, but the consistent calculation under all of them is the good of others. Especially her children and their families. Nor have her sons with all their good intentions succeeded in making her aware of her rights. The more they have tried, the more have they failed. She continues to keep her fasts, worry about others, sacrifice all comforts, be bent over rather than straight....

So what is a *mother*?

It is not that either the author's text, or this discussion, has an answer to that question. It is that we are both *interested* in the question. My reading of the text, and my reading of my mother-at-home above, suggests that a mother is, at the most elementary level, both weakness and power, innocence and manipulation, self-denial and self-interest. It is the paradoxical reciprocity of the two that creates a version of the master-slave dialectic, that leads to confusion on the part of observers, and miscalculation by both 'oppressors' and 'reformers'. *Mai* goes to the heart of the paradox.

Anthropologists, sociologists, scholars of religion and history, other academics with an interest in the constructiveness of gender roles, all have their perspectives, and give answers to this question. It would be outside the agenda of this discussion to survey the literature in detail but we could note the constructions very briefly. First we have the earliest, most realist, economistic studies according to which there are two clear-cut sexes, of which woman's is the oppressed one, and this remains stable across time and place. There are numerous inflections in this approach, such as those that question the effects of development, of multinational production and trade, and of modernist ideology. The most sophisticated is certainly the Marxist one, such as used by Claudia von Werlhof. She writes,

The 'true essense', so to speak, of this division and its starting point is nothing more than women's natural monopoly: their child-bearing capacity. In no mode of production throughout history is the child-bearing capacity, the prerequisite of production of humans, so central as in the present. It is no accident that capitalism's so-called 'Population Law' is considered to be nothing less than the 'general law of capitalist accumulation' (Marx). It is this law which turns women into child-bearing machines and is responsible for the so-called population 'explosion' (von Werlhof 1988: 178).

In this view women have developed 'a specifically feminine capacity for work' because 'they *had* to develop it' (von Werlhof 1988: 178). Everything that women do, however, and the way they do it, is for the benefit of 'the system'.

The friendliness, submissiveness, being-always-at-others'-disposal, healing-all-wounds, being-sexually-usable; the putting-everything-again-in-order, the sense of responsibility and self-sacrifice, frugality and unpretentiousness, the renunciation in favour of others, the putting-up-with and helping-out-in-all-matters, withdrawing-oneself and being invisible and always there, the passive being-available and the active 'pulling-the-cart-out-of-the-mud'— the endurance and discipline of a soldier (ibid.; 179).

On this super-capacity, rests the whole system of capitalist accumulation. One might extend the same terminology to add, of feudal exploitation as well. It is a hair-curlingly accurate picture of Rajjo, the mother. This is what the mother I have at home is.

In a second approach to mothers, the database is not, as in the above, international statistics of how many hours women work versus the wages earned, illuminated by insights into their subservient behaviour. The data is ideas about women, in literature, mythology, sculpture, painting, rituals, and politics. These 'images' of women, it is argued, shape the 'reality' of women's lives. And though some correspondence between the two can be empirically discerned, there is just as often contradiction, and no particular technique is used to demonstrate either relationship except of informed hypothesis. Ideas or images of women—of South Asian women, for instance—as in Tulsidas, regional literatures, Bankimchandra, Tagore, Gandhi, and so on, can themselves be notoriously contradictory and also predictable. The mother, particularly, is imaged in the following ways: (i) as a deity in Harappan civilization, the putative origins of the mother goddess in South Asia; (ii) as *Shakti* or embodied power, by Shakta sects and practitioners of Tantra; (iii) as a parent who can be either (a) benign, as one would find in biographical and apocryphal literature, or (b) violent, as Hindu mythology cheerfully informs us, (iv) as the nation by late nineteenth-century nationalists, particularly Bengali, and finally, (v) as invisible and voiceless, according to some recent scholarship.

The third approach to the mother would be one that would turn over the preoccupations of the second approach above, by first casting doubt on the relevance of the data through a theory of reading, and then on the conclusions which use androcentric models in good faith and with naivety. This perspective would question models, concepts, language itself, redefine the premises, reframe the dominant questions, and re-examine the facts.

Mai hints at using many, or all, of these perspectives in turn, but none of them exclusively or consistently. It plays a kind of trick on the reader. It leads the reader from holding one view with full conviction to moving around to the other side and viewing its reverse. Each time that a watertight case is made for the motherhood, mothering, and mother's destiny of her whom for lack of any other name in the book but *Mai*, we will call Rajjo, the author turns around her correct politics and questions this status.

But, somehow, with the peculiar genius of literature, *Mai* also gives us a character who encompasses at least two faces—maybe three—without the negative implications of inconsistency. She opens up for us a past of girlhood and freedom, then a present of bondage and servitude, then a future yet unknown but full of potential.

Mai shifts the question from 'What is a mother?' to 'What kind of a person is this mother?' Rajjo is behind a purdah, but, as the novel gradually suggests, it is a curtain that provides serenity and privacy, and contains behind it a bustling world and life. The world goes back somewhere into the past, before she was a mother, before even she was a wife. In this hidden world she had—she *has*, because the text keeps her 'fire' alive (or, if I may be allowed a witticism, as my laptop informs me occasionally, 'word' is saving 'mai')—a selfhood, smiles and laughter, loves and losses. A selfhood is a fire that smoulders. It can be turned inside, as Rajjo does, and becomes invisible because it is behind a permanent curtain. Or it can be turned outside, as the daughter Sunaina does, when it sets fire to the curtain itself and becomes visible, maybe engulfs some territory involuntarily. That no one at all is privy to Rajjo's selfhood makes her all the stronger. The fire smoulders as strongly, none the weaker for being contained.

This, one may argue, is not necessarily an emancipatory vision. Sunaina's fire, turned outside, does not immediately seem to explicitly illuminate anything or lead her anywhere. She is, at the end, consumed by frustration, her mind filled by fog. Rajjo's fire might give her an inner peace, but outwardly she is broken. She has a bent back. Like 'the woman who walked into doors' she has her own satisfactions and life of the mind, but she cannot claim that she was free to make her choices. Others do build up walls around her, close doors, erect barriers, 'oppress', and 'maltreat'. Rajjo is praised by her mother-in-law, but oftner abused by her husband, for her very silence. Does Rajjo's case suggest that all mothers and wives who are only dutiful and silent, are supremely fulfilled? What about the argument that:

A woman's heart has secrets that even the funeral pyre cannot reveal. Suppressed continually by the opposing forces of religion, society, even destiny, they finally explode within her. Like weeping without tears, living without breathing, like a mountain of fire that cannot give out smoke, they are contained inside her and shatter her inner being (Antharjanam 1998: 45).

A fire is a difficult metaphor. Unlike the narrator in *Mai* we do in fact associate it more with explosion and consumption and a final reduction to ashes than with a quiet containment behind a curtain— that most combustible of things.

Or in a more universalist vein, the argument can be put thus:

Is this enough? Is it to live?...Does virtue lie in abnegation of the self? I do not believe it....Each human being has his share of rights. I suspect it would conduce to the happiness and welfare of all, if each knew his allotment, and held to it as tenaciously as the martyr to his creed. Queer thoughts these, that surge in my mind: are they right thoughts? I am not certain (Jacobus 1986: 41).

Fot those who think these thoughts, such as Sunaina, the question is a live one, and finally a confusing and unanswerable one. So the question, 'Is this mother's life enough?' is not answered, neither by the author nor by the protagonists. For me what the book suggests is the bigger question: 'Whose question is this'?

My mother-at-home's, *ma's*, case should tell me. (I would give her a name too, because to merely name people 'mai' and 'ma' is to deny them their lives beyond their roles of mothering—and yet I feel constrained by the Indian idea that you do not call elders by their names. So I cannot call my ma by her name but I can call 'mai' Rajjo. I am an insider to the former context and an outsider to the latter. An insider is one who can respect out of conviction, that is, who can accommodate the irrational within the rational. An outsider is one who strives to be purely rational.) The one thing I knew best about ma was that 'she was a very good student and always stood first in class'. Then I knew also her practices: how she held her son's chin as she combed his hair, what she fed her sons and daughters, how she cooked spinach. Who told me all this about her? Her children, exactly those who wanted to make her into something. When she speaks to me, it is never about herself. She will never say, 'I was a good student'. Or even, 'This is what I consider a good breakfast and what I gave my children'. Her talk is always about her children, and, to her credit, about me.

Does she have a mountain of fire within her? Does she have the question if her life is 'enough'?

It would be going against the grain of all my empirical knowledge about her to say 'yes'.

Ma, and mai, may both simply exemplify a familiar annoying characteristic of mothers. They will never say what they want. They will outguess you at the daily level and put you before themselves. They will refuse to assign themselves preferences, tastes, and choices. They retreat from accepting subjecthood. They will not to the end admit even whether they were the ones who ever decided or not, and then, having travelled a certain path, were fulfilled or not. Did they, do they, ask the question or not?

We will not know.

A mother like Rajjo seems precisely the dissolution of the subject.

But perhaps dissolution of the subject is only what our limited vision suggests?

Vivekanand's response to a question regarding how he would help widows, was, 'Am I a widow? What is the logic of asking me? Do not widows have the intelligence and the will to themselves decide how they would be helped?' What *Mai*, the novel, like Vivekanand, is raising is a very large discussion on the question of 'the subject' and its desirability. And a related questioning of the viability of the project itself, when the problematization and the solution both come from others. Are the subjects here the questioners, or is the subject Vivekanand, or are the subjects the widows? Obviously it is not the widows, and Vivekanand refuses to take up the mantle, so it is the questioners. But why is Vivekanand's simple point so difficult to keep in mind in scholarship, even feminist scholarship? Why is silence taken for absence? Why, in the imagery of the novel, is a curtain short-sighted, unimaginatively misunderstood to be not only a barrier, but a barrier behind which there is *nothing*?

Rajjo undoubtedly has a fire inside herself. But she has done more with her fire than simply turned it inside for herself. She has tended someone else's fire, allowed it to grow, and even arranged the curtain in such a way as to allow its flapping to incite the flames. Sunaina is free because of her mother—free to use what she likes of the past and discard the rest. She does not even realize perhaps, by the end of the book, how free she is. But we feel, we suspect that she will go on ever onwards, and still hold on to her past as bestowed to her by mai.

Mai can speak eloquently when necessary and can be adamant and persuasive through other means when she wants to be. She *chooses*, however, most of the time to be silent. Even when there is no speech, the assumption that speechlessness is not a choice is unjustified. Mai demonstrates, again and again, that silence is a weapon. It can be used to aid or to hinder. It can purposefully make the other angry or en-thused. It can stand for approval or disapproval. It can indicate resis-tance as much as complicity. Rajjo, like the mother I know, and the women I have studied (Kumar 1994), is a master at silence. A silence does not indicate non-communication or unreadability. The potential here is analogous to that of translation, where a text is not untranslat-able because it has not been translated, but is simply, as it were, awaiting its ideal translator (Benjamin 1985).

The novel *Mai* is certainly the posing of an intellectual's question, an author's and a reader's. It is an intellectual's discovery, as the narrator, of herself, including her widening comprehension of her mother and her relationship to her mother. *Mai* is not the mother's voice. As novel, it is a meta-fiction, on how a novel may be written in search of the mother's voice.

But as a translation of the mother's silence, it gives a wonderful insight into how silences can be pursued. Here, the daughter has enough at stake, in rootedness and pain, to keep pursuing her mother's mystery. Apparently, in intellectual endeavour, there is far less motivation. But what if there was to be that passion for the unspoken, or that instinct that tells that after all everything is not spoken in words?

Perhaps the clue lies partly in the difference between the brother, Subodh, and the sister, Sunaina. He is scholar of sorts, apart from being a man, and relies, one supposes, both professionally and person-ally, more on words. Sunaina is a painter, apart from being a woman, and seems to trust images that are incomplete, suggestions of move-ment, shadows, and clouds.

What the novel *Mai* suggests to us, I submit, is that the method should follow the subject. We do not know *what* mothers are, we do not know if a given mother is 'fulfilled' in what she does, or what else she 'wants'. But we could progressively know whether to ask certain questions, how to ask some others, what any of them might imply, how to refrain from asking and retract, how to pause and begin to comprehend little glimpses better. We could start evaluating silence differently than how our dichotomous, rationalist world, much like

Subodh and Sunaina's, tells us to. We could question agency, strength, and weakness anew. We could take the plurality of each of these things seriously. *Mai* is partly about a mother, and largely about the methodology (a social science term that the novelist, I suspect, would not like) of asking about mothers.

*   *   *

There are at least three other mothers in *Mai* apart from Rajjo: the grandmother, *dadi*; the servant, Hardeyi; and the aunt, *bua*. Dadi is laughable. She adores her son so much that it blinds her to any possible shortcomings in him or virtues in others. She is a terrible mother-in-law because she is such a devoted mother.

Hardeyi is a failure in a very precise way because her son dies, the implication being that it is because of her poverty and ignorance. She is destined, and through her, her son, to be lost to history. But she shows solidarity with other mothers, and women generally, by routinely co-operating in Rajjo and Sunaina's efforts to live lives maximally ordered by themselves.

Bua does not have her children around her. She interferes, unsuccessfully, in her nephew and niece's life. They shrug off her voice as irritating, but it is also internalized, at least by Sunaina, as the prototypical voice of the order that is trying to make her into a puppet. This is also a mother. A mother who speaks for patriarchy and the non-freedom of women.

No comparisons are made or suggested. But *Mai*, like life itself, poses the conundrum that the problem of the mother is created, most volubly and aggressively, by mothers themselves: for Rajjo and Sunaina by dadi and bua.

Mai plays this other trick as well, then. It shows us a range of mothers. But it calls only one of them 'mother'. It calls itself by that title, that is, makes itself the story of this *one* mother. This is a trick played not only by this novel but by all fiction and real life itself, or rather, by our ability to read fiction and to read real life. We can analytically see in the book that all mothers are not alike (such as Rajjo and dadi) just as all non-mothers are not alike (such as *dada* and Babu). We can see the same in innumerable variety all around us in real life. Yet we forget that, both every day in our own lives and while we read *Mai*. Popular consciousness has it that mothers are nurturing and sacrificing. A hasty report on or version of *Mai* could be that it is the tale of Rajjo as the archetypical mother, not dadi, or bua.

But though she is nurturing and sacrificing, there is nothing archetypical about Rajjo's versions of these processes. She nurtures her children towards questioning and independence. She sacrifices with conflict-free self-confidence. The result of these processes is the surprise. As archetypical mother she would have glorified these very virtues. But her children condemn them and her daughter will not 'be like her'. She can produce change, that is, through her own preferred tactics, and do it so effectively that we are not quite aware how it occurs.

Equally significant are the non-mothers in the story. Dada is the foremost, repressing all the women for his own pleasures, confirming fear in the heart of his son to keep him subservient. He is a monarch who does not have to bow before anyone—opposite in this sense to dadi, who, monarch as she is in her own way, is ready to wash the soles of her son's feet.

Then there is Babu, supremely tangential to his children's socialization and upbringing, to an extent that in spite of his rare feeble efforts, he does not win them over to even a basic empathy with him. Only in relation to the domineering habits of his father does he seem mildly attractive, or perhaps tolerable. Otherwise, throughout, he is the weakling, who cannot eat heartily like his parents, take care of his own clothes, puja, or other needs, and cannot speak his mind directly to his son and daughter. He seems capable only of commanding his wife, albeit in a feeble or indirect way. But this non-mother presents his worst side in the non-nurturing, non-supportive, and non-socializing role he plays with regard to his children. He is their enemy. We can almost see how this damages him as it does them and how it weakens their relationship. He is merely a victim of a certain structure of parenting that is understood to be the norm. He seems to have the inclination for more gentleness and love than he himself or others expect of him and give him a chance to easily display. Thus, denying and being denied his androgynous possibilities, Babu suffers from being distanced from his children, not achieving either the excessive masculinity of dada nor an individually formulated sense of self-worth.

Last, there is Sunaina herself, the narrator. Unmarried and unattached in any stable relationship to the end of the story, she is determined to be not like her mother, presumably including in the central characteristic of maternity. She, together with Subodh (also a non-parent) is chided often by her mother for not understanding, not letting her alone, for kicking down her house of sand, as it were. The suggestion is partly that Sunaina is immature, that she lacks some insight that comes form Rajjo's involvement with the complexities of childrearing, from the protection that only mothers can give to children from cohorts and seniors out to destroy them.

Yet, of these second generation non-mothers, if I may be excused for the awkwardness of the phrase, Sunaina stands closer to the mother-heroine. Why? Is it because, of the two non-mothers, she is the daughter? Because this makes her bear the mantle of her mother's legacy, some connecting thread that does not snap however much pressure it has to bear, of reform, reason, and rationality? What is the perception Sunaina has of her mother's, grandmother's, and other female forbears' shadow upon her, their beings mingling with hers? Are we back to the argument that there is a sisterhood of women, that one is biologically programmed towards certain traits and characteristics from being born a woman?

Even Rajjo seems to share this profound belief. Her mother-in-law is her harshest critic, and particularly virulent in denying to her the possibility of her having, in the past or present, a life as anything but a servant of the family. Dadi, in her love for her son, pours scorn on the previous existence, the virtue, and truthfulness, and every single possible good quality, of her son's wife. Yet, after the bitterest of these attacks—and they are violent, abusive attacks—Rajjo turns the other cheek. She comes with a bottle of oil to massage her mother-in-law's body, or to oil her hair. Sunaina's incredulity is answered with an explanation that leaves us equally incredulous. Dadi and she, says Rajjo, the mother and the daughter-in-law, are one *jati*, one caste or genus. They have to stick together.

One *jati*? All women? All mothers? All wives? All daughters-in-law? Rajjo's elaboration is of the last two points. When dadi was young, she was physically hurt by dada, repeatedly enough for her to have a bald patch on her head from where he dragged her by the hair. Her own mother-in-law admired her—in dadi's version—but also clearly only because dadi left no stone unturned in her dedication and service of this highly important personage, whose status she is interested in promoting since it is now her own status. So dadi is what she is because it is her fate as woman, and in turn it is Rajjo's.

Sunaina lacks a vocabulary for saying this. With that, maybe thanks to that, she lacks the confidence for saying it. She remains confused and wondering to the end—where is mai to be found? Who or what was mai? What is her own relationship to mai? Why can she not kick away the past and be free? Why is she held prisoner by the house and mai's memory?

What is mai trying to tell her?

Surely it could not be that Sunaina should be like her. Had Rajjo wanted that, she would have behaved differently towards her daughter and other family members right from the beginning. She stood up to her sister-in-law and father-in-law, antagonized her husband, contradicted (tactfully) her mother-in-law, kept endless secrets, lied and dissimulated, all so that Sunaina could be free to explore and maybe discover 'herself'. We may not be clear about what the mother saw Sunaina as possibly doing. But we can be clear that she did not try to reproduce herself in her daughter.

It is, we might say, simply the mother's love again. That particular impossible quality of maternity: 'I love you but I am so self-sacrificing that I do not want even you for myself. Be free.'

Yes, but this is not as simple as it seems on the surface. This seemingly impossible quality, in fact, says, 'Be free, but you will always be attached. Because you will realize, the stronger you grow in your freedom, that I did not have to hold you by force. You were held by your own will.'

The freedom of Sunaina and Subodh is a reflection of Rajjo's own freedom. She makes herself free by not taking possession of them. We see this in the powerful contrast between her and the others in the family, especially Babu. He is utterly weak, even wretched, because he cannot let them go. He cannot be free of his own possessiveness and his own jealousies.

Rajjo adopts the very difficult course of actually hindering her children in their plan to 'save' her. She saves herself instead, from the inside, as it were, in her own way, with her own priorities as well— something that they are sure to recognize in the afterlife of the novel.

The question of sacrifice illustrates another twist: how mai does not try to reproduce herself in her children, but how the reproduction does happen. She succeeds somehow in teaching her children her values, including that of self-sacrifice. More importantly, she succeeds in teaching them that hers is not the losing side and the opponent's the winning side. After their years of pursuit of reason, logic, individualism, secularism, modernity, and self-fulfilment, she leaves them—and specially her daughter—with serious doubts about 'taking', about self-centredness, about possible misunderstanding of relationships in the world and balance in the universe. She leaves her daughter wondering about penance, fasting, sacrifice, and bending.

With this we come to what else lies at the heart of *Mai* besides the matter of the mother. It is the saving (*bachana*) of her, the pulling her out (*nikalna*) of the house, the whole business of reform (for which there is no colloquial Hindi word). That is, the novel has two foci: the mother, mai, and the saving of her, or creating of the non-mai. Its two foci are mai and non-mai. Mai is—in the early narrator's voice— hollow, an absence, nothing. Non-mai, or the saving of her, stands for fullness, for choice and personhood.

This could be an abbreviation for the whole narrative of reform in nineteenth-century India, except that the main actor in the case of *Mai* is, unlike in history, a daughter and not a son. But the novel strives to make the point that the two, son and daughter, were a unit initially and made plans to rescue mai as one. If we can overlook this gender differentiation and imagine the siblings as one, what emerges is the simple proposition, 'The children want to improve the mother's lot, but they cannot'. They themselves become free, largely thanks to the mother. They grow beyond the bonds of class, caste, and religion, and are physically free. Then something happens. The daughter decides that she does not want a tug-of-war between them and their mother, and she would like to be neither the winner nor the loser in such a war. So she dedicates her life, instead, to discovering why it was that 'improving their mother's lot' was a fallacious proposition.

I am anticipating the next section here when I say that this is a good summary of much of what comprised the reform movements in nineteenth-century India, and less dramatically, what goes on today. There seem to be two clear-cut sides, the progressive reformers and the conservatives. Between these, women seem to be the passive objects of reform that yield or not to different degrees. Usually they resist, they act as obstacles to reform, they seem incomprehensible in their recalcitrance. In *Mai* both Subodh and Sunaina realize that their pity for their mother has gradually a new element of annoyance in it, but it is Subodh particularly who begins to be bitter about her 'weakness'. Both, however, for most of the book, feel frustrated.

She simply refused to understand. She refused to change, to escape. We would fight for her again and again, and she would herself betray us. Babu, from whom we scurried around trying to save her, was exactly the one she would submit to.... She was trapped. She was in chains (pp. 91-2).

And what does Rajjo herself have to say about this? She tells them at different times that this is her work, that the work is in the interest of everyone, not of only the one oppressor or two that they seem to identify, that she enjoys it and takes pleasure in doing it well. The work, precisely speaking, is housework, cooking, serving, childbearing, childrearing, hospitality to guests, and all other odd jobs that arise in the house, such as massaging her mother-in-law's legs or oiling her hair.

As liberal, egalitarian readers, do we not all share her children's dismay that the mother should be slave to this routine of work? Do we not feel convinced that her life should be reformed?

Rajjo does have a reply regarding the satisfactions of her work, but she does not address the other question implied by her children: that she had no choice in being allotted these tasks, that she is additionally abused instead of praised in the performance of them, and that her voice does not figure at all in the chorus of demands and expectations that resound in the house. She seems to understand the abuse as a ritual or cyclical one—one generation to another—and as largely formal. She seems to content herself by being a dignified victim.

In fact, what she is, is an unusual agent of change. She stops the cycle of abuse not merely by not being the kind of mother-in-law that those in the previous generations have been, but by showing no interest in being a mother-in-law at all. She may have liked the idea of her children married and bearing grandchildren, but she does not let it influence her behaviour towards them. She could continue, cyclically, the path shown by bua: since all women are barred in their youth from active choices—in bua's case, of a career, in Rajjo's presumably, of a marriage of her choice—they use themselves as role models for their juniors. This is the fate of women, they will say. Mai does not give herself these satisfactions. She has other satisfactions. Most of all, perhaps, that she has herself never controlled. Sunaina, at her end of the book, inherits no bitterness or acrimony from her. She will build her own life in unspecified ways.

Similarly, Rajjo is an agent because no matter how preferable silence is to response in the case of some kinds of abuse, she is discriminating. She does not let bullying go beyond a point. One may draw a kind of map of what matters enough to her to speak up for, and what does not. When the abuse is addressed to her children particularly, she retorts and fights back, and is immediately effective. When it is addressed to her other identity, that of wife, she again acts, and has to be pacified.

But regarding her lack of choice during her whole adult life, starting from her marriage itself, she is silent. So silent, that her children do not know anything of her past, even about her parents. How can this be? Why did she not tell her daughter at least? We may suspect that it was because the children were not good listeners. They formed their opinions too strongly, too soon, and she did not want to disturb the trajectory of their lives: They did not give her enough space, enough time. Maybe it was equally because she did not believe the past to be worth anything. Most women in South Asia who are not 'modern' would date their lives only from their marriage, and consider the time before as an unimportant part of the narrative of their lives. If so, then Rajjo, in considering her past 'nothing', is indeed, as her children imagine, 'nothing'. Their desire to rescue her includes giving her a past, and if their failure in this is partly due to their insensitivity, it is also partly due to Rajjo's refusal to pursue their vision.

But Rajjo, with the limited past that she has—exactly one letter, and them the reawakened desire of the father to see his granddaughter—is not a non-actor. She keeps the letter instead of destroying it, and somehow by the end, conveys to her children that they should listen more carefully to the whispers of the past.

Now, if we have to interpret this particular stand of women like Rajjo—I will not speak or fight for what you think I should be—and interpret it in a way different to the rational, reformist, children, that is, different to the early Sunaina and closer to the later Sunaina, we may come up with something like this. Women have their calculations of what the spaces for them are, where their freedoms lie, and how certain satisfactions may be maximized through certain manipulations. They, too, wish for change on many counts. But, while we know the scattered efforts of women in the history of reform that were more or less direct in nature, we lack a vocabulary for stating, and a methodology for uncovering, the efforts that were less than direct. In *Mai*, as we see, it would be a fallacy to say that the mother, Rajjo, does nothing towards her own emancipation and only hinders her children's efforts—as certainly seems to be the blunt case on the surface. It seems to me that Rajjo transmits the burdens of her containment, her repression, her burdens, very effectively. She uses, to put it in its most daring form, her children as weapons in her fight against society. But she does not reveal this, maybe does not admit it to herself, and they, certainly, imagine that are the ones in charge, the ones with a vision.

What they do not grasp, and what all of us scholars of the reforms in nineteenth-century India have not grasped, is that a woman and her life is not raw data, to be then taken up and interpreted by the reformer. She and her life are already interpreted, and in analogy with the informant's interaction with the ethnographer, the resulting text—in this case, reform or change—is the product of this interaction. The story of the reforms in nineteenth-century India is largely a story of the wills of those to be reformed, who, like Rajjo, partly taught others what had to be reformed, and largely refused to be taught themselves.

In addition, there is another kind of reform that might go unnoticed, that of ending certain cycles and not passing on cruel or thoughtless treatment received oneself to others structurally similarly placed. Just as abuse towards women comes from women as much as men, one could wake up and see that perhaps reform of women's conditions comes from women as much as men.

There are these different aspects to the mother, then. She seemingly 'sacrifices' for her children to be 'free'; it would be more accurate to say that she labours. She could do this with physical labour, which might bend or break her body. She could do it with nurture and support. More subtly, she does it often not by fighting but by resisting getting involved in fighting.

She reveals to the children what is so abused about her life, what is empty, chained, in pain. Again, she does this not through direct statement, through no strategy that anybody can point to or cite. But she shows what she wants to, although they do not always realize or read it as such.

At the same time, she does not make those whom she is educating and bringing up, sufferers of the same fate that she has had. Indeed, she reverses their future for them.

Finally, she has her own life and existence which is quite separate from them, even unknown to them, even unguessed by them. She can even scold them about belittling her hidden life, but typically she is closed about it. To their regret, they realize only later that not only did she have a life of her own, but that she had many sources of strength.

* * *

We must try to resolve this confusion about silence, as well. Is silence weakness, or is it strength? Is it something that emanates from the subject, or is it a product of the subject's associates' and reformers' inability to comprehend messages?

Rajjo's silence is interpreted by different characters differently. Babu sees it as the result of her lack of education (about which he is imprecise) and her insufficient exposure to the world. This, together with her subservient personality, results for him in her seeming a supremely dumb, passive object, comparable to a round eggplant rolling around on a plate, or a spoutless pot that can be pushed in any direction one whishes. Subodh labels his mother's silence 'weakness', calls her a 'weakling', and shouts at her to speak, to speak out, to say something. Sunaina hesitates to label her mother's silence as anything. She notices instead the calm that accompanies the silence, the dignity on the face, the strength of the silence contrasted to the incessant nagging from others.

Rajjo has her own explanation for the silence. She might say, shortly, 'I have nothing to say', when Subodh, particularly, shouts at her, but she elaborates, tellingly, 'If I listen to one side, I have to listen to others as well. Then it is difficult to act.' This importance of hesitating, of balance, is exactly what Sunaina discovers as she instinctively shies away from being either a 'victor' or a 'loser'.

The silence is contrasted mildly with dada's garrulousness, loud voice, love of monologue, authoritarianism, and opinionated personality. Where he would belittle others, including for their caste or family, Rajjo silently respects them. Where he bullies, she wins over. Where he fails to communicate, she succeeds.

The silence is more clearly contrasted with dadi's common speech, her selfish formulations, and her screams and efforts to draw attention to herself in pain. Rajjo is in pain too, but silently. She works much harder than dadi, but unnoticed. She seems to accept victimization as the target of dadi's sarcasm, but the sarcasm is such that silence could be the only dignified response.

Most of all, the silence is clearly contrasted with Babu's whimpering and whining, his confused statements and contradictory propositions. He tries various ruses to eavesdrop and elicit information, whereas mai in her silence has to try none—she gets the information she wants. He is evasive in spite of his volubility, and she is direct in spite of her silence.

Finally, the silence is contrasted with Rajjo's own clear speech at points when strictly necessary—but also, one must not forget, with her own ordinary joking and laughter with her children, proof that they were a threesome for them, and for us that she was simply an ordinary person and no tight-lipped heroine.

Silence certainly emerges as a communicative practice, one of many, and one used strategically. Given the way that the novel makes its comparisons and contrasts, and given all the implicit and explicit conceptualizations of silence, we are obliged to realize that silence is in no way inferior to other practices, but is stronger, more voluntary, and deserving of much soul-searching on the part of others.

* * *

Finally, we have to take seriously another problem that the matter of the mother gives rise to: of interpretation versus life. I state it as baldly as this, because domination works in both and is not adequately recognized as such. I have suggested above that our 'natural' interpretation of a mother like Rajjo, as of her children, is that she is weak, but that other interpretations should be formulated whereby her own spaces and strengths are recognized. Now I wish to suggest that while in interpretation we must thus 'bow down' to mai, to the 'silent, repressed women', and change the whole interpretation of reform, passivity, and freedom in nineteenth-century India; we must equally question what we want women to be. Should women be like Rajjo? Strong, dignified, and good. But also forced to marry against their will, in purdah all their lives, abused by their parents-in-law, ignored and poorly treated by their husbands? I have deliberately kept these definitions to the barest, and excluded mention of 'power', 'strength', 'freedom', and so on. I think I may presume to suggest that all the readers of this text would agree that women should not be in this position. Therefore, what the dilemma seems to resolve itself to is the following question: would the cause of women be better served by critiquing their existing conditions, or would it be better served by showing a sensitivity to its hidden compensations and positive features?

It would seem that to critique means to ignore some things, to distort others, and to finally draw back from balanced assessment. It would seem that to speak with respect and sensitivity means to hold double standards: some things are all right for others and we even appreciate them, but we would not like them for ourselves. Where we interpret a life positively, we refrain from living that life.

This seemingly familiar feminist dilemma itself gets a new twist by looking at the case of mai, and also gets a new energy in a possible impact on the studies of reform and social change in India. The new twist for feminism would be to see how, even within certain repressive structures, women can not only tolerate and act for themselves, but actively change the course of the future by refusing to participate in the repression. Many widows, as I have found, wished precisely to change the future for other potential widows like themselves (chapter 7). Then, the history of 'reform movements', as they are called, and indeed the whole history of modern India, would benefit from an enlargement of its methodology inspired by a feminist search for not only women's action and agency that is identifiable as such, but that which is more daringly defined as such.

Why, one may ask, should one bother? Novels are read not for us to judge whether we would choose the protagonist's life for ourselves. Obviously the discourse is being shifted here to one of the subject position in history. Doing that, are we not justified in inquiring after the positioning of the self, the actor, vis-à-vis that which is being studied, interpreted, reformed? In *Mai*, the positioning is as follows: young man and young woman want to reform their mother. They understand the mother as pitiable. At a certain point, the young man and young woman part company with each other: he continues to regard the mother as before, she revises her perspective to wonder whether the problem was as simple as had seemed. The book ends with her dilemma.

Although the gendering of the two reformers perhaps overstates the case—the siblings could have been two sisters and behaved exactly as do the brother and sister—one crucial factor here is certainly gender. Sunaina has the body and, she fears, the spirit of her mother, and previous ancestresses. Subodh has neither. He has inherited, if anything, his grandfather's roaring voice and spirit. Sunaina therefore has an advantage. But we can do away with this asset and perfectly well suggest that an observer of either sex could come around to seeing the problem as not that simple, the strong saving the weak. It is also the problem of vision and strength, and of understanding.

To sum up, then: *Mai* suggests a methodology for pursuing the mother, for asking a question and problematizing whose question it is. Given that it does not give the mother a direct voice, it might seem to confine her as the object of our gaze. But some of us will feel, I think, that it is not we watching and objectifying mai, but it is rather she, throughout the book, watching others, albeit non-judgmentally.

The problem is actually equally ours. For the book and its project it may be that of the 'daughterly perspective'. Its solution? Not to reinstate the mother as the subject, but the future telling of the story by the mother and daughter together, the reformer and the to-be-reformed. For us the problem is how to accept being non-judgemental, passive as that position seems. The solution? To extend the topic of study into the methodology for studying it.

II

HISTORY, ANTHROPOLOGY, AND *MAI*

Mai does what every good novel does: it serves as brilliant ethnography. It creates a world that convinces us of its reality. It is full of people with energy and conflict, it has tastes and sounds, it has clashes and resolutions, and weaves a complex net of relations between people, emotions, artifacts, and symbols. There is the credibility of the complexity, untidiness, and motion, but also the structure, weight, and holism, of everyday life. In this sense, it does, like every good piece of fiction, more than what ethnography does, because the latter, counter-intuitively, aims to tidy up, simplify, render inert and stable, and classify elegantly, and in the process, render what we know as 'life' less credibly. Since I am appreciative of the particular tasks of ethno-graphers, I will not belabour this point. What concerns me here is not any comparison, implicit or explicit, but how social scientists (anthropologists, sociologists, political scientists, historians, and others) might 'use' *Mai*. Again I am not concerned with whether they should or should not, and whether it is good or proper to do so. I recognize that fiction is used all the time by social scientists, in the classroom and in writings, and want to explore one particular case of how it could be so used.

It is easy to see that the novel works on two levels: the literal and the metaphorical. It is literally about a family in a north Indian small town over three generations, their house, fields and orchards, their place in society, the children's education and escape to wider horizons, and the inner hierarchies of the family where their mother is particularly the victim. It tells us about caste, religion, gender, colonialism, and modernity—all the staples of various branches of South Asian studies.

What it does additionally is to present layer upon layer of data that we can read metaphorically as well as literally.

The house is a metaphor for domination, repression, and freedom, at different times. The food is a metaphor for choice, service, and modernity in various contexts. Clothes are multi-vocal. The body can symbolize diverse states of being. Language, speech, and silence tell us more than they seem to on the surface.

The house has the structure of a courtyard, lined by verandahs and rooms facing inside, a passage from the inside to the outside, and an external *baithak* or sitting room where hospitality reigns. This is the design we know from histories and ethnographies, for some of us from travel and living in India. What does it do to human relations? It comments on them, of course. But, as *Mai* allows us to glimpse, it constructs them also. There is an active interaction of the house design with human lives, even a causal relationship. Dadi, when broken-hipped and in pain, can still lie there on a chaise lounge and supervise domestic activities with her sharp tongue the whole day. If she had a separate room she would be isolated and at the mercy of those who chose to come and sit by her.

Dada, like dadi, enjoys the pleasures of age and retirement: talk, food, bossing, pontification, and music. He entertains whom he likes and gets what he wants. That he does not have a closed room to bathe in and was thus observed by his grandchildren is a minor disadvantage. He is the one who has honed the inside-outside pattern to perfection. The inside is both literal—no womenfolk ever appear outside—and metaphorical: women do not sing or dance or do anything 'public'. Nothing in their inside should turn to the outside except, ironically, their teeth.

It is equally true, though unstated, that dada, the archetypical male, would not appear inside. Babu does, but in passing, to eat, to change, to greet his mother every day and chat with her, to pass to his wife purchases for the house. He has his own room there, though at sometimes he sleeps in dada's. Dada does not have a room inside. It is fair to say that in terms of 'freedom', the women are free in their own specialized space as the men are in theirs. Yes, the 'outside' does sound bigger. It allures as open and unfettered. The idea of escaping from inside to outside grows with the children. But, as Sunaina discovers, it does not benefit the bird in the sky to have a vast expanse around her, if she can cover only a small compass anyway, and sometimes as she observes, not even that, but flutter her wings in the air and remain stationary.

Mai, of course, does not need a house for confinement: she is in a purdah of her own. And yet it is the very design of the kitchen, the storeroom, and courtyard that necessitates her being bent over always. She develops a weak spine—both metaphorically and literally—from always having to pick up, clean, sort out, grind, mix, cut, and cook things bent over. And in her case the open location of these activities is not an obvious advantage. She can always be observed by dadi, who keeps up a running commentary on what she observes, ironical and implicitly critical. If mai had a closed kitchen with modern counters, she would not only have never bent over, she would have had the privacy to order her activities in her own way.

There are mixed blessings for her in other aspects of the house design. There is no master bedroom in the house, which would have of course created a twosome on the one hand and a separation from the children on the other. Like this, she stands alone, supported progressively by her children, but certainly not as a conjugal couple with her husband unless at the rare times of going out to the club. On the other hand she does not have to spend a lot of time with him, including at night, and can indulge in horseplay and crazy jokes with her son and daughter as a threesome. In 'their' room, theirs and hers. The absence of a conjugal bedroom may suggest pre-modernity and attendant lack of freedom and privacy to some. But the novel makes it clear that freedom may lie in sharing with the children instead of the spouse. Certainly the adults in the novel have not discovered companionate marriage, though there is a discernible progress through the generations: bua and *phupha*, and Babu and mai have discovered it more than dada and dadi, and Sunaina and Subodh will no doubt go on to discover it far more than any of these.

The children have infinite resources for freedom. They have the fields, the roof, the courtyard, everywhere except beyond the gates, where they go only with permission or under escort. Their experience of animals, of fruits and vegetables, no less than of human activities, is a product of the house design. When they grow up and leave, it is the house that haunts them, particularly the roof, its views, low hanging branches, the fields, the trees around, the changing seasons. In each memory, located physically in the house, is the spirit of mai.

The house has in a way created mai, at least by giving her a bad spine. but it is mai who has created the house, and neither can be said to be a prior creation. The way the house runs and every detail of its functioning is mai's personal responsibility. It runs one way when dada and dadi are alive, and another after their death—in both cases because mai wills it so. It is not mindless labour, it is not habit, and it is not simple-minded service on her part. It is what she is: someone who thinks of the house and its functioning as hers. Her activity in this regard is reconfirmed by her absence outside the house.

The house can also then be viewed as a power engine for generating sensibilities, practices, and selves, but, importantly, a power engine masterminded by mai. If we are going to make the identification of mother with home, domesticity, and the inside, as it seems from all evidence that we have to do, then we should at least re-evaluate the home with some sensitivity. Sunaina supplies us with some clues by observing at regular intervals throughout the book, that she simply had not thought about the apparent contradiction of mai's obvious strength in the middle of their more apparent weakness. Or, as she puts it yet more relevantly, she had not thought about the thought.

But the house goes beyond mai. There is an identification of the house with childhood, and with life itself. Like one's childhood and one's life, the house is suffused with something extra-material, something mystery-filled, maybe ghost-like. Old, dead ancestors appear in it, fogs and clouds enter its doors and windows, its walls echo with voices, its corners look on as if with eyes. There is a familiar image for Hindi film-goers:

ma ka dil ban ke kabhi sine se lag jata hai tu
phir kabhi nanhi si bitiya ban ke yaad ata hai tu
[You take me sometimes to your bosom like a mother,
then at other times you haunt me as if you were my little daughter (Gulzar 1961)]

It is both mother/parent and daughter/child in turn. It bears the children, it binds them, it makes them grow, it suffocates them. All they dream of is escaping it. When they escape, all they dream of is returning to it. When they are almost free, chance brings them back and binds them to it. It may not be obvious why they feel so rooted in it. The house, even while a reflection of mai and the life she has created for the children, has an independent existence: its life revolves like the seasons and continues beyond mai. But of course it is not beyond history, and when the time comes, it becomes a ruin and is abandoned by all.

We certainly have insufficient discussion in anthropology yet of how spaces work, how homes are created, lost, and remembered, how homes can control lives, and how they can become, even more than the parent, the locus of childhood and the past. Mai reminds us of this lack.

In the history of modern India, the 'public' and the 'private' are supposed to be colonial, modern creations. The novel does not shed direct light on the subject, but certainly gives us interesting insights into their working. When change has to be shown, it is through the 'creation' of a modern bathroom: what has never been private before is made so by modernity. The creation of 'privacy' through doors and partitions, as in the new dining room and bathrooms, may be the signifier of modernity, but has multilayered repercussions. Mai is the ultimate private person. Her observance of privacy is such that even her daughter has never seen so much as her naked back. Is this modern or pre-modern? We have noted that husbands and wives do not have private bedrooms, but the children and mai do. Should we interpret conjugal privacy as modern and parent–child privacy as pre-modern?

A significant denoter of modernity is the written word. The two ways in which this appears in the novel are as forms: application forms to be signed and acceptance forms to be received, and as letters. Forms are markers of passage from one phase of life to another, signed by the more co-operative parent, mai, who thus makes possible all the important changes in the lives of her children. Acceptance forms are received facilitated by her 'sacrifice' and that of those emulating her. Letters are the ultimate bearers of truth. Mai begins to write one but never does write it, and her children suspect it was a farewell note to a suicide or an escape. She has received exactly one letter ever, and for this she has no private repository. The fire-hot messenger from her past is merely tucked away within the yellowing paper of a photo frame. Sunaina writes many, by contrast, about her new life and all its dramatic events, and receives many, including from boyfriends. These are her private property, and must not be opened or read by anyone. One could suggest that modern education has made the difference. The pre-modern Indian, the 'essential' Indian of E.M. Forster who cannot resist idly perusing a letter lying on a mantelpiece while awaiting his host, and the Babu who deliberately reads every letter received by his children, is replaced by the modern Indian who expects and demands that what is addressed to her should be for her eyes only. But this suggestion is belied by the character of mai. She is not modern-educated, but she fully and sincerely respects the privacy of letters. Similarly she respects other 'modern' conventions, of the privacy and inviolability of friendships and other love relationships.

What dominates the novel, the reader may feel, is the constant creation of food. From the very beginning, people are what they eat, except mai, who is what she cooks. Dada and dadi's gourmet tastes mark them out as hedonists, as Old World non-realistic self-indulgers, who scoff at mundane notions of diet and exercise.

The contrast between East and West, old and new, is drawn simply and lightly. Most importantly, it is not the only line of division. That is, foods could be classified according to: whether they were approved by dadi or not; easy for mai to produce or not; nutritious according to Sunaina or not; digestible by Babu or not. A food from 'England' or 'the village' would be better represented on these grids rather than as Indian or Western, modern and pre-modern. Dadi demonstrates perfectly how one could enjoy any Western or modern dish without making a dent in her 'indigenous' preferences. Sunaina and Subodh, when both emancipated and free, miss their old foods and, it is implied, do not give them up.

Dada and dadi's abandonment with food reflects not only their carelessness with their own health, but their carelessness with others' convenience as well. Subodh and Sunaina are obliged to eat over-greasy, overcooked foods, and mai, most of all, to produce whatever may strike the fancy of the elders, so that she is 'always cooking'. Babu, in his spartan choices, displays the complicated nature of domination. It is not always with gentleness and quietness as well. His food demands are the opposite of dada and dadi's, but equally exploitative of mai.

As for other treasures in the novel about other staples of enquiry: caste, language, religion, the rural–urban contrast, I do not think I would like to belabour them, but simply to suggest their potential.

Caste is a shadow presence throughout the book—as one may argue it is in India itself—through allusions to servants, unseemliness, the outside, people's pasts and futures, and the unembarrassed prejudices of dada's jokes. Mai does not have to be a modern, educated character, simply a humane, practical one, for her to have the dirty dishes scrubbed by a sweeper woman when necessary. Equally, we can imagine that dada, for all his prejudices, would not forfeit the pleasures of music or conversation—or rather, of monologues to a captive audience—simply because the people in his sitting room belonged to castes lower than his own.

The languages in the house include chiefly Bhojpuri, 'clean' Hindi, and English, and then some mixtures of these. The range from them is plotted on an axis of education and exposure to the outside.

Dadi is presumably unlettered and speaks only a rural dialect, which I as the translator of this book unfortunately have no talent to represent in another code. Her being uneducated means no lowering of her power or status, no shortcoming in her self-confidence, and no lack of knowledge on any topic of relevance, from housekeeping to religion to ethics.

Mai is a First Arts pass, that is, a graduate of class 12, and speaks clean Hindi like her husband and father-in-law, who have seen the world. She dresses the same as her mother-in-law, in a traditional style *sidha palla* (the sari end over her right shoulder), and acts the same as homemaker and server, but speaks differently to her. We can see this difference in language and speech reflected in the unmitigated suspicion that dadi harbours towards mai. She is even accused of corresponding with her former suitor, one suspects because of her education.

Babu and dada, in spite of their firm adherence to the superiority of age and sex, are consumed with a love of the symbols of modernity, most of all the English language. To some extent, dadi and mai share this love as well, but they have almost nothing to lose. The story of dada and Babu's losses at the feet of the goddess of English, as it were, is in a way the whole narrative of modern India. Did not every generation in turn feel that the next generation should learn English and its wider culture better than themselves, and that this learning would somehow be confined to a technical mastery and not spill over to the rest of life? That the young man or woman would merely attend a fancy college but not then take dreams of freedom seriously and want to break away from 'home'? That the young person would not discover a 'self' that had to be further discovered and satisfied, rather than be satisfied with the self reproduced on the model of his or her forbears?

As I see it, every generation of the educated classes in India has done this to different extents (Kumar 2000) and has refused to face the obvious conclusions to be drawn from the lessons of other generations. That no one can learn merely a language. When the language learnt stands for a culture, then it is particularly difficult not to take what 'words stand for' to heart. It is not just that Sunaina and Subodh become fluent in English and use English words. It is that they take 'English' or 'Western' concepts of the self utterly seriously, seek freedoms, and discover truths that come with their new language. There is thus, in the book, not merely the play of Bhojpuri, Hindi, and English languages and their mixtures, but the play of Bhojpuri,

Hindi, and English discourses and English discourses and their mixtures.

The rural–urban continuum is related to that of the languages, in that the rural end is connected to Bhojpuri, and the urban, culminating in London, to English. The rural–urban contrast is drawn fleetingly with regard to the nature of consumption in the small town, displaying its rural poverty of taste in some of its markets and cinema halls. But it is drawn more powerfully with regard to the town's village-like lack of sophisticated educational institutions. Sunnyside Convent does have nuns, but they read Barbara Cartland. Only Subodh's school in the larger city can teach English properly and has all the classics in its library. Students broaden their minds on them and develop an intimacy with England along the way, and so do the women in their family through their assistance.

Then there is the insight that a novel like *Mai* gives us into the meanings of religion in India today. Rajjo, as the dutiful daughter-in-law of a high caste Hindu family, keeps scores of fasts, almost exclusively for her husband and son's well-being, and like all such wives and mothers, believes in keeping them. The power that accrues from fasts and the accompanying lifestyle, as I argue (chapter 7) includes both the power of the image of such a person (even dadi respects her daughter-in-law for her lifestyle) and the internal power of the ascetic whose energies are increased by such concentration. Sunaina believes that the image is fallacious, but that the internal power is real. A summation, we might say, of a change in Hinduism which is powerful as social structure, but not as cognitive structure.

Babu fasts and prays too, but with an evocatively described reliance on his wife's prior preparations, and a simple pleasure in the culmination of the fast. The description of his eating can make us only relate to him with bemusement. There is, by contrast, no description ever of what mai enjoys, only of what she wants to eat because it is stale or leftover. But Babu has another hang-up: superstition. He takes literally prohibitions against proceeding with an action in the face of a sneeze or other obstacle, and more seriously, is devoted to a holy man. None of the holy man's miracles will hold up to enquiry, but Babu is not only simple-minded enough to never challenge them, he goes one step further and claims that his particular guru is the origin of all religions everywhere. His exaggerated simple-minded religiosity is a counterpoint to the suave pleasures of dada, to the aesthetically enjoyable practices of mai, to the mechanical scriptural recitations of dadi, and to the rationalistic questioning of the brother and sister. If we add to this the professionalism of the guru, and the imputed backwardness of the servants Hardeyi and Bhondu, we might have exhausted the larger part of the varieties of religious practice in India.

An important dimension of Rajjo's character is her refusal to take up the gauntlet thrown by her husband regarding the dangers of the various liaisons of their children. The one with the foreigner is dangerous, but the really threatening one is the one with the Muslim. Who is he, how serious is Sunaina, is she planning to marry him? These are Babu's questions and no amount of prodding from him will make mai ask them of Sunaina. This is the other dimension of 'religion' and 'rationality' in India. A relatively uneducated, untravelled person like Rajjo, herself cast as a shadow and a victim, does not have any problem in respecting her daughter and daughter's choices of friends, no matter who or what they are. She does not ever pass judgement but waits patiently for them to reveal themselves, and then rests. Respect for 'difference', it is suggested, does not lie only with the modern, nor, paradoxically, does humanism, but rather the reverse.

Mai comments on the colonial aspect of India equally succinctly. The patriarch, dada, has made his image as a 'freedom fighter' and informally as well, bested several Englishmen at various things, even while doing whatever is necessary in the British mode, such as having a portrait made, or having dadi get an artificial hip. He is resolutely non-anglicized in his lifestyle, to the extent of having a distaste for gadgets, and a pronounced taste for 'feudal' servitude and hierarchy. It is a familiar personage, one that makes us question the virtues of resistance to modernity, even if it is colonial modernity.

Babu's is the other resistance, but similarly convoluted. He prefers his wife in purdah, his daughter silent, and he himself subservient to his father. He worships a godman, eats austerely, and is the proverbial good son. But he frequents the club, and admires his son's burgeoning competence in a global world.

Close in importance to the major themes of house and food is the body. Many bodies 'break' at different points and it is difficult to classify them simply. Indeed they work towards different purposes. The longest lasting is the problem of Rajjo's body. Rajjo stoops, and her stooping, from the first line of the book, is a metaphor for a weak will. That she is always bent over is her choice and leads, as expected, to constant, incurable pain and a habit she cannot and will not change.

It goes with her sacrificing herself and her putting herself second before all, to prostrate herself metaphorically before all, to negate herself in favour of their needs and wishes. To a historian of British India, the metaphor evokes the similarity between women and the colony. The colonized were seen, and to some extent grew to see themselves as 'small', 'servile', 'effeminate', as opposed to the colonizers, who were tall, upright, and manly.

Dadi's hip breaks in a fall and her limp and accompanying enforced leisure is merely a part of her aging. But, important to note, the aging is not mental aging at all. Even without teeth and in spite of the doctor's orders, she eats with gusto and adores everything new. Similarly she can keep up her matriarchal discipline in the house without the use of good legs. We understand that her disability is an asset to her in disguise, because she now cannot do any work and mai, perforce, must do everything.

Babu's case tells us a great deal about the sources of women's strength, therefore, of their weakness. He becomes disabled in an accident and mai spends the rest of his life waiting on a helpless invalid. The significance of this lies in the rude extension of her servitude by fate. She cannot do anything but be at Babu's side all the time now, even to the point of having to now share the same bedroom—which was one bond she had been free from so far. Yet, mai is not unhappy. To be at the helm of affairs brings out her hitherto dominated strengths. She speaks louder, she commands, she expects and gets obedience. The death or invalid status of the husband can become, we realize, a new lease of life for the wife or widow. The once-powerful man can become an empowering figure for the woman when broken. There is a new freedom and vitality for the female with the death, or disfigurement, of the male,

So, Rajjo was not *inherently* a spineless creature, as the author seemed to have suggested. Indeed, as I write, I look out of the window (in India) and see in the space of one minute two working women striding along with baskets on their heads. They walk tall and could be models in a finishing school. A question regarding being 'bent over' comes to mind. Does the posture of the women get transferred to their actual strength, in their family, community, and world-at-large? If they are strong and straight in their walk, surely they do not cook and serve others at home 'bent over'? If they don't, if they remain as deliberately upright as on the road, then we know we are dealing with a class issue. Rajjo is what she is because she is part of a certain kind of middle-class patriarchal household. Hers is not the problem of 'Indian women', or of 'mothers', and certainly not of 'women'.

But if they do, that is if the working women are tall and straight-backed on the street and bent over at home, then we must question the correlation between physical cowering and psychological cowering. Bending over may be a habit for the woman, may be even a convenient habit, it may be a pose or attitude; it may transmit some gratification, as of a role well played, a value well enforced, a self-satisfaction enjoyed. It does not denote that she is cowering inside, or is actually subordinating herself. It could be like the purdah, or any other play-acting, device, or impersonation. It has its uses and conveniences. You observe yourself doing it. It does not make you into something that you are not. Yes, it could become oppressive if, like a permanent mask, there is no escape from it. But it could have its compensations.

Rajjo's bending over seems to be of this latter kind. She is in fact the strongest character in the book, insofar as she has amazing principles that she never betrays regarding her children's privacy, their right to decide and choose, and the dignity inherent in them and indeed in every human being. She is even heroic and is certainly enviable in this strength of hers. Plus she is superlative at the more predictable things: keeping everything synchronized and harmonious in the house, everyone satisfied, all wheels oiled and rolling.

Again, we are not surprised. We come back to the matter of the mother. Mothers are known to have strengths, most ostensibly to decide, control, manipulate—none of which is particularly hidden. Yet they seem to be puppets who dance to everyone's tune, even when they are known to have solid cores, definite shapes, and rock hard resistances. We have repeatedly suspected that mothers are pretending to more weakness than they deserve pity for.

The feminist reader is given a puzzle, which is exactly what the social scientist must deal with. Mai, the mother, is not as weak or helpless or in need of rescuing as would seem by every objective criteria. She has immense reservoirs of strength, which can be observed at odd times and even all the time with some insight. But besides that, there is a problem of definition. What is strength? What is bondage and what is freedom? If Rajjo does not need to be rescued, is it because she is placid and ignorant and suffers from false consciousness: or is it because the narrator has few tools of empathy and experience to interpret the rewards of Rajjo's life as being lived by her? Who is wrong, the old/traditional/unquestioning woman or the young/modern/ questioning woman?

The author seems to pronounce judgement in favour of the old, and seems to describe the younger woman as regretting her simplified, one-dimensional view of mai. But, do we not feel convinced that, given the nature of the house, her husband, her in-laws, and her duties, Rajjo is indeed confined? She had a lover once and cannot even write to him or see him again. She is belittled as a cook and housewife by her mother-in-law. She is forbidden to hum or sing, to dress up or to go out, by her husband and father-in-law in turn. She is supposed to have no powers to take decisions and is therefore not expected to. Only when the older people die off and her own husband gets bed-ridden, does she take more and more decisions, explores more of her personality. This is a familiar generational cycle for Indian women. But she does not have even a name, and she does not care that her daughter, too, has one that will partly be erased. Between her cooking and feeding, no matter how excellently, and her namelessness and her silences, no matter how peaceable, do we not pity her?

Maybe it just underlines the hidden side of history, what many historians would acknowledge but not do anything about. And others besides historians, because

maternity has always been the repressed term in the family plot. Just as the matronymic is blanked out by the patronymic, just as the mother's lineage is forfeited to the father's and just as maternal discourse has been governed by paternal law, so the mother herself has had to die to narrative possibility. Associated with blood, flesh, materiality, she has appeared so intransigently imminent, the literary, indeed cultural, authority has been predicated on a transcendence or a repudiation of her being (Gilbert and Gubar 1994: 378).

Mai presents us with a mother-heroine, like Sethe (Morrison 1987), who can leave us questioning the joys of motherhood.

If this can remain an open matter—to pity or not to pity Rajjo— then we have literature here that teaches social scientists something. It supports my long-felt agreement with what Virginia Wolf says in *The Pargiters*, 'It would be far easier to write history [than fiction, but] that method of telling the truth seems to me so elementary, and so clumsy, that I prefer, where trust is important, to write fiction' (Woolf 1967:9).

This may be easier said of the matter of the mother than all the other ethnographic stuff in the novel. After all, whose is the representative voice on 'India'—the author's, the narrator's, the characters'? How do we readers know it speaks with authority? At which point should we suspend our disbelief willingly?

I am interested in childhood and mothering and associated processes. I recollect, on reading *The God of Small Things* (Roy 1998) that while I loved the depiction of childhood in that novel, I thought there had been a grievous mistake in drawing the character of the mother and her lover. Or, one could have a familiarity or even intimacy with a place or a people and therefore either trust the author, or suspect the author of making a mistake regarding them. I know weavers, and specially the weavers of Banaras, and Abdul Bismillah in *Jhini Jhini Bini Chadariya* (1996) gives a masterful portrayal that wins my sincerest admiration and envy. But I know Lucknow too and feel little empathy for Amritlal Nagar's Lucknow. Because I know too little? Because I do not know the kinds of people he is writing about? Because he has failed?

What this tells me is to be prepared for what the fiction text does versus what the social science text does, and what each does not. The former does not systematize, theorize, or generalize. It is not in search of reality, because it *is* a reality. Reality lies within it. The latter worries about all exceptions (worries, if not in the text itself, then in the critique of it). It wants to present what reality is, either as statement or as negation. Because a text, as Umberto Eco would say, is a lazy machine that expects its reader to do some of its work. The reader must assess some of her own needs and expectations when approaching the text, and of course, her competence. We may say that there is a complementarity of emotion and objectivity that has to be supplied to the text and by the text, and the particular mixture must be worked out in each case.

Having said all of which I would not say that I know what a work of fiction *is*, or what a social science text *is*, and wherein therefore lies the exact, the *is-ness* of, difference between them.

III

ON TRANSLATION

I am uncomfortable with the role I seem to be performing—that of the critic certain of the 'nature' of literature and of the way to read it, convinced of the mimetic view of literature, holding the belief, as it were, that: 'The task of literature is to render life, experience, and emotion in a potent way; the job of criticism is to reveal the true value and meaning of the rendition—a rendition at once contained within the literary work and yet, paradoxically, needing the critical act to reveal it' (Rice and Waugh 1989: 2-3).

This humanist, empiricist, and idealist view that takes language to be transparent and experience to be prior, is exactly what I would like to eschew. Unfortunately, I do not know of a way to do so as translator, and as a social scientist who wants to deliberately 'use' *Mai*. I accept that my translation is an interpretation, and along with this more direct discussion, is obliged to repeat the endlessly repetitive agenda that reading literature comprises, never to reach a certain or final reading of the text, and certainly not an explanation of it.

Mai is of profound interest to me because it does at the level of fiction what I strive to do through history and anthropology: to show that although public voices 'decree that the course of history should shape itself this way or that way, being manfully determined to control the course of events', private domestic lives move silently forward, whose importance we do not always have a vocabulary to convey (Woolf 1978: 172 in Gilbert and Gubar 1994: 17). The strength of supposed weakness, the splendour of supposed dullness, the paradox inherent at the heart of power, is what many vocabularies do convey, but social science can do only approximately. Marianne Moore is only one instance of many artists when she emphasizes this paradox, as when celebrating, beyond the envious will to self-aggrandizement that constructs history, 'the power of relinquishing/what one would keep; that is freedom' (Moore 1967: 144).

Then it is of interest to me because *Mai* is a feminist novel, not only a novel about women or speaking to women. Its feminism works at different levels. It takes gender to be socially constructed, and therefore capable of being reconstructed. Rajjo is brought to our consciousness through the burgeoning consciousness of her daughter, as someone with a past, someone who was many things in potentio before she became 'only' a wife, daughter-in-law, and mother, although she seems to be only these things par excellence. She herself does not cultivate these identities in her daughter.

Mai uses some of the tropes of feminist writing, such as the narrativizing and problematizing of the past. *Mai* is about the past, seemingly about a world passed and gone, but actually about its construction, what it *seemed*, its meanings, its uses.

The protagonist, while thus establishing her relationship to the past, breaks with it and redefines it in overt ways. The mother is herself not very educated, does not read or paint or discuss, and equates the world outside her kitchen with 'school and college'. The aunt scoffs at painting. The grandmother despises everything that is not measurable by the yardsticks of men, specially her son. The daughter, in contrast, begins to paint to portray facelessness and (to write?) to give voice to silences. She is doing so not to produce a commercially marketable cultural artifact (as her brother wants to push her to do) but to express herself. This expression runs into a lot of trouble with questioning of the relative gain and loss. She gains freedom, but there is suspicion of a possible 'loss of women's inheritance' (Jacobus 1979: 10).

Lastly, it could be seen to be feminist in a narrower sense. The author and translator/critic of the book are certainly consciously producing cultural artifacts, but through them both coming to terms with the paradoxes of 'woman' and breaking in little possible ways with historically established denials of women to artistic and literary discourse. The writing itself both articulates protest and enacts it. But even so, they make themselves part of the universal process of the 'historical' and the articulated feeding off the 'a-historical' and the muted. It is the conditions of the 'ordinary women's life' that they write about. It is a presentation and interpretation of that which bestows importance on 'the ordinary woman' but also importance, through her non-subjective presence on the author and translator (Woolf 1967: 142).

The question is a large and all-encompassing one for women and feminism, partly intuited, partly understood. Strength can well lie outside oneself, in connection with details 'outside', typically humbler and duller than 'history'. Whether this is a durable difference appropriately labelled 'the feminine', or only historically so, it is certainly a deliberate and reflexive difference with other sorts of strengths.

* * *

As if I was already not being ambitious enough in this introduction, I cannot resist musing aloud on my experience with translating, particularly with the transitions of a cultural nature that occur when translating from Hindi to English.

The reason I am interested in the Hindi to English question is because of its embeddedness in a politics. The politics arises from a history where colonialism has decreed that the Orient, India, its languages, its imagery, its very ambience is to be ranked lower than the Occident and *its* languages and imagery.

I want a character in a book to be true to herself. Rajjo is that, Sunaina is that, Babu, dada, and dadi even more so. But that is as long as they speak their own language. When we turn their speech into English, the syntax goes wrong, the vocabulary becomes absurd, and one would have to labour without rest with every single image to get it just right without any guarantee of succeeding. I believe there is no escape form this problem. I believe the problem is exacerbated by the fact that English is used regularly in India and has a wealth of connotations—syntax, vocabulary, and image-related. But I think the problem is really bigger. Because, why, otherwise, would it infest not only the speech of characters but everything else in the book as well?

Why cannot one describe a house in English without tremors of dissatisfaction (I crave pardon for sounding melodramatic if I do, but I trust some of my readers at least will share my totally physical reactions to language use)? Because there is an untransability to *angan*. I can be a woman of my time, even one with a remarkable post-modernist consciousness, and wonder in my angan every day. But an American woman of the present cannot possibly walk in a courtyard unless she goes to the Cloisters for the purpose. Even as I say this I seem to suggest that the angan/courtyard is from the past; if it exists today there is an incongruity, a quaintness. What I would like to say is that there is an orientalist fog we cannot escape whenever we present India in English, if the consciousness of the narrator has been originally expressed in an Indian language. And there is a modernist fog which creates a hazy hierarchy. Residents of the Western world would quite regularly rank India both as 'non-modern' and 'lower' than a Western country. In the English language, then, all the things of India—courtyards, brass pots, lamps and wicks, bamboo curtains, fruit juices—are not simply things with various properties, they are things that belong to an inferior, non-modern world.

We can accept that there are in Hindi—as in other Indian languages, but I will speak of Hindi from now as a case—some examples of certain genres, say, of detective thrillers, which are written in a way that when translated might read exactly like an English language thriller, sans all image or ambience of anything non-Western. I don't know. Because I don't know what really is Indian or Western and therefore what may be non-Indian or non-Western. Not because the distinctions and the essences don't exist. But because they lurk everywhere, they defy all definitions, they defeat categorization, they spill over and stain boundaries.

There are words such as *prasad, charanamrit,* and *gangajal* for which this fact can be explained as part of their religious connotations. But there are others, which probably *seem* to have a religious connotation, and this is precisely part of the problem, such as *anchal* or *desi ghee.* If we try to translate 'apron' into Hindi, we come up against a comparable situation: there is no one corresponding word; the word in the original is too multi-vocal to be rendered by a tight translation; its beauty lies in its complex symbolism, stretching back into centuries, and forward into changing lives, and all this can never be conveyed without a veritable dissertation of a footnote. Which, for some of us at least, should have an etymological content, something like the unabridged OED.

Much of the time, however, the meaning 'changes' hopelessly. This usage of a term connoting a fixed nature or essence, is permissible only to the 'insider', one who is savouring as her 'own' certain images and expressions, and then, equally as an 'insider' in the other language, is struggling to assert her mastery over language by approximating these images as best as possible. She 'knows', as would any unusual reader who actually sat down to compare the two versions, that the meaning changes even with the best of intentions and efforts. There is then, not so much an essence, as a structure of relationships that gets wrenched loose from the slight adjustment of any of its parts. The new structure may be elegant, convincing, otherwise faultless, but it is 'different'. When Babu says, '... *nahin karenge bhai...*' (translated evasively be me, p. 52), there is a complex of sensibilities—class, gender, age, and personal—that cannot be carried over intact into any expression in English. He says *karenge* and not *karunga* (an aspect of class and region), he says *bhai* and not *Sunaina* (gender, age, and personality), and he gives his statement an overall abstractness and passivity that is his personality. This is an exercise that could be prolonged into book length, analyzing every nuance of the original for its history, philosophy, and narrative thrust (as in Damsteegt 1997). I do not pursue this line at all because I am not interested in how the author says what she does, or the translator does what she has to, but in what the author says and we can know through the translation.

Therefore, interested much more in the content than the form, my discussion is doomed to appear like a fixing or pinning down of the real or actual intent of the text. The problem with a translation is that it is based on the assumption of non-availability of the original and the corresponding monopoly of the translation to convey the meanings of the text. I see no recourse from this. In this discussion, however, I would like to emphasize *this* hierarchy, of all the hierarchies of discourse that inevitably exist within and surrounding a text. I emphasize that *Mai* in the original, and hopefully in the translation, is not a realistic text, unreflexively privileging one discourse as true, conflict-free, and therefore superior. I hope, further, to position myself in a way that what I am making here are 'propositions' and not enunciations, propositions based on the recognition of the 'stereographic plurality' of the text (Barthes 1983).

* * *

Then we come to another aspect of translation. We are reading as women, that is, being constructed and constructing ourselves as female readers. We are writing as women, as feminist, postcolonial, in my case, ethnosociological consciousnesses. But where does this consciousness come from, what is it grounded in?

I can answer for myself. Hindi is my mother tongue. I realized for the first time while doing this translation why the cadences of 'Indian English' sound so natural to me: a mistake, but a natural mistake. *'Mai se zyada ham hi dyorhi men mandrate rahte'* will naturally occur to a Hindi speaker as 'More than mai it was we who kept hanging around the house'. A Brit might say; 'We were the ones who, rather than mai, seemed to be unable to leave the house.' A Brit and maybe some of us Indians who have been trained in schools like Subodh's. The point is not a comparison of Indians' English versus English people's. Professor Higgins confirmed years back that only foreign people can speak correct English because they are trained in it unlike English people. I have two quite other points to make. First, whatever my natural desire in translation might be, I will choose to use correct English because, simply speaking, the characters in the novel, as well as the narrator, are all using their language 'correctly' and without a hint of exoticism, quaintness, awkwardness, etc. To do this I have to know this correct English, which only one who has been in the privileged class of Indians with a certain education can know. Second, most such Indians themselves do not know their own mother tongue as well, either currently or colloquially. They function, including writing creatively, think, and dream in English.

I am not interested in the merits or demerits of this right now. What I want to puzzle about is, how then do we know this mother tongue (second or third language as it becomes) at all, and what status does it have? It has a peculiar pull, is my claim, for embedded within it is a political commitment known in shorthand as 'mine' and 'my'. Generations of Indians through the nineteenth and twentieth centuries, five to nine generations by a rough count, have had this experience. Their formal training has been totally in English, and they have picked up their mother tongue on all sides alongside. From their relatives, their servants, the streets, popular events and culture, more elevated arts, the sounds of the world around them. This builds a base and a love, both together the motivation for a politics. Then, with maturity, there has taken place a self-education, and a learning, through books, if not a teacher, of the mother tongue in adulthood.

· This was the course followed by me and others I know personally. This translation is infested by a double politics: that which allowed me to have an involuntary knowledge of English better than my mother tongue, involuntary on my side and due to the decision of my *mother* and father. And then, in the second turn of the screw, when I understood the implication of this state of affairs, sensed dimly some injustice in the world, and sought vaguely to rectify it by blundering around with some kind of self-education in Hindi. I must note for the record that as a spoken language I always associated Hindi more with my mother than my father. Fathers in general are more educated formally and therefore more fluent in English which they then try to speak to their children. Apart from English, what my own father spoke was Urdu; what he had studied was Arabic and Persian. I cannot to this day say I have ever seen a Hindi word written in his hand, apart from the shaky *Om Ganeshay namah, Om Lakshamay namah* that he wrote on a new notebook every Diwali puja.

In South Asian history and politics, the sociological position of the mother, and the work of the mother beyond what is stereotypically understood as 'mothering', must be taken seriously. She does not simply nurse and nurture, feed and socialize. She teaches and transmits a language correctly in this context known as the mother tongue, even though, given the capital possessed by formal schooling, she does this only incompletely. But she builds a base that the grown child's burgeoning politics can build on.

That the child 'acquires language through interactions with the linguistic autonomy of a maternal rather than paternal figure' (Gilbert and Gubar 1994: 391) has significance beyond the case of South Asia. Kristeva would argue that the symbolic linguistic order being primarily partiarchal, the maternal can never have a voice within it except through the very structures which repress it. Thus, 'As long as there is language-symbolism-paternity, there will never be any other way to represent this nature/culture threshold, this instilling the subjectless biological program into the very body of the symbolizing subject, this event called motherhood' (Kristeva 1984: 241-2). But my language is more my mother's than my father's and the obstacles in representation of motherhood are more historical and cultural than eternal or essential.

I feel the need to call my Hindi my mother tongue. Is English, then, a later accretion, the father tongue, the language of formal schooling, career and advancement, formality and reason? Or, even as Thoreau (unwittingly) put it, when those in my position rediscover the mother tongue, is it that 'The one is commonly transitory, a sound, a tongue, a dialect merely, almost brutish, and we learn it unconsciously, like the brutes, of our mothers. The other is the maturity and the experience of that; if that is our mother tongue, this is our father tongue, a reserved and select expression' (Thoreau 1973: 95).

The 'problem' of the mother is also the problem of the 'mother' tongue. And equally insoluble. But equally, I hope, worthy of being pursued.

10

Learning Modernity?
The Technology
of Education in India

Let us begin by taking an ethnographic journey in pursuit of schools in a non-metropolitan urban centre in north India, which I shall call by the apocryphal name of Janabad. The first thing that strikes us is the amazing variety of schools. The most prominent are the so-called English-medium schools. Their names range form Tiny Tots to Oxford Public School, including a Harvard and a Cambridge, two St Joseph's, a St Mary's, a St John's, a St Atulanand, and a St Vyas. There are Temple Bells and Glorious Academies, and innumerable Little Birds, Sun Beams, Moon Rays, Golden Boughs, Margaret, Thomas and Don/ Dawn 'Public Schools', 'Academies', and 'Convents'. The names of these are not normally heard in public life in Janabad, my suspicion being that the names do not sit comfortably on the tongues of those referring to all these schools generically as 'convent schools'.

Then there are the Hindu, Urdu-Arabic, and Sanskrit-medium schools, each of which also pronounce their status by their nomenclature. The Hindi schools are typically named after role models such as Tulsi Das or Madan Mohan Malaviya. But the cultural fund to be gained from such naming gets lost as children and the public reduce the names to undifferentiated barebones: TVS, CHS, DPS, and so on. Madrasas are typically springs, gardens, and centres of learning in flowery Arabic. Non-madrasa Muslim schools are non-committal about religion in public, and even severely nationalist, calling themselves City Girls' School and National Public School. Sanskrit schools all name the patron and only the patron, thus: Rani Chandravati, Goinka, Marwari, and Sri Nandlal Bajoria Sanskrit schools.

Naming can provide insight into history, even the history of the nation. Within a survey of the names of schools in any provincial Indian city is summed up the history of education in South Asia. And not just the narrative of the colonial state's administrative history, but the parallel narratives of the march of missionary education, the fate of vernacular education, and the hidden histories of family and community. In any provincial town of north India there is the following pattern. The oldest schools will have been set up by a local *rais* or aristocrat, if a raja or maharaja was not around, and will be named after his father or grandfather. The other large schools will have been founded by: the Agrawalas, the Khatris, the Marwaris, the Thakurs, the Kayasthas and other upwardly mobile castes or caste clusters, by organic intellectuals from within the community, educated in indigenous ways often called 'illiterate' in government records. Some of those based on caste will be actually founded by widows, who have deliberately used their marginal status to occupy subject positions for themselves. The madrasa and non-madrasa Islamic schools will be differentiated among themselves according to sect and emphases on modernity. In the provincial capitals and larger towns, the most popular schools are certain to be the Christian missionary ones. If the town is too small to have any, there will be the simulated versions, that is, non-Christian, but sporting 'Saint' in their names or with names that are self-indulgently cute. My favourite is 'Kiddy Convent'.

Names of course have more serious implication yet. As in other cultures, past and present, names in India are regarded as isomorphic with reality or even able to create reality. Thus names are not just images, as images are not just images, but transfer unpredictable force and meaning to objects which are thus named. A name can bring an object to life. We should remember that even the Hindu College (f.1817 in Calcutta, today's renowned Presidency College) was given that name by the founding committee because that was understood to demonstrate its 'Hindu-ness' although the curriculum was the secular one of government schools and what the school became renowned for was its anti-Hindu stance. Similarly there are schools today that declare themselves to be based on Montessori principles. Others evoke the Vedas, some the Qur'an, yet others the New Testament. Some conjure up the names of Gandhi, Tagore, Krishnamurti, and Sir Syed Ahmad Khan, who, together with Vivekanand and Aurobindo Ghosh, are the names listed in compilation of 'Great Indian Educators'.

Our first stop, then, on our ethnographic journey (all the excerpts below are from my fieldwork notes):

The classroom is a kind of shed, though the campus otherwise is beautiful and idyllic with old, airy buildings. In this classroom walls are broken, windows have grills like a jailhouse, and there is no lighting (the bulb is constantly stolen, says the teacher). There are typical benches and tables with no space for huge bags or books, no place for the children to climb in and out. There is a broken blackboard, broken cupboard, broken shelf and nothing on the walls but cracks and greasy spots—yet it is pleasanter than the smart Little Flower House or Kiddy Convent... .

This is the Annie Besant Theosophical School, called popularly BTS, founded 100 years ago by Annie Besant, Hindu missionary and reformer, builder of the modern nation, preoccupied with the synthesis of science and religion.

The second example:

In the Principal's office, I notice with a shock that near my feet is a metal waste paper basket from which is leaking some liquid. Looking more closely, I realize that it is pan juice, and the basket is not only wet but totally rusted at the bottom with the remains of many pan spittings. Many spittings must have also missed their mark, because the mat outside and under is liberally sprinkled with pan juice, chewed ingredients and much else... .

This is Dayanand Anglo–Vedic College, or DAV, the most impressive of the reformist–progressivist schools in terms of plant and philosophy, the plant resembling an English public school's, the philosophy that of synthesis between the most valued in traditions and the best in modern Western knowledge.

A third example:

The Montessori apparatus in the pre-school section is all packed away and I am allowed to view it in its abode of ground level shelves covered with cloth curtains. The nun explains that Montessori practices have been dropped 'in view of the preparation for the higher classes', the apparatus packed away because 'the children are of Indian background' (as she is). 'Is Montessori not a suitable method then?' I ask innocently. 'Very suitable', she tells me, 'but the place, the atmosphere, have to be suitable'. Meanwhile, it is a parents' meeting day and mothers have been dropping in. The first one has a daughter, all of four years old, who cannot learn the Hindi vowel signs and got them all wrong in dictation. She has been labouring at home continuously from then on, under the guidance of her father as well as a tutor, and gets everything right now. Sister Gita squashes this claim from the mother with no compunction. '*Abhi apko bahut mehnat karni hai. Isko nahin ata, nahia ata...*' ('You have to work much harder with her. She still doesn't know the stuff...').

This is St Mary's, a Catholic school, the actual model that every provincial school strives to follow, with its indisputably dedicated nuns, unmatched Church endowments, and invincible philosophy of rationality, uniformity, and punctuality (these qualities measured by size and action: it has the largest gates of any school in the city and they are closed the most punctually in the morning to shut out all latecomers).

I am interested in using the cases above to illustrate and discuss a series of problems today under the rubric of 'technology' and 'modernity'. Technology, as we know, is some artifact or set of artifacts related to a context of human action, including techniques of use. I include within my discussion of 'technologies' non-material circumstances as well, in the anthropological belief that dreams are as real (and as hard) as rocks.

I distinguish my approach from three major ones in the study of schooling in South Asia. Many studies describe graphically how step after step was taken on the path of building a progressively better system of education in India without questioning the actual building, that is the texts comprised by the brick and mortar of school building. But these aside, most studies do pay attention to technology if they do not call it that. Some studies describe the efforts of nationalists and conservatives to set up alternative institutions. For the nineteenth century, we have evocative studies of the Deoband madrasa (Metcalf 1982), and the Aligarh University (Lelyveld 1978), and for the twentieth century, the Krishnamurthy school in Rishi Valley (Thapan 1991), respectively. Each institution comes alive in its technological setting, Each is placed in the history of Hinduism or Islam, or nationalism, but then there is no discussion of the political and discursive effects produced within its walls. That is, what kind of subjects do they produce? Other scholars of education such as Krishna Kumar, do an interesting job of interpreting the colonial and the nationalist projects, but then leave out completely the 'how to' of these projects, so that we cannot visualize the overall sites of these projects, leave aside any details of classrooms or playing fields. That is, we know of the subjects, but what is the technology? Then finally there is the fascination ethnography of Doon School by Sanjay Srivastava, which is called, tellingly, Constructing Post-Colonial India (1998) which focuses precisely on the school as creator of a national subject. Here we have a salutary distancing from a straightforward class reproduction model of Paul Willis and the social interactions approach of most education studies. Srivastava looks at the school as the space for the production of the citizen, of the nation, and of modernity. In doing this, he does not accord the processes sufficient specificity: what makes a pedagogic institution different in so far as it is a space for children, and children are in their turn actors, albeit subaltern ones, and the commodity being produced is not only citizenship but also intelligence and stupidity, and the control of languages and narratives. That is we have both the technology and the subjects, but there is no agency and no pain. A focus on elite institutions, moreover, that are only the illusion of a real (a real that exists nowhere), shuts out illusions of other realities and there is no space left for non-elite institutions.

I choose to speak of technology because it permits me to weave together the material, the political, and the meaning-creation aspects of the process of education. And I speak specifically of non-elite institutions in a provincial city.

To simplify, let us say at the outset that the minimal technology of schooling consists of: buildings and spaces, furniture and textbooks, teachers and curricula, routines and rituals. I will not be able to touch on all these areas in my essay, and will focus on buildings and spaces, as in the first two ethnographic descriptions, and some rituals, as in the third. The purpose can be accomplished with just these few: to demonstrate how a particular kind of modern subject gets created, and a particular discourse of modernity, precisely at the sites of these classrooms and the interactions of these teachers with their students gets famed and created by the technologies of the school. My purpose is to question the nature of this subject, and the nature of our anthropology in pursuing this subject.

MAPPING

Although they are all fundamentally one, as I shall be arguing, the apparent diversity of schools in a small town requires some mapping. One division would be into the public or recognized and the private or unrecognized schools, each then further divisible according to management. There are at least five major Boards that recognize and affiliate schools. In a city like Janabad with a population of one million, there could be easily over 200 schools, counting only those that exist for at least a decade. Why there are so many is because of the phenomenal growth in the market demand for schooling, both in absolute terms and proportionate to the population.

Of the 200 plus schools that I am aware of, in a city like Janabad, 64 per cent are unaided and unrecognized. Apparently the conflict between the requirements for government recognition, and the needs of a neighbourhood, continues today, some 150 years after the system was first set up. Schools that 'survive', including unrecognized ones, cater to local needs which consist of English language and a modern syllabus. Good academic results are also needed but are seen to depend on the family's initiative, not the school's. Other considerations, such as a playground, extra-academic activities, innovative teaching or reliance on extra resources and method, do not constitute a 'need'.

The requirements for recognition, on the other hand, include facilities such as library, laboratories, and playground, which private schools do not have. What is significant is that recognized schools do not have them either. They may have them 'in name', that is there are spaces that may be pointed out to the visitor as 'games room' or 'library', or 'laboratory' but are never used by the students for the named purpose. Real facilities, actually used by the children, as required for the running of a modern, liberal school by any of the Boards, do not exist in any schools in the city.

If we were to look at the Board requirements as they are presented on paper, we might say that the rules were well meaning as premises for a liberal, modern education. Given the demand for modern schooling, the paucity of funds with public bodies to aid schools, and a popular ideology not congruent with the colonial, the rules became for the last over 100 years a non-constructive restraint and a progressively bigger bottleneck that had to be overcome by circuitous routes. Schools recognize these routes today to be—exertion of influence or power, running around to, and repeated humiliations from officers, sheer time, and perhaps bribery. In this they are playing the discursive game that characterizes all public life in India: a recognition of the utility and I will add, even of the *pleasure*, of a second parallel plane of functioning to the officially articulated one. This Indian is the 'flexible subject' who thrives with élan in condition of insecurity and seeming doubletalk, willing to accommodate contradictory demands.

In the case of schools, this duality is significant because of the 'naturalness' of the absence in all schools of the very facilities required by government boards. The cultural assumptions that underlie recognition rules are modernist ones, concerning the nature of childhood, the nature of learning, and the duties of educators. Schools and their public *do not share* these assumptions.

BUILDINGS AND CLASSROOMS

The most obvious instance of technology is perhaps the building. In India, buildings have been the citadels and indeed statements of empire. The choice of sites for studying in the early part of the nineteenth was labouriously listed by various surveyors of the indigenous scene and is available in the Reports of Howell, Kempson, Monteath, Reid, and Thornton. These sites were popularly: teacher's house, parent's house, other's house, temple, mosque, *chabutara* or garden. The subtext of the listing of these sites was a critique of their non-specialized nature and their primitive continuity of the outdoors with the indoors. The discussion invited, not any appreciation of its rationality, but only opprobrium. The critique of the possible plurality of sites was so complete that it did not have to be even articulated. A coded allusion was sufficient: 'There are no proper school buildings'. This comment summed up the negative assessment of the total educational practice.

From the middle of the nineteenth century onwards, there was a discursive shift from older legitimate understandings of teaching to a newer one. This 'progress', as it was considered by both the British and Indians, was marked by the earliest schools such as Hindu College in 1817, Jai Narain Ghoshal in 1816, to the Universities of Calcutta, Bombay, and Madras in 1857, each approximating the definitions of proper institutions in Europe. By 1900, there was no conflict or questioning left regarding the norm of the proper school building. The case of Bombay is archetypal. The architect of the Central Hall and Library of Bombay University was the famous Sir Gilbert Scott who had never visited India. He adopted a style which was 'a free variety of the eighteenth century adapted as far as I was able to judge to the exigencies of a hot climate'. The building, therefore, embodied rationality and science, paying attention to the broad points of temperature, wind, and water currents: and confirmed the authority of European architectural principles, the weight of the Greco–Roman heritage, and, of course, the authority of the colonial state. He emphasized what he saw as 'all practical considerations', such as making the Tower the loftiest and most conspicuous in the city.

In the case of each building, the foundation ceremony was now conducted with great pomp and circumstance, with hopes expressed loudly for the future of the institution as an instrument of acculturation and profound change. Lord Mayo said in Bombay: 'The building now commenced will give a fresh impetus to these objects for which the University has been founded', described otherwise as 'a moral and social training.... The native student... receives unconsciously each day a thousand moral and social as well as intellectual impressions. Only by personal experience of College life can it be known how great a change in the character is so produced in a few years' (Chatfield 1876: 226; Tikakar 1984: 30).

The new architecture was the single most dominant mark of the new era. There has been no conflict or questioning left of the model for at least 100 years. When I stress this, I am saying that this ideal of a closed, box-like school building (for gradually no more turrets or verandahs were possible) with heavy gates in front, both proclaiming some terrifying rules of discipline that can only be maintained if all is insulated from interference of the world outside, is the *norm*. However, when we look at the urban scene in the 1990s, we see—to use one of my favourite metaphors—that the stick of modernity with which the place was going to be beaten into shape has received a beating of sorts itself. Even while the normative school building in Janabad is the only model of a good school, the majority of schools, or 95 per cent of them are acceptable and popular even without their fulfilling the criteria of this school building or its corollaries: adequate playgrounds, classroom space, ventilation and lighting. 'Saraswati dwells even in little rooms' is the convenient expression of the acted out ideology.

Most schools in Janabad are housed in residences that have been donated to the school by philanthropists and do not even pretend to emulate the model. But as opposed to the tolerance expressed for these, antagonism is aroused by a building that may seek to be deliberately different, to offer an alternative to the code of heavy masonry and closed doors and suggest, perhaps, openness to the outdoors, child-centred spaces, or climate-appropriate materials such as tiles and bamboos. There is a threat inherent in this, which cannot be met except by a refusal to participate in a new dialogue, to respond to a challenge to ideas beyond a stubborn conviction of 'rightness'.

The historical explanations are the easy ones. One is the role of philanthropy in old urban centres in India, leading to schools like Bipan Behari Chakravarty Higher Secondary School, housed in an old, ornate, early twentieth-century aristocratic home with deep verandahs and high ceilinged shady rooms—all wonderful but positively not suited for use as classrooms. Such buildings are donated, and accepted, with grace and gratitude. As expansion becomes inevitable, new classrooms are created with tin or asbestos siding, on the roofs, all around in the compound, and spawning all over corridors and verandahs. I wish to emphasize the range this includes. There is W.H. Smith Memorial School founded by an Englishman's widow and immensely popular because of its suggested resemblance to a 'convent'. There is Sir Syed Public School started by the Aligarh Old Boys' Association as a 'reply' to Christian and Hindu schools. In both cases, all semblance of the original plan has been lost as classes meet in the verandahs, in the courtyard, in front of offices, and literally in nooks and crannies—in the case of residential buildings, in bathrooms and garages. Historically, any acquired space may be used for any stated purpose, and failure or success in achieving the purpose is not attributable to the space. While I use the term 'historically' loosely here, I mean it as both a discernible characteristic of 'The History of India' and also of the awareness of tradition with which people choose. In all these cases, the crowding is of no interest to the educators, including all those who enthusiastically discuss 'the problems of Indian education' where space, classroom, or building finds no mention. No educator or alumni of a school ever commented voluntarily on the physical properties of their school, either with relation to its excellence or mere satisfactoriness and, never at all, inferiority.

Such a persisting pattern in history might provoke us to attribute the indifference to space to a notion of non-materiality. Are Indians, both Hindus and Muslims as we see, but additionally Sikhs, Jains, Buddhists, and Christians, characterized by an unarticulated cultural grammar of the possibility of any and all achievement merely through internal resources, and not external ones? One may also pose another question of great contemporary relevance to the anthropology of the nation state. One's common sense understanding is that the ideology of the nation state is transmitted and reproduced in actual sites: the office, the railway, the newspaper, the school. But its propagation may well be achieved through images, not even the images on a screen or in a book, but in the mind and in the rhetoric of words. The grandiose architecture of a neo-Gothic style college set up in the nineteenth century may be reduced to local tropes through posters on the walls, peeling paint, overgrown flora, garbage, and cows depositing their dung freely around the campus. Yet the only imaged ideal of a 'college' that is positively reinforced in the whole population remains that of the colonial-style college.

This particular fate of the modernizing project in small towns in India is significant. These small towns are India, with their seeming resistances, compromises, and maladjustments. 'India' is not the postmodern rediscoveries of variety in traditions and the arts, such as regularly encountered in the metropolitan centres. Yes, the different composition of symbolic capital in the metropolises and provinces of India may give us an insight into the problem. Veena Das's argument for continuing the focus on local experiences and practices as constitutive of contemporary human existence in postcolonial societies is indeed a powerful one, one which she then works out in her own study of the suffering of the victims of Bhopal (Das 1996). What I seek to do is to extend the meaning of 'critical events' to go beyond tragedies and disasters easily recognizable, such as the Babari masjid demolition and the response to the Mandal Report, to the everyday disaster and tragedy of life in small-town India, such as in its classrooms. If the nation is the simulation of the real and acts itself out in theatres such as elite public schools, the threat to it comes not only from specific action of the communal, the ignorant, and the chaotic, but continuously from the populations of small towns (which are of course, according to this terminology, ignorant and chaotic).

People in Janabad, even while paying lip service to the ideology of the nation state, do not modify modern school buildings beyond recognition, because they are *ignorant*. In modifying them or finding alternatives, they are distancing themselves from the play-acting of Delhi, and theatres like the Doon School. They are sceptical of the liberal nation state, openly dismissive of its civilizational claims, and finally, not overly threatened by its coerciveness. There is certainly a clash of two contrary discourses: a modern one of properly conducted specialized space, and an anti-modern one indifferent to the specific qualities of organized space. There is also a double loop: the mimic-man of Macaulay is the one produced in the provincial school. We can interpret this as mimesis if we also question the implicit claim that there exists a purer model of which this is an unstable copy. I prefer to regard mimesis itself as the ultimate in creativity, when a representation satisfying certain criteria, functional and aesthetic, is made by the actor, not particularly because he is a certain 'kind' of actor—colonized, South Asian—but because mimesis is the condition of life. How real does a copy have to be? These schools fail our realist tests; they show no fidelity, in the sense of both accuracy and loyalty. But the magic of mimesis lies in that while the copying may be quite imperfect, it is nevertheless effective in acquiring the power of the original (Taussig 1993), *as well as* accomplishing some further purpose of the actors.

Let us look briefly at an Agarwal school in the heart of the city. The founder is an idealistic woman who has no other interests in life but personally supervising every detail of its running, one of the widows mentioned by me as turning around the discourse of widowhood to her advantage (chapter 7). Her single-mindedness is confirmed by her turning to me to exploit me as a resource, as would any good educator to her environment. 'What is an intsy wintsy spider? What is a tuffet?' she demanded of me. The meanings of some of the nursery rhymes 'taught in the convent schools', as she put it, were not clear. And she insisted on minute explanations rather than my evasion that many were supposed to be nonsense anyway. Here the English nursery rhyme is taken by her as symptomatic of the 'modern': opaque and incomprehensible, but unchallengeable and with some material reference to meaning and power that was simply undisclosed yet, but could be captured through mimesis.

This particular school was impressive in its obvious effort to emulate innovative techniques such as the use of visual and aural devices, and emphasis on art and music, an increased participation by children by seating them in semicircles, and so on. The problem, for the anthropologist, was its inadequate space and related inconveniences. In an old residential house in the densest part of the city, every space is used as a classroom, some shared by two, some on a rotating basis as classes go elsewhere for dance, music, and physical training. Dance classes are held in the courtyard of the owner's house. Music is taught in the owner's bedroom, bare of anything but a string cot used by the teacher and her instrument. PT (Physical Training) is conducted in the front courtyard—in turn, as the space can accommodate no more than ten boys. The children take all this totally in their stride. The teachers are matter-of-fact, the owner non- committal. The anthropologist's feelings of unease are shared by no one.

The anthropologist has the dilemma of whether to take the point of view of the school administrator, dedicated to the proposition of a good school through sheer commitment of her own house, funds, time, and energy. She does not seem to notice that children in her classrooms cannot bend over, stretch out, or move their legs. She will not see that the teacher cannot move around among her students or display her illustrations to all of them or that there is insufficient light in the classroom, once the natural light has been restricted by iron grills on the windows and the artificial light economized. In her practice, she is not 'modern'.

Or, should the anthropologist take the side of the school children who need a spokesman since they do not themselves know or can say what is best for them, but could find a voice in the anthropologist's report? But that would of course make the anthropologist a modernizing colonial-type authority on educational matters, a role that restricts her options in many ways. Or should the anthropologist be the old-fashioned detached observer, taking the most prominent voice as the authentic informant's? The crises of legitimating and representation which beset our discipline are well displayed here. Who is the subject? Who is being spoken for, and to whom?

As we take leave of Mrs Agrawal and move on I will re-emphasize one point. Clearly the description of the domestic facilities of the owner doubling as school facilities evokes the image of the old indigenous school where the teacher taught in his own home and space naturally overlapped between different functions. The conflict I wish to highlight is that the owner in this case in not striving to recreate the indigenous. She would consider the indigenous a poor alternative to the modern, implying specifically poor physical surroundings even though she may refer positively to some ethical values transmitted 200 years ago. In her articulation of the matter, she is a deliberate modernizer seeking the colonial Western mode, even when this mode is not comprehensible as in the case of nursery rhymes or buildings. The grandiose liberal, humanistic discourse of education with its large, built-up, specialized space and its ideas of engaging the children in sport, must be taken seriously by the anthropologist (as it is in name by the educator). Equally seriously must be taken the lived-in culture of the city where it is believed that a child can be taught anywhere, with no material help, as long as there is moral dedication.

PLAYGROUNDS AND GARBAGE

Let us enrich our observations on the non-materiality of Indian small town modernity further, remembering the conventional truth that human beings inhabit discursive worlds of culturally constructed significance, including their construction of a differentiated terrain. Almost all schools make the effort to provide some sort of open space for their children: in a sample of fifty, twenty do so with what may be called 'playgrounds', twenty-three do it with courtyards. The remaining either cannot or do not need to. The schools which cannot are located in the Chauk and market-places of inner cities and possess no semblance of free space. Those which do not need to are the madrasas which have no open-air or physical activity as part of their curriculum. They have successfully institutionalized an attitude that is in front in the minds of many Indian educators and parents, but that suffers from being buffeted by a contrary ideology. The attitude is that mental drilling is sufficient and physical drilling is unnecessary. The ideology that buffets it is that PT and games are part of the modern curricula and therefore necessary to fashion the modern (English-medium) individual. This duality has roots in both history and culture. The Hellenistic legacy of competitive sports has been integrated with local culture, and funding has ensured a national legitimacy for both. The history of the ideology of wrestling and bodybuilding in provincial India has seen the following pattern: first, the exclusion of females and its installation as a male prerogative some 300 to 200 years ago. Then its typification as a lower-class practice from being that for all males some 200 to 100 years ago. Finally, the loss of patronage and cultural capital for even the lower classes over the last 100 years. Now neither do modern sports, nor Indian bodybuilding, find a niche in the practice of city schools.

Of the twenty schools with playgrounds, thirteen do not use or maintain theirs at all. Some look like overgrown wildernesses, others like dusty fields. The cultural attitude enshrined here is not simply one of indifference, but a discursively complex one. 'Jungles', as they are called, have a privileged status in local life. The opposite of brick and mortar structures is not the cultivated flower garden, but the 'jungle', meaning not necessarily a verdant forest, but any natural place, unspoilt by human hands (Dove 1994). The British ideal of the culture of nature has never made any impact on Indians outside the metropolitan centres. Uneducated or vernacular-educated Indians, such as in our small town, regardless of region, religion, or caste, continue to have their own ideal of cultured nature which is a contrast to the modern one. There is a common-sense comfort with mud and water in context, such as of the *akhara* or the well or river. The student of the modern school learns to despise this in concept through exposure to a discourse of sports-with-all-your-clothes-on, but in practice gets neither of the two worlds to embrace and experience.

The schools that do use their playgrounds are either populous boys' schools where the boys in their enthusiasm find it a fine site for as many as one dozen cricket games going on simultaneously; or the Christian missionary schools which, through their system of 'houses', have as their annual event not a cultural programme as do all other urban schools, but a Sports Day. The few other schools with ill maintained front grounds use them exclusively for morning assemblies.

Because these assemblies are rituals that are confined to fixed spaces, they deserve to be mentioned briefly here. The assembly, with its emphasis on straight lines, silence, and correct uniforms, is an exercise in making the child respond to instructions unclear in principle, such as 'stand at ease!', 'attention!', 'keep arm's distance!'. Indeed the distortions of these dreamt up by children in various degrees of playfulness and even seriousness are marvellous. What children experience at assembly time is that certain rules have to be obeyed in that one context and that one space, bur not transported over to others. The discipline of the assembly becomes restricted to and associated with the space in which it is held. The school assembly, if taken as a formal disciplining site for future adults, makes it possible to explain the chaos of public life in urban India. School-goers as children, and then as educated adults, can never maintain even a fraction of the discipline they are/were subjected to at assembly time when they find themselves in other spaces, such as when boarding trains or buses, buying tickets, or entering a narrow gateway. Here we have extra-materiality: too close an associating of a discipline with its physical location.

I come then to a discussion of garbage. The average citizen of a small town insists on his freedom to disregard the rule of law that is supposedly institutionalized in the city (these citizens include law-makers, such as policemen). Most also display ignorance about basic science, and seem uneducated about sanitation and the germ theory. Small towns in India are quintessentially dirty places, originally with recyclable waste, at present further degrading the environment through a liberal disposal of plastic bags and non-recyclable waste. The indif-

ference to cleanliness and sanitation in the city spaces is perfectly replicated in the spaces of the school. Modern education should pose a threat to this freedom and this ignorance but it does not.

The question then, reflected in the invasion of garbage everywhere, is why, for all the lip service paid to modernity in the form of buildings and banks, offices and schools, roads and traffic signals, citizens prefer to remain at a pre-civic level of involvement with the city, demonstrating a passivity to soluble problems, and even actively celebrating their perpetuation of garbage.

Again the history and culture: Indians may have always had a strong notion of 'own' versus 'other', related to well developed ideas of hierarchy, pollution, and contest-based appropriateness. The experience of the colonial state over more than a century as both invasive and foreign may have created an indifference to public spaces which were clearly under colonial control; and a need for private spaces which were not. A postcolonial state then failed to dispel, and perhaps nurtured further, the infancy-syndrome in its citizens bred from decades of dependence on the colonial state. Thus the average small-town Indian has no interest in public spaces, no belief of contiguity regarding them, and no concept of his own rights or power to do anything regarding them.

Again, there is a dilemma for the anthropologist. We could empathize with local practices and refuse to accept or comment on the problematic nature of garbage because our informants thus refuse. Or we could be colonizers who believed in difference, and maintaining our own preserved enclaves elsewhere, in leaving the natives alone to wallow in their own cultural preferences. Or we could react, again as with classroom space, by striving to engage those in control in a dialogue regarding what arouses us but not them.

This possible critique then takes us into deeper waters. We cannot but glimpse a similarity between us and other intellectuals in the past, both nationalist and colonialist. These intellectuals are routinely deconstructed for their seemingly un-reflexive reliance on 'tradition', 'history', 'science', and 'progress'.

But, if we were to take the problem of garbage seriously, what can we propose we would do in the place of these intellectuals and social traders in the past? When one searches for ways to transmit the principles of cleanliness to children and uneducated adults, one thinks of teaching about the germ theory and about environmental pollution.

One ponders on various rituals that breed pride in one's own, but where 'one's own' can be defined in a wider way to include public spaces. One's mind turns to various resources, to traditions, for instance, of nature worship, corpuses of stories about trees and animals, to the images of ashrams and philosophies of oneness with the environment.

That is, one moves towards the logic behind the occasional effort to strive for the scientific subject in India; to design rituals that expand the 'our' into the national; to use the resources of literature mythology and philosophy to construct a 'tradition'.

We then go beyond the deconstructionist historian who would critique modernizers in the past for their promotion of science, or question the whole allegiance to progress displayed by the educated elite. Judging from our survey of schools and the invasion of garbage today, should we not wonder instead: why was science not loved and promoted 'more'?

Similarly, as anthropologist we need to steer clear of essentialism when judging the behaviour of the ordinary Indian at face value. I am on record as having marked my break with ethno-sociology when I realized that I did not share many of the values of my informants (Kumar 1988). That, after I was through interpreting the aesthetics and freedom, I was finally critical of the violence, often fatal, as in the ignoring of garbage. A critic of my work narrates the following incident. He interfered in a young man's dumping of garbage on the road and was bemused at the youth's challenge to him. 'Is this England?' The academic was rendered silent, trailing off in his narrative, implying that demanding a cleaner surroundings in India is tantamount to an elitist, objectifying conflation of India with England, based on an ignorance of Indian 'indigenous' culture (Chakrabarty 2002). I want to conclude this section on garbage by suggesting rather, another set of consideration with which this Indian youth's comfort with garbage dumping could be treated. Maybe we could consider that there are more complicated equations than the intuitively perceived ones of garbage dumping as equaling 'freedom' and cleanliness as equaling external control. The young man's notion of what is English and what is not in our anecdote is clearly uninformed and has resonance of protest against upper class control. But can we afford to forget that this essentialist notion of the English and the Indian was itself bred by colonialism? That by being generous to purer, native values, we are perhaps confusing the indigenous with the essentialism of colonialism?

The framework we are obliged to adopt is clearly one of modernity. I suggest that there is no other path for the Indian state or its
citizens to follow than one leading towards science (but an environmentally sensitive science); technology (but a culturally appropriate
technology); and progress (but a progress aimed at redressing gender
and other inequalities). And that if this placing is not recognized by the
anthropologist, she is still placing herself, but on the side of science,
technology, and progress *without* the caveats mentioned above.

THE DISCOURSE OF CHILDHOOD

The technologies of education allow us to glimpse the discourse of the
child in India.

Sanskrit schools and madrasas eschew all symbolism, because they
are themselves icons and signs of the religions they substantialize.
Catholic schools are abundant with crosses and bleeding hearts and
pink, blonde children cuddling kittens. But in non-religious schools,
the only representation is of Hinduism and a closely allied nationalism.
The favourite personage depicted is Saraswati, the goddess of learning,
with close favourites being Vivekanand and Tagore, Gandhi and
Nehru, and Krishna in pursuits arguably adult. The philosophy of
childhood evident here is an unreflective one based on the educators'
predilections towards a combination of a bhakti style and a reformist
Vedantic Hinduism, and a pre: BJP Congress Hindu nationalism. The
philosophy is comfortable therefore with symbolism that has no local
referents, thus there are lotuses, swans, and Mughal or Victorian
gardens. The child, it is maintained confidently, can be unilaterally
worked upon. He or she is a blank slate with no context in everyday
life and can be written on.

The child is understood to be chaotic, destructive, and unstructured. When there are framed pictures or flowerpots or other destruct-
ible items in schools spaces, they are at a height or in places beyond the
reach of children. The supposedly innate capacity of children to violence is regarded with tolerance and pragmatism. There are no *theories*
of how the child can be brought within discipline, short of growing
older. Rationality, orderliness, and respect for the law, do not characterize the child, and it is not that he must therefore be made over
from the inside, but that he must be controlled and opposed in all his
impulses from the outside. There is thus a non-negotiable belief in
authoritarianism. The most important aim in the classroom is obedi-

ence. When some allegedly new-fangled ideas are introduced such as seating children not in straight rows but a circle, or having them brainstorm or discuss, the purpose of these ideas is not understood. Educators claim disciplinary difficulties with practising them, and the vote always goes in favour of 'discipline'. This is just the opposite of the discipline of Foucault which is a transcendent self-discipline and works through a mystique of the everyday. Self-discipline in space and in time is the characteristic of the modern citizen, and endless supervision from the top through coercion and threat is the characteristic of its Other. The ground is therefore not made ready for the creation of the modern subject of postcolonial nationalism in the schools we have been looking at. Such a ground is only made ready elsewhere, in boarding schools in the mountains, in Delhi or Bombay, but not in provincial towns. The explanation given by both metropolitans and provincials is that in the provinces there is simply too much disorderliness, religion, irrationality, and backwardness allied with sheer cussedness.

Prior and more significant than even the above discussion is the observation that in doing an ethnography that may seek to focus on the child, one would be pursuing the unrecognized, trying to locate the undefined. The 'child' or 'childhood' have no resonance in small-town India yet. It is not clear how to ask about them in languages: *bachcha, shishu, larka-larki, vidyarthi, chhatra-chhatri?* It is clear from all evidence, linguistic and otherwise, that the overall discourse in society is emphatically not of discrete, self-sufficient individuals and of the child as one such individual in the making. She has typically no choices and no status outside that of her family, community, and local history. Without belabouring the point, I would claim, as I have done elsewhere, that the modernist invention or discovery of the child and of childhood has not occurred in India yet outside metropolitan centres, and that the non-relevance of some categories on enquiry tells us of the subject itself.

PAIN

What is it that the nation state is afraid of, that is seen by the national elite as a threat to the democratic, secular order? That is further characterized as primordial, communal, ignorant, and factionalist? That is privately also known as vernacular, with the greatest divide recognized as between English and provincial languages? The threat is

typically discussed with reference to events and happenings: demolition of Babri masjid, Roop Kanwar's self-immolation, rural tragedies in Bihar. But the threat lies, for this national elite, in very familiar, mundane, quotidian sites, where subjects are produced and reproduced who have no access to and no vision of the secularism, liberalism, and nationalism of this elite. They are accessing a range of other options, none of which are certainly primordial or ignorant. They are *also* modern, but also specific as both threatening to the modernity enshrined in nationalist discourse, and creative of a via media between larger cultural processes on the ground and larger global processes. We have to discard dichotomies, especially of the real and the mimicking modernity, of the centre and the periphery, of colonialism and the indigenous. It is not that there has been a struggle or resistance against a model modernity that resulted in peculiar local versions of the modern. There has appeared rather a 'formation of modernity' that is as legitimate as the more globally familiar variety, and is more than simply protest. It is constructed and hybrid as much as any modernity is constructed and any construction is hybrid.

The power structures at the national level work out in terms of both repression and subversion. As repression, they keep the larger part of the population out of the accounting for ruling the nation (though for different reasons than Myron Weiner gives in his class analysis [1991]). As subversive potential, however, they may well prepare a script leading to a larger upheaval in the national-global model of democracy if not capitalism, sometimes summed up as 'Lalu Raj' and 'Mulayam Raj' named after new and powerful provincial leaders.

I want to end, however, by suggesting a legacy of colonialism and an interrogation of modernity that is less familiar to us than the tropes of mimesis, alterity, and subalternity, that is experienced by the subjects of the nation as 'pain'.

There are two obvious experiences of pain for the child at the micro level, each constituting an unbroken tradition for 150 years. One is the paraphernalia of 'convent schools', that is the some 200 schools in our city, of blazer, tie, belt, badge, socks and shoes, ostensibly the marks of a disciplined identity. The power of these artifacts in producing meaning is displayed by the opposition to them of the few schools with a rigid ideology behind them, such as Rashtriya Swayam Sevak Sangh Hinduism or Wahabi Islam. They are decisive in their condemnation of Western Christian gadgets, but they do not realize the power these gadgets potentially exercise, a power that has eluded the critics. The critics discover, as they think, appropriate symbols in the past, and are simultaneously convulsed by the realization that the symbols themselves, say, white *pajama-kurta* with *topi* in one case, *salwar-kameez* and *dupatta* in another, or a local language in a third, spell marginalization. Meanwhile, the ethnographer notes that the synthetic, tight-fitting pants, shirts, socks and shoes do *not* in fact suit the climate, and notes that adults accept heat and discomfort for their children as celebration of the victory of modernity—and further notes that elite metropolitan Indians celebrate *their* modernity with the comfort of loose cotton garments and sandals.

The second micro-level tradition of pain comprises the rote learning. Schools had become synonymous with rote learning already 150 years ago, both because of the previous legitimacy of memorization in the Sanskrit and Arabic curricula, and because it was not possible to perform well in the new schools until the new language had been somewhat mastered. But while there was legitimacy for rote learning in the Sanskrit and Arabic learning systems, in English studies it was rued from the beginning. To tackle English was launched a technology that has become elaborated further and further over the past 150 years: of private tuition, notes, translations, commentaries, and other guides for everyday work and final examinations. The spiral of insecurity that is built at the outset for a student is typically never broken, as demonstrated in my third ethnographic example of St Mary's. There are no possible rewards for effort or improvement, only total success or failure, the constant expectation of being judged, of competing ceaselessly, and for most, of not being good enough.

This is at the micro-level. I have been ethnographically stressing the local. Such pain might seem to be the fate of every student everywhere. The particular colonial gloss on it is that 'the greater pain' lies in the denial to children of the rewards of the national-global. At the national-global level, or the level of power, there are clearly winners and losers, both economic and symbolic. Provincial schools do not succeed as little theatres of the nation to play out, or little workshops to create, the spokesmen, the elite, and the intelligentsia. They reproduce the pan-chewing, pan-spitting headmaster of DAV College, who stars in my second ethnographic example—a free and satisfied human being certainly, but not the progressive, successful citizen of the nation.

The problem is not merely, as postcolonialist critics put it, that this is the cultural strategy of the postcolonized nation state. The problem is that the schools create pain, at the level of both the local and the global. This modernity deserves to be ceaselessly interrogated.

11

The Space of the Child
The Nation, the Neighbourhood, and the Home

INTRODUCTION

In this preliminary anthropological study of the structure and imagining of space in the lives of children, I go through the following stages of discussion. First, I consider how the construction of an environment is used to discipline the body and the self. The child, who finds herself subject to a certain space in the home, is being taught to be a certain kind of being. This is the politics of age domination. The child can only manoeuvre within it, and it is only as adult that she can manipulate or change it, and then in turn make it an instrument of teaching for her children. Given this positioning vis-à-vis space, I feel confident in talking of a specific experience called 'childhood', and in regarding it as a specific aspect of education that can be retrieved.

Two, I discuss the location of the child in the nation, and how an initial difference appears in the imagining of the nation between the schooled and unschooled child. But the difference produced by schooling is offset by the learning that is in common, for instance from the media; and partly offset by the sheer poverty of schooling across the whole range of schools. This pedagogic poverty equals the failure of the nation state. The nation is far more interestingly imagined in films and songs.

Three, other spaces that produce a common experience for all children are the neighbourhood and the city. My city is the provincial city, not the metropolitan one, characterized par excellence by garbage. There are commonalities in the technology of space, as well as in metaphor and imagery, that cut across class. The neighbourhood, at least of the provincial city, might be one of the most powerful sites for the learning of a common habitus.

Four, given all these commonalities, and turning back to the home, I find that the most crucial lines of division within a class called children are between girls and boys: girls privilege the home, boys the neighbourhood; girls know they have more than one home, boys that they will forever wander. Their personas, and their lives, as male and female, are shaped by the spaces they find themselves in, the spaces as they read and live them, and the spaces they anticipate.

AGE AND CONTROL: THE FACT OF CHILDHOOD

In seeking to talk about children, I am proposing a belief in some form of 'age culture', and that 'children' or 'childhood' are somehow a reality. As a discursive proposition, I have argued elsewhere, this reality needs questioning for South Asia (Kumar 2000). However, I will postulate here, as an anthropologist, that a demonstrable 'children's culture' and 'world of the child' exist, in that there is observable action performed by children, games and activities, participation in social life and indeed, lifestyles (for Germany, see Fuchs 1995). Whether these are accepted and sanctioned by adults is relevant, but not central to the proposition.

What is central is the creation of much of the child's world by adults, or the politics of age. Space, in the home, the neighbourhood, the city, and the nation, is constructed and provided by adults for children. Even when involuntarily done, this involves control and domination of the child, and the effort at disciplining. Benignly speaking, we may call it 'teaching'. The uses of space by adults are all aspects of a teaching strategy by which effective socialization is carried on, and the body is adapted to the constructed environment.

THE CASE OF ZEENAT, A WEAVER'S DAUGHTER

In class III of the Madrasa Hamidia Rizvia for girls, I watched how the teaching consisted of writing answers on the blackboard for children to copy—some explanations having been thrown in for my benefit—and then the teacher going into a kind of doze while children wrote at their own speed, or not at all. Those at the back played, gossiped, and exchanged objects of value. Those in front must have been the better, or best, students, because their entertainment consisted of jerking their pens to form pools of ink, scrambling to share the ink, asking each other for ink, discussing the shortage of ink, and then with a pout bending down to write.

Zeenat was right under my nose so I picked on her. Or, rather the teacher did first, asking for her book and her copy to show me. She would not have chosen a bad student, so the choice of Zeenat was partly because of her location and partly her scholarship. She had indeed a fine hand and also an aesthetic sense, writing all the questions in green and the answers in blue. She looked very serious and would not respond when I tried to make her smile or laugh. Through her teacher I got her to invite me at her home.

Her house was just across the road, an excellent arrangement by all considerations. She seemed so 'good' that I took for granted that she was from a 'good' family, by which I meant without reflection, a comfortable, middle-class, upwardly mobile family in a clean, spacious set of rooms that I could look at approvingly. We climbed up four flights of steep stairs of a house with an opening in the middle like a well and rooms all around. It was the all-too familiar design of all old homes in Banaras, seemingly more of Muslim homes but that only because more Muslim homes were old-fashioned. We climbed up and up and on each floor women and children gathered and stared at us without reservation (I mean, stared at me).

The room she took me to was equally familiar. There was a cooking space on the landing outside. The room had no furniture and was barely seven or eight feet wide on each side. The father sat on his haunches against a wall. The mother sat against another. A mat was spread against the third wall. The fourth wall was taken up by the door and a window through which peeped family members constantly. In other words, it was cramped and poor (see Figure 1)

They had five children, Zeenat being the middle one. The oldest boy, Wasim Riaz, and the girl, Shahina Parveen, had both dropped out of school early because they did not have the inclination for studies. They were bright in other things? I prompted. Neither mother nor father responded, although we had excellent rapport otherwise. Wasim wove and Shahina did housework. Zeenat and her immediately younger brother Mukhtar Naim went to school, she in class III in

1st Floor

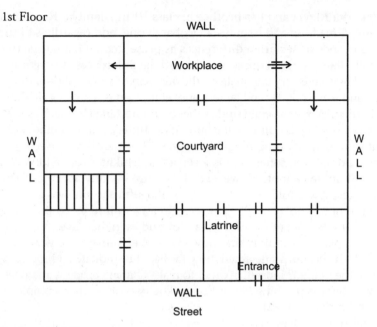

2nd and 3rd Floors

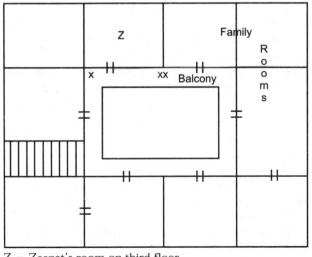

Z = Zeenat's room on third floor
xxx = Cooking spaces

Figure 1. Zeenat's house

Hamidia Rizvia and her brother in class III in Islamiya. Rizvia is a Barelwi madrasa and Islamiya a Deobandi one, and regardless of the importance of sectarian differences as presented by maulanas, this family, like many, did not seem to regard the differences as significant.

They were very articulate on the question of some children studying and some not. By and large school education is seen as useless and a burden. While the child studies she can do nothing else, such as sewing or cooking. Because of the burden of studies, many families keep tutors also. Anyway, some children *can* study—they have the *zehen* or inclination—and some *cannot*. Zeenat and Mukhtar can, and Wasim and Shahina cannot. However, all four are equally accepted. The youngest, I was told, a toddler of two, Shagufta Yasmin, was going to be the best scholar of all—she was already so interested in books. When I asked about the whole place of studies in their lives, Waheeda Bibi explained candidly that nowadays when a marriage was being fixed, the groom's side asked, how far has she studied? Did she complete the Qur'an? Indeed, in order to make Shahina properly marriageable, she was teaching her at home. The two others had completed their Qur'an courses.

Qur'an courses were held in the house of her *bari Amma*, or senior mother, grandmother, or aunt, with at least twenty girls gathered under a *maulani*. Classes took two hours a day, from 2.30 to 4.30 or 5 p.m. There were no charges, but there was a gift given on graduation, and sweets at other occasions, and when the student would get married, a set of clothes. The *ustad* was to be honoured next only to the parents.

Zeenat was sitting close to her mother and looking more serious by the minute, so I tried to speak to her at which she seemed to draw into herself all the more. She must have been so hungry, having eaten whatever she did before 7 a.m. and then carried a mere tiffin to school. But there was no sign of lunch; indeed there were chunks of raw meat showing no input of preparation. Perhaps that was for dinner. So, lunch? I asked carefully. Oh, it's early yet, I was told. We'll eat at 1.30 or 2 p.m. They served me Crackjack biscuits and tea. I hurriedly gave the two school children a biscuit each, under protest. The little baby wanted tea and got some.

I turned to Zeenat because I was her guest after all and there because of her. What were her games, her toys? She didn't budge (too hungry?) but her brother brought down a lovely doll's chair and bed, and then a doll. Then he brought down a suitcase full of little clothes stitched by the children, every bit as good as those sold worldwide by

companies like Mattel. The baby played with everything as I exclaimed over it. I suddenly realized that Zeenat was too old; by a rough calculation, the youngest was two, the next ten, Zeenat twelve, the next children eighteen and maybe nineteen. None looked their age. All were small built, thin, and tired looking, except the mother who was plump and glowing. Wahida Bibi was educated, since she had spoken of teaching her daughter. But she had not gone to school or madrasa, rather learnt at home from female family members, as they had learnt before them.

She stitched everything at home: her clothes, the children's clothes, the linens, everything. Only the gent's clothes had to be bought. How had she learnt? How would her daughters? She had learnt just by doing. That was how everyone ever learnt. Zeenat was too busy with her studies to sew, but when the madrasa was closed she did whatever she wanted. By such doing, one learnt. Her sister had lots of time once she left school and was an expert seamstress.

The room in which the family lived presented a huge problem. What was the little Zeenat learning? In school, watching her, I had thought that she was destined to study far and was perhaps nurturing ambitions inside her serious little brain and that she would break her family tradition in some way. After all, I had only just met several women teachers, such as Safia Sultana, who had completed her *Maulvi*, *Alim*, and *Fazil* courses/degrees while living in a hostel in Maunath Bhanjan, sent there by her family in north Banaras, and who had been teaching since, even with two sons one and two years old.

But upon seeing Zeenat's family, I realized that the little girl's seriousness at school was destined to pass like a happy dream. Whatever she did, she would do very well. What she did now was school work; what she would do later was housework and childcare. All the time she was learning as conscientiously at home as in school. In school, she was learning the reading and writing of three languages, and some other subjects. At home, she was learning cooking, sewing, keeping baby, serving, tidying up, running for errands, all the details of how a home works and what in their 'culture' and 'community' a homemaker should do. She had finished with the Qur'an and although that is learnt only by rote, there was other intangible teaching that goes along with it that she had imbibed.

Zeenat was learning how to deploy herself in the one room her family lives in, to share the bathroom on the landing with the extended family, to cook with her mother, and gradually by herself in the space

outside their door, to clean up each time and leave the space un-
marked, and otherwise practise a total non-specialization of domestic
spaces. The room and its outside were swept morning and evening or
when littered, whichever came first. All materials were put away after
use. No space was called after its function, as the place 'for' some
particular activity, including sleeping. The room became, in turn, a
bedroom, a dining room, a sitting room, a den, a study, a workplace,
a dining room again, and again a bedroom. Zeenat was mastering the
discourse perfectly without a word being spoken on the subject. She
was learning further where and how to spread out the rugs for those
who would work or sleep, and those who visit. She was learning how
every niche and cranny of the room has its uses.

Zeenat is as a child, and will grow up into an adult, a being
perfectly comfortable and 'natural'. When she is transported into
another, foreign space, is when she might, miraculously, become
awkward and unnatural, as described by Abu-Lughod of the Bedouin
family in a glamorous upper class home full of artifacts (Abu-Lughod
1993: 120).

But she will also go to another space that will be interpreted as
'natural', a place that will become 'home' to the extent of her replacing
this home with that one. Her married home will be a home configured
initially by others, such as her mother-in-law, and then gradually (and
dialectically, we hope) both be constructed by her as it is constructing
her too. As I note about a different household and its mistress elsewhere
(Shree 2000: 183-6; see Figure 2), it is the very design of the house that
can impose a discipline on the daughter-in-law. The *mai* house has a
central courtyard with verandahs and rooms on three sides, that
ensures that the mistress of the house is in confinement because she
can always be observed and criticized by the bed-ridden mother-in-law,
sitting strategically on one side of the courtyard. If mai, our protagonist
in this story, had initially had a closed kitchen with modern gadgets
and a counter—all of which she got, but too late—she would not only
not have had the bent spine she got, but would have had the privacy to
order her activities her own way. But there are other, more mixed,
results of the house design. In the absence of a master bedroom and the
companionate marriage that implies, mai has the freedom to spend
time with her children, in their room, hers and theirs, and build an
inter-generational solidarity. Such a solidarity is the stuff of the socio-
cultural training which constitutes 'tradition' in families, equalling a
lack of freedoms in a certain perspective but other freedoms in a

different perspective. For the daughter in this story, Sunaina, and maybe for Zeenat in the future in ours, there comes to be an identification of the house with childhood, with life itself, with something that haunts and keeps coming back. The house bears the children, it binds them, it makes them grow, it suffocates them. They dream of escaping from it. When they escape, they dream of coming back to it. Homes, even more than parents, control lives, and become for the children the locus of childhood and the past.

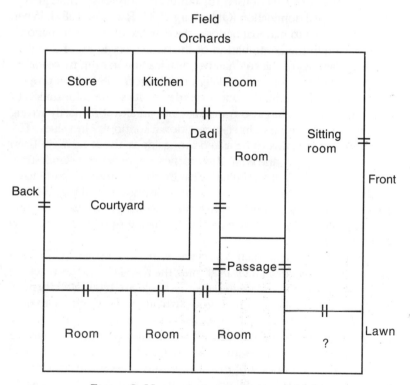

Figure 2. House design in the novel *Mai*

Much of the culture that anthropologists locate, including lifestyles, values such as of interpersonal relations, personal identity, honour, and shame, are all aspects of the functioning of the environment and its bio-politics. We have insufficient discussion in anthropology yet of how spaces create and control lives, even as Henrietta Moore pointed out in her interesting study of the Marakwet of Kenya

(1986), 'It is now axiomatic that spatial relations represent and reproduce social relations, and it is the view that relations of likeness exist between social distinctions and spatial boundaries that link the study of gender to the study of space' (xi). The thrust of the research on space, or rather, buildings, as a political technology for the exercise of power by organizing and canalizing bodies in space derives its inspiration from Foucault (1975, 1984; Rabinow 1984). This is taken forth to the case of colonies like India to show how architecture, city planning, and aesthetic forms were used for culturally and epistemologically-oriented colonial domination (Oldenburg 1984; Rabinow 1982). When brought forward to national periods, the exercise of power by national states is seen in the continuation of the same techniques of architecture and planning of the colonial periods, leading to even more elaborate control of the domains of daily life (Holston 1989). I am proposing a discussion of a more subtle, everyday politics: the colonization of children by adults that also translates into an extraordinarily strong socialization, resulting in inter-generational continuity in values. The question that remains to be asked alongside is about how children reappropriate space, and what their tactics are, overt and clandestine, to escape the nets of disciplining. How do they themselves participate in their socialization? Because....'the pedestrian's walking, like the flaneur of Walter Benjamin...is the spatial acting out of place, creating and representing public space rather than being subjected to it' (Low 1999, 113–14).

Useful for my approach is also the work of Bourdieu (1977) and the concept of *habitus*. 'In his examples, the Kabyle house becomes the setting in which body space and cosmic space are integrated through metaphor and symbolic homologous structures. Through the experience of living in the spatial symbolism of the home, social structure becomes embodied and naturalized in everyday practice....Bourdieu also examines resistances and the effect of feedback on the social system. Since the concept of habitus spatially links social structure to the human body and bodily practices, the possibility of resistance to these practices becomes more apparent (Giroux 1983)' (Low 1999, 114)

EDUCATION: FLAWS IN TEACHING THE NATION

Because, specifically, of the colonial history of India in the last two centuries and the ways that modernity was defined and used, schooling came to play the part of the archetypical signifier of the nation state, progress, and upward mobility. The space of the school came to be a fetishized one. It became a ritual space where a wonder was supposedly enacted. Because it was, and continues to be, closed and hallow, no one may look inside and almost no one has a precise idea of what is enacted within, especially not the parents. But a magic was/is supposed to occur, indeed, the biggest magic of modernity: education can apparently change a person from one kind of being to another.

One would expect, then, that the child's understanding of space also varies according to whether the child is schooled or unschooled. This interesting proposition of the school as marking the social division in India between two parts of the population can be investigated with regard to the nation.

The nation for the school child is visualized as a geographical space: a map of a certain space that can be brought to life with images of mountains and rivers, plains and countrysides. This map and this collage of images could be encountered routinely by the child in the school, and in a spectrum running from strong to weak to non-existent, its presence gets diluted from the most modern (a missionary school) to the least modern school (a municipal school). The nation, as I have discussed elsewhere (chapter 2) does not exist as a physical, material concept for the unschooled child.

Further, a child going to school can answer questions about the nation, that is, he can *imagine* the nation. An ironic characteristic of schooling in India is that the more powerful or effective the schooling is, the more it has to ignore the local. Schooling does not so much battle with the local as render it invisible, which is of course one of the strongest symbolic weapons to wield. 'Progress' and 'modernity' are measured with regard to the distance from the local. This distance could carry one well beyond the nation into the terrains beyond (called the global by us, but not my informants), and this is exactly what happens.

Let us look very briefly at the play of national and spatial symbols in three schools: St Johns, Gopi Radha, and Jamia Islamiya. St Johns has 'foreign' pictures of romantic landscapes, from the same repertoire as its others of cuddly animals, blonde infants, and bouquets of flowers. It also has a large concrete map of India on the wall, discoloured by being outside where the assemblies are held, and a flag of India that is unfurled on ritual occasions. The 'houses' students are divided up into for competitive sports and other activities are named after national heroes: Gandhi, Nehru, and Tagore. Elsewhere, in Loreto, they are

Carmel, Fatima, and Lourdes, and in the Ramakrishna Mission School there is Vivekanand and Netaji Bose. When questioned, the students had no idea what role 'houses' were supposed to play in their lives, and the map of India was consensually relegated to the unwanted margins, but both do exist.

In Gopi Radha and provincial schools which are either Hindi-medium or are English-medium only 'in name' (not in fact), there are pictures of Krishna in various contexts, the choice falling, ironically, more on Krishna as adult than as child. There are pictures of Saraswati, the patron of learning and the arts, blessing without discrimination. There are idols closer in history, such as Gandhi, Nehru, and Tagore, always straight-faced and forbidding. There are landscapes of mountains and fountains, the idealized scenery never typically seen by the children. The principle seems to be to maximize the distance from the mundane and the real, and immerse them in an adult world of the desirable. But 'immerse' is hardly the right term because the effort is technologically so flawed. The posters and pictures are not at children's eye levels but at adult height. Anything remotely prone to damage, such as of glass, clay, or paper, is safely removed from within touching distance. There are no colours, patterns, or images in tune with children's mental worlds, and certainly nothing produced by children themselves.

Jamia Islamiya, like all madrasas and Sanskrit schools, eschews deliberate symbolism, and effortlessly creates a continuity of sorts with the child's home environment. This includes floor sitting, a demonstration of poverty in unwashed walls and mats, a noise level and disorder that is more benign than a modernist disciplining, and the absence of any modern artifacts or images, including a common sense of the very impossibility of them. In the novel *Mai*, we are told: 'Dada's sitting room had been converted into a drawing room. His two portraits and sword in a leather sheath were still on the wall. But around them were English landscapes framed by Babu in golden frames. Apart from this drawing room there were pictures on the wall only in the puja room. *We had not developed a tradition of hanging things on walls with a view to decorating the place*' (Shree 2000:99; italics mine).

This lack of wall decoration is a closely held ideal in the madrasa, and something that matches exactly the lifestyle of every student and teacher. I must not be misunderstood as suggesting that the madrasa is not a 'modern' institution. In all those aspects which characterize a modern education: age-graded classes, predetermined and centralized curricula, examinations and report cards, the dominance of the textbook, and the irrelevance of any particular teacher, it is as modern as all the other educational institutions which proclaim themselves as that. It is also modern in the historical Indian way that I have mentioned: in spite of a cultural-spatial continuity with the home, the madrasa school, like all schools, has a strained relationship with guardians (see Figure 3). Each party in the relationship, the school and the home, blames the other for the inadequate socialization of the child into the self-conscious, confident, participating citizen of the modern nation state.

When we go beyond the symbolism of the spaces and look at the curricula and rituals, all the schools, from madrasa to missionary present a set of patterns. The schooled child learns early on that the name of her country is 'India', that it is 'her' country, and that it is 'great'. The child sings songs to that effect, maybe marches or parades or salutes the flag, and takes part in celebrations on Independence Day and Republic Day. By class III or IV the child studies about the thirty-two different states and union territories of the Indian Union, the boundaries, physical and economic features of each, and a bit about the costumes and festivals. Apart from the two all-India Boards that are popular in all towns, there are separate State Boards, which give more attention to the geography and history of the particular state the school is located in.

My argument, however, is that the pedagogy of the nation is flawed. The efforts of all those who seek to create a new Indian citizen in the school have historically been lacking in technology, both its execution and its very conception. Their politics, for nationalists, have been correct—we must build up consciousness of and loyalty towards the nation—but their pedagogy has been insufficiently developed. Consequently, what has actually been offered to the child in the classroom has not been of the standard to produce the results desired. The schooled child in India has not developed that consciousness of the nation or that loyalty which was supposed to be produced. Although this argument could be demonstrated by citing the assessments of educators themselves, I have tried to look into explanations for it as well. Through ethnography in the classrooms, I show elsewhere that children in madrasa, private school, and public school, all experience a distancing from their history and geography that is a product of poor pedagogy. They cannot envision their country, cannot draw it, cannot

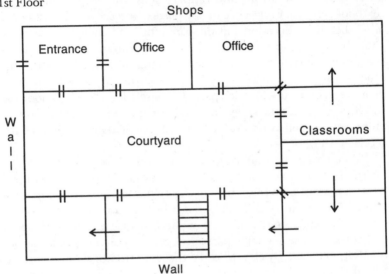

1st Floor

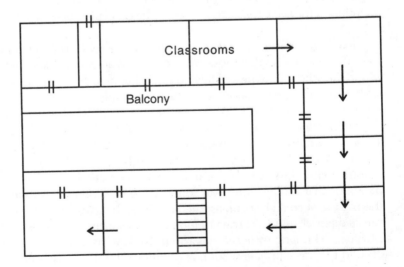

2nd and 3rd Floors

Figure 3. Madrasa Jamia Islamia

refer visually to its physical features, cannot relate to its characteristics, or conceptualize any continuities—even ironic or subversive—between it, the nation, and themselves in their experienced, lived-in lives. Through interaction and interviews with children I found that even those children who had mastered the arts of answering adult questions and spinning narratives within test procedures ('Name the five largest rivers of India'; 'Where does it rain the most?') showed no ability to construct connections between their own biographies and their nation's history (chapter 2).

If adults in India have not thought of pedagogic strategies that could successfully teach the nation, how do they react when they are directly taught the strategies, as in a workshop for the interactive teaching of nationalist history, such as I witnessed?

There were several reactions. The first was of agreement, a confirmation of knowing the same approaches, perhaps of having attended several workshops, of having taken training courses and got degrees. There was an agreement which seemed duplicitous, because there was a slight masking in the eyes and lack of volubility about precise work. There was an emphasized separation into 'theory' and 'practice' and the response was saying, 'These are great ideas in theory *but not in practice*. I know the theory quite well, thank you, but I am clever enough to also know that practice is different.' If we translate the discourse, it runs as follows: Of course, India is a nation, and a great, ancient one, the best in the world. But we Indians are too clever to fuss around with that. The real challenge to us lies in our confrontation with the problems of everyday life. Let us go on with resolving those. That is the practical. All this rhetoric about the nation et cetera is fine, but is only theory. (Not that the nation is theory, but to talk about it in this solemn, quasi-religious way will never happen with us, and is thus theoretical.)

EDUCATION OUTSIDE THE SCHOOL: HERE COMES THE NATION

When the child does not go to school, there are two main ways in which she encounters the nation, which are shared by school-going children too. One is in movies and the other is in songs, typically heard over radio, television, or over loudspeakers amplifying their sounds generously in streets and neighbourhoods. In contrast to the movies of the fifties and sixties, there are fewer nationalist plots today that elaborate on citizens' duties towards national development: the building of roads, dams, and high structures. That was perhaps not 'realism', but only idealism. Setting up a city in the jungle is a long-standing cultural ideal and was transferred from the king to the government. Movies of the nineties onwards are continuous with the older ones in their evocation of the natural beauties of the land: mountains, deserts, and waterfalls. But they are new in their direction of responsibility, not towards development, but to the protection of the virtue of the land and of its borders. Enemies are all those located outside: Pakistan which would seek to plant terrorism and attack the borders; and Europe, America, Australia, and New Zealand, which are enticingly beautiful just like India but fail in virtue when compared with India. In movies such as *Pardes, Dilwale Dulhaniya Le Jayenge, Jeans, Hum Dil De Chuke Sanam, Pyar to Hona hi Tha, and Kabhi Khushi Kabhi Gham,* India is not celebrated through its nature, but with a new confidence, through its value.

In this, the media, movies, television, and taped music, are all more advanced in nationalist rhetoric than school textbooks, which still continue to equate nation to nature. Textbook poetry asks: 'What does "nature" teach us?' and then answers with reference to the different parts of the national imaginary: 'The Himalayas teach us to stand firm. The rivers teach us to nourish. The trees teach us to protect. The clouds teach us to share....'

Which is so much less resonating than the dialogue from one of the above films: 'Are you a German?' 'No.' 'Are you an American?' 'No.' 'Are you a Russian?' 'No.' 'Then?' 'I am "an Indian".' The latter speaker has decided to fight for the girl's virtue, in contrast to the other nationalities evoked that presumably would have failed to. There are numerous variations of this theme.

THE NEIGHBOURHOOD: GARBAGE AND BEAUTY

A trip through the mohallas or neighbourhoods of the city, along its main roads as well as its several lanes, inside the campuses and compounds of its main institutions and then a very close investigation of the official, commercial, residential, and recreational areas shows us that Banaras is a modern city with a particularly unified character. That is, not that it is not recognizably divided into inner and outer, upper and lower class, ethnic or caste, and educationally and occupationally separated areas. It is that the divisions, insofar as they exist, are secondary to other unifying characteristics, which, in the interest of brevity, are the following, illustrated by ethnographic glimpses.

When I watched from my balcony at 7 a.m., I saw five or six women winding their way to and from between the houses of this colony. They were maids who worked in different houses, typically as domestic help, to do the sweeping, mopping, washing of dishes, and occasionally clothes. I focused on one woman who was just leaving a house. She must have been one of the 5 a.m. workers. She was carrying a packet of garbage in her hands. I knew exactly what would happen. She walked to the empty plot one house away in front of our house and aimed unenthusiastically towards the ground within. She missed, as do most women and men. The garbage landed on the roadside, to join the growing piles on both sides, most of which had spilled out from its containers and blown and spread around. The twenty or thirty yards of the road at that part were a garbage dump itself.

Similarly, I watched and talked with this woman and that, including our landlady, our neighbour, our maid, miscellaneous workers and loiterers, and confirmed that *all* of them took it as a law of nature, God, and society that garbage should be thrown wherever no one personally stood as occupant of the land. It is the first unifying fact about the neighbourhoods of the city. The difference that could arise, say out of regionalism, is slight, and subverted by other processes.

Vishvajit Chatterji, in class IX of Anglo-Bengali Inter College, lives with his family in an ancient, crumbling house in a tiny *gali*. The house was in the corner, so they had some open space around their first-floor rooms, but there were other equally tall or taller, and older, houses a few yards away, so the room upstairs was dark and closed, in spite of its windows and balconies. More than half the room was taken up by a double bed, on which most of the social and educational activities were carried on. On the other side there was a fridge, a steel almirah, and a dressing table. Visvajit and his brother Surajit cannot help noticing that their home looks different to their non-Bengali friends' homes, and similar to their Bengali friends'. Other points that might strike them as part of their Bengali identity are that their mother chops and cuts with a *boti*, not a knife. She cooks rice all the time, and fish regularly, as well as several other dishes in a Bengali way. They speak Bengali at home, and the children seem as fluent in Bengali as in Hindi. They celebrate Durga Puja in a big way. They go to Calcutta once a year and have relatives there. The mother's friends are almost all Bengali, although the father, being also a BJP worker, moves across all sectarian lines. Where they are no different to all their neighbours is in their respect for the city's ethical codes about garbage, and its relationship to freedom. This is not articulated by them (as much of the above is not) and can only be observed. Father and son share the city's ethos, which in a nutshell, is the positive proposition: the more garbage, the more freedom, and vice versa.

Second, there is no discernible separation into public and private spheres of activities. That which may be considered a private activity at one place, for instance, bathing or massage, is explicitly a public one at another, and vice versa. That is to say, the code for public and private does not exist, and the city's ethos is unified in that it holds *one model* of the public and private: the lack of interest in a fixed division into public and private.

There is therefore no specialization of spaces by activities. Inside the house, cooking, eating, resting, and sleeping, gives place to working or meeting, without prejudice to any principle. Outside, every space from side of street to centre of street to park or empty public land may be used interchangeably for work, celebration, meeting, storage, and so on. There is perfect unity of social code and social practice.

Third, some arguably modern values, or more precisely, metropolitan modern values, are recognizably absent, including: the observance of rules of precedence in traffic, recognition of symbols for discipline, obedience to appointed lawmakers, and a sense of that internalized control that would preclude, for instance, throwing garbage in any public space.

It has been my argument that the nature of schooling, across the spectrum of all kinds of schools, is such that the discipline often boasted about or alluded to positively by schools and educators is not the discipline of Foucault's argument, that permeates the self and transcends conflict and consciousness, that empowers even as it controls, and makes the disciplined person a true subject of modernity. Rather the child in a provincial school learns only to be subjected to authority, and this authority is arbitrary both in composition and actual action, and arbitrary in its deployment of symbols. Thus, when free of scrutiny, the lessons of the school such as punctuality, straight lines, silence, cleanliness, or maintenance of codes of discipline, are totally unobserved by him. They are a kind of game that must be played only if those in authority are watching. This is not the phenomenon described by Paul Willis of working class kids reproducing their class through resisting a certain socialization (Willis 1977). Rather, the children in a provincial city collaborate with the adult authorities to put on a show of learning discipline, and both collaborate in a kind of humanity that precludes learning the discipline, and in terms of the child's experience actually empowers him—within the provincial world.

But there is more to the teachings of the neighbourhood, and my fourth point is about the aesthetics of everyday life. A religious institution called the Gayatri Shaktipeeth had a grand celebration lasting for three days. It is one of hundreds of such sectarian public organizations, and they all have their periodic celebrations. The Shaktipeeth had dozens of loudspeakers spread over four neighbourhoods. They had two full days of chanting, lectures, yoga, meditation, puja, sermons, *prasad*, and singing. The theme was *'Mahila jagriti'* or the arousal of women. The speakers explained how important it was for women to rise and take up their full share of building up the society and the nation. The nation was taken to be homogeneous, with no difference of caste, class, or creed, as the cliché goes. The event was crowded. The arrangements were expensive and efficient. The sermons were articulate and powerful. The singing was tiresome.

A tent was erected in the field of a local school, where the public sat, women or the sisters, on one side, and the men or the brothers, on another. There were stalls of power-building *chyavanprash*, of incense and *yantras* and rings, of pictures of the founding teachers, and of books on the topics of the day. The stage on one side had six young women in saffron, playing, singing, and preaching. The audience was absorbed and often clapped or chanted alongside. At the edges children ran around playing their games.

What did these children learn from this event? Regardless of its specialized nature, it is the same as large scale feasts and rituals like weddings. Children could certainly catch odd things from the mikes on *mahakal*, on *Shakti*, on the problems of contemporary society and their solutions. But what else? I would like to interpolate here an observation based on myself as an informant.

When I was small I often hung around till late at night at such events, sometimes falling asleep on the sofa or *dari*, running around with cousins if at home, with utter strangers if elsewhere. I always caught something of what was going on. I saw Indian dances first at such occasions, heard non-film Indian music first on such stages through such loudspeakers, and built up involuntarily my intellectual world with knowledge such as: What was so distinct about each of the Pandava brothers? Why did Mira hate her husband's family? How did Yashoda react to her son's naughtiness?

I learnt these things because I saw them repeatedly and not just once. But even more, I learnt how such events should *feel*, and the correct, normal ambience in them. If as an adult I came to arrange any large-scale ritual, it did not feel successful if it did not feel like that. Like what? With a tent (or marquee, as Salman Rushdie calls it) in the night, food served outdoors, people coming and going, amplified lights and sounds, and a sense of liminality. A oneness with nature, a continuity of space, an endlessness of time, the outdoors transformed into the indoors, but so much more exciting than the everyday indoors. These were things I learnt that were as concrete as what I learnt in school.

THE HOME: CLASS

The sensual, symbolic, and metaphoric world of the provincial child learnt by her in the neighbourhood is shared across gender and class. By sensual I mean experiences such as those of the monsoons, of eating mangoes, of swimming in the river, and of playing in the streets. The symbolic is a continuation of the same, in that it constitutes and does not merely denote: the food, colour, sound, and liminality of festive occasions as necessary for both ritual correctness and the good life. By metaphoric, I mean the almost classical-by-now metaphors of the *ghazal* and the cinematic world, such as the cluster around love: stars, night, thirsty eyes, sleeplessness, tossing in bed, crying, calling out a name, responding. This world of the senses and metaphors is learnt also in the home, simply because the home is continuous with the neighbourhood.

The home of Gulistan and Gulfesa, ten and six (see Figure 4) was surrounded by a sea of water one day in August. The only reference I heard about the water was that the two girls would not be going for their tuition that day because of the water. Perhaps that was why they were happily playing cards instead. Gulistan and Gulfesa do not experience shortage of space or difficulty in any job at home because they have grown up in this house and they are totally used to it. This is how space and time are, as normal as sun is sun and water is water.

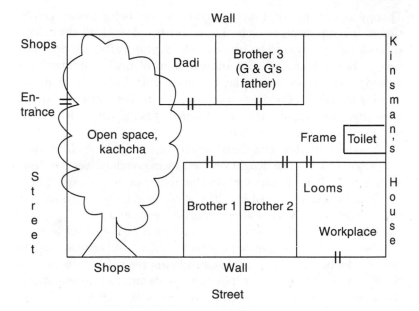

Figure 4. Gulistan and Gulfesa's house

   When I was small and visited my ancestral house in Kutchery Road, Lucknow, I never thought of its surroundings as a crowded street with open gutters on either side, and food shops which were made on wooden benches on top of these, the refuse from these shops going directly into the gutters underneath. There was a Thakur who brought around his cart every evening, ringing his bell as a special signal, and we would rush, if we could afford it, to slurp up his shaved ice and cream and syrup, never imagining that it was less than sanitary. The *only* consideration, ever, was, can I afford it? Only when I was grown up, did I hear this beloved Kutchery Road described as 'dirty' and children being warned not to eat the *nali ki chat* (snacks of the gutters) or hang around by the roadsides. Moreover, all my cousins in this Kutchery Road house slept in smaller, darker bedrooms than did I in my cantonment bungalow, but I did not think their situation pitiable. Rather, it seemed wonderful and enviable. The eyes I have now to discern clean and dirty, spacious and crowded, well-lit and dingy, are not the eyes that children ever have, no matter who they are.
   When I was small, the rainy season was a time of magic. Clouded skies, breezes, drizzles and sprinkles, a kind of magic quality in the air.

There was a chance of 'rainy days' and school being unexpectedly closed. It was possible to sit in the verandah and work all afternoon, without being bothered by heat or cold. A child, after all, does not have to be conscious of adult monsoon problems like mildew and mould. I remember many play kitchens, with little clay or metal cooking utensils, leaf and clay foods, picnics, real and make-believe. I remember swinging on the charpoy swing, or being safe under a roof, soft greens outside.

Maybe Gulistan and Gulfesa are enjoying their childhood monsoons equally. The delight on their faces certainly seems to bear witness to it. This, despite the fact that their house is broken down, very cramped, surrounded by filthy water, and they are themselves resource-less, poorly fed and nightmarishly educated.

Of course, class is important. The toilets of poor people are a problem—for the outsider, but maybe for them too. Some are totally outside the home, in the worse cases being the side of the nearby pond. Little children in poor localities are encouraged to defecate on the wayside, and almost all children to urinate anywhere. When slightly better, homes have toilets in the courtyards, entrance ways, and staircases. They are dark, with non-flushable commodes in the ground, of the squatting 'Indian style', with stored water to be dispensed with a mug. The child learns to manoeuvre among all this matter-of-factly, and never actively suffers.

Bathing places are not specialized either. The tap or well is not in a closed space. Men and women bathe routinely in courtyards, with some items of clothing on. In other cases, there is no private well or tap and buckets are brought in from outside. There is a preferred place for keeping them, but obviously a bucket could be kept anywhere. Thus a child could one day be bathed on the roof and another day in the corner of a room. The Ganga is a vast reservoir for one's private use, including brushing of teeth, washing of clothes, and soaping and scrubbing oneself clean.

The night spaces in the cramped rooms get messy and are slowly transformed. A thorough *jharu* (sweeping) is done on all the floors, by the mother or an elder sister, never by the father. Sheets and blankets are folded up and stacked away. Mattresses and *chatais* are rolled up and put away. Some beds are stood up; others are left flat for daytime rest. Where there are permanently placed beds, they serve as sofas, couches, divans, and are just like the floor in bed-less places. The floor everywhere is made clean enough to sit and eat at. Nowhere do people wear shoes into the house or living areas.

But class socialization is much weaker than gender socialization. Unlike with gender where both the parents are simultaneously present for comparison, there is no other model before the child except that of the home she is born into. Those whom she visits are other members of the family or close friends, and are typically of the same class. Or she assimilates, as in my childhood visits to the ancestral house, two different lifestyles as equally 'natural'. Only the adult suffers pragmatically from shortcomings, and only the outsider interprets spaces, processes, etc. to be limited or cramped. For the child, they are normalcy itself and she finds them not remarkable in the least.

THE HOUSE OF BACHHE LAL, A PAINTER, AND THE PROCESS OF GENDERING

I will suggest that all children do *not* share the same experience of space, nor express themselves similarly with regard to it, but that the lines of divisions are not those that are the strong, evident ones of education and class. Neither the difference between the schooled and unschooled child, or the child in elite public school versus the child in the madrasa; nor the difference between the elite and lower-class child, if both products of the provincial city, is the crucial axis of division. Children are, on the national plane, divided according to whether they belong to metropolitan or provincial cities, towns, and villages, because the nature of neighbourhood and community life and teaching differs in each case. Within the provincial city, the experience of space and the expression of space vary according to the sex of the child.

In the house of Bachhe Lal (see Figure 5), a painter, there live his mother and father, and his five brothers, of whom two are married and have seven children among them. The house is an open space with three separate rooms or huts, all *kachcha*, of mud. The open space is like the water in a map of the earth with some land interspersed in between. On one side is usually spread a curtain on which Bachhe Lal paints typical studio scene of buildings and roads with artificial flowers sprouting in the foreground. It is very iconical of the much discussed modernist tropes of the road leading to the new India (see Srivastava 1998). On the other side lie some masks drying, in symmetrical rows of deer, bears, monkeys, lions, and so on.

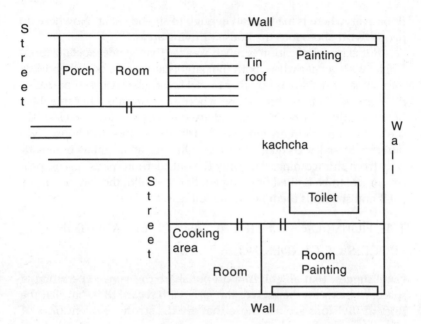

Figure 5. Bachhe Lal's house

The treatment of children in this family was a puzzle. Again and again I was assured that nothing of the family craft was taught to them until they were much older, and that even then they just picked it up from watching. The children seemed to have little to do, with no toys (Bachche Lal chose to interpret my question about toys as the masks and dolls made in the family and shrugged about how satiated the children were with those) and nothing child-size in the house that I could see. They were not allowed to touch any of the materials. There were, of course, no separate spaces for children at all. It seemed self-defeating to not provide them with anything of their own and then scold them incessantly for trespassing into the adults' worlds. They would stand around, feel the pressure of bottled-up energy and surge forward to touch something or act upon something, and be shooed or struck out of the invaded space again. Adults were forever creating a centre from which children were barred and of which they were supposed to stay in the margins.

Bachhe Lal had actually made a children's landscape that was ordered, purchased, and now hung up in the neighbourhood school.

He took me to see it. *It was exactly like the landscapes he made for his photo studio clients.* There were mountains in the background, a stream in front with boats on it, a bridge on one side, trees and a settlement with huts on the other. There were bright colours, a sunset, flowers, shadows. There were no people. It was abstract and distant and frozen in time.

On Diwali day, it felt that the activities going on were no different to other days. The house was not cleaned up or decorated. The family behaved like the producers of the objects being celebrated—images, clay lamps, and toys—with attention to others' consumption in the market rather than on their own consumption. In the middle of my mid-morning visit, they packed up two crates with these things, ready to go. One was picked up by the youngest brother, a boy of about eight and one by the father. They headed for Khojwa market, where two other sons had set up Diwali stalls. I followed. The little boy walked fastest, and led the procession. Khojwa, even after hundreds of visits, can remain a mystery with its lanes and byways, all suffused with garbage. The last time I had to find a place, I was also led by a boy of maybe ten, who led me all along back lanes in the interest of saving time and showed me another world than I had known existed, this one with even more garbage.

Then I remembered other incidents from my fieldwork. I remembered all the scores of times I had been sent to wherever I needed to go under the guidance of little boys. Or, when I had asked directions at a shop or on the road and a little boy had stepped forward with alacrity to guide me, and adults had taken it as a given that he should. Then other consistent patterns: little boys of even four or five sent out for pan and tea to the corner shops. Women's voices echoing throughout the day inside homes, calling out to sons, nephews, and little brothers to fetch them this or that from the market, from outside.

Before beginning an analysis of the inside-outside division, one must repeat that in India there is no exclusive space for children, of whatever age. When they are small they are not taken anywhere special by their mothers/parents, as, for instance, to a park but to places where everyone goes, such as markets, or others' homes, or the ghats. When they are independent, from just three or four onwards, they wander into each others' homes, congregating wherever convenient, say on rooftops, or in the lanes themselves. At slightly older, they seem to take over vacant lots, neighbourhood squares, and burial grounds, but only temporarily, because they can be and are chased out regularly from these places. The same spaces are used for work, such as drying yarn, selling or demonstrating wares, and for adult recreation, ranging from the most informal to the most formal. Then, when they are adolescents, the children have absolutely nowhere to go. Embarrassed to play in open places, they congregate in tea or pan shops, on ghats and streets.

At the early age of six or seven, the category of 'children' gets divided into 'boys' and 'girls'. The Hindi word for children, *bachhe*, tends to be used thereafter only for boys, and thus have I used 'children' above. The separation is on many counts: clothes, speech, body language, activities, and even food. But its most dramatic dimension is in its location of children: in the 'inside' for the girl and the 'outside' for the boy.

At the times of the day when school begins and ends, both girls and boys will be visible on the streets, coming from or going to school. Girls walk openly, or cycle, or ride rickshaws, scooters, or buses, apparently in equal numbers to boys. Sometimes they walk in groups and seem to take over parts of the street like boys do. The difference lies in where this takes them, if I might be forgiven this pun of mobility. Apart from travelling to and from school, mobility is not a structural characteristic for girls. They do not go out for pleasure, for hanging out, or to pass the time. There would be nowhere to go. A street side, pan shop, tea shop, or any open urban space is not the provenance of the female of any age, unless they are professionals or otherwise have work. From early morning to late night, females are visible on streets as sweepers, garbage collectors, vegetable sellers, and hawkers, and of course, shoppers in transit. But they do not stand around without work, as men and boys do.

The little boy in Banaras gets the training to be a flaneur early on in his life. The city is his oyster, starting from his neighbourhood. One could write extensively on the subject of men's activities in the city (Kumar 1988); what would remain to be added is that the socialization into this occurs early on for children. There is scanty literature on this, even as for girls there is the proposition that in colonial times they came to belong to the inside, to stand for the home, purity, and the nation that cannot be colonized. At this point I can only give tiny ethnographic insights regarding the gendered ways of the working of space.

All children, for example, wake up to the sound of their parents. Gender socialization begins at that point, because the mother is typically filling water, doing the dishes, or sweeping the floor, and soon lighting the fire for the first meal. The father is either still asleep, or else busy. In some cases his work entails going before dawn to buy the raw materials for his business, such as pan, vegetables, or milk. In some cases, he has to start setting up his shop by carrying things out. In other cases, he might spend the first few hours of the day in grooming himself and preparing for the day, whether with a newspaper and cup of tea, or a leisurely toilet, or preparing what he needs for the day at home. *In no case* is the father the person who is responsible for the morning meal and the children getting fed and sent off with their tiffin boxes.

The only exception is when the mother is ill, dead, or absent because of an emergency somewhere. Then the father does take over, ready to pass on the job to the oldest female. An occasional informant, such as Lajjavati, might narrate how her father brought her up completely after her mother's death and how he remains the best cook she ever knew. All the women of Assi, my research neighbourhood, get a welcome break from cooking when they are ill or having their periods. As their daughters grow up, however, such as Lajjavati's Chunni, which means when she is as little as nine or ten, the daughter takes over the substitution work from the father.

The mechanisms of all this are clear enough to the child, and the gender socialization is stern and unalterable. The gender socialization, as with class, seems natural and is not remarked upon. Almost all children take for granted that the mother should provide all the services at home, as well as be around the whole day like an anchor for the various vessels to come back to and tie themselves up temporarily. They do not consciously think that the woman's situation could be compared to the man's or any constructive ideas generated from the comparison.

But there may be more commonalities than we imagine between the sexes too. I will end with one woman's and one man's song. The first is a *vidai geet* or the lament of parting from her family by the bride as she leaves for her new home. The second is the man lost in the world, ready to wander. Uprooted as they both are, could it be that the pain is so great only because they would both *like* to be fixed in a place?

The woman sings:

.... sakhi sakhiyan bachpan ka ye angna guriya jhule
koyi bhi to hoga sabnam

chhupaungi aansu kaise bhigege kangna
sakhi sakhiyan re....

...my friends, my girlfriends, the courtyard of my childhood, the dolls, the swings....

How will I hide my tears [as I depart]?—my wedding bracelets will get soaked...

my friends, my girlfriends....

The man sings:

ai dil mujhe aisi jagah le chal jahan koyi na ho
apna paraya meherban ya meherban koyi na ho...
duniya mujhe dhunde magar mera nishan koyi na h0

Ah, my heart, take me to a place where there is no one

There is no one of mine, no one other, no friend or supporter at all...

where the world would keep searching for me but there is no sign of me....

POSTCOLONIALISM

12

The Scholar and Her Servants
Further Thoughts on
Postcolonialism and Education

The hypothesis of the paper is twofold. By juxtaposing the two subject-positions of mistress and servant, moving between one and the other to highlight how each is largely constructed by the interaction, we illuminate the questions of margin and centre, silence and voice, and can ponder on how to do anthropology better. But secondly, to the work of several scholars who propose various approaches to these questions, I add the particular insight offered by the perspective of education. Because one of the subject-positions is that of 'the scholar', someone professionally engaged in knowledge production, the new question I want to consider is regarding the formation of this authoritative knowledge, its seemingly autonomous history, and the existing and potential intersections of that history with the history of the 'non-scholar'. If I study India, the question is how the history of India impinges on the history of the subjects involved in the study. The solution proposed is a radical one. Might one consider that the fancily educated, labouriously trained Western or modern indigenous scholar who is in the field to do her research for degree or publication may contribute something to the necessary education of her less-than-perfectly educated informants? If this sounds illegitimate or unfeasible, I suggest that it is so because of certain problems in our understanding of 'colonialism' and 'culture', and that these could be resolved particularly by reflecting further on several histories. My suggestion then is to work to create what I call a postcolonial context, defined by the attempt to minimize the dichotomy between the scholar as subject and her non-scholarly, indeed, unschooled, subjects of study.

THE SCHOLAR *LEARNS*, AND THE INFORMANT— *KNOWS*?

The relationship of the scholar and her informant, each, to education, has multiple dimensions. As my heading above announces, however, the basic division between the two is reflected in the fact that the scholar is the dynamic being, and the informant the static one. This is not only in terms of the obvious mobility of the scholar travelling to the research site and making contact and uncovering data, while the informant is already settled there and travels nowhere. It is in terms of the dynamic quality of learning versus the static quality of 'knowing'. Apart from busily acquiring knowledge through school, college, and university, the scholar is educated in the field, through her fieldwork, which serves to complete a degree, advance a career, or simply project her as now (even) more knowledgeable. It used to be not explicit as to what role the people in the field play in this education.

More recently, not only does the discipline problematize the position of the researcher vis-à-vis the research (Asad 1973; Borofsky 1997; Clifford and Marcus 1986; Marcus and Fischer 1986; Obeyesekere 1992; Rosaldo 1989) many anthropologists specifically acknowledge the education they have received from their informants in new, human, terms. Unstated in most cases is that the informants in question were far less 'educated' than the scholars, and this in at least two ways. One, that the informants were formally less educated, that is, they were less schooled. Not only is every scholar in this situation either a candidate for, or actually possesses, one of the highest degrees, a Doctor of Philosophy, she has typically acquired it or its candidacy in a modern institution (Western or based on Western premises) with rigorous standards of examination and graduation. Two, she is also typically a member of the intelligentsia and in the view of an anthropologist of the West like myself, to be clearly distinguished from the general public in her society. Such a member of the Western intelligentsia has many characteristics, among them broad-mindedness and belief in cultural relativism. She goes beyond, or strives to, the trappings of her modernity. This difference between the Western intellectual and the average Western citizen is hardly noted, whereas the parallel difference between the modern, say, Indian intellectual, who is secular, democratic, progressive unlike most of her fellow citizens (it is claimed), is unfailingly mentioned by scholars (see Van der Veer 1994, specially pp 159–60, 163–4). The bulk of the population in societies like the USA's are ill-informed and prejudiced about other societies and cultures. Higher education and research serve to de-nationalize the scholar to the extent of being publicly and professionally (not necessarily personally) open to alternative values and lifestyles. Without being necessarily personally interested in the practices of her informants (indeed she typically is not), the Western scholar does view these 'foreign' practices with neutrality and professional interest which translates in the scholar–subject relationship into respect for the informant and a lack of ethnocentricity. Thus the scholar is better educated twice over: formally, in schools; and ethically, in a humanistic, scholarly tradition that would not accept hierarchizing other cultures as lower than one's own. The informant is worse educated because even if formally schooled, the school is likely to be an average or poor one, or, if excellent, in an indigenous, alternative-to-modernity mode (of shamans, pandits, midwives). And the informant is likely to seem ethnocentric and narrow-minded about her beliefs, without the desire or capacity to put them in a universal, comparative perspective. I say 'seem' rather than 'is', because poor and informally educated people in countries like India can, and do, have amazing tolerance for those with unheard of backgrounds and habits. This, important as it is, is not a structural characteristic, as I argue in this paper; it does not empower them in structural ways as it does a déclassé Western or indigenous intellectual.

Many anthropologists acknowledge the subtler education they receive from their informants. At the simplest level, this may be a case of mastering a language, or translating a text or discourse (Trawick 1990:14-40). At a more abstract level, it would be learning discourse in the wider sense, as epitomized in the image of the anthropologist enacting the role of a child in order to learn a culture from the inside. A more personal version of the same is the scholar admiring the etiquette, poise, and interactional finesse of one or more informants and comparing them unfavourably to his/her own bumbling and tension (Geertz 1973; Gold 1988: preface; Kumar 1992).

I am not aware of discussions that link the paradigm of orientalism with this particular experience or choice of scholar–subject relationship in the field, but it seems like an obvious link to make.

The native of Bali, or Ghatiyali, or Tamilnad, is supposed to be simply 'different', more rarefied, less temperamental a being, to 'know' something, which the scholar then tries to 'learn'. Gold is more subtle in her suggestions that it was her own particular background and personality that created the confusions that initially arose for her in the field, and both Gold and Raheja then successfully incorporate their fieldwork experiences in a search for the particular subject-positions of their informants (Raheja and Gold 1994: Preface). Geertz's other-ing is certainly benign as compared to that of those implicated in colonial forms of orientalism, but it is no less obfuscating about the self-reflexive nature, will, and agency of the native. What is definitely missing from his account is the possible wish of the informant to also learn, or what I would like to call 'the will to education' of the informant.

Yet another kind of education occurs particularly for women ethnographers in the sense of learning from 'the strong, self-possessed Indian women who have been our teachers' (Gold 1992: 27) even when the scholar acknowledges herself to be less than sweet, obliging, and even-tempered, that is, a strong woman herself (Trawick 1990: 5). Finally there is the more recent case of developing new ethnographic strategies as by Abu-Lughod (1993) who patiently allows women's own narratives their voice without injecting comments, analytical or judgemental. Again, the women with the narratives are wiser. What I continue to find problematic is the implication that these women informants 'know'. They have wisdom. It would seem that they will not perceive something new in what they encounter, as the scholar has just done; that they do not also learn and change, as the scholar does; that they have no will to education, as the scholar does.

THE SUBJECTS OF THIS STUDY

In this essay, I am talking, on the one hand, about the anthropologist as an informant, a professional teacher of, say, twenty to thirty years' standing, possessed of the ambition to know and learn endlessly, and broadcast this knowledge to the world. This subject, here, I, includes within it its history: those responsible for its formation, in this case two main groups of people and their knowledge systems; her teachers, mostly men or normatively male women, the ones who literally taught and guided her, and the innumerable (male) writers she learnt from in quieter ways; and her 'teachers', the mother-figures who have filled in her epistemologies and cosmologies, literally innumerable aunts, great aunts, other relatives, friends, and voices all around.

Her subjects, on the other hand, are her servants as informants, the products of certain systems, materials and cultural, of production, in a north Indian small town. There is a clear overlap between the two subjects. Although poor, the informants are from the same pool as the mother-figures. Mothers and aunts are typically not professional scholars and, even if upper class, share the 'cultural world' of women of classes lower than theirs. Then, the scholar–subject might be actually 'taught' by servants as she is growing up, or by others in her environment who form her common sense and epistemology in numerous intangible ways.

My argument is a precise one for the indigenous scholar, part of a possible larger argument regarding the formation of an indigenous intellectual class, from among whom would come all the Indian scholars who work on India. Recent discussion of the positioning of the indigenous scholar does not specifically discuss her history as class formation, and the implications of this, for instance, in India, of class as related to education. As I discuss below, it is crucial to incorporate the history in any possible strategy of purposefully negotiating that history, of fashioning a postcolonial politics to overcome the rampant colonialism of the present.

The case of Western scholars abroad is a more complicated one that I can only broach here, but is totally related. There are several ways to open up this discussion. One could argue that 'We [the West] have never really been Modern' (Latour 1993): that so-called modernity consists of 'hybrids' and not pure forms, of rationality, science, and so on. One could argue in a historical vein to show that the Western scholar is also taught and socialized in ways and by people who bear a strong resemblance to those who will be her informants when she is a professional adult. More structurally, one could argue that if one sees the world as a whole, the very identity of the Western scholar presupposes the identities of those who are her Others and that she is constructed in every possible way by the historical trajectories that have produced what seem like different worlds but which all flow into and form each other, not least through colonialism.[1]

Although my immediate arguments concern an indigenous scholar working in her own society, and these above approaches can only be opened up in this paper, one of the most obvious overlaps between even the Western scholar and her poor, Third World village informants that suggests itself is that of gender. When the scholar is a woman and is studying women, it seems difficult to imagine that she can remain indifferent to this commonality of gender even as other very stark differences, of civilization, culture, development level, and education between her and her informants yawn constantly in front of her in her research. Then, as the commonality of gender presents obstacles, it should become apparent that more central to the relationship still is class. But in the case of the 'international' research relationship, class difference becomes fallaciously translated as national difference, but is in any case not discussed as class[2].

   With that, I turn to the specific Subjects of this discussion, the scholar/informant and her servants/informants. The problems I present here arose from some one decade of my own work with poor women in north India in which I was trying to discover their experiences of work, leisure, and everyday life. I encountered an obstruction in the practice of what I was used to respecting as the ethnographic method, that of attending carefully to the informants' representations and taking it seriously as my data. The problem I had was the following.

   First, the question of gender consciousness, as reflected in personal biography. What when the thought processes of the informants are patently lacking in some awareness that occurred to the scholar herself in her own quite recent memory? My mother-figures too tried to teach me of the virtues of self-sacrifice with illustration from the cases of Sati and Savitri, the north Indian Hindu models of domesticity and husband-worship. I could plot quite reflexively and ironically the course I followed in my development in shaking off the repressive dimensions of such teachings to realize that I could be 'good' and 'normal' without buying into this discourse of self-sacrifice. So, when my informant tells me seriously that what is special about Indian women is that they are all potential, struggling Satis and Savitris, I see in her the woman not yet questioning and reflexive. I see her as susceptible to new awareness and change, and not least because of experience with precisely such processes of gender awareness on the part of myself and others in recent years. If she is younger than me, I have no hesitation in ascribing her restricted beliefs to age and that takes the burden off my shoulders. But if she is of my age, or senior, or more typically age unknown but senior enough, I face the dilemma: should I orientalize her, by constructing her as simply 'different', as 'naturally' tied to certain ideas? Should I be distanced in my cultural relativism and pretend that whatever she says is harmless? Should I take on my feminist politics and treat her as an involuntary member of the women-of-the-world circle whose consciousness must be raised? Or should I try something new: treat her as an equal to me where as two equals we subscribe to two different discourses and in respect to her, I must share mine with her as she is sharing, innocently, hers with me? Her discourse could be less than innocent too, in cases where the informant is self-righteous or merely chock-full of her seniority, and implicitly or explicitly condemns me and my (imagined) principles and seeks to educate and dominate me in/with something better.

Second, the question of History, with a capital H, as in the History of the nation state with its processes of education and class formation. The History of India has been characterized by the separation of classes on the basis of their access to colonial English-medium education, together with its disciplines such as Western sciences, philosophies, and histories. The elite are those who have this access, and the underclass and provincialized are those, educated as they may be in other knowledge formations, do not have this access. An informant who voices certain ideas regarding, for instance, menstruation, is a good case in point. I am aware that ideas about menstruation are part of the cultural systems that anthropologists regularly study, and that 'scientific' ideas themselves are not gender-free or culturally neutral. I am aware of the generations of missionary women who have come to South Asia and felt upset by the distorted limbs, weakened bodies, and unsuccessful childbirths that resulted from ignorance about the female body. The lines of such noble professional colleagues and ignoble colonial foremothers should effectively silence one against speaking out against an informant's cultural beliefs. My argument is that this informant is not different in 'culture' from the scholar, but the product of the same history of class formation that has produced her and the scholar as certain kinds of knowledge products. To show her a drawing of a woman's bodily systems and explain how certain processes occur and are not morally marked is also a potential part of her history and therefore her culture. When she is aware of many possible explanations, as supposedly the scholar is, she could still choose to discard some and retain others. But at the moment, as a result specifically of the history of the state she belongs to, she is ignorant.

But, third, there is the very possibility of becoming déclassé through an understanding of History and class. What when the scholar becomes aware of no fear of 'culture' any more? Partly because of the questioning of the culture concept that is so familiar to us by now, and partly from my reflections on my own placing vis-à-vis my informants, through prolonged work with them, I for one am comfortable with a profound scepticism of the 'real' and the 'authentic'. The 'real' (body, culture) is as much mine as theirs. The culture has, and has always had, room for difference and variation, ranking and self-questioning. For every woman who says, 'A female body is a fragile clay pot', another woman can, and does, say, 'A woman's body is her own for her to define'. Nothing I say or do makes me feel inauthentic, 'un-Indian', or out of touch with people from my society.

The discomfort now is greater. Not because I am so different and distanced from the people I study and blame myself for it, but because I am aware of gender, History, and class, that together make me complicit with a structural violence at the heart of the scholar–informant relationship that I no longer wish to be inept at dealing with.

One source for my present comfort/discomfort in my questioning is that I have had some twenty maidservants over the years and have been closely involved with them and their lives, and it is to some of them that I now turn.[3]

Stage 1: The fear of contamination

Among the first servants I had during my initial fieldwork was a maidservant named Shyamdulari. She came from a family who rolled cigarettes called *biris* for their income. She was poor and low caste. I realized quickly that my relationship with her was destined to be different to those of other servants I had encountered in my past, pre-fieldwork life. These others had been merely professionals doing a job, hence two-dimensional for me and lacking in any social and human depth. Shyamdulari was exactly the kind of person I was actually studying.

I made the following observations. Artisans, given their occupation, were carefree and knew that they were so. They could tell the interested researcher like me of their concepts of *mauj*, *masti*, and *phakkarpan* (carefreeness, *joi de vivre*). They liked to be masters of their time and scoff at rules from external sources. Almost none of them took up service jobs in shops, homes, or factories, avoiding them as hell-like or jail-like choices at the very bottom of the ladder of choices when impoverishment struck. *Naukri*, as service was called, meant literally to be someone's 'servant', to have a 'master' controlling you. To earn four rupees a day instead of ten or fifteen was acceptable, but not to lose one's freedom over time and action by doing *naukri*.

Shyamdulari was such an artisan. She was a lovely, interesting person but a poor servant. She arrived late and wanted to leave early. Many days she did not arrive at all. She would sit and dream, or chew tobacco, or disappear. She did her jobs at snail's pace. She had a sense of humour but I got tired of sharing jokes with her as the work was left unattended. Her not doing her work meant my not doing my own, because hers was more essential so in her place I would have to do it.

Basmati followed Shyamdulari and took over charge of crucial domestic work, including watching the baby in the mother's absence most of the day. She was a wisened old woman, who miraculously grew younger over time, even as her mistress definitely grew older. She was drawn from a suburban village, a village of ex-fishermen and new sari weavers, and was an artisan to the core. She loved poetry, music, dance, and colour. Our baby was probably more comfortable with her than I had bargained for, and while grateful for the physical latitude this gave me, I was also, I realize in retrospect, resentful of the local, indigenous socialization my firstborn and precious child must have been experiencing.

Basmati assessed her indispensability quite accurately and bargained effectively to raise the level of her wage and vacations, until we reached a point when she was, as it were, in pensioned retirement, back in her hut in her village attending to pressing family matters, visited by us periodically to plead our case regarding her return, reappearing periodically to keep the fact of her indispensability intact—and all the time able to demonstrate aesthetic sensitivity, warmth, love, and even loyalty.

Of course, we could not fine, or fire, her for her absences because she, and her whole village including the headman, were so inexpressibly poor. The huts made one dry mud continuum with the earth. They were almost totally bare inside. She stayed young because she was not old to begin with, and only looked wisened like so many poor people who look much older than their age. But the poverty was difficult to relate to in an uncomplicated way because of her 'exploitation' of it. I was silently enraged that people like her felt no need to have a work ethic at all. Silently, because the dawn of such a feeling surely put me on the side of the 'outsiders', the merchants who sneered at the backwardness of weavers, the visitors to the city who hated its non-purposeful philosophy and meaningless zest for life, and the officials who for over a hundred years had been writing about its chaos and vulgarity. I did truly feel drawn by this zest, chaos, and craziness, but was appalled at its destructiveness. It was not a problem with her or with me. It was a structural problem where for the beauty of her world she had to be who she was, but for the representation of this world in the academic world I was part of, she needed to do her job in order for me to do mine.

Apart from carefreeness, artisans, like every other class of people, had their own culture of food and drink. Their favourite dishes were very interesting to me and I noted their high use of pepper, red and green chillies, mustard oil, and many spices. I myself never ate like that nor did I want to start. Our cook for one year in my second round of fieldwork was a mother–daughter couple from a wood-carving family. Indeed they were the mother and daughter of my star informant, Tara Prasad, who had died suddenly, leaving them with nowhere to go. The mother, Lilavati, had been a housewife so far with little knowledge of anything outside, and the daughter, Mangra, a school dropout of twelve years. I offered them a job, and used the weapon of our honorific kin ties, Lilavati my sister-in-law, Mangra my niece, to ensure that they could not refuse. I knew that I would 'treat' them more kindly and pay them better, than wherever else they could find a place with their limited knowledge.

The year was spent in an ironic reversal of the previous four years of research. From teaching me about their culture, they were now being taught my culture. They had been obstinate and strong-willed about what they believed. Now, it turned out, so was I. We had frequent clashes. Thanks to Mangra, who unselfconsciously proved one of my main dogmas that only children can really learn anything, the clashes were over quickly without a residue of resentment. A frequent one, for instance, was about the making of tea. They valued a heavy creamy sweetened drink that had turned tea leaves to poison, as I saw it, by boiling them (a drink unjustifiably popularized as 'chai' in the USA today). I could not and would not accept it. As a drink it was probably all right, because whenever I had tea in someone's house, this is what it was. But as a staple of life and a symbol of the self, this sugary soup was oppressive to me if served matter-of-factly to me in my own house in lieu of my steeped just-so tea.

I call this section 'Fear of Contamination' because the only lesson I drew from these experiences was that one must keep servants and informants separate, and the two relationships free of each other. That there was a part of me that was the professional, who would listen patiently and respectfully to all that my informants valued and did. And that there was a part of me which was my own and which would keep her preferences to herself. But a servant is a very intimate category. One needed servants. They tended to be around in intimate places for intimate jobs. I quickly realized that almost anyone I got in my small town melting into its rural suburbs would not only have to be taught the job she was being hired to do, but that she would then proceed to teach me about my heretofore ambiguous relationships between me and 'my' culture, and between me and 'her' culture—both of which I had foolishly taken for granted so far.

Why 'ambiguous'? What is wrong with compartmentalization? Since we are talking about seemingly trivial things like tea, this is not self-evident. I mention the tea case because it marked the beginning of my awareness on the issue, but the question is a much weightier one of relative choice and power. At one level we are all the same: we enjoy walks, friends, conversations, music, and we all enjoy life to the hilt when not in sorrow with the heartbreaks of death, parting, longing, frustration, and confusion. But there is a systemic inequality built into the equations: Shyamdulari and I; Basmati and I; Lilavati and I. We can all of us be free and happy, full of *mauj* and *masti*, exercising our free will. But only I, and not Shyamdulari, Basmati, or Lilavati, am additionally empowered through the power of literacy and then a multifaceted education.

Are 'they', the 'unlettered' informants, and 'we', the educated scholars, then alike? Is not the difference of education the greatest difference altogether for what else *is* the difference between me and my maidservant except that I have had a certain education and she has not? Would Lilavati ever have been a maidservant if she had had an education? And if she has not had the privilege of an education, is it not because of the History of the nation, deriving from the History of the world, with its contemporary chain of schools, ostensibly open to all, but not in fact?

It is difficult to tolerate the language that speaks of informants and scholars as 'they' and 'us'.[4] If not immediately then after sometime in the field all do indeed appear equal, although not the same (Rabinow 1977). Yet, there remains the crucial inequality of education. If scholars and informants share the same interests, but the scholar is better educated, and is empowered by her education, which indeed creates the inequality that she lived off, how can she not acknowledge it? How can the informants not be called what they were, as heretofore denied this education? And how can they be denied this education further?

Is not, then, the only solution for a private individual to undertake some education, on however small a scale, to reduce the inequality, by however tiny a notch? Because, once the realization presents itself, to not act is of course to act, in preservation of the existing system. In my case I did not act because I considered myself fortunate to have discovered the world I was writing about and would have done nothing to jeopardize being the unprejudiced observer of it. The consideration that my informants were 'poor' in terms of choices, or mobility, or power, certainly crossed my mind often but was a set of thoughts put aside in the interests of a larger, elegant deconstruction of their culture. To be afraid of these considerations as a contamination of my work, and a contamination of their culture, when the worst possible contamination was entrenched already, created an impasse for me that led to the next stage.

Stage 2: The fear of domination

The British had a healthy fear of servants. Behind their very masks of inscrutable servitude, servants' obedience probably hid deep revolt. With the end of colonialism and other social changes, masters and servants continue but not with the same meaning to those names. They can often not be differentiated, and the recognizably unifying factors between masters and servants increase at every step.

Both Shakuntala and I were aware of this, that we were basically one people, I her *didi* or older sister, she my younger one. But both were attuned to niceties; it would be difficult to say who the more, but she certainly at least in speech. Thus, her demeanour towards me was, appropriately as she would consider it, 'Didi, you are great. You have money, home, health, education, job, fancy possessions, and status. Look on me kindly, who have none of these desirable things.' My demeanour towards her was, 'Shakuntala, you old poser, get on with your job. I know you people well. You, specially, need not put on these stage effects for me.' She was single and earned well, lived with her family so spent all her earnings on clothes and make-up, was a smooth talker, flirted with all men, and had supreme self-confidence.

Shakuntala also came from an artisan family. Her father and brothers were blacksmiths. Her mother cleaned grain for a living. Her sister and she herself made extra money by stitching and mending. Shakuntala displayed another important characteristic of artisans: she learnt fast those things that had to do with the eye and the hand, she had a knack for crafts, and she did not feel rooted in a particular manufacturing profession but felt that all crafts were hers to master as and if necessary. A little studied craft is that of bodily decoration. Shakuntala specialized in that.

To my chagrin, not only was she always turned out like a cover girl, with plucked eyebrows, cream and lipstick, coiffured hair, and carefully chosen clothes, she constantly lectured me on the virtues of being like that, and my two daughters on the brink of teenage. In my opinion Shakuntala was the perfect example of the woman in a man's world, one who judges her worth by the gaze she can attract from men, who consumes whatever the cosmetic and clothing industry presents as necessary and desirable, and who have no thoughts of an independent mind which may possibly reject some of the premises of this male misogynist industry and this world.

I could have treated her merely as a professional servant, restricted my interactions with her to her work, despised her in the privacy of my thoughts, and got along with her and myself. But, as I said, a servant is an intimate person. At this stage, Stage 2 for me, I also became aware that it was *not* all right to compartmentalize. To pay Shakuntala a handsome wage which, if smoked away as by Shyamdulari, was somehow sweet and tolerable, but if used for a hairdresser's and L'Oreal and Max Factor by Shakuntala, was not, had to be thought about. Her very presence in my home for some eight hours a day meant a level of interaction where our different stands on women and their bodies could not be ignored.

But Shakuntala was both more determined in her beliefs than me and more certain of her right to hold them. I was often lost in reflection and questioning. She was totally sure. I became resentful of her power to dominate. I became downright angry when I understood fully how her certainty was in direct proportion to her ignorance.

Her slavishness to new products was all the more objectionable because she could neither say their names nor read their labels, but recited their virtues like scriptures. She was totally illiterate. She seemed to manage fine without literacy and, disregarding my mild strictures on the subject, constantly increased her aura of self-confidence.

With all kinds of doubts and questions in my head, I expressed tolerance for this different way of being and let her free to indulge, as I called them, in her own follies. But they had a short life. When I saw her last year, she was visibly older and more tired. Having left our employment four years ago, she had freelanced with the things she knew best: stitching, mending, hairdressing, make-up, and massage. Now she would be employed for three months at a beauty parlour, now for a day at a wedding. I think I should have pushed her more. Somehow forced her to be minimally educated. Somehow bullied her into learning more about what a woman can be. Somehow exposed her to other job possibilities and helped her into something. I should have owned up to the recognition of her as innately intelligent, self-'educated' and 'wise', dynamic as a learner, and a powerful resister to the glib, elitist discourse of the global cosmetic industry. But I was afraid of the domination she regularly practised on me and very uncertain about my own dislike and possible domination. I knew that I wanted to be fair to her but the uncertainty lay in the nature of this fairness. Should I let her be as she was because she was, after all, only related to me by being my servant and from the same class as my informants, that is, should I let her culture be in peace? Or should I treat her (as I would like to put it), with more respect, as I would someone from my own class with whom I had such long, intimate ties, say, my friend, and engage her constantly in a reciprocal exchange of ideas even if she did not seem to understand my ideas. I know that a different anthropologist would not have bothered, would have been interested and amused by her, and would have written about her with irony and delight. But she, whatever fodder she might provide for writing, was and is not destined for a comfortable life, mostly for structural reasons to do with the inaccessibility of education. If anyone could help her, which is always doubtful, it would be someone like me, because she did respect me in her own way. But I did very little because I was angry at her domination of me, and afraid of similarly assuming a role of the dominant with her, rather than that of a non-interfering, supremely tolerant intellectual being.

Phase 3: The fear of modernization

I realize that all my readers' sympathies will be with my informants/ maidservants. That is because *I have made it so.* Like most people in my position, I recognize myself as a product of a capitalist world sys-

tem and am afraid of its percolation into my innermost being. Therefore when I see other sensibilities and priorities I rush to elaborate on
their many riches. There are, it would seem, aesthetic, philosophical,
and political justifications for doing so. Plus in a clash between one's
own culture and another's, it is the latter that deserves more space.

Yet I am haunted by the condition of my servants/informants. What
does it behoove a woman to be carefree and happy if she does not
know enough about her body and her rights vis-à-vis medical experts
to claim an averagely long life and steady health for herself? We may
not have to deal with the spectre of sati on an everyday level any
longer. But the pain of the subjected body remains, subjected by
ignorance which is more elusive but as domineering as more tangible
workings of patriarchy. Anger at this everyday pain is therefore equally
deserved as by the extreme case of sati. I do not have statistics at hand,
but all the poor women I interacted with spent staggering amounts on
doctors and medicines and *in no case* understood the treatment they
were receiving. These amounts were proportionately about fifty to a
hundred times more of their incomes than I ever spent on medical
treatment; thus if I spent 1 per cent, they spent 50 to 100 per cent, and
even got into debt. The qualitative data I have documents that they
speak of 'pills' (*tikia, goli*), 'injection' (a word incorporated into
Indian languages now), syrup, all summed up in a folded piece of paper
tied up in a corner of the sari called the *purja*, the prescription, as if
these were fetishes. They have magical properties and whether they
work or not is as impossible to predict as in the case of rituals, but
they are all equally targets of faith.

All my maidservants spent and behaved like this. I am thinking
specifically of Shanti, wife, then widow, of a mason, who will be in
debt all her life because of her misguided treatments, and Kanti, wife
of a rickshawalla, who has lost her youth, energy, and beauty in a few
years before my eyes from popping any kind of pills the neighbourhood
doctor prescribes for ailments that probably deserve no pills at all.

The ignorance of these women is produced because of a certain
structure of relations in which they involuntarily participate. It
includes the hospitals and clinics, and the rows of pharmacies outside
the hospitals and clinics. Equally it includes the universities and
colleges, percolating down to the schools, where even if they send their
children to at least the elementary sections, the women are always
outsiders because themselves illiterate. An illiterate mother will *never*
go to a parents–teachers meeting in her child's school, or interact
with it in any way; she fully expects to be scolded or even thrown out

of the premises. Or, if she goes, she goes as a supplicant, ready to accept whatever is handed out to her. The structure includes the law courts where many uneducated people circle under the gaze of various kinds of legal and semi-legal middlemen, in each case as supplicant grateful to receive guidance. It includes all government offices and, now, non-governmental organizations that work with, patronize, or bypass to various degrees, the poor.

The ignorance of these women is produced actively in interaction with these structures of knowledge and their practice of power. Of these structures, the scholar is an inextricable part. The poor woman is there because the scholar is there. The same world that has produced the academy and its brilliance has produced the poor woman-subject and her ignorance. This world, with its medical, legal, and educational institutions, has produced the discipline of anthropology that would construct the (poor, ignorant) woman as informant but eschew any aim of changing her as a result of the encounter. The changing, the education, the self-improvement, the widening of horizons, the final achievement, have all to be the scholar's, and not the woman's.

On a calmer level: a divide between indigenous and scientific knowledge is held by all of us, whether formulated as such or not. Indigenous knowledge is concrete, enabling the holder to exist in some harmony with her environment. It matches seasons, natural materials, and familiar life trajectories. It is functional and contextual, and typically non-dichotomous and non-individualistic, tolerant of variety and heterogeneity. It is woman's own territory, non-official, and therefore a space for her own agency. One should approach this realm of knowledge with sensitivity and be prepared for patience to master its workings.

But what if at various stages, including when there have been years spent at this sensitive decoding and mastering, one feels dismayed and troubled? I will take the case of Shakuntala Patel (different to the beauty Shakuntala), who worked very briefly for us, and Mangra, the little girl of Stage 1. Shakuntala has six daughters, the youngest only three, the oldest married but still not sent away. The mother works full time and also goes out for pleasure whenever she wants, making the point that she is dispensable to the running of her household. The oldest daughter looks after the younger ones and cooks and organizes the housework. After getting to know their family, spending time with them on various occasions and sharing their stories and jokes, I found myself visiting one day when they were all glued to their television set watching an Oriya movie that no one could linguistically understand (being Hindi and Bhojpuri speakers). The plastic bags of the whole neighbourhood were littered in their spacious compound making it, as indeed was the case with the whole village, an urban slum. The scene provoked me to voice many unasked questions. I asked about marrying the daughter off in her early teens—why? The mother said that she was herself thus married; no one argues with adults on this score. The rational reasons are that the choice of boys is greater and the dowry to be given will be therefore less, and one may negotiate, and also act exactly when one was properly ready with the dowry. No one would take an older girl anyway. It is good for the girl also because she gets broken into her new home gradually. She visits it for longer and longer, starting with one day, then a few, then one week, then a few. Everything continues as before, with her actually belonging in her old home, but making the transition to the new. Of course, there is a tussle. The mother-in-law and sisters-in-law, or the boy's side, express their need of the bride and demand her presence. The mother and other family members of the bride express their reluctance to send her. Occasionally the tussle can expand into a rift with neither side willing to compromise, and the girl is left on one side or the other. The young girl begins thinking of her *sasural*, her married home, as her home typically when either the first child is born, or one parent or both on either side dies, or the brothers on either side separate, creating the space for property ownership, and a conjugal unit.

I listened with full attention and was pleased that I 'got it'. Existing marriage practices certainly had their logic. It became only very slowly clear to me that as long as one does not interfere in the practice of child marriage, one is putting one's invisible weight in support of it.

Or that one has to actually ask the question: how far may one benignly accept the practices one encounters? Shakuntala's daughter will mature to be like her mother: most probably earning, but in any case, free, strong-willed, confident of herself. She will know less than her mother about matters such as keeping her courtyard clean. That is, if women in an 'older' system, including of early marriage, are supposedly in tune with their environments or competent in certain lifestyle practices that are benign and nurturing, there is some kind of a case. But when they are prisoners of the most perverse accoutrements of modernity, such as plastic bags, and more serious effects, then we may have no case at all. The most serious of all the effects of 'modernity' are supposedly new, smart ideas of child-rearing.

Mangra, who was the raw adolescent in my fieldwork in the eighties, was the housewife and mother of maybe 25 years in my later fieldwork in the nineties. Mangra's son Vijay, affectionately and in the modern spirit, called 'Vicky', has been going to school since he was three, indeed, going to *schools*, one the formal one, and then one at home with a tutor. This is what all aspiring families in urban India do for their children. The double pressure was perhaps partly responsible for him developing an ulcer which had to be operated on, leading him to miss a school year at the age of six. After that, the pressure on him was increased. Now he revolts against schoolwork and is condemned by Mangra as incorrigibly destructive. In his presence she keeps talking of him as *badmash* (a rogue), *harami* (a bastard), and *sunta hi nahin hai* (totally disobedient). Both her discipline and her punishment are different, and I would argue, worse, than her mother's were, because of the changed circumstances. Mangra and her husband own many more amenities than their parents did, but there is also a more tangible gulf between desires and fulfilment. The lack of desirable resources in the home—delicious meals, space to sit or play or rest in, attention in and out of school, money to fix the cassette player broken by the destructive child—creates an underlying sense of tension. The mother acts as if in charge, but she is also a victim. She is afraid of pushing a resentful child; she shares the child's frustration; she cannot admit her mistakes. Hence, her inability to refuse the child anything, to actually control or discipline, her ceaseless personal comments, her consistent blaming.

Abu-Lughod (1993) narrates her experience of mother and children, including the mother's indifference to the children except to shoo them off or scold them or slap them. This helped me put my problem in words: why may not the scholar interfere? Interference could take numerous forms, starting from a casual conversation during a visit, to the rather formal extreme: an interactive workshop for neighbourhood mothers. The categories 'workshop', even 'mothers', and certainly the idea of interference in 'mothering', all seem foreign and strange and totally out of place in an anthropological essay. But why are they? Government and non-governmental organizations have been experimenting with them for years, and when interactively conducted, produce some results. I suspect that scholars would not like to be put on the same platform with them, perhaps to be judged by similar criteria of success. Women's magazines for middle class readers in India regularly teach about bringing up children. Lower-class children and mothers are aware of these lessons, albeit only of their more marginal messages. Thus Purnima, poor and illiterate maidservant and proud mother of a son, like Mangra, told me she knew how 'birthdays' should be celebrated. 'You put on a conical cap, you have balloons, you get a cake with icing, and you sing and give presents.' To the extent that they can afford it, 'they' will also try, once they have heard of this system, to copy it. Why not?

So, there could be discussion of, even exposure to the arts and sciences and philosophies of, or any other problematization of, child rearing that dealt with more substantial issues of self-esteem and disciplining rather than merely birthdays, although those too are important. Many such good and bad discussions already fill the air and impress everyone variously, to say nothing of more insidious marketing and consumption structures. If the scholar's fear is that by discussing with mothers how to mother, she will be violent and complicit with the worst in modernity she could debate whether the best favour to do the people (not 'the culture') is not to respect and accept their wishes for modernization and share with them some of the spoils that we, the 'more' modernized people have accrued in spite of our critical attitudes towards it. Modernity, after all, has largely created the problems, but also empowers by teaching critical techniques to produce resistance. Modernity makes available discourses of knowledge, including some that deconstruct it. That is how I learnt any 'post'-modernity, to give the devil, modernity, its due. To not share the discourses available to me with Mangra, or Shakuntala, or Shakuntala's daughter, is to live off their problems.

At the end of the spectrum are cases that are surely more troubling still. Parvati worked at two jobs, in our home and elsewhere, because she had to feed and clothe the family. But the long hours of work meant that she could not watch her son. Over the years of eight to twelve, he progressed from being merely naughty and missing school, to being incorrigibly indisciplined, to being a prototypical school dropout who looked, talked, and behaved rough, gambled, and got into fights, and had/has a very dim future ahead. Parvati also suffered abuse from her husband. Of these multiple problems, I may have no resource to tackle many, but I certainly cannot claim that about the problem of her son. I am, after all, studying the precise topic of education and children. I have devoted my adult life to the study of Indian history and society. I teach and speak as an expert on the subject. What is it that keeps the problem of Parvati and her dropout son outside the purview of this knowledge and expertise? What is my excuse for not knowing what to do about this, and if I know (which I surely would make it my business to know if the matter mattered to me), why do I not do something with this knowledge? I have increased my store of learning immensely, thanks to Parvati. She, in turn, continues not only to know not much more after contact with me, but to have this son whom she has not been able to keep even in school. Because *of me*, I feel like adding. Because I do not interfere in her life out of my fear of modernizing her. The same is true of Shakuntala, Durga, Mangra, and their children, all of whom have educated me, but not I them. Not because they do not have the will to learn, but because I imagine that only I do. In doing so, I am not being 'myself'. I do not extend myself; I do not make of myself and my presence in the field all that it could be. Certainly they learn at their own pace, but as far as my positioning goes, I do not co-operate with them in their move, I do not give of myself.

Phase 4: The fear of politics and the myth of non-interference

The fear of modernization could more accurately be called a fear of politics, based on the 'myth of non-interference'. As a term used to describe Indian colonial-nationalist policies after 1857, this myth presupposed a private, domestic. typically religious or ritual space not influenced by colonial rule (Sinha 1995: 141). There was, of course, no such space, inscribed as all spaces were by the same legal and administrative codes, infused by the praxes regarding land, property, migration, occupation, and written over by colonial discourses of identity and public–private separation. There was no way in which the colonial presence and rule would not impinge on the 'private', and the defence of this private, typically woman's sphere was a convenient strategy of the nationalist elite to entrench patriarchal institutions and practices.

There is a similarity between that situation and the situation today where there can be said to be nothing uncontaminated by modernity and the nation state. Yet many classes of men would defend their rights to run their affairs and they will shy from 'interference', either of the government as in the Shah Bano case (for example, Das 1995), or of voluntary reformers. Many women would themselves claim their right to their separate worlds and from quite transparent platforms of igno-rance, or echoing the voices of patriarchy, position themselves as inferior and objectified. Scholars are not colonizers in either material or discursive ways. Yet they seem to buy into the discourses of contemporary nationalist masculinity and patriarchal structures at several levels, some of which are apparently understood as 'women's culture'. They would not interfere even in their capacities as feminists apart from their feminist scholarship. Thus, they would collude with patriarchy in a way similar to the collusion of colonial and nationalist masculinity.

Colonialism has left many kinds of legacies in South Asia. Today there are many questionings of an involuntary condoning of social inequity in the name of culture (including by Asad 1975; Hatch 1983; Gellner 1985). Yet, such is the legacy of colonialism that there *is* a split between not only classes or cultures but between worlds. As an educated member of the Western/global world, the scholar feels strangely reluctant to interfere with local cultures because she may be acting like a colonial. Even when she can see quite clearly that the situation demands interference on humanitarian, feminist, political grounds, yet such is the whole structure of this colonial discipline of anthropology that a separation is sincerely maintained between what we the scholars prefer, need, and tolerate, and what we are happy to report them, the informants as preferring, needing, and tolerating. And not everything can be lumped together. There are practices, the larger number of the total, which are best left alone. There are only some that need to be argued and debated. There are the few that exceed the pale of tolerance. Yet, for these last, the scholar muses, maybe she simply does not understand them, maybe she needs to work harder at her exegeses or even simply data collection and interviewing? Maybe there is justification for hitting children or abusing them or neglecting them? For not educating them, getting them employed, or marrying them off? If we were to seek to interfere, might we not come dangerously close to implying that they are inferior in some ways to us?

Colonialism has truly polarized the world. Diversity is surely good, plurality likewise, variety and heterogeneity, *yes*. But simpleminded tolerance in the excuse of nothing but tolerance itself is another matter. A lack of a practising politics is another matter too. And another matter yet is an academic technique that wins as reward the best in modern amenities for the scholar and her dependents, from electricity and gadgets to longevity and top health care, to say nothing of freedom and mobility, while leaving the informants maximally untouched, as close to possible as we found them, that is, without any of the aforementioned benefits.

Colonialism has taught us to forget how to discriminate between levels of practice according to how they matter for life. Everything is lumped together as 'culture' regardless of how life-threatening it is, how resilient it is, how hierarchical and contested it is, how precious or dispensable it is. In the name of culture, we see differences where none may exist. So I go to study village women because they are nicely different to me. But if I teach them something I happen to know about childcare, say that something called paracetamol exists (a knowledge that could save babies' lives and mothers' pain, just like babies and mothers anywhere), I am: (a) not going to succeed in changing their religion overnight, so that fear need not prevent me; (b) if I and such as I, do change their religion in the long run, we are simply some of the many circumstances that regularly play a role in history to thus keep everything in flux, and we need not rate ourselves any higher than that; and (c) if this argument seems suspiciously like what the colonial state could have said in its own defence, as part of the larger aim, 'civilize! reform! emancipate!' we have come around exactly to my argument: that such is the legacy of colonialism that the very fear of seeming to resemble colonialism prevents us from taking necessary action. But (d) a recognition of equality means seeing that we do not in fact dominate, that they are capable of sifting and judging for themselves, and should be respected as being capable of *choosing* to have our advice and not simply of having it forced onto them. We need to shift the focus from *us* to *them*. That is what would make our inter- actions with them different to the work of missionaries, colonials, and modernizers.

We would also almost certainly do a more nuanced, richer ethnog- raphy, as we would uncover layers of thought that were left untouched when we only probed the surface features of 'culture'. A difference in the observers' view and the informants' more pragmatic, engaged view has occasionally been suspected. A simple example is Engels report (1996: 126) that Indian women explained their poor birthing condi- tions as due to specific reasons, whereas Europeans would ascribe them to customs and traditions.

Am I suggesting, then, that there are certain universals, such as death and pain, freedom and pleasure? Is Veena Oldenburg correct to make her sweeping claim that there has never been an authentic sati? (Oldenburg 1994) Maybe we do not need to be able to answer this question and it is still too early in the stage of human knowledge to know about universals. Maybe it is enough that there are different versions of some things that are pretty universal, such as respect for human life, avoidance of unequally experienced pain, respect for the environment; that there is something describable as structural violence (Farmer 1996). Maybe it is possible to lay our excited conscience to rest by reminding ourselves constantly that there is and should be a give and take, that if we teach, for example, a fact about cleanliness, we are not necessarily emulating our colonial forebears who believed that all their beliefs were superior without the benefit of enquiry, but we are indeed keeping up a complex, ongoing enquiry, are forever willing to learn and change, retain our irony and scepticism, but are willing to take the risk of being put in a mistaken role meanwhile for what may be certain gains, such as the prolongation of a life. Is it more important to preserve a culture, after all, or a human life?

And *why* do we have this notion of preserving a culture rather than boldly negotiating with it? Is it not a (convenient) fear of politics?

Phase 5: The fear of poverty

Why do I not speak my mind out though? The so-called fear of politics is in fact a fear of poverty. I went to the house of Kanti, our one-time cook, whose husband drives a rickshaw, his brother weaves saris, and the other brother is a Home Guard. Going through the muddy main road of the predominantly Untouchables' neighbourhood, now broader and well lit, thanks to the World Bank and Chief Minister Mayavati, champion of the Dalits, then through the narrow lane bursting with people, to reach her house, I turn the corner and find myself in what seems an idyllic village centre with a pond and spreading trees and houses in a semicircle all around, some clay, some *pukka*. 'How pretty!' I exclaim. 'There's even a pond!'

'Pond!' laughs Kanti bitterly. 'It's not a *pokhra* (pond). It's a *pokhri*.'

I am reluctant to confess my ignorance of the exact difference between *pokhra* and *pokhri*, what an 'i' can do, in short. But I grasp the difference right away. It's between a clean, pretty body of water such as it seemed to my short-sighted eyes in the gathering gloom that it was, and a dirty, somehow-collected body of water that no one wants. Indeed it is wanted so little that everyone is trying to fill it up. The way to fill it up is, by common consensus, to throw all garbage in it. *Pokhri bhari ja rahi hai,* everyone tells me in the passive voice: the undesired pond is being filled up.

The homes I have passed in the lane are so small, so dismal, that I am afraid of what I will find at Kanti's. Yes, I am actually afraid. What will I write? How will I express my sorrow and my sympathy, my sense of a history gone wrong, and regret at being at a simple receiving end of the spectrum? But I am pleasantly surprised. Kanti's is a brightly lit single room of concrete, new and clean. The floor is so clean you could mix batter on it. Indeed the cooking is going on, on it at that very moment. Rice is done, *dal* is on the fire, *bhindi* is being chopped. All around are shelves built into the walls lined with the Sunday glossies from newspapers. Canisters are kept in one, gleaming pots and pans on another, stainless steel plates and bowls on the third. A new wooden bed is on one side; a bicycle at its foot. These are symbols of prosperity; indeed everything in the room is. I feel distinctly foolish to have mentally and outspokenly ignored the efforts of those, like Kanti, who provide themselves with a clean, safe environment, pleasant with light and air, comfortable with the amenities for rest and pleasure. This is what Kanti is very deliberately doing when she covers her shelves with the glossies and stands-up her steel ware, museum-like, against it. Or, when she buys the bed and puts it in her room in a way that indicates it is partly an exhibition piece. To be precise, she did not *buy* the bed. She negotiated for it, probably very strictly, with her daughter-in-law's family. This was, of course, 'better' from the anthropologist's point of view as data regarding a cultural practice, but 'worse' from a lived-in point of view in that women are commodified.

Kanti's niece sat in her place to cut the okra and entertain me while the aunt went off to get me appropriate snacks. Usha was in her early twenties. She had borne three children, none of whom had survived. The case of the last was typical. Usha had been 'full of water'. She was 'like an elephant'. But she felt she was actually only swollen full of air. She had no blood. Her baby died upon being born (being deprived of the mother's blood) and she was given up as dead. Her coffin had been sent from her natal home. People were weeping and crying. Then they took her to the hospital and about three buckets of liquid were drained from her. Blood was pumped in: *khoon charha*. It was like coming back from the dead.

And the other two babies? I faintly asked.

They would be delivered at seven or eight months and die forthwith. Usha looked unhappy but resigned. She had delivered all her babies at home, in the presence of a *dai* (midwife). In books arranged under *Stri Shiksha* (Women's Education) in the local archives, I had read that women in the nineteenth century were ignorant and uninformed about pregnancy and childbirth and often made grievous mistakes, fatal for their babies. Dais were likewise uneducated and were trusted blindly more than they deserved. Some concrete examples were given. Apart from common problems such as tetanus, from which there were as many as 50,000 deaths a year less than a hundred years ago, there were less tangible problems regarding diet, nutrition, and so on. If a child grew up less than normal in certain ways, it could almost certainly be blamed on the ignorance—the satisfied ignorance—of the parent.

Parents just like Usha. Her husband caters and cooks for weddings. He is a *halwai*. The work is sporadic, the earnings feeble. He hardly provides enough for the two of them to live on. They have one room on the edge of the filthy pond that is being filled in with garbage. They have no electricity. I am full of pity. It is the double blow of the lack of education/knowledge: not permitting her to get a job (except always as a maidservant) and not permitting her to have babies.

Then there is the more ambiguous case of Kanti herself. She married off her son; one would think a very important person, judging from the fact that as dowry he received a bed and bedding, a cycle, a TV, a watch, an almirah, clothes, utensils, and cash. When I exclaimed, Kanti said, determined to be non-defensive, 'Well, they are giving it all to their daughter, aren't they? Is it to us that they are giving?' At which her neighbour, sitting alongside her, murmured matter-of-factly, 'Well, you get the cash don't you?' This second person herself had a young son soon to be of marriageable age, presently training to be a carpenter, and she looked studiously practical about the topic at hand.

A vision opened out before me of how women were themselves powerless, from the days of Manu at least, and of how their only power lay in their motherhood. So they not only lavished all their care on their sons in order to be revered and obeyed the rest of their lives, but worked in numerous intangible ways to support the ideology that decreed that a son should worship his parents, *and specially his mother.* Manu and his fellow rishis all proclaim that women are good for nothing but to serve their husbands, and in the same breath, that it is the duty of every male to put on the highest pedestal his mother. For those women who could not protest the first of the proclamations, which means every woman, it was a boon to have the second idea.

But although there is such a thing as a prescription for women and for femininity that goes beyond class and location, there is more emphatically a prescription for *poor women* and for *uneducated women*. The noose tightens the more uneducated the women-subjects are. I know in my guts that poverty, or class, is bigger than gender. I can glimpse how the recognition of poverty, and the fear of poverty, could lead one quietly to take refuge in gender. How much the female researcher and her female informants could share in spite of differences! Why, then, we should talk about the woman scholar and her *manservants*, or the man scholar and *his* servants, men or women. If one were to do it (it would have to be done elsewhere, not now, here), one would not, I suggest, significantly revise or reverse any of my claims in this essay. The presence of men in the argument, as either of the two Subjects, the Scholar or the Servant, would still lead to the stages as I have described them: the Fear of Contamination, of Domination, of Modernization, of Politics, of Poverty, and then, perhaps, of Love. In my analytical model, a manservant would show himself to be first a servant, then a man. A master would turn out to be first a master, then a woman or man.

Phase 6: The fear of love, the victory of professionalism, and the pursuit of postcolonialism

I love my maidservants/informants. This is a confession so difficult to make to anyone I know. Colleagues look embarrassed, and Indians, particularly those who have experienced similar servants, profoundly sceptical. Moreover, to my own embarrassment, there is a clear resemblance in my statement to the genteel attempt to deny class, and protest kinship—'Oh, *my* servants are like my family members.'

These women do not all love me, not at all. There is a Chamela, who lives in a broken, one-roomed house, but beams with pleasure when she sees me coming down the street and rushes to pull me into the room and bring me tea and *dalmoth*, and protests when I am ready to go; all this so consistently for so many years that I know it is not only the good manners her parents taught her but her own feelings. There is also a Lakshmi, living in only a slightly better one-roomed house with a fatherless child and several other discomforts, who definitely does not brighten up on seeing me, and on the occasion of my last (intrusive, as I understood) visit was reported as having told her colleague, 'Does she think she has *bought* me?' And there is a

Parvati, whose feelings I am not sure of, except that she humours me in my various efforts but consistently follows her own different path, while all the time concerned and affectionate about me, indeed, definitely condescending.

'Love', overused a word as it is, may be the wrong word. My informants/servants/friends (if I dare to say it) haunt me. I cannot even take an aerobics class in the USA without plotting in my mind how I could teach them some aerobics when I am next back there, how they would laugh and joke, but also how some of their aches and pains might disappear. This is a pleasurable haunting, not a horrifying one. It enables me, I am beginning to feel, to suggest what I have vaguely and vainly pursued from the beginning of my scholarly career: how to construct a postcolonial methodology.

There are authors interested in the intersection of gender with colonialism (Mohanty 1988; Sharpe 1991; Suleri 1992), whose work I see as inspiring, but limited in one way. They see the main encounter as an 'East-West' one and are troubled by the West's negation of, blindness to, homogenization of, and consequent distortion of and fallacy about, the East. They correctly see that the whole 'culture construction' of scholarship, and the common-sense view of culture and everyday life of the West, is formed and imbued by the colonial encounter, but never admitted as such. To fight this unjustified distortion of history is certainly an important task.

But these scholars, in so far as they see this fight as leading to-wards a postcolonialist resolution (and the literature on postcolonial approaches is vast; see specially Frankenberg and Mani 1996; King 1999; Loomba 1991; McClintock 1992; Said 1989; Shohat 1992; Spivak 1999) have too literal a reading of difference and its negation. Postcolonialism would have to be an active going beyond colonialism, not merely be a description of it. It is a labour, a construction, as I see it. Colonialism does not characterize merely civilizational, military, social and epistemological encounters between nations or states, but also those of class and gender within a nation, state, or even commu-nity. I find institutionalized scholarly research, particularly the anthro-pological method, fundamentally colonial, which is not to deny the fact that there are many more sites of colonialism that are larger scale or more injurious (Tenhunen 2003). Scholarly research, however, is what concerns us today.

I have argued that the product of these class formations in the case of one individual scholar doing her particular project is demonstrably characterizable as colonialism. In doing so, I have focused on the relationship of mistress to servant, not only because I experienced it, and made it an object of reflection and study, but because it highlights something in class/national difference that is obfuscated in less explicitly hierarchical interactions. Further, it is important to look at the servant case because the intimacy and simultaneous tension it produces highlights another feature of the informant-scholar relationship not always visible. Let me take a moment to expand on this.

I said at the beginning that the scholar is the mobile one and the informant the static one. But in the master-servant case, the scholar is the one who sits at home and waits, literally, for the servant to appear at the agreed time, and the servant is the one who takes off and disappears on a daily level, and one day simply leaves the job. Why else do you think I had some twenty maidservants in twenty years! This mobility and exercise of agency and the scholar's reluctance to admit it is a reflection of the scholar's reluctance to admit how much she actually does not know about her informants, how they have eluded her, and may be even betrayed her, how many she dropped and changed, and why.

But a greater reflection of the exercise of the servant's agency is glimpsed in the case of one of the most famous servants of all, Jeeves, and his dreadful master, Bertie Wooster (as in Wodehouse 2000). Jeeves, the butler is the intellectually sophisticated one, and we would rather take his side than the inane, rich, and insufferable, Bertie's. But who is really cleverer, Jeeves or Wooster? Some would say that Bertie Wooster is. He is the narrator, like the anthropologist, and he has to have two voices, or two mouths. One, to say those silly, brainless things. The other, to present himself readably and credibly as someone who would say these things, making it so that we respond in the way intended. Like the anthropologist, but in a different style, he says winningly, 'Wow, Jeeves is really clever. What do I know?' Note, he always does well.

By which I mean the moulah. Bertie has not only enough, but he has enough to keep a mastermind like Jeeves at his elbow, murmuring, 'Yes sir', and 'Very good sir'. The moulah *never* gets transferred. Now, there is a delicate question of excess here. Bertie talks and exclaims too much; he has too much voice. Jeeves is imperturable and says almost nothing. Can he, as the subaltern, not speak?

We know this to be absurd because he is the key figure, the one who makes the story happen. He chooses not to speak because it suits him. He does not need to speak; he *suggests*; and his master voices his ideas. Another side would say, then, that it is Jeeves who is the cleverer. Very likely he even keeps his own journal, with *his* narrative of what is transpiring. As for power, he has it twice over: one in this silent, invisible form, and the other in the form of the expressions Bertie voices on receiving his subtle communications.

This particular case of the master and servant seems on the surface analogous to the relationship of the scholar-master-narrator and the informant-servant-narrated on its ambiguity. But the real analogy is in the impossibility of a resolution of the ambiguity of who has the power, the intelligence, and the voice. My suggestion is that we will never know, that we should be content to let the ambiguity stand, and that we should work for a postcolonial methodology in which there is always this tension of two subjects, and a division of power.

I find the discussion of master and servant useful because it thus mixes up the categories of 'master' and 'servant'. Let us anthropologists also do so, if we can. Let scholars in the field *serve* their informants, not have the informants only serve them, the scholars, with data on their lives and raw material for their learning. Let the scholars be at the informants' *service* in whatever way needed by the latter, but at the most basic, with simple, necessary education. Let the scholars *produce* something useful in the field, and not merely *consume*. Let them *educate* and not merely *get educated*.

My arguments then have echoed and re-echoed the proposition that one must understand the informant's situation beyond the definitions of the scholar, and expand the scholarly activity to deal at all time with two Subjects. We would then recognize the Scholar as the Subject engaged in 'authoritative theoretical production' (Spivak 1988: 66), but also understand the other Subject to be not 'silenced', as if 'silence', or its opposite, 'speech' or 'voice' or 'authorship' had a transparent allusion to something fixed and recognizable, and we had to do no work to distinguish and recognize it (Shree 2000: Afterword). That it was only one of the Subject's, the scholar's, prerogative to insist on the proper definitions of 'speech' and 'silence'.

Postcolonialism, then, should be the effort to forge methods in our disciplines that can preserve the best in them while moulding them in ways to go beyond their founding moments in colonial sites which seemingly formed their (arguably) core approach forever. In proposing this additional labour for the scholar where she attempts to understand the informant beyond the formulation that she brings with her to the field, I am also pushing for my preferred strategy of 'education'. By this awkward term, which suggests activities forced and unpleasant, I mean in fact a very wide discourse and a huge range of activities. The discourse of education in South Asia includes the idea that people are fundamentally changed by their education, and strange though the idea may seem to a classless West, it is important to take it seriously from the South Asian case.

It is a frightening prospect to undertake any educational work and make the interaction truly two-sided. Imagine the grubbiness of poverty, slums, disease, ignorance, small-mindedness, all not disturbing so much for their material difficulties as their intellectual disturbance to our emerging—existing systems of knowledge. Imagine not being in control and being actively resisted. Imagine not being able to just step off, but having a burden to carry. Then imagine the awkwardness, worse even than all the above, of the self-consciousness of finding oneself with the grandiose aim of trying to change the world.

But that need not be the aim. The single aim need be only to be a better scholar and do one's professional job better. All that I have been saying is in the interest of furthering scholarship. My point is not a transparently ideological or political one, but rather a theoretical one, which needs, at this moment of constructing postcolonialism, this ideology and politics. A postcolonial approach is, precisely, the discovery of the speech of the subaltern. It is a discovery that this speech is a process. *Who*, I want us to ask, is this informant-subject I am studying? Is she the one I see, or think I see, before me, today, now? Is she as static as I am presuming her to be? Or is she the one I could glimpse as emerging, if I tried, a process I could also decipher, but would have to refine my approach further in order to catch successfully in my vision? Is she the one I think I hear, or is she the other tenor (too) that is trying to sound and is practising its cadences before suddenly sounding out loud and clear? Many people make a preparatory sound in their throats before they speak. Many express themselves through sounds that cannot be quite transliterated. Many sounds definitely exist around us but are near-inaudible until we are past a certain training. The theoretical point here is about the history *within* each of us, interacting with the history that has produced us. A person is not a being nor a becoming; and at any rate, not a fact, or the end of an enquiry; but a *history* negotiating with itself, or an ongoing enquiry. Scholars, of all people, know that they are learning and therefore in movement all the time. So, they must accept, is the informant part of a process, and looking for change.

NOTES

1. Ruth Behar (1996) suggests that there is a vulnerability of scholars to what they observe because of human, if not more specific social and historical connections. Her point, made particularly in the first chapter, seems to me valuable, but particularly true for the US population, made up of so many diasporic and global emotional and material movements.

2. There is an in-between situation, that of the diasporic scholar who goes to study the society she has 'left behind' (for India: Chatterjee 2001; Narayan 1993; Visweswaran 1994). I do not fully share the discomfiture of these scholars as insiders-outsiders, partly because their situation does not seem to me generically different to that of scholars from either the same society or from one totally different (all are insiders-outsiders); and partly because the historian in me resents their positioning as a simplification of the class and educational histories of the societies concerned that has produced scores of intellectuals who live in several worlds just like these diasporic scholars but are not related to.

3. A word about servants is necessary. An Indian scholar in the field might have no desire to live in the field in the self-denying, mistakenly-authentic 'Indian', or simply American, ways adopted by scholars from the USA. As narrated bluntly in the fieldwork memoirs called *Friends, Brothers and Informants* (1992), many of the Indian author's American colleagues denied themselves elementary comforts adopted by all Indians who can afford them: to deal with the weather in different seasons, eat and sleep in preferred ways, arrange spaces for their maximal comfort, and treat India as a civilized country of creature comforts. Americans' tolerance for discomfort and even garbage, as something 'natural' to India, was astonishing to the author of these memoirs. One part of my own chosen lifestyle, as far as allowed by one's research grant, of course, was to have the servants I deemed necessary, servants being an accepted necessity by those of us who know South Asia, like purified drinking water, and refrigerators, and air coolers in summer. My choice of servants was based on chance and availability, and it was a (wonderful, sad) coincidence that they were from the same large class of people from whom came my informants.

4. At several places Marcus and Fischer (1986) speak of 'us'/'our' and 'them'/'other' (such as ix–x, 1) which is perhaps meant only to highlight the contribution of anthropology in overcoming these distinctions, but surely these entities are not as bounded, discrete, and transparent as the language suggests.

13

A Postcolonial School
in a Modern World

This essay is about a school, taken not only as an educational project
but as an active historical intervention. A discussion of the school could
elsewhere help in resolving the problems of contemporary schooling.
Here we discuss how it helps us: (i) to interpret the history of education,
and perhaps all history, with new insight; (ii) to understand the nature
of modernity in a provincial city; and (iii) to fashion an approach to both
theory and practice that could be called postcolonial.

VIDYASHRAM—THE SOUTHPOINT

The school originally called Southpoint Vidyashram, later changed to
Vidyashram—The Southpoint, was set up in 1990 simply as 'A school
for boys and girls', extending in the first year from pre-nursery to
class 5. Its site was a provincial city that none of the founders belonged
to. The school was not set up with an intention to express some grand
philosophy of life or nation-building. It had nothing to pronounce of a
fixed nature about the history or past of India, or which way the future
should go. The people in the small founding committee were serious
people motivated by a zeal for improvement on several fronts. But they
were sceptical of grand aims. Perhaps they would intellectually argue
that in the long run we are not only dead, but that our well-meaning
work dies with us too, and not that action is futile, but that we cannot
claim to have found the secret to life's problems with our action. They,

or at least the authors, felt unconvinced by the aims of all prophets and visionaries, ideologues and missionaries. They simply wanted to see a job well done.

Perhaps the school was set up in a moment of naiveté, when we—the authors will speak for themselves from now on—convinced ourselves that intellectuals, too, must act. As parents, we had the imminent problem of a nine-year-old and a four-year-old daughters' schooling in a city where investigation into some one dozen reputed schools had revealed to us depths of pedagogic violence unknown to us from our own experience, later to be confirmed by years of formal research on schools. As Indians, we had the question to face of 'What are "we" doing about it?' whenever we engaged in a discussion on the anomaly of the continuation of colonialism into our lives in the present. And certainly there must have been an assurance and a pride. Although not trained school educators, we were well read in literature, philosophy, and the social sciences, and had faith in our powers of observation and learning as we taught ourselves the skills of educating children. We could not help but believe that the level of activities that went on under the rubric of 'education' around us could not but be improved by our well-considered efforts.

So, the intention of founding the school was to create a space where, unlike in the institutional spaces we saw around us, children could be comfortable and happy as they learnt. Where children would not be dominated by arcane authority structures, and not be subjected to mindless rote learning and testing. Where a green and beautiful space could surround learners, and where they would learn to take the responsibility for their environment in every sense.

That the school could be called 'postcolonial' occurred to us later. Just as colonialism was not natural or accidental (it did not have to happen, but it did not happen by chance either), so is postcolonialism not merely a point in history. It is actively *constructed*, by intellectuals and critics, professionals and ordinary people. Vidyashram Southpoint is a school that actively seeks to be postcolonial, in two ways. One, we see colonialism as responsible for a poor pedagogic technology, with excessive dependence on textbooks, examinations, authoritarian teachers, mentalities of dependence, and an inability to make connections between texts and experiences. To be postcolonial is to break the cycle of reproduction of these colonial structures and seek to construct new ways of teaching and learning (which are not new on the surface of the earth, only in the colony). Two, we see colonialism as a relationship that dominates interpersonal relationships, and even the person to herself through her discourses and histories. To be postcolonial is to refuse and reverse these relationships of domination. The ways in which this is done are elaborated below, in the course of other discussions.

The school has grown over twelve years to class X, and those, like our older daughter, who was in class V at its inception, are even done with college now. It has been successful with its students, in that they have all become active learners who believe in taking initiative and have gone on to good high schools and colleges. But it has not had many students, and most have left after a few years for more mainstream schooling. Its teething problems with funds and a stable teaching staff have not vanished with the years. It has not created a major revolution in the city's society, and continues to be questioned and misunderstood by parents. But it has not made compromises on its simple/complex aims of child-centredness and postcolonialism. Below are discussed under separate headings, what the case of a school we would call 'postcolonial', located in a context which can be understood as 'modern', can teach us about history.

SPACE, BEAUTY, AND GARBAGE

When you walk into Vidyashram Southpoint, you find it very pretty, with a greenness and shadiness all over. Some can instinctively feel its difference to the outside, and murmur vaguely something to the effect of, 'This is how a school should be'. Most do not comment on the greenness. Perhaps if they did they would have to further make some logical connections on how it is produced as compared to the garbage of the world outside its walls.

Every school in the city, in contrast, lacks a green and well-tended space. Some have sizeable grounds, used enthusiastically by children. Others have smaller open spaces, used equally happily by children. The happiness of children parallels that of the adult residents of the city who cannot see the mess they live within as amenable to change. Adult citizens boast of their freedom in living as they like in their city, that is, in throwing garbage wherever they like, spitting, and urinating. Children inside the schools also share this idea of freedom, and schools do an inadequate job of disciplining them into other ideas of citizenship and responsibility, as should be their mandate. Schools are the vehicles of modernization and nation-building, but their spaces, and the public spaces of the city, do not reflect success in this.

A simple proof of this is a modern 'colony' (residential neighbour-hood) in this provincial city, which looks as garbage-ridden as the worst 'slums'. In the colony live every kind of educated, well-placed, prosperous people: doctors in the best hospitals of the city and Ayurveds; professors and teachers in modern institutions and Sanskrit pandits; businessmen; government officers; private executives; university students and foreign scholars. Yet, the public space in the colony, especially the sizeable space left in the centre for a 'park', is a horrible mess of stagnant water, mud, overgrown grass, and most indicting, the garbage of all the households. No one in this colony has learnt the lesson of civic responsibility.

The two questions that arise are, if you do have a space that is different, how does your different space help explain this garbage? And what possible lessons can be learnt about changing the rule of garbage?

The invasion of garbage in every public space can be seen to be the intertwined result of, so to speak, culture, history, and nature. Culture: systems of caste and ritual definitely lead to well-developed ideas of division, hierarchy, and pollution. History: these systems were selectively exacerbated instead of being weakened during colonial rule. A further notion of 'my own' was engendered by the experience of the colonial state as both invasive and foreign, which made 'outside' spaces not my own. A dependency syndrome was also generated whereby it was not oneself but the 'parent' state that was supposed to take care of public life. Systems of civic activity decayed at every level. Garbage in public spaces increased. Nature: modernity in the sense of obedience to external, blind, objective rules, is not 'natural', but de-rived, learnt, and internalized. It is 'natural' to throw your waste materials just anywhere. Why is it worse to do that, as every single person in the city does, rather than in a specially designed receptacle? It is not, unless the receptacle rule has been made, has been taught to everyone, and then there is a check on its violation. Contemporary modernity is such in provincial India that, international banking and internet café notwithstanding, such rules have not been made, taught, or enforced.

The way to change the merry dominance of garbage in public life is, most simply, to make, teach, and enforce some rules. Most modern schools in Banaras have not done this. Those that have then should face up to the second level of the problem. How do you make the rule 'natural'? Observation of the behaviour of students of disciplinarian schools reveals that their behaviour changes radically outside school grounds. They associate certain rules with school space and when outside that space, relapse into other ways of thinking. It is a problem of both space and time. Chintamani Mukherjee, the founder of the local Anglo-Bengali Inter College, may have been a superlative slave-driver in forcing order and beauty into the spacious grounds of his school fifty years ago. But insofar as the sense of respect for the surroundings was not institutionalized in the school family, after him, *le deluge*. The grounds of Anglo-Bengali look today like no-man's land.

When one searches for ways to transmit the principles of cleanliness, beauty, and respect for the environment, one is forced to think precisely of 'science', 'tradition', and the 'nation', to fight with 'nature', 'history', and 'culture'. Science because it is necessary to overcome the naturalness of certain ways of living by teaching age-appropriate versions of the germ theory and environmental pollution. Tradition to fight colonialism, not only by turning to certain resources in the cultural fund of the population—to stories of nature worship, the images of ashramas, river banks and forest retreats; to the poetry of oneness with nature and the emotions of seasonality—but also to pre-colonial processes of self-help and public responsibility. And the nation to overcome 'culture', because the definition of 'self' and pride in 'one's own' is bred largely through rituals, and rituals can be defined in a way that the self is made larger. Yes, the nation can be threatening to those excluded, but such exclusions are not natural but constructed processes. Rituals can produce definitions that are positive, non-threatening, and non-exclusive, but constructive of a clean, garbage-free environment.

Searching for these ways, we realize how history can help us. Similarly, we can help, so to speak, history–writing. To make children take germs and the environment seriously means to strive for the scientific individual. To design rituals that take pride in 'our' land means to promote some brand of nationalism. To use the resources of literature, philosophy, and mythology means to propagate some sense of 'tradition'. Action in the present obliges us to take science, nationalism, and tradition more seriously than we would otherwise do. Such action and responsibility towards positioning show us that we are embroiled in a history that is continuous with the past. We see in a more rounded way that history-writing needs a humanitarian effort of the imagination and not merely a sterile and brilliant intellectual effort. And yet academics have fallen into an analytic habit of distancing themselves from the history and ideology of past actions as if they have stepped outside history and ideology altogether, and could merely inspect it out of their free will. Instead of acknowledging the continuity with the past, they assume themselves to be sceptical and reflexive, and others in the past as making only utilitarian choices with no imagination, reflexivity, or doubts attached to them. In the simplest terms, they never ask as a hypothesis, 'What would we have done in that position?' The difference between us and the academic who thinks she is uncommitted and merely looking on at history or society is that she is taking a position without acknowledging it and is involved in action by default, whereas we are quite clear that we are in favour of science, reform, and nationalism; and we are able to use the tool of empathy for those who were so in a study of the past or the present, even while critiquing them or deconstructing them.

Our position is radically different from that of the bemused academic who interferes in a youthful dumping of garbage on the street, and is rendered silent by the youth's challenge, 'Do you think this is England?' to trail off with the implication that demanding a cleaner environment in India is tantamount to being untrue to India. In contrast, we suggest that such an ethnocentric non-historical youth who considers garbage control as tantamount to westernization, could be taught the following considerations:

(1) There is a certain trajectory to history which puts into question static ideas of what is 'England' and what is 'India'. In countries such as England, certain norms were set in the eighteenth and nineteenth centuries dictated by the bourgeois state, the capitalist system, and mass education, which made for what is now—but was not always—a clean, green England. We may not want a bourgeois state or a capitalist system without qualification, but mass education? What will be the nature of our choices if we want approximately the same kind of garbage-free society as resulted in Europe but without similar class and gender divisions, profit accumulation, and colonialism? That is, we must respect History and not Essence as being at the heart of the form of things, even as we recognize that History is not a template or a roller coaster that moulds everything impassively, and can indeed be moulded.

(2) The young man's notion of what is 'English' and what 'Indian' are short-term and ahistorical. But to have a longer perspective means to evoke a past and a tradition that might give us the inspiration to overcome the indifference to garbage. We have to tread a fine line here between an ethnocentrism that celebrates an essentialist and ahistorical notion of what is India in opposition to the West; and an imaginative confidence that what is *Indian* is largely what we *construct* as being so. That is, we need to shed all fear of being outsiders just because we are reformers, because reformers there have been all the time; and to shed the fear that we may be inventing tradition, because that is one of the healthiest relationships to have with tradition.

The arguably limited case of garbage is important because it highlights that modern schools in a provincial city are failures as agents of the nation-state because they cannot teach the skills of discipline, civil society, and the discourses needed by mobile citizens in a globalizing world. The schools are failures before a street culture, exemplified in the physical spaces of the school being influenced by the physical look of the street, rather than vice versa. This street culture, however, is not 'authentic', being produced by a discernible interplay of nature, culture, and history. By attributing authenticity to it, the historian would limit her vision of a complex, conflictual process to merely one particular construction.

It seems clear to us that we stand at a moment in time (at a 'crossroads' as the imagery goes) where the only valid choice of path seems to be one leading towards science, but environmentally sensitive science; technology, but culturally appropriate technology; and development, but development aimed at redressing gender and other inequalities. We must recognize that to not act also is an action—in support of science, technology, and development, without the qualifications above.

Now this action, in favour of science, tradition, and nationalism, has also to be taken in a particular way. Such is the nature of provincial modernity that a building and a space which tries to execute the above qualifications and also use child-centredness as a central criterion is treated with suspicion. A modern school in India means a box-like building with a large gate that is shut securely. The whole thing should be closed and solid, unattuned to the climate, wasteful in its use of materials, uncomfortable to its users. Vidyashram has evolved over the years from smaller to larger spaces, and is unusual in its odd angles, use of bamboo and clay tiles, open feel, and colourful finish. People are perhaps afraid that it is not 'modern' enough, and they look on it askance. They cannot imagine anything but a solid, concrete, box-like structure as being 'modern'. No one in a provincial city is impressed.

There could be three reactions to this dilemma. We could assume that 'they' are like that, and leave them more or less benignly to their own ways while we enjoy our more compatible structures in other places, either in enclaves within the city, or in other cities, or in other countries. This was partly the colonial attitude, and today is the tourist's, and to some extent the anthropologist's. Or we could do 'them' a favour and try to educate or reform 'them' into what we might consider a higher consciousness. If we were dealing with the poor, we would simply pity their deprivation, including of ideas, and give them some basics. This was also partly the colonial attitude, but mostly the missionary's and the reformer's.

Or, thirdly, we could not rest content, and be ready to admit at any given time that there is no simple solution. We could strive for an interaction where we are not interacting with 'them', but are all in a mess together and can only resolve it together. To run away or to act 'upon' 'them' are not solutions. To act together is the key, which includes argument, difference, mutual efforts at domination, and slow understanding of the common aim. This aim cannot be a common-sense proposition such as 'the health and prosperity of the child', but rather consists of negotiations over 'health'. 'prosperity', 'success', etc., and certainly 'child'.

A postcolonial school is one that does not give in to local culture, as local schools do all the time, arguing that 'such is the place, such are the people'—'kya kare, ye log hi aise hain'. Nor does it bully local people into submission arguing that 'such is necessary'. Both these are colonial approaches. It recognizes the dilemma but resolves it without the distancing from the other which is at the crux of a colonial-colonized relationship.

CITIZENS AND THEIR GUARDIANS

There are some students who are consistently under-achievers in whose case it is easy to see that it is their guardians who are to blame. The over-rich and molycoddled aside, these are children of families where minimal importance has started to be given to schooling; where both parents or at least the mother is uneducated; where the nature of the father's profession and lifestyle preclude giving time to the children; where the norm is to be a precocious child who if not working in childhood is engaged in similar pursuits of freedom and pleasure as adults. It is impossible to communicate adequately with such parents, nor is it the school's business to try and educate them in how to run their families.

In our school, however, we do a remarkable job of trying. In a way unprecedented in the city we have parents–teachers meetings where we try to draw the parents into discussions of their responsibilities towards the children. Within the school, the teachers regularly discuss each child in the context of her home conditions.

The real solution to the problem of under-achievement lies largely in a classroom structure where time is provided to deal with social needs. If necessary, the time has to be provided outside but as an adjunct to the class. The solution lies largely in making the classroom activities of such high levels of attractiveness that motivation arises from even among those indifferent to learning. The solution also lies, and in connection with the above, in pulling together the real-life experiences of children with the academic skills they need to learn.

None of these solutions is tried in provincial schools today. Indeed the notion of 'under-achievement' does not exist. The child is simply labelled 'dull' if he fails to achieve and the family labelled 'backward'. Having become familiar with such children in our classrooms, we are inclined to judge with more alertness the pedagogic failure of schools all around. This failure is multiple. The simplest is the failure to try any pedagogically astute or appealing techniques in the classroom. The reason for this all-India provincial phenomenon is usually understood to be 'poverty', but may be better diagnosed as the continuation of a colonial mindset and culture. The teacher acts as a colonized adult, that is, not as a free and responsible agent in her space, the classroom, but as a slave to other's agendas. She performs her role reluctantly, almost in anger, referring to the curriculum and textbooks as prescribed by 'them', as being mistaken, and as the mistake being made at her cost. In this situation, to expect her to devise more successful methods of teaching is to be unrealistic. Here the antagonists are the state and the educators, with the children a passive, suffering population victimized by the former via the latter.

The more complex failure of most provincial schools is their distancing themselves from even the most basic teaching of languages and disciplines, even in the most rote-learning-based way. As they dispense with their responsibilities they successfully make a norm out of an exception: the engaging of private tutors for their students. Parents expect by now that they must pay for private tuition for their child, achiever or not, and that they cannot engage in any dialogue with the school on the subject. A system of parallel schooling or duplicate schooling has fully been institutionalized, with the child going to an ordinary school in the daytime for five to six hours, and to a second one in the form of a tutor in the evening, or night, or morning, and sometimes at two of these times.

Such is the nature of provincial modernity that these private tuitions have become a prized consumer good, decried for their expense but valued as a status symbol. For those who simply cannot afford them, they have become the real obstacle to an egalitarian society, because schools are not judged by how much they cost, but rather by how much private tuition their system needs. So-called English-medium schools apparently always need so much private tutoring that they are effectively closed to modest-income families.

Such, further, is the nature of provincial modernity that there does not exist a single parents' organization in any school in the city, or any kind of forum that could speak for the child's needs from the point of view of the parents. Our research shows an amazing vacuum in communication. Almost all parents without exception complain of the lack of attention to their children by the school, of oversized classes, of negligent teachers, of an over-heavy curriculum, of unrealistic extents of homework, parents' help, and cramming. Some minor complaints are volubly made such as the carrying of ridiculously weighty bags to and fro, but no larger issues reach the status of public debate. On the other side, almost all educators and administrators without exception complain of the lack of co-operation of parents, and their inability—being not educationally sophisticated by the school's standards—to do their share in the education of their children.

Here the antagonists are the parents and the educators, as each blames the other for not doing their part of the job. This is but a con-tinuation of the colonial set-up in which the modern school originated as an arm of the colonial state and was held at a distance, and treated with awe, by the people. There was no possibility of questioning the school's workings, and there is little understanding of such a possibility now. Indeed, schools are divided up into the 'better', more highly disciplined schools, and the looser ones. The former tolerate no interference in their policies, and exercise their 'discipline' against parents as well as students. The latter are local institutions where guardians feel more powerful. There is also an unequal market relationship between demand and supply that makes schools a precious partner in the relationship that may not be aggravated. Culture, that is, the culture formed in history, adds to the workings of economics. Organizations based on region, language, caste, and profession, do start schools in response to demand. Once they formally do so, the same organizations become now the agents of an external, mysterious process. All formal schools remain in provincial India a foreign, colonizing power that have to be obeyed and pandered to.

We emphatically do not want more of the 'local' institutions only because they are kinder to the family, because the amount of violence exercised by them in terms of damaged self-esteem and damaged prospects of security and mobility for children is immeasurable. Nor are we critiquing the 'better' schools because of the perverse Foucauldian kind of control they exercise over their tie, belt, socks, shoes, badge, and buckle clad students. We are critiquing them, ironically, because they do not perform their modernizing mission successfully. Just as they do not teach about garbage disposal, they do not teach the disciplines, and they do not teach the discipline of self-reliance and responsibility. They do not teach English, as they all profess to do. The few children who seem to learn all this while attending them do so because of the labour of their parents and private tutors. This lopsided reliance on the family for the actual education while denying the family the right to participate in formal schooling whether through advice or any other form of participation is a double blow to the modernization project in India. It further widens the colonial gap between school and family and poses them as adversaries of each other. It trashes those families that will not or cannot take over the education of their children at home, and these are the vast majority of families. The population of India is at present divided up into those who can teach their children through their own resources, and those who cannot and therefore rely fruitlessly only on schools or stay away from schools as impossible propositions.

A postcolonial school is a difficult thing to run, as is anything 'postcolonial' because of the legacy of colonialism. But we use the lessons of history to suggest some concrete steps that are all being tried.

First, the postcolonial school does not discriminate between children on the basis of their family background, including through subtle features like the name or appearance of the school, the fee structure, the dress code, and most of all, the expectation of home-education from parents.

Then, starting from the bottom up, it actively strives to woo those children to learn who have never encountered book learning before. There is a series of pedagogic strategies for this, and the aim being clear, they are all developed with tireless labour and tried variously. For the faltering performance of children from families where there is no previous education and there is also active resistance to the culture of the modern school, the children are not faulted. We are in this histori-cal situation together, and nothing about the modern position is trans-parently unquestionable. So, the school revises much curricula and procedures to incorporate the home culture, which like any culture, is full of a wealth of potential for any possible use.

THE RAMMOHAN ROY SYNDROME

Rammohan Roy wanted to be taught everything of Western learning because the other Eastern knowledge was already accessible and, as we understand him, it is better to belong to two worlds and be universal than to one and the less powerful one. He was not so much western-ized as a westernizer.

This desire has stayed with ambitious Indians since, but no one has worked out a formal pedagogic strategy for the implementation of it. The school, as the main production unit of this project, given that it controls curricula, books, rituals, and language, should be able to demonstrate a stronger strategy than it does.

Rammohan Roy was a polemicist and a reformer. He was not an educator in the sense that he had not spent hundreds of hours teaching children and observing the effects of his teaching (which we claim educators must do). His call for Western learning for Indians consisted simply of the introduction of the English language and European philosophy, science, and history into schools based on the British organizational model in which Indian children should now study.

The problem with this approach was, and is, that it is a layman's solution, not a pedagogically skilled or a technical one. We are not condemning the history but taking it for granted. All peoples and nations adopt 'foreign' norms and forms and forge new syntheses that prove functional and, eventually, even aesthetic. Because of a complex of economic and political circumstances in the eighteenth century, there was a strong move in India towards Western learning and ideas. But judging by today, one cannot be sure the adoption has worked. The problem is not merely aesthetic or political. It is of substance. It is not that we have no working educational strategy, and no great Indian model of schooling. It is that we have little learning altogether. There is occurring a massive waste of human resources.

In Vidyashram we have children from backgrounds as authentically 'Indian' as you could want. They are familiar with Hindu or Muslim mythology; have a holistic attitude to nature; are in touch with the countryside, even visiting ancestral villages frequently; know Hindi and usually Bhojpuri well; and are comfortable with their identities. We try, in Raja Rammohan Roy's mode, to downplay this knowledge and taken-for-granted identity, and push for comfort with the English language, Western ideas, images, stories, concepts. Like Rammohan Roy, we feel that because they have a sufficient dose of 'the Indian' at home and are never exposed there to 'the Western', that is, 'the universal', we must compensate for this by using up the school time as a balancing mechanism. This is probably a simple but fair description of how all good schools, including ours, have operated from Rammohan's day.

But there is a difference in our school. We are openly uncomfortable about this home-school split and the fact that it has continued for some two hundred years, with the only challenges to it coming from religious schools that exclude non-co-religionists and belittle their knowledge formations. So we take the next necessary step of creating new rituals for children, consciousness-raising for teachers, and new texts for both—and not as 'we' against 'them', but together. The staggering dimensions of the task, and simultaneously the indispensability of it, make it comprehensible how insofar that it was not tried, there was only inefficient pedagogy.

To reduce the Rammohan Roy syndrome to basics—Western learning in the school, Indian at home—and then to go beyond it with different curricula is one thing we try. The other, more intangible, thing again also refers to a certain understanding of history. The school and home have been locked in a battle for these two hundred years, but have each done their job more or less. The school has been more powerful for the elite, and the home more powerful for the majority of India's provincial and rural population. But if we interpret the history of learning as positive and productive, and see how much has been gained by the nation in 'preserving' entrenched knowledge (the success of the home, the failure of the school), and also how much has been gained by assimilating English and Western knowledge into the Indian systems (the success of the school, the failure of the home), we can have a vision of how the home and the school need not be counterposed and could work together very productively. This needs a tremendous comfort with history, a lack of shame at 'what happened', a confidence that it was, and can be, moulded, and a recognition of ourselves inside it.

THE POWER OF RITUALS

The practice of running a school convinces once and for all, with a firmness beyond dispute, of the importance of everyday rituals as a hidden curriculum, that is, as responsible for as much of the teaching occurring in the school as the more explicitly stated curricula.

Once this point is digested, it is not possible to interpret efforts either in the past or present towards building up a certain kind of person or consciousness by any other yardstick but: did they institute the proper rituals? Failure cannot be judged harshly, because, again, practice tells one that appropriate rituals are difficult to construct. But *efforts* can be so judged, and educators' statements can be analysed carefully for the seriousness of these efforts.

Almost no group at any time, in the whole history of education in India, submitted mechanically to new colonial constructions or follow unthinkingly a colonial citizen or other similar model. Groups, whether region or caste or language or occupation or ideology-based, all tried experiments in synthesism. They understood the power of naming and the power of bestowing meaning in various ways. They wished to pick and choose and adapt and combine names, symbols, and rituals for their purposes. In the case of schooling, however, as far as history tells us, they did not demonstrate pedagogic acumen. Observation in schools today confirms that the same weakness persists. Educators continue to make bold statements about the 'Indian citizen' they wish to produce, and then have almost no thoughts on how this alchemy will occur. Indeed, modern Indian educators still have to resolve which of several conflicting messages we wish even to present to our students.

A modernizing nation has always used the power of rituals together with more directly conveyed messages to socialize its younger generations in desired values. We in India have still to decide, which values? To become aware of the fact that we were teaching some values already anyway, only not reflexively, would hasten our choices and decisions, but this awareness itself is lacking. Observation in a U.S. school for one day would make it self-evident that the values being taught with consistency are: individualism, competition, consumerism, occasional environmental friendliness, the 'us' as modern, rational, advanced, and American. Observation in a provincial Indian school for one day would lead us to believe that what was being taught was: indifference to surroundings; the absence of any authority but the teacher; no sense of self-worth; the mindless following of instructions; the expectation of being judged all the time; the 'us' as moralistic, but otherwise undetermined and left for private determination at home.

To be instrumental in changing this, as said above, those involved in schooling have to be aware of the problem first. But even the simplest technical difficulties of the 'East-West' synthesis are not recognized by anyone. Hence, in the some one hundred schools of a medium-sized Indian city, the paraphernalia of tunic, tie, badge, belt, buckle, socks and shoes is used to support rituals like morning assembly, marching, raising hands, stopping at doors, and so on. The hollowness, indeed the perniciousness, of this is recognized only by those with a solid ideology behind them, such as Gandhian nationalism, Ahl-e-hadis reformist Islam, or Rashtriya Swayamsewak Sangh Hinduism. They are decisive in condemning Western 'gadgets' that do not suit our climate or culture, but they do not realize that they then have to *invent* substitutes, not discover them in the Vedic, Qur'anic, or traditional village past. All other teachers and parents in a provincial city, of whatever sex, age, class, or community, speak only acceptingly of the whole packet of what are called 'convent' practices—meaning colonial derived, theoretically English-medium schooling—and would not dream of challenging the smallest, most mistaken aspect of this structure.

We say 'mistaken' not because we are fond of the 'pure'. Processes of syncretism, hybridization, and creolization are precisely what constitute history, and should be considered central and not peripheral to its workings. The experience of a subject decides where the centre lies, and her experience is likely to be that of hybridity. But in terms of power, both economic and symbolic, there are definite winners and losers. Thus, while the whole of Indian history has surely consisted of domination and adaptation, assaults and responses, interaction and synthesis, the violence of this is larger in scale in the colonial period and also directed to very vulnerable groups. As a result, there is a distance from the target aimed at by both sides, the colonial and the nationalist. The modernity and the disciplining aimed at by the colonial forces did not evolve, but neither did an 'Indian' modernity aimed at by the nationalists.

The problem is not, as both nationalists and intellectuals would have it, that there is westernization, and we were, and still are, imitative and derivative. The problem is that there is vacuousness. Children, and their educators and parents, do not know why they are wearing, repeating, responding, behaving in a certain way. The rituals and symbols of the school are unallied to the home and street, and children are non-creative and awkward with them. The rituals and symbols being in this sense meaningless, the children create their own meaning in them, which is: 'This is what is demanded of you. Do what they ask, lie low, then go about your preferred business.' Colonial education created, and continues to create, two faces in the educated Indian: the public 'yes' and the private 'no'.

Our active practice shows us clearly what often escapes academic study: that rituals and symbols are always created and manipulated and are never natural. When looking at a certain time in the past, say the establishment of British rule, a scholar might find that indeed, that was a time of symbol constructions, but then inferentially regard previous constructions as natural. Involvement with schooling teaches that at each time, just like today, leaders, reformers, and educators had to make an active choice about symbols. Where they were not alert or active, they made mistakes.

The other argument is about change. The average teacher, belonging to the same pool of adults who unreflectively condone and perpetuate existing structures, is not the person to expect to change schooling in this regard. Only a very talented or experienced teacher could, from the lessons that emerge to her from her practice in the classroom, do so. Otherwise it is only the postcolonial thinker who has to deploy her understanding towards fashioning rituals and materials for the creation of the future by negotiating with the past in the immediate present.

THE POWER OF THE TEACHER

Rituals, symbols, and the philosophy they reflect are the determining components of a school, and each educational system maintains its legitimacy and power by these means. Until the nineteenth century the natural seeming discursive formation of Sanskrit education for the elite and *pathshalas* for the masses, seemed to be unshakeably entrenched. Yet it did get shaken and replaced. Apart from being a simple comment on the vagaries of history, this teaches specific lessons for schooling today, and the schools that result have lessons to teach about history.

In the shift from Sanskrit and vernacular teaching to colonial education, the power of the teacher was taken over by the administration. The power of the text was replaced by the power of the textbook. And the power of the word went to the power of the examination.

What if today, almost 200 years after the reverse process was launched, we want to restore the power of the teacher? This is what our postcolonial school is trying to do, and we face at least three problems. First, unlike the British, who came in from another system with their own baggage of meanings, we are bred within our own system. Every single person acting in India today has been produced within its educational system, which as we have claimed above, breeds an insidious effect of obedience of authority, dependence on others, lack of self-worth, moralism, etc. The techniques of escape from a cycle of reproduction are not well understood yet. The closest we have is to the notion of the postcolonial, the reflexive, and universalist intellectual who is in the business of deconstructing colonial and colonial derived discourses. This is also our solution, to which is added very emphatically the postcolonial insight missing for most such intellectuals: that history does not stop and we are not outside it.

The second problem is that we need the unassailable economic and political power to assert our right to meanings, such as the British had when they asserted their equivalent right. And third, we need to fight on a cultural front the persuasion already imbedded in people's minds that the colonial modes of schooling are the only ones possible. These notions are strong because mental formations and relations persist even after the legitimizing authority behind them has retired, and specially if retired from a position of strength. So, even if we can imagine being a government in power with sufficient economic resources, we need to marshall the support of conviction that existing educational techniques are not the only ones possible.

These insights help us to understand history better. The British, we can now suppose, had a much harder time in trying to install their system of schooling against the existing Indian ones than is generally supposed. It took long and occurred in slow phases as their cultural legitimacy grew. It was resisted for varying reasons in most provincial towns and cities. And when it was accepted, it was accepted with modifications.

We share then a feeling of difficulty with change similar to nineteenth-century British efforts. But there is another ironic problem also to be compared, and we would like to end with a possible solution to that. The justification of colonial action lay in that the existing system was inferior in their view and they had a duty to set it on a correct path in the cause of civilization and enlightenment. We are similarly calling an existing system insufferable and implying that we have a 'duty' towards children in changing it, though we would prefer not to name any legitimizing agendas. The colonial move is typically condemned as political: they actually needed cheap clerks, a westernized consumer market, a loyalist citizenry and overall brainwashing into accepting the British. And we? Are we the less political? We may not need the modernizing bourgeoisie's efficient labour force and docile public such as present-day Indian schools should, arguably, try to produce but dismally fail to. But we do want to teach the virtues of environmental protection, concentration on the job at hand, control over one's life and responsibility towards others, and an attitude of creativity and achievement. These are no less political goals than the colonials', only different ones. We may consider them infinitely superior to colonial and modernizing ones, but even so, in the conflict they arouse between the unreformed Indian adults of the provinces and we educators, they are also 'colonial'.

It is not in the content, therefore, that we can overcome colonialism. Any intervention in contemporary problems, any action in history and life, is violent and destructive of others' beliefs and rights, and therefore partly colonial, no matter how glorious the cause.

It is only in the process that we could be postcolonial. Schooling is itself a process, and is colonial. Moreover the schooling has to be carried on at several levels, not only of adults towards children. At all levels, then, there has to be no toleration of the following relationship: the subjects, reformers, acting upon the objects, those to be reformed. To be actively postcolonial is a never-ending challenge. Teachers cannot be forced to take responsibility in their teaching spaces, as they were once forced out. They have to *understand* the power of this responsibility and adapt it to their needs (which means that they can fail to do so, or actively refuse). Maids cannot be forced to keep the rooms clean because such is the new need of the nation. They have to be permitted to choose the work, by being moved around (after being trained in) different jobs. (But they can refuse to co-operate.) Children cannot be forced to stand in line because that is one of the few visions of a possible disciplining. They have to be given sufficient time by adults to interactively comprehend and develop rituals (and will provide unforseen challenges in doing so). Failure is tolerable on all these scores if a germ of change occurs with it. Failure is temporary in the *longue durée* of history. Our school is 'postcolonial' because it believes in the method. It might fail in immediately overcoming its modern, colonial surroundings. It succeeds in producing change, albeit slowly.

Bibliography

PRIMARY LITERATURE (ACCORDING TO REPOSITORY)

From Nagari Pracharini Sabha, Varanasi

'Adhunik bharatiya striyon ki dasha', *Khatri Hitaishi* November 1938.

'Angrezi shiksha', *Kavivachan Sudha* 29 August 1881.

'Apni bahano se', *Kamala* 3–5 no 5 (August 1941): 428.

'Ashlil sithaniyan', *Khatri Hitkari* 31 December 1906: 2–3; 31 March 1907: 2–7.

'Bharat ka nari jagaran', *Jyotsna* 3 no 1 (January 1950): 83–7.

'Bharat men shiksha prachar', *Saraswati* 1 April 1914.

'Bharatiya shiksha padhati ka patan', *Kurmi Kshatriya Diwakar* 10 no 12 (February 1935):13–15.

Central Khatri Education Committee, Kashi, *Khatri Hitaishi* November 1938: 43–5.

Chandra, Ram. 1904. *Stri Shiksha Shiromani*. Bombay.

'Devarshi Narad', *Kalyan Shikshank* 1988: 432–3.

'Dharma Shiksha', *Khatri Hitaishi* November 1937: 16–17.

'Diwakar dvara jati utthan', *Kurmi Kshatriya Diwakar* 10 no. 8–9 (October–November 1934): 2.

'Doha', *Kavivachan Sudha* 14 February 1887.

'Gali gane ka shauk', *Kamala* 3–1 no. 1 (1941).

'Gandhivad aur stri andolan', *Kamala* 2 no. 3 (June 1940): 232–3.

Gupta, Maya. n.d. *Bapu aur nari*. Patna.

'Hamari dasha', *Khatri Hitkari* 31 March 1907.

'Hindi sahitya aur mahila samaj', *Kamala* 2 no. 1 (April 1940): 72–4.

'Hindu samaj men vidhwa', *Jyotsna* 1 no 11 (July 1948): 624–6.

Indravati, Babu Sharma. 1940. *Kanya Sudhar* Part 1. Itawa.
'Kashi ke Maharashtra', *Hans* 4 no 1 (1933–34): 161–6.
'Kashi men samajik sudhar ke prarambhik udyog',
    Hans 4 no 3 (1933): 173–4.
Kaushal, Ranswarup. 1936. *Saheli.* Delhi.
'Kya striyon ko shiksha dena murkhta hai?', *Saraswati* 1 January, 1914: 54.
Lal, Ram Prakash. 1900. *Bal Bodhini.* Meerut.
'Maharaj Manu', *Kalyan* 1988: 439.
'Nari aur satyagraha', *Grahasta* July 1940: 217.
'Nari aur shiksha', *Jyotsna* 2 no 7 (June 1949): 22.
'Nari aur uske rajnaitik adhikar', *Jyotsna* 2 no 2 (December 1948): 43–6.
'Parda: prachinkal men', *Jyotsna* 3 nos 9–10 (October 1940).
Pathak, Devnath. 1917. *Stri Subodhini.* Allahabad.
'Prachin Bharat men nari shiksha', *Jyotsna* 2 no 9 (August 1949): 14–15.
'Prachin Bharat men nariyan', *Kamala* 1941: 272–5.
Ramkrishna. 1866. *Stri Shiksha.* Allahabad.
'Samaj men stri ka sthan', *Kamala* 1 no 1 (April 1939): 38–40.
Sampurnanad. 'Striyon ki madhyamik shiksha', *Kamala* 2 no 2 (May 1940):
    115–19.
'Shiksha prachar ki avashyaktayen', *Kurmi Kshatriya Diwakar* 9 nos. 1–2
    (March 1933): 21–5.
'Shikshit stri samaj', *Hans* 4 no 4 (1934).
Sinha, Rameshwari Devi. 1939. *Mahila Kalpadrum.* Mathura.
'Stri samaj aur shiksha ki avashyakta', *Kurmi Kshatriya Diwakar* 10 nos. 8–9
    (October–November 1934).
'Stri samaj ki sadbhavnayen', *Khatri Hitaishi* November 1937.
'Stri Shiksha', *Kurmi Kshatriya Diwakar* 10 nos 8–9 (October–November
    1934): 15.
'Stri shiksha aur samak', *Khatri Haitaishi.* November 1939.
'Striyon ka adarsh', *Grahasta* 2 no 3 (1940): 244–5.
Suman, Ramnath. 1931. *Bhai ke Patra.* Allahabad.
—— 1943. *Kanya.* Kashi.
'Suyogya pati', *Jyotsna* 2, no. 2 (December 1948): 17–19.
Tripathi, Chandra Dipnarayan. 1934. *Stri Shiksha sar.* Kashi.
Verma, Mukulbihari. 1956. *Bahan ko Sikh.* Delhi.
Verma, Parpurnanand. 'Bharat men prachin shiksha tatha adhunik shiksha',
    Kalyan 1988: 225–30.
'Vidya', *Khatri Hitkari* March 31, 1907.
Vidyalankar, Prem Nath. 'Shiksha kyon avashyak hai', *Nagari Pracharini
    Patrika* 23 no 1 (July 1918).
'Vivah men gali', *Khatri Hitkari* October 31, 1906.
'Wah!' *Grahasta* 2 no 8 (November 1939): 237–9.
'Yatha nam tatha gun, yatha gun tatha nam', *Jyotsna* 1 no 2 (1943).

From Banaras Municipality, Sigra, Varanasi

Annual Administrative Report of the Banaras Municipality for the years 1910–38.

From U.P. State Archives, Lucknow

Allygurh Institutional Gazette July 8, 1870.
Indian Statutory Commission. 1930. *Report of the Indian Statutory Commission. Voume 1—Survey.* London: His Majesty's Stationery Office.
Education Department Files (Education and Education A) 1880–1940.

From U.P. Regional Archives, Varanasi

Education Commission. 1884a. *Report of the Bengal Provincial Committee.* Calcutta: Superintendent of Government Printing, India.
Education Commission. 1884b. *Report of the Bombay Provincial Committee.* Calcutta: Superintendent of Government Printing, India.

From the British Museum and Library (materials formerly in the India Office Library)

Howell, A. 1872. *Education in British India prior to 1854 and in 1870–71.* Calcutta.
Kempson, M. 1877. *Report on the Progress of Education in the Northwestern Provinces for the Years 1867–68 to 1876–77.* Allahabad.
Monteath, A.M. 1867. *Selections from Records of Government of India (State of Education in India).* Calcutta.
Reid, S. 1852. *Report on Indigenous Education and Vernacular Schools.* Agra.
Thornton, R. 1850. *Memoirs on the Statistics of Indigenous Education within the Northwestern Provinces of the Bengal Presidency.* Calcutta.

From Centre for Studies in Social Sciences, Calcutta

Census of India 1901–1981

From Centre for Postcolonial Education, Varanasi

Hamara Itihas aur Nagarik Jiwan. 2000. Basic Shiksha Parishad, U.P.
Hamari Pothi. 1982, many reprints. Delhi: Markazi Maktaba Islami.
Jamia Salfia Markazi Darul Ulum ka Sankshipt Parichay. 1998. Varanasi: Jamia Salfia.
Nomani, Maulana Abdus Salam. n.d. *Geographia District Varanasi* (in Urdu). Varanasi: Nomani Publishers.

Satyalok: Silver Jubilee Souvenir of Gopi Radha School. 1987. Varanasi.
Shubhabhinandan Patrika. December 1986.
Sri Agrasen Kanya Vidyalaya Swarna Jayanti Smarika. 1972–4.
Sri Arya Mahila Hitkarini Mahaparishad. 1962.
Srimati Satyavati Devi Abhinandan Grantha. n.d. Varanasi.
The Punjab University Calendar for the Year 1920–1921. 1920. Calcutta: Baptist Mission Press.
Vasantshree (Annual Magazine of Vasanta Kanya Mahavidyalaya). 1980–1.

Miscellaneous

Siddiqi, Mohammad Ishat. n.d. ms on the history of weavers in Banaras. In private possession of Mujees Ahmad Sahab, Pandey Haveli, Varanasi.

Oral Interviews (by first name)

Dubeyji and Mauryaji. 1986.
Gayatri Devi. 1986.
Leela Sharma. 1986, 1988.
Rama Bhattacharya. 1988.
Rustom Satin. 1986.
Satyavati Devi. 1986, 1988.
Shah, Karuna. 1986, 1988.
Sundari Bai. 1986.
Vidya Devi. 1986.

SECONDARY LITERATURE

Secondary Literature (published)

Abu-Lughod, Lila. 1993. *Writing Women's Worlds: Bedouin Stories*. Berkeley: University of California Press.
Aggarwal, J.C. 1976. *Indian Women: Education and Status*. Delhi: Arya Book Depot.
Ahmad, Aijaz. 1992. *In Theory: Classes, Nations, Literatures*. New Delhi: Oxford University Press.
Ahmad, Imtiaz (ed.) 1978. *Caste and Social Stratification among Muslims in India*. Delhi: Manohar.
Aklujkar, Vidyut. 2000. 'Anasuya: A Pativrata with Panache', in Mandakranta Bose (ed.) *Faces of the Feminine in Ancient, Medieval and Modern India*. New York: Oxford University Press. pp. 56–68.
Ali, Yusuf. 1900. *A Monograph on Silk Fabrics Produced in the Northwestern Provinces and Oudh*. Allahabad: NWP Government Press.
Alter, Joseph S. 1992. *The Wrestler's Body: Identity and Ideology in North India*. Berkeley: University of California Press.

Amin, Sonia Nishat. 1996. *The World of Muslim Women in Colonial Bengal, 1876-1939.* London: E.J. Brill.

Ansari, Ghaus. 1960. *Muslim Caste in Uttar Pradesh.* Lucknow: The Ethnographic and Folk Culture Society, U.P.

Antharjanam, Lalithambika. 1998. *Caste Me Out If You Will.* Translated with an introduction by Gita Krishnankunthy. Calcutta: Stree Publications.

Arendt, Hannah. 1978. *The Life of the Mind. Vol 2: Willing.* London.

Aries, Philippe. 1973. *Centuries of Childhood.* London: Jonathan Cape.

Asad, Talal (ed.) [1973] 1975. *Anthropology and the Colonial Encounter.* London: Ithaca Press.

Bagchi, Jasodhara. 1990. 'Representing Nationalism: Ideology of Motherhood in Colonial Bengal', in *Economic and Political Weekly* 20-7 October: WS 65-71.

Bandopadhyay, Bibhutibhushan. 1968. *Pather Panchali: Song of the Road.* Translated by T. W. Clark and Tarapada Mukherji. Delhi: Harper Collins Publishers.

Banerjea, Surendranath. 1878. *Lord Macaulay and Higher Education in India.* Calcutta.

————1925. *A Nation in the Making: Being the Reminiscences of Fifty Years of Public Life.* London.

Banerjee, Sumanta. 1989. *The Parlour and the Streets: Elite and Popular Culture in Nineteenth Century Calcutta.* Calcutta: Seagull Books.

Barthes, Roland. 1971. 'Réponses', in *Tel Quel,* 47. pp. 89-107.

————1983. *Mythologies.* Selected and translated from French by Annette Lavers. New York: Hill and Wang.

————1989. *The Rustle of Language.* Translated by Richard Howard. Berkeley: University of California Press.

Basu, Aparna. 1974. *The Growth of Education and Political Development in India, 1898-1920.* New Delhi: Oxford University Press.

————1982. *Essays in the History of Indian Education.* Delhi: Concept.

Basu, S.C. 1925? *Problems of Primary Education in India: A Study.* Calcutta: Sen Brothers.

Bayly, Susan. 1999. *Caste, Society and Politics in India from the Eighteenth Century to the Modern Age.* Cambridge: Cambridge University Press.

Benjamin, Walter. 1985 [first pub. 1968]. 'On Translation', in *Illuminations: Essays and Reflections.* New York: Schocken Books.

Berman, Marshall. 1988. *All that is Solid Melts into Air.* New York: Viking Penguin.

Bhabha, Homi K. (ed.) 1990. *Nation and Narration.* London. New York: Routledge.

————1994. *The Location of Culture.* New York: Routledge.

Bismillah, Abdul. 1996. *The Song of the Loom (jhini jhini bini chadariya).* Madras: Macmillan.

Boman-Behram, B.K. 1943. *Educational Controversies in India: The Cultural Conquest of India under British Imperialism.* Bombay: D. B. Taraporevala Sons and Co.

Borofsky, Robert. 1997. 'CA Forum on Theory in Anthropology', in *Current Anthropology* 38, pp. 255–82.

Borthwick, Meredith. 1984. *The Changing Role of Women in Bengal, 1849–1905.* Princeton: Princeton University Press.

Bose, Pradip Kumar. 1996 [1994]. 'Sons of the Nation: Child Rearing in the New Family', in Partha Chatterjee (ed.) *Texts of Power: Emerging Disciplines in Colonial Bengal.* Calcutta: Stree Publications.

Bourdieu, Pierre, and J.C. Passeron. 1977. *Reproduction in Education, Society and Culture.* Translated by R. Nice. London: Sage.

————1977a. *Outline of a Theory of Practice.* Cambridge: Cambridge University Press.

————1990 [1970] 'The Kabyle House or the World Reversed', in *The Logic of Practice.* Oxford: Polity Press.

Bruce, J.F. 1933. *A History of the University of the Punjab.* Lahore: n.p.

Bunzle, Matti. 2004. 'Boas, Foucault, and the "Native Anthropologist": Notes toward a Neo-Boasian Anthropology' in *American Anthropologist* 106 no 3 (September), pp. 435–42.

Burton, Antoinette. 2003. *Dwelling in the Archive: Women Writing House, Home, and History in Late Colonial India.* Oxford: Oxford University Press.

———— 1994. *Burdens of History: British Feminists, Indian Women, and Imperial Culture, 1865–1915.* Chapel Hill: University of North Carolina Press.

Burton, Scott L. 2003. 'A Case Study of Lexical Borrowing Between Language Families in the Southern Philippines', in *Philippine Journal of Linguistics* 34(1), pp. 29–67.

Callinicos, Alex. 1995. *Theories and Narratives: Reflections on the Philosophy of History.* Cambridge: Polity Press.

Carron, Gabriel and Ta Ngoc Chau. 1996. *The Quality of Primary Schools in Different Development Contexts.* Paris: UNESCO.

Carstairs, Morris. [1957] 1961. *The Twice Born: A Study of a Community of High-Caste Hindus.* Bloomington: Indiana University Press.

Chakrabarty, Bidyut. 1990. *Subhas Chandra Bose and Middle Class Radicalism: A Study in Indian Nationalism, 1928–1940.* London: London School of Economics and Political Science in association with I.B. Tauris.

Chakrabarty, Dipesh. 1992. 'On Modernity, Garbage, and the Citizen's Gaze', in *Economic and Political Weekly.*

————2000. *Provincializing Europe.* Princeton: Princeton University Press.

————2002. *Habitations of Modernity: Essays in the Wake of Subaltern Studies.* Chapel Hill: Duke University Press.

Chandra, Sudhir. 1998. *Enslaved Daughters: Colonialism, Law and Women's Rights.* Delhi: Oxford University Press.

Chatfield, K.M. 1876. *Annual Report of the Director of Public Instruction in the Bombay Presidency for the Year 1874–75 and 1875–76.* Bombay: Government Press.

Chatterjee, Kalyan K. 1976. *English Education in India.* Delhi: Macmillan.

Chatterjee, L. and S. Mukhopadhyaya. 1931. *Representative Indians.* Calcutta.

Chatterjee, Partha. 1989. *Nationalist Thought and the Colonial World: A Derivative Discourse?* Princeton: Princeton University Press.

––– 1993. *The Nation and its Fragments.* Princeton: Princeton University Press.

Chatterjee, Piya. 2001. *A Time For Tea: Women, Labour, and Post/Colonial Politics on an Indian Plantation.* Durham: Duke University Press.

Chaube, S.P. 1965. *A History of Education in India.* Allahabad: Ram Narain Lal Beni Madho.

Chodorow, Nancy. 1978. *The Reproduction of Mothering.* Berkeley: University of California Press.

Chowdhury-Sengupta, Indira. 1992. 'Mother India and Mother Victoria: Motherhood and Nationalism in Nineteenth-Century Bengal', in *South Asia Research* 12.

Clifford, James and George E. Marcus. 1986. *Writing Culture: The Poetics and Politics of Ethnography.* Berkeley and London: University of California Press.

Cohn, Bernard. 1992. *An Anthropologist Among the Historians and other Essays.* Delhi: Oxford University Press.

––––1996. *Colonialism and its Forms of Knowledge: The British in India.* Princeton: Princeton University Press.

Conlon, Frank. 1977. *A Caste in a Changing World: The Saraswat Brahmans.* Berkeley: University of California Press.

––––– 1986. 'Indian Renaissance beyond Bengal', in Margaret Case and Norman G. Barrier (eds) *Aspects of India.* Delhi: Manohar.

––––1994. 'Hindu Revival and Indian Womanhood: The Image and Status of Women in the Writings of Vishnubawa Brahmachari' in *South Asia* Vol. 17 (2), pp. 43-61.

Coontz, Stephanie. 1992. *The Way We Never Were.* New York: Basic Books.

Cowen, Ruth Schwartz. 1983. *More Work For Mother.* New York: Basic Books.

Crosby, Christina. 1991. *The End of History: Vico and 'The Woman Question'.* New York: Routledge.

Dalmia, Vasudha. 1997. *The Nationalization of Hindu Traditions: Bharatendu Harishchandra and Nineteenth Century Banaras.* Delhi: Oxford University Press.

Damsteegt, Theo. 1997. *Giriraj Kisor's Yatraem, A Hindi Novel Analysed.* Groningen: Forsten (Gonda Indological Studies VI).

Das, Veena. 1996. *Critical Events: An Anthropological Perspective on Contemporary India.* Delhi: Oxford University Press.

De Beauvoir, Simone. 1961. *The Second Sex.* New York: Bantam.

De Certeau, Michel. 1984. *The Practice of Everyday Life.* Berkeley: University of California Press.

Dharampal. 1983. *The Beautiful Tree: Indigenous Education in the Eighteenth Century.* Delhi: Biblia Impex.

Dimock, Edward C, et al., (eds). 1974. *The Literatures of India: An Introduction.* Chicago: The University of Chicago Press.

Dobbin, Christine. 1972. *Urban Leadership in Western India: Politics and Communities in Bombay City 1840–1885.* New York: Oxford University Press.

Donald, James. 1996. 'The Citizen and the Man about Town', in Stuart Hall and Paul du Gay (eds) *Questions of Cultural Identity.* London: Sage.

Doniger, Wendy. 1980. *Women, Androgynes and Other Mythical Beasts.* Chicago: University of Chicago press.

–––– 2005. *The Woman Who Pretended to be Who She Was.* New York: Oxford University Press.

Dove, Michael. 1998. [1994]. '"Jungle" in Nature and Culture', in Ramachandra Guha, (ed.) *Social Ecology.* Delhi: Oxford University Press. pp. 90–115.

Dube, Leela, Eleanor Leacock, and Shirley Ardener (eds). 1986. *Visibility and Power: Essays on Women in Society and Development.* Delhi: Oxford University Press.

Duranti, Alessandro. 1997. 'Indexical Speech Across Samoan Communities', in *American Anthropologist* Vol. 99 (2), pp. 342–54.

Dwivedi, Sivnarayan. 1917. *Rammohan Roy.* Varanasi: Haridas and Co.

Eickelman, Dale F. 1978. 'Royal Authority and Religious Legitimacy: Morocco's Elections, 1960-1984', in Myron J. Aronoff (ed.) *The Frailty of Authority.* New Brunswick: Transaction Books. pp. 181–205.

––––1986. 'The Art of Memory: Islamic Education and its Social Reproduction', in *Comparative Studies in Society and History.* Vol 20 (4), pp. 485–516.

Engels, Dagmar. 1996. *Beyond Purdah: Women in Bengal 1890–1939.* New Delhi: Oxford University Press.

Fabian, Johannes. 1983. *Time and the Other: How Anthropology Makes its Objects.* New York: Columbia University Press.

Fabian, S.M. 1992. *Space-Time of the Bororo of Brazil.* Gainesville: University of Florida Press.

Farmer, Paul. 1996. 'On Suffering and Structural Violence: A View From Below', *Daedalus* 125(1). California: Sage Publications. pp. 261–83.

Ferro-Luzzi, Gabriella E. 1987. *The Self-milking Cow and the Bleeding Lingam*. Wiesbaden: Harrassowitz.

Forbes, Geraldine. 1996. *Women in Modern India*. Cambridge: Cambridge University Press.

Foucault, Michel. 1975. *Discipline and Punish: The Birth of the Prison*. New York: Vintage Books.

—— 1980. *Power/Knowledge: Selected Interviews and Other Writings 1972–77*. New York: Pantheon Books.

Frankenberg, Ruth and Lata Mani. 1996. 'Crosscurrents, Crosstalk: Race, "Postcoloniality" and the Politics of Location' in Padmini Mongia (ed.) *Contemporaray Postcolonial Theory: A Reader*. London: Arnold.

Fuchs, Dieter. 1995. 'Training and Continued Education—Children's Culture.' *European Education Summer* 26 (2) pp. 5–17.

Gallagher, John, Gordon Johnson, and Anil Seal, (eds). 1973. *Locality, Province and Nation: Essays on Indian Politics 1870 to 1940*. Cambridge: Cambridge University Press.

Gangopadhyaya, Sunil. 1981. *Those Days*. Delhi: Penguin.

Gaonkar, Dilip Parameshwar, (ed.) 2001. *Alternative Modernities*. Durham: Duke University Press.

Garner, Shirley, Claire Kahane, and Madelon Sprengnether (eds). 1985. *The Mother Tongue: Essays in Feminist Psychoanalytic Interpretation*. Ithaca: Cornell University Press.

Garrett, H.L.O. (ed.) 1914. *A History of Government College, Lahore*. Lahore: The 'Civil and Military' Gazette Press.

Garrett, H.L.O. and Abdul Hamid. 1964. *A History of Government College Lahore 1864–1964*. Lahore: The 'Civil and Military Gazette' Press.

Geertz, Clifford. 1973. *The Interpretation of Cultures: Selected Essays*. New York: Basic.

Ghose, Jayatri. 2000. 'Satyavati: The Matriarch of the Mahabharata', in Mandakranta Bose (ed.) *Faces of the Feminine in Ancient, Medieval, and Modern India*. New York: Oxford University Press. pp. 33–47.

Ghosh, Archana. 1989. 'The Education of Women' in *Arghya*. Banaras: Durga Charan Girls' School.

Gilbert, Sandra and Susan Gubar. 1994. 'No Man's Land: The Place of the Woman Writer in the Twentieth Century.' *Vol. 3: Letters from the Front*. New Haven: Yale University Press.

Giroux, Henry A. 1983. 'Theories of Reproduction and Resistance in the New Sociology of Education: Critical Analysis', in *Harvard Educational Review* 33, pp. 257–93.

Glenn, E.N. 1994. 'Social Constructions of Mothering: A Thematic Overview', in E. N. Glenn, G. Chang and L. Forcey, (eds) *Mothering: Ideology, Experience, and Agency*. New York: Routledge.

Gold, Ann G. 1988. *Fruitful Journeys: The Ways of Rajasthani Pilgrims*. University of California Press .

————1992. *A Carnival of Parting*. Berkeley: University of California Press.

————1994. 'Gender, Violence and Power: Rajasthani Stories of Shakti' in Nita Kumar (ed.) *Women as Subjects: South Asian Histories*. Charlottesville: University of Virginia Press, and Calcutta: Stree Publications.

————2002. *In the Time of Trees and Sorrows: Nature, Power, and Memory in Rajasthan*. Durham: Duke University Press.

Goswamy, Manu. 2004. *Producing India: From Colonial Economy to National Space*. Chicago: University of Chicago Press.

Gramsci, Antonio. 1971. *Selections from the Prison Notebooks*. Edited and translated by Quintin Hoare and Geoffery Nowell Smith. New York: International Publishers.

Guha, Ranajit. 1997. *Dominance without Hegemony: History and Power in Colonial India*. Cambridge: Harvard University Press.

Gupta, Dipankar. 2000. *Mistaken Modernity: India Between Worlds*. Delhi: Harper Collins.

Gupta, Narayani. 1973. *Delhi Between Two Empires 1803–1931*. Delhi: Oxford University Press.

Handler, Richard. C. and Daniel Segal (eds). 1990. *Jane Austen and the Fiction of Culture: An Essay on the Narration of Social Realities*. Tucson, Arizona: University of Arizona Press.

Hansen, Kathryn. 1988. 'The virangana in North Indian history, Myth, and Popular Culture', in *Economic and Political Weekly* 23 (April 30) pp. 25–33.

Harlan, Lindsey and Paul B. Courtright (eds). 1995. *From the Margins of Hindu Marriage: Essays on Gender, Religion and Culture*. New York: Oxford University Press.

Hatcher, Brian A. 1996. *Idioms of Improvement: Vidyasagar and Cultural Encounter in Bengal*. Calcutta: Oxford University Press.

Hawley, John and Donna Wulff (eds). 1982. *The Divine Consort: Radha and the Godesses of India*. Berkeley: University of California Press.

Hays, Sharon. 1996. *The Cultural Contradictions of Motherhood*. New Haven: Yale University.

Holston, James. 1989. *The Modernist City: An Anthropological Critique of Brasilia*. Chicago: University of Chicago Press.

Hughes, Thomas Patrick. [1885] 1988. *The Dictionary of Islam*. Delhi: Rupa.

Indian Worthies. 1906. Bombay: Manoranjak Grantha Prasarak Mandali.

Ingold, Tim. 1995. 'Building, Dwelling, Living: How Animals and People make themselves a Home in the World' in Marilyn Strathern (ed.) *Shifting Contests: Transformations in Anthropological Knowledge*. London and New York: Routledge. pp. 57–80.

Jacobus, Mary (ed.) 1974. *Women Writing About Women*. New York: Barnes and Noble.

———1986. *Reading Women: Essays in Feminist Criticism.* New York: Coumbia University Press.
Jeffery, Patricia. 1979. *Frogs in a Well: Indian Women in Purdah.* London: Zed Books.
Jenks, Chris. 1996. *Childhood.* London and New York: Routledge.
Jetter, A., A. Orleck and D. Taylor, (eds). 1997. *The Politics of Motherhood.* Hanover: Dartmouth College: University Press of New England.
Kakar, Sudhir. [1981] 1989. *The Inner World: A Psycho-Analytic Study of Childhood and Society in India.* Delhi: Oxford University Press.
Karlekar, Malavika. 1991. *Voices from Within: Early Personal Narratives of Bengali Women.* Delhi: Oxford University Press.
Karve, D.K. 1963. *The New Brahmans: Five Maharashtrian Families.* Berkeley: University of California Press.
Katten, Michael. [2002] 2005. *Colonial Lists/Indian Power: Identity Formation in Nineteenth-century Telugu-speaking India.* New York: Columbia University Press.
Kaul, Maninder, Sukhdev Singh and S.S. Gill. 1996. 'Facets of Primary Education in Rural Punjab', in *Journal of Indian Education* XXII no 3 (November), pp. 1–14.
Kaviraj, Sudipta. 1995. *The Unhappy Consciousness: Bankimchandra Chattopadhyaya and the Formation of a Nationalist Discourse in India.* New Delhi: Oxford University Press.
Khanna, Madhu. 2000. 'The Goddess-Woman Equation in Sakta Tantras' in Mandakranta Bose (ed.) *Faces of the Feminine in Ancient, Medieval, and Modern India.* New York: Oxford University Press. pp. 109–23.
King, Richard. 1999. *Orientalism and Religion: Postcolonial Theory, India and 'the Mystic East.'* London: Routledge.
Kinsley, David. 1997. *Hindu Goddesses: Visions of the Divine Feminine in the Hindu Religious Tradition.* Berkeley: University of California Press.
Kolhatkar, C.G. and D.K. Karve. 1963. *The New Brahmans: Five Maharashtrian Families.* Berkeley: University of California Press.
Kopf, David. 1969. *British Orientalism and the Bengal Renaissance: The Dynamics of Indian Modernization 1773–1835.* Berkeley: University of California Press.
——— 1979. *The Brahmo Samaj and the Shaping of the Modern Indian Mind.* Princeton: Princeton University Press.
Kristeva, Julia. 1984. *Revolution in Poetic Language.* Translated by M. Waller with an introduction by L.S. Roudiez. New York: Columbia University Press.
Kumar, Krishna. 1991. *The Political Agenda of Education.* Delhi: Sage Publications.
Kumar, Nita. 1987. 'The Mazars of Banaras: a New Perspective on the City's Sacred Geography', *The National Geographical Journal of India* 33, no 3.

—— 1988. *The Artisans of Banaras: Popular Culture and Identity.* Princeton: Princeton University Press.

——1992. *Friends, Brothers and Informants: Fieldwork Memoirs of Banaras.* Berkeley: University of California Press.

—— 1992. 'Class and Gender Politics in the Ramlila', in Indian Economic.... 29(1).

——1994. (ed.) *Women as Subjects: South Asian Histories.* Charlottesville: University Press of Virginia, and Calcutta: Stree Publications.

—— 2000 *Lessons from Schools: The History of Education in Banaras.* New Delhi and London: Sage Publications.

—— 2001. 'Families, Languages and Communities: The Plural Learning of the Nineteenth Century Intelligentsia', *Indian Economic and Social History Review*, Special Issue, 'Explorations in Colonial and Precolonial Intellectual History', pp. 81–103.

Kumar, Sunil. 2003. *The Present in Delhi's Pasts.* Delhi: Manohar Publishers.

Laird, M.A. 1972. *Missionaries and Education in Bengal, 1793–1837.* Oxford: Oxford University Press.

Lalitha, K. and Susie Tharu (eds). 1991. *Women Writing in India, Volume 1 and 2.* New York: The Feminist Press at the City University of New York.

Latour, Bruno.1993. *We Have Never Been Modern.* Harvard University Press.

Lelyveld, David. 1978. *Aligarh's First Generation: Muslim Solidarity in British India.* Princeton: Princeton University Press.

Littlejohn, J. [1960] 1967. 'The Temne house' in J. Middleton (ed.) *Myth and Cosmos: Readings in Mythology and Symbolism.* New York: American Museum of Natural History London: Routledge.

Loomba, Ania. 1991. 'Overworlding the "Third-World"', *Oxford Literary Review* 13 (1–2).

Low, Setha M. 1999. 'Spatializing culture: the Social Production and Social Construction of Public Space in Costa Rica' in Setha M. Lowe (ed.) *Theorizing the City: the New Urban Anthropology Reader.* New Brunswick, New Jersey: Rutgers University Press.

Mandelbaum, David. 1970. *Society in India.* Berkeley: University of California Press.

Marcus, George E. and Michael M.J. Fischer. 1986. *Anthropology as Cultural Critique: An Experimental Moment in the Human Sciences.* Chicago: The University of Chicago Press.

Marriott, McKim. 1998. 'The Female Family Core Explored Ethno-sociologically', *Contributions to Indian Sociology* 32. pp. 279–304.

Mayaram, Shail. 1997. *Resisting Regimes: Myth, Memory, and the Shaping of a Muslim Identity.* New York: Oxford University Press.

Mazumdar, Shudha. 1977. *A Pattern of Life: The Memoirs of an Indian Woman.* Delhi: Manohar Book Service.

McClintock, Anne. 1992. 'The Angel of Progress: The Pitfalls of the Term "Post-Colonial"' in *Social Text*, 31–32, pp. 84–98.

McCully, Bruce T. 1940. *English Education and the Origins of Indian Nationalism*. New York: Columbia University Press.

McDonald, Ellen (Gumperz). 1966. 'English Education and Social reform in Late Nineteenth Century Bombay: A Case Study in the Transmission of a Cultural ideal' in *Journal of Asian Studies* 25, no 3 (May).

McGee, Mary. 2000. *Inverted Identities: The Interplay of Gender, Religion, and Politics in India*. New York: Oxford University Press.

Metcalf, Barbara Daly. 1982. *Islamic Revival in British India: Deoband, 1860–1900*. Princeton: Princeton University Press.

Mies, Maria, Veronica Bennhold-Thompson and Claudia von Werlhof. 1988. *Women: The Last Colony*. London: Zed Books.

Minault, Gail. 1986. 'Sayyid Ahmad Dehlavi and the "Delhi Renaissance"' in R.E. Frykenberg (ed.) *Delhi Through the Ages: Essays in Urban History, Culture and Society*. Delhi: Oxford University Press.

———— 1994. 'Other Voices, Other Rooms: The View from the Zenana' in Nita Kumar (ed.) *Women as Subjects: South Asian Histories*. Charlottesville: University Press of Virginia and Calcutta: Stree. pp. 108–124.

————1998. *Secluded Scholars: Women's Education and Muslim Social Reform in Colonial India*. New Delhi: Oxford University Press.

Mishra, Yadunandan Prasad. 1917. *Raja Rammohan Roy Ka Jiwancharita*. Prayag: Onkar Press.

Mitra, Peary Chand. 1880. *Life of Dewan Ramcomul Sen*. Calcutta: I.C. Bose.

Mohanty, Chandra Talpade. 1988. 'Under Western Eyes: Feminist Scholarship and Colonial Discourses', *Feminist Review*, 30. pp. 49–74.

Moore, Henrietta L. 1986. *Space, Text and Gender: An Anthropological Study of the Marakwet of Kenya*. Cambridge: Cambridge University Press.

Moore, Marianne. 1967. *The Complete Poems of Marianne Moore*. New York: The Viking Press.

Morris, Jan (text) and Simon Winchester (photographs and captions). 1983. *Stones of Empire: The Buildings of the Raj*. Oxford: Oxford University Press.

Morrow, Susan Brind. 1997. *The Names of Things: Life, Language, and Beginning in the Egyptian Desert*. New York: Riverhead Books.

Mukherjee, Haridas and Uma Mukherjee. 1957. *The Origins of the National Education Movement 1905–10*. Calcutta: Jadavpur University.

Murickan, Jose. 1995. 'Education for Social Change' in Denis Coelho (ed.) *Changing Perspectives in Education*. New Delhi: Indian Social Institute.

Nagar, Amritlal. 1973. *Ham phidaen Lucknau: Lucknau ki visishta sanskriti men range jana-jivana par rocaka kahaniyan* (I am crazy about Lucknow: Interesting Stories on the Special Culture and Everyday Life of Lucknow). Delhi: Rajapala.

Nair, Janaki. 1990. 'Uncovering the Zenana: Visions of Indian Womanhood in Englishwomen's Writings, 1813–1940' in *Journal of Women's History* Vol 2(1), pp. 8–34.

Nanda, B.R. 1977. *Gokhale: The Indian Moderates and the British Raj.* Delhi: Oxford University Press.

Nandy, Ashis. 1980. *At the Edge of Psychology: Essays in Politics and Culture.* New Delhi: Oxford University Press.

————1987. 'Reconstructing Childhood: A Critique of the Ideology of Adulthood' in *Traditions, Tyranny and Utopias.* Delhi: Oxford University Press.

————1999. *The Intimate Enemy: Loss and Recovery of Self Under Colonialism.* New York: Oxford University Press.

Narasimhan, Sakuntala. 1999. *Kamaladevi Chattopadhyay: The Romantic Rebel.* Delhi: Sterling Publishers.

Narayan, Kirin. 1993. 'How Native is a "Native" Anthropologist?' in *American Anthropologist,* New Series 95 no.3, September, pp. 671–86.

Naregal, Veena. 2001. *Language Politics, Elites, and Public Sphere.* Delhi: Permanent Black.

Nehru, Jawaharlal. 1960. *The Discovery of India.* New York: Anchor Books.

Nicholson, Linda. 1986. *Gender and History: The Limits of Social Theory in the Age of the Family.* New York: Columbia University Press.

Nurullah, Syed, and J.P. Naik. 1951. *A History of Education in India.* Bombay: Macmillan.

————1964. *A Students' History of Education in India, 1800–1965.* Bombay: Macmillan.

O'Hanlon, Rosalind. 2002. *Caste, Conflict and Ideology: Mahatma Jotirao Phule and Low Caste Protest in Nineteenth-Century Western India.* Cambridge: Cambridge University Press.

Oakley, Ann. 1974. *The Sociology of Housework.* New York: Pantheon.

Obeyesekere, G. 1992. *The Apotheosis of Captain Cook: European Mythmaking in the Pacific.* Princeton: Princeton University Press.

Okin, Susan Moller. 1981. 'Women and the Making of the Sentimental Family' in *Philosophy and Public Affairs* Vol 11(1), pp. 65–88.

———— 1991. 'Gender, the Public and the Private' in David Held (ed.) *Political Theory Today.* Stanford: Stanford University Press.

Oldenburg, Veena Talwar. 1984. *The Making of Colonial Lucknow, 1856–1877.* Princeton: Princeton University Press.

————1994. *Dowry Murder: The Imperial Origins of a Cultural Crime.* New York: Oxford University Press.

Orsini, Francesca. 2002. *The Hindi Public Sphere: Language and Literature in the Age of Nationalism*. New York: Oxford University Press.

Pandey, Gyanendra. 1990. *The Construction of Communalism in Colonial North India*. Delhi: Oxford University Press.

Papaneck, Hanna and Gail Minault (eds). 1982. *Separate Worlds: Studies of Purdah in South Asia*. Delhi: Chanakya.

Paranjpye, R.P. 1915. *Dhondu Keshav Karve: A Sketch*. Poona.

Phoenix, A., A. Woollett and E. Lloyd (eds). 1991. *Motherhood: Meanings, Practices and Ideologies*. London: Sage Publications.

Pintchman, Tracy. 1994. *The Rise of the Goddess in Hindu Tradition*. Albany: SUNY Press.

Pollock, Sheldon. 1993. 'Deep Orientalism' in Carol Breckenridge and Peter Van der Veer (eds) *Orientalism and the Postcolonial Predicament*. Philadelphia: University of Pennsylvania Press.

Primary Education in India. 1997. Washington DC: The World Bank.

PROBE: Public Report on Basic Education in India. 1999. Delhi: Oxford University Press.

Punday, Daniel. 2003. *Narrative after Deconstruction*. Albany: State University of New York Press.

Quigley, Declan. 1999. *The Interpretation of Caste*. Delhi: Oxford University Press.

Rabinow, Paul (ed.). 1977. *Reflections on Fieldwork in Morocco*. Berkeley: University of California Press.

——1982. 'Ordinance, Discipline, Regulation: Some Reflections on Urbanism' in *Humanities in Society* 5: 267–78.

——1984. *The Foucault Reader*. New York: Pantheon Books.

Raheja, Gloria G., and Ann G. Gold. 1994. *Listen to the Heron's Words: Reimagining Gender and Kinship in North India*. Berkeley: University of California Press.

Ranade, Ramabai. 1963. *Ranade: His Wife's Reminiscences*. Translated by Kusumavati Deshpande. Delhi: Publications Division, Ministry of Information and Broadcasting, Government of India.

——1938. *Himself: The Autobiography of a Hindu Lady*. Translated by Katherine van akin Gates. New York.

Ranciere, Jacques. 1994. *The Names of History: On the Poetics of Knowledge*. Minneapolis: University of Minnesota Press.

Rao, P. Raghunath. 1983. *History of Modern Andhra*. New Delhi: Sterling Publishers.

Ray, Rajat Kanta (ed.) 1995. *Mind, Body and Society: Life and Mentality in Colonial Bengal*. Calcutta: Oxford University Press.

Ray, Raka. 1988. 'The Contested Terrain of Reproduction: Class and Gender in Schooling in India' in *British Journal of Sociology of Education* 9 no 4 (1988): 387–401.

Reagan, Timothy. 2000. *Non-Western Educational Traditions: Alternative Approaches to Educational Thought and Practice*. Mahwah, New Jersey: Lawrence Erlbaum Associates.

Redfield, Robert and Milton Singer. 1954. 'The Cultural Role of Cities', in *Economic Development and Cultural Change* 3. pp. 53–73.

Renu, Phanisvaranatha. 1963. *Maila ancal: eka ancalika upanyasa* (The Soiled Hinterland: A Provincial Novel). Delhi: Rajakamala Prakasana.

Restructuring of Elementary, Primary and Non-Formal Education in the Context of the New Panchayati Raj: Commission Reports. 1996. New Delhi: Institute of Social Sciences.

Rice, Philip and Patricia Waugh (eds). 1989. *Modern Literary Theory: A Reader*. London: Arnold. pp. 248–258.

Robb, Peter. 1993. 'Texts, Communities, and the History of Change in Modern South Asia' in Peter Robb (ed.) *Society and Ideology: Essays in South Asian History*. Delhi: Oxford University Press.

Rosaldo, Renato. 1989. *Culture and Truth: The Remaking of Social Analysis*. Boston: Beacon Press.

Rothman, Barbara Katz. 1994. 'Beyond Mothers and Fathers: Ideology in a Patriarchal Society' in E.N. Glen, G. Chang and L.R. Forcey (eds). *Mothering: Ideology, Experience and Agency*. London: Routledge.

Ruddick, Sara. 1980. 'Maternal Thinking', in *Feminist Studies* 6.

Said, Edward. 1979. *Orientalism*. New York: Vintage Books.

——1989. *Musical Elaborations*. 'Wellek Library Lectures in Critical Theory' at the University of California at Irvine.

—— 1993. *Culture and Imperialism*. New York: Knof.

Sarkar, Sumit. 1998. *Writing Social History*. Delhi: Oxford University Press.

Sarkar, Tanika. 1992. 'The Hindu Wife and the Hindu Nation: Domesticity and Nationalism in Nineteenth Century Bengal' in *Studies in History* 8.

——1995. 'Hindu Conjugality and Nationalism in Late Nineteenth Century Bengal' in Jasodhara Bagchi (ed.), *Indian Women: Myth and Reality*. Hyderabad: Sangam Books, pp. 98–115 .

—— 1998. 'A Book of her Own, A Life of her Own: Autobiography of a Nineteenth Century Woman', in *History Workshop Journal* 35. pp. 35–65.

—— 1999. 'A Book of her Own, A Life of her Own: Autobiography of a Nineteenth Century Woman', Kumkum Sangari and Uma Chakravarti, (eds). *From Myths to Markets: Essays on Gender*. New Delhi: Manohar Publishers and Distributors.

—— 2001. *Hindu Wife, Hindu Nation: Community, Religion and Cultural Nationalism*. New Delhi: Permanent Black.

Sastri, K.A. Nilakanta, (ed.) 1965. *A Great Liberal: Speeches and Writings of Sir P.S. Sivaswami Aiyer*. Bombay: Allied Publishers.

Seal, Anil. 1968. *The Emergence of Indian Nationalism: Competition and Collaboration in the Later Nineteenth Century*. Cambridge: Cambridge University Press.

Searle-Chatterjee, Mary, and Ursula Sharma, (eds). 1994. *Contextualising Caste: Post-Dumontian Approaches.* Oxford: Blackwell/Sociological Review.

Sen, Ashok. 1977. *Ishwar Chandra Vidyasagar and His Elusive Milestones.* Calcutta: Siddhi Publications.

Sen, Keshub Chunder. 1940. *Life and Works of Brahmananda Keshav.* Calcutta: Navavidhan Publication Committee.

Sen, Samita. 1993. 'Motherhood and Mothercraft: Gender and Nationalism in Bengal' in *Gender and History* 5.

Shah, A.M. 1973. *The Household Dimension of the Family in India: A Field Study in a Gujarat Village and a Review of Other Studies.* Berkeley: University of California Press.

—— 1998. *The Family in India: Critical Essays.* Hyderabad: Orient Longman.

Sharma, Ursula. 1999. *Caste.* Buckingham and Philadelphia: Open University Press.

Sharpe, Jenny. 1991. 'The Unspeakable Limits of Rape: Colonial Violence and Counter Insurgency' in *Genders* 10.

——1993. *Allegories of Empire: The Figure of Woman in the Colonial Text.* Minneapolis: University of Minnesota Press.

Sheehan, Paul. 2002. *Modernism, Narrative and Humanism.* Cambridge: Cambridge University Press.

Sherring, M.A. 1975. [First Pub. 1868]. *Benares: The Sacred City of the Hindus.* Delhi: Cheap Publications.

Shils, Edward. 1961. *The Intellectual between Tradition and Modernity: The Indian Case.* The Hague: Mouton.

Shohat, Ellah. 1992. 'Notes on the Post-Colonial' in P. Mongia (ed.) *Contemporary Postcolonial Theory.* London: Arnold. pp. 321–333. Also in *Social Text* 31/2, pp. 99–113.

Shorter, Edward. 1975. *The Making of the Modern Family.* New York: Basic Books.

Shree, Geetanjali. 2000. *Mai.* Translated by Nita Kumar. Delhi: Kali for Women.

Shweder, Richard. 1991. *Thinking Through Cultures: Expeditions in Cultural Psychology.* Cambridge: Harvard University Press.

Sinha, Mrinalini. 1995. *Colonial Masculinity: The 'Manly Englishman' and the 'Effeminate Bengali' in the late Nineteenth Century.* New York: Manchester University Press.

Sjoberg, Gideon. 1965. *The Preindustrial City: Past and Present.* New York: Free Press.

Skaria, Ajay. 2001. *Hybrid Histories: Forests, Frontiers and Wilderness in Western India.* New York: Oxford University Press.

Some Noteworthy Indians of Modern Times. 1992. n.p.

Southard, Barbara. 1995. *The Women's Movement and Colonial Politics in Bengal: The Quest for Political Rights, Education and Social Reform Legislation, 1921–1936*. Delhi: Manohar.

Spear, Percival. 1971. 'Bentinck and Education' in Thomas Metcalf (ed.) *Modern India: An Interpretive Anthology*. London: Macmillan.

Spivak, Gayatri Chakravorty. 1988. *In Other Worlds: Essays in Cultural Politics*. London.

————1999. *A Critique of Postcolonial Reason: Toward a History of the Vanishing Present*. Cambridge: Harvard University Press.

Srivastava, Sanjay. 1998. *Constructing Post-Colonial India: National Character and the Doon School*. London and New York: Routledge.

Stone, Lawrence. 1977. *The Family, Sex and Marriage in England 1500–1800*. New York: Harper and Row.

Strathern, Marilyn. 1992. *After Nature: English Kinship in the Late twentieth Century*. Cambridge: Cambridge University Press.

Suleri, Sara. 1992. *The Rhetoric of India*. Chicago: University of Chicago Press.

Sundar, Nandini. 1998. *Subalterns and Sovereigns: An Anthropological History of Bastar 1854–1996*. New York: Oxford University Press.

Sundaram, V.A. 1956. *Golden Jubilee of the Banaras Hindu University*. Varanasi: n.p.

Tagore, Rabindranath. 1962. *Rabindra Racanabali Volume 2*. Kolkata, n.p.

————1990. 'Streer Patra (Letter from a Wife) (trans.) in Kalpana Bardhan (ed.) *Of Women, Outcastes, Peasants, and Rebels: A Selection of Bengali Short Stories*. Berkeley: University of California Press. pp. 96–109.

Taussig, Michael. 1993. *Mimesis and Alterity: A Particular History of the Senses*. New York: Routledge.

Tenhunen, Sipra. 2003. *Secret Freedom in the City: Women's Wage Work and Agency in Calcutta*. Quebec: World Heritage Press.

Thapan, Meenakshi. 1991. *Life at School: An Ethnographic Study*. Delhi: Oxford University Press.

Tharu, Susie and K. Lalitha (eds). 1991. *Women Writing in India: 600 B.C. to the Early Twentieth Century*. New York: Feminist Press.

Tikakar, Aroon. 1984. *The Cloister's Pale: A Biography of the University of Bombay*. Bombay: Somaiya Publications.

Tillotson, G.H.R. (ed.) 1998. *Paradigms of Indian Architecture: Space and Time in Representation and Design*. Richmond, UK: Curzon Press.

Traub, Valerie. 2002. *The Renaissance of Lesbianism in Early Modern England*. Cambridge: Cambridge University Press.

Trawick, Margaret. 1990. *Notes on Love in a Tamil Family*. Berkeley: University of California Press.

Trumbach, Randolph. 1978. *The Rise of the Egalitarian Family*. New York: Academic Press.

Van der Veer, Peter. 1994. *Religious Nationalism: Hindus and Muslims in India*. Berkeley: University of California Press.

Viswanathan, Gauri. 1989. *Masks of Conquest*. New York: Columbia University Press.

Visweswaran, Kamala. 1994. *Fictions of Feminist Ethnography*. University of Minnesota Press.

Walsh, Judith. 1983. *Growing Up in British India*. New York: Holmes and Meier.

Weiner, Myron. 1991. *The Child and the State in India*. Princeton: Princeton University Press.

Werker, Janet. 1989. 'Becoming a Native Listener'. *American Scientist* vol. 77, pp. 54–9.

Willis, Paul. [1977] 1981. *Learning to Labour: How Working Class Kids Get Working Class Jobs*. New York: Columbia University Press.

Wodehouse, P.G. 2000. *Right Ho, Jeeves*. New York: Penguin.

Wolf, Eric. 1997. *Europe and the People Without History*. Berkeley: University of California Press.

Woolf, Virginia. 1967. *Collected Essays*. London.

Yule, Henry. 1995. *A Glossary of Colloquial Anglo-Indian Words and Phrases. Hobson-Jobson*. Richmond, Surrey: Curzon Press.

Zastoupil, Lynn and Martin Moir (eds). 1999. *The Great Controversy, 1781–1843*. Richmond: Curzon Press.

Zelliot, Eleanor. 2000. 'Women Saints in Medieval Maharashtra' in Mandakranta Bose (ed.) *Faces of the Feminine in Ancient, Medieval and Modern India*. New York: Oxford University Press. pp. 192–200.

Secondary literature (unpublished)

Fahimuddin. n.d. 'Globalization and Growth of Madrasas in India.' Occasional Paper, Giri Institute of Development Studies, Lucknow.

Gumperz, Ellen McDonald. 1964. 'English Education and Social Change in Late 19th Century Bombay, 1858–1898', Ph.D. dissertation, University of California, Berkeley.

Kalam, A.P.J. Abdul. 2002. Speech given in Hyderabad. July.

Kumar, Nita. 1998. 'Liberte, Egalite, Fraternite: Nationalist Education in France and India.' Lecture delivered at the Centre for Social Sciences, Calcutta, organized by the Alliance Francaise. August.

Lee, Chris. 1999. ' "A Promise in the Name of Bearing Witness": Urdu Poetry, Memory and the (Re)Construction of Muslim History in Varanasi, India.' Paper delivered at the University of Wisconsin South Asia Conference, Madison, October.

Monius, Anne. 1997. 'U. Ve. Caminataiyar and the Construction of Tamil Literary "Tradition".' Paper presented at the University of Wisconsin South Asia Conference, Madison, October.

Secondary literature (Miscellaneous)

Gulzar. 1961. *Ai mere pyare watan* (music composition). In Bimal Roy, *Kabuliwala.*

Ray, Satyajit. 1964. *Charulata: The Lonely Wife.* Film produced by R.D. Bansal, based on 'Nashtanir', a short story by Rabindranath Tagore.

Index